Sandra –

It has been a pleasure to join you in this program. I particularly enjoyed the board engagement that occurred during your presentation. Well done!

Good luck with your music, running, and Mandarin. See you in Shanghai.

Steve

More Praise for
Surviving and Thriving in Uncertainty

"*Surviving and Thriving in Uncertainty* is proof that effective risk intelligence doesn't have to be an arcane venture requiring a Ph.D. The authors' practical, common sense insights and actionable methods make efforts to improve decision quality and manage enterprise value not only achievable, but oddly enjoyable. Simplifying complexity is perhaps one of the book's biggest strengths. Whether you're an experienced director, a seasoned executive, or just starting out, this book is a must-read."

—Chris DePippo, ERM Director and Chief Compliance Officer,
Computer Sciences Corporation (CSC)

"Funston and Wagner's excellent user's guide for managing risk in today's rapidly changing global business world is also a great tool for how to win in high-threat competitive environments. As skilled practitioners, they provide just the right mix of insightful reflection and timely practical guidance for readers to incorporate into their own disciplines."

—William O. McCabe, former B-52 commander,
Pentagon official, and DuPont executive

"*Surviving and Thriving in Uncertainty* provides a refreshing risk-management framework. Funston and Wagner provide unique insights into creating the Risk Intelligent Enterprise. Their focused questions and real-world examples transferred easily to our own risk program. The common sense approach resonated with our board and staff and rapidly advanced the WSIB's risk program."

—Theresa Whitmarsh, Executive Director,
Washington State Investment Board

Surviving and Thriving
in Uncertainty

Surviving and Thriving in Uncertainty

Creating the Risk Intelligent Enterprise

FREDERICK FUNSTON

STEPHEN WAGNER

WILEY

John Wiley & Sons, Inc.

Published by John Wiley & Sons, Inc., Hoboken, New Jersey.
Published simultaneously in Canada.

For general information on our other products and services or for technical support, please contact our Customer Care Department within the United States at (800) 762-2974, outside the United States at (317) 572-3993 or fax (317) 572-4002.

Wiley also publishes its books in a variety of electronic formats. Some content that appears in print may not be available in electronic books. For more information about Wiley products, visit our web site at www.wiley.com.

Library of Congress Cataloging-in-Publication Data:

Funston, Frederick.
  Surviving and thriving in uncertainty: creating the risk intelligent enterprise/ Frederick Funston, Stephen Wagner.
    p. cm.
  Includes bibliographical references and index.
  ISBN 978-0-470-24788-4 (cloth)
  1. Risk management. 2. Uncertainty. I. Wagner, Stephen. II. Title.
  HD61.F86 2010
  658.15′5—dc22   2009046301

ISBN-13 978-0-470-24788-4

Printed in the United States of America

10 9 8 7 6 5 4 3

To our wives Irina and Charlie for their unflagging support
and sage advice throughout this journey.
To the partners, principals, and directors of the Deloitte
firms for their support of this project.

Contents

Acknowledgments

We wish to express our sincere appreciation to the following people for their support:

To Elizabeth Harrington, John Cardis, Ellen Hexter, Debbie Van Opstal, and John Olson for their insights and advice.

To Tom Gorman, Max Russell, and Samantha Clutter for their editorial assistance.

To Barbara Tysell for her research and fact checking throughout numerous drafts.

To Bill Sandy and George Peck for reviewing early drafts and providing highly constructive feedback.

To Mike Gardner and Jim Laney for their willingness to be partners in developing these concepts.

To Duncan Galloway and Bill Foote for the years of collaboration that formed the initial foundation of the risk intelligent enterprise.

To Alex Zmoira, Ian Waxman, Lane Kimbrough, Linda Igarashi, and other members of the Governance and Risk Oversight team for their support in researching various aspects of the manuscript.

To Kristy Coviello, Jack Burlingame, and Mark Baylis for their help in taking this manuscript through to publication.

To John DeRemigis, Emilie Herman, Chris Gage, and the entire team at John Wiley & Sons for their efforts and support.

And lastly, to the innumerable directors and executives we have met with who have shared their experiences, their challenges, and their visions.

Foreword

During my tenure as the first Secretary of the U.S. Department of Homeland Security, much of what we did to secure the country and its citizens centered on risk assessment and risk management. Dealing with risk, whether in the public or private sector, is a daunting but critical task. At the Department of Homeland Security, of course, risk management is required in order to keep the country adequately protected while simultaneously contributing to its capacity to be competitive and productive. What you will see in the following chapters is an insightful view of how risk management, when intelligently applied, can help the private sector achieve the same outcomes.

Every day, people, businesses, and governments assess, manage, and prepare for risks. Any business, in my view, that does not have some measure of risk assessment and risk management embedded in its operational structure and culture is most likely a static and non-innovative enterprise. It has no true situational awareness and thus, in the long term, will have no long term—because it will have neither means for preventing and mitigating crises nor for identifying and optimizing opportunities.

At the governmental level, one of the challenges of risk management is building bridges and promoting shared communication among the intelligence community. Consider the National Security Agency, the Federal Bureau of Investigation, the Central Intelligence Agency, and the Department of Defense. Each has its own set of intelligence sources. But if these separate agencies don't share information, their effectiveness in identifying and managing risks is diminished. The same is true of different business units or departments within any corporation.

It isn't easy to run any federal department as a business, particularly when you consider that 535 people, the Congress, act as an informal board of directors, appropriate dollars, and dictate where the department or agency spends them.

However, it is possible and even necessary for government to apply certain business principles to its overarching and departmental missions. That begins with identifying risks. Each day, on the way to the White House, I would receive a matrix that addressed potential threats. Homeland Security doesn't generate intelligence information; it is a consumer of information provided by various intelligence agencies. But the question for the leadership of any enterprise is how do you evaluate risks and the impact each could have on your business or enterprise?

The first consideration is credibility. How credible are your sources? Have you received information from a given source before, and did that information prove to be accurate? Second, can this intelligence be corroborated? Can you verify this information with another source? Third, how exposed are you? How vulnerable are you at that particular point? Have you performed certain preparedness training? Have you built security and safety measures to substantially mitigate the risk? Fourth, what's the actionable threat? What are the most important things you can do to deter the risk immediately? Is this action consistent with your culture, your reputation, and how you do business? Will it have a good or bad economic impact on your enterprise? Will taking action make your enterprise safer or more productive? The answer is usually both.

Effective risk management is not about forecasting events with 100 percent accuracy. That would be a fruitless and impossible goal. But in many cases, erring on the side of caution, even when your information might not be as reliable as you would like or when your intelligence cannot be verified by a second source, is simply the smart thing to do. Before and during the 2003 holiday season, Homeland Security cancelled a number of flights due to intercepted "chatter" that al Qaeda had plans to hijack an airplane and attack a target in the United States. Was this information credible? We thought so. Was it corroborated? Not really. Yet the context and content were so unique that the threat could not be overlooked. We found out roughly nine months later that the intelligence we intercepted was, in fact, not accurate. But given the potential risks, we couldn't afford to ignore the possibility that such an attack was being planned.

Finally, an aspect of risk management that is often overlooked is the notion of being too cautious—walling up like a fortress, precluding opportunity. An example, perhaps, of being overly vigilant can be seen in the obstacles U.S. businesses face as they attempt to bring in professionals from other countries. In a post-9/11 world, it has become increasingly difficult for foreign professionals to navigate the rules and regulations that would allow them to enter this country to do business.

The key to risk management is managing risk before it manages you. Individuals, national governments, and international enterprises face this challenge every day. But it's a challenge that is becoming increasingly complex and complicated, particularly given today's global and interdependent marketplace. Additionally, the concept of risk as a two-edged sword is as true at the corporate level as it is at the governmental level. However, risk management, when done intelligently, not only allows businesses to build in resiliency and protections but also to inspire innovation and create value. The following pages provide practical strategies and approaches that can help enterprises do just that.

THE HONORABLE TOM RIDGE
First Secretary of the U.S. Department of Homeland Security
Former Governor of the Commonwealth of Pennsylvania

Preface

A ny clear-eyed assessment of the state of risk management today would have to conclude that the field is more notable for its spectacular failures than its ability to keep businesses—and the executives who run them—out of trouble. Innumerable organizations have been staggered by risks that, in hindsight at least, could have been recognized and mitigated; their names are well known and need not be repeated here. Equally disturbing perhaps, these organizations often touted their risk management processes as state of the art, an assessment frequently seconded by analysts and commentators and accepted at face value by eager investors.

Standing amid the rubble of the latest financial ruin, two troubling questions arise:

1. Why can't the cycle of scandal, speculation, greed, and recklessness be broken? Devastating business failures have occurred frequently throughout the last century, yet the most-recent wave always seems to catch the business community off guard.
2. With countless sums spent on conventional risk management, why does it consistently fail at critical junctures? Executives, investors, and regulators are justifiably skeptical about continuing to invest in approaches apparently so fundamentally flawed.

The answers to these questions, as you might have guessed, can be found within these pages. Rick Funston and Stephen Wagner have spent most of their careers helping top executives, boards of directors, and audit committee members bring clarity and efficiency to their risk management programs. In this book, the authors clearly describe the risks unaddressed and the warning signs unheeded that have brought erstwhile respectable companies to their knees. More important, the authors devote much of the book to practical advice that allows companies not simply to survive in a risk-fraught business environment, but to thrive in a climate of uncertainty and peril that sinks poorly prepared organizations.

However, perhaps the greatest value of this book lies in its power of demystification. As the authors note, the failure of enterprise risk management (ERM) can often be tied to needless complexity. Business executives frequently complain that ERM is too complicated and too big; that a typical ERM infrastructure is by its nature bulky, creaky, and likely to collapse under its own weight. Due to the misconception that it's virtually impossible to get one's arms around ERM, many organizations take a piecemeal approach, with risk specialists in various business units lacking a harmonizing, oversight, or "big picture" view and approach. This "silo" phenomenon often yields predictably fragmented results, as it is unable to address aggregate or cascading risk scenarios. (For example, a credit risk that impacts treasury that in turn affects cash flow, accounts payable, supply chain, production, inventory, and sales.)

Yet, as Funston and Wagner convincingly demonstrate, a risk infrastructure need not be bloated. Indeed, the best risk management programs are often the simplest, in both design and execution.

The full picture has been carefully drawn by the authors in this book. Their insights and practical knowledge will benefit those directors and executives who seek to tame the risks and capture the rewards that await their enterprises.

HENRY RISTUCCIA
Managing Partner
Governance, Regulatory & Risk Strategies Services
Deloitte and Touche LLP

Introduction

There is no security on this earth. Only opportunity.
—Douglas MacArthur

The pursuit of opportunity in any human endeavor means leaving the security of the status quo, the safe haven, the tried and true. General MacArthur's statement above implies that fact of our professional and personal lives. Moreover, his statement explicitly describes security itself as nonexistent. Efforts to achieve security by standing still, hunkering down, or attempting only that which has been attempted in the past will not produce security. Indeed, such actions will generate risks of their own. Yet, as we all know, risks also accompany the pursuit of opportunity.

Managing the risks that accompany the pursuit of opportunity—or, more precisely, the pursuit of value—is the main subject of this book. Executives and board members understand that risk accompanies this pursuit, yet they often misjudge, mismanage, or simply avoid that risk. Indeed, risk avoidance has traditionally been the foundation of risk management as commonly practiced in enterprises. As a result, events in the business and financial world over the past decade clearly demonstrated that risks encountered in the pursuit of value are rarely fully appreciated or properly managed.

Executives and boards mainly accustomed to risk avoidance—or to gauging and addressing risk by means of mathematical models—often failed to identify, appreciate, and manage the risks that attended the pursuit of value. This occurred across a range of industries, and it was chiefly a result of conventional approaches to risk management.

Conventional Risk Management

Relatively few board members and senior executives, including those of many major corporations, take what we call a risk intelligent approach to managing the risks their organizations face. Conventional risk management, with its focus mainly on avoiding risk and protecting existing assets, is necessary but not sufficient. Worse, risk management as practiced rarely focuses on ways to identify, develop, seize, and exploit the most promising opportunities for the enterprise to create value. Indeed, most leaders and risk managers do not see risk management as part of value creation, and that is a major reason we've written this book.

The proper aims of risk management in business are to preserve existing value and to enable the creation of new value. Implicit in this view of risk management is the recognition of the reality that value and risk are inseparable. Risk attends every attempt to protect and create value.

Yet conventional risk management takes value preservation as its main purview and leaves risk taking for value creation (the reason that the enterprise exists) largely out of risk management. This leaves most directors and executives with a skewed view of risk and with only one set of tools—asset preservation tools—when they need another set to deal with the risks that accompany their efforts to create new value.

Conventional risk management has failed, most recently and spectacularly, in the well-chronicled housing bubble, subprime crisis, and credit crisis of the 2000s, with exacerbating effects on the business cycle. When we began writing this book in late 2007, we set out to warn that conventional approaches to risk management presented serious dangers and that leaders' understanding of risk management—and risk itself—had to change.

Now that we all have experienced what by many measures was the worst financial and economic crisis since the Great Depression, those "warnings" have been issued. We also set out to offer a more pragmatic approach to risk management through a deeper understanding of value and risk. That approach and that understanding is what you will find in this book.

A Risk Intelligent Approach

Executives and boards must make important decisions in the present, without complete information in a complex and rapidly changing environment characterized by uncertainty and turbulence. Uncertainty is a state in which the outcomes are unknown and perhaps unknowable; the more distant in time, the greater the uncertainty. University of Chicago economist Frank Knight described two types of uncertainty: first, that in which probabilities are known or knowable, which he called risk; and, second, uncertainty, which is not known or knowable.

This bifurcation has led to much of the current wisdom on which conventional risk management is founded—that is, probabilities based on normal distributions. Thus extreme cases are typically ignored.

Unfortunately, such wisdom has failed us, as improbable and extreme events have occurred while probable events have failed to occur.

Turbulence is a state of extreme instability characterized by sudden and violent change. It cannot be modeled outside of the laboratory. It is characterized by high speed. Together, uncertainty and turbulence generate risk, that is, the potential for failure. In the case of the enterprise, it is both the failure to protect its existing assets and the failure to create future value.

Thus, improving ways of anticipating and managing risk in uncertainty and turbulence is the subject of this book. To help leaders operate effectively in that environment, we present—under the rubric of risk intelligence—proven methods from a wide variety of disciplines by which they can exercise better judgment and make superior decisions under risky, uncertain, and turbulent conditions.

The risk intelligent enterprise recognizes that risk intelligence and risk management are not ends in themselves but a means toward the ends of creating and preserving value and surviving and thriving in uncertainty. Risk intelligence is an approach to conducting business that improves decision making and judgment in vital areas and initiatives. After all, to be enterprising means to be bold and willing to undertake new initiatives that involve risk.

In fact, according to Webster's New Collegiate Dictionary, the word *enterprise* means "a project or undertaking that is esp. difficult, complicated, or risky" or "a unit of economic organization or activity, especially a business organization." Too many enterprises appear to bear the second definition in mind but not the first.

Risk intelligence is dynamic. There is no set of rules to follow, no permanent certification, no way to insulate the organization from the forms that uncertainty and turbulence will take in the future. Rather, there is only a path to creating value and managing risks that enables better decisions.

The Approach of This Book

This book aims to stimulate and contribute to the discussion of risk by presenting factual, informative, provocative, and sometimes challenging views on the subject. In that spirit, we present a number of realities that organizations must confront if they are to survive and thrive.

In addition, we provide a multifaceted, panoramic way of viewing risk, one that encompasses both asset preservation and value creation. We have repeatedly heard directors and senior executives express their desire for new skills and their need for updated tools for addressing risk proactively rather than reactively. We introduce such skills and tools in this book and provide a context in which to use them in the form of the risk intelligent enterprise.

A risk intelligent enterprise takes a broad view of risk, assesses the full range of risks across the enterprise, matches risk management resources to the priority of the risk, and thus more effectively manages the risks of value creation as well as asset preservation.

We address ourselves primarily to boards and senior executives because they hold primary responsibility for the success or failure of the enterprise. They, and only they, hold the power to promulgate risk intelligent practices in the enterprise because they define the direction and develop the strategies by which the enterprise creates value. They also make the major decisions regarding the initiatives that the organization will pursue, the resources to be allocated to those initiatives, and the risks that are inherent in those initiatives.

As to method, we draw upon our collective years of client work and research experience in Deloitte & Touche and throughout our careers, and draw upon on the intellectual capital of the firm. We've met with hundreds of directors and senior executives to obtain their perspectives on issues such as resilience and agility, asset preservation and value creation, and corporate governance and risk management.

We also sought the perspectives of combat pilots, first responders to crises, race car drivers, sailors, mountaineers, explorers, and astronauts—people with a vital interest in managing risk. And we drew upon extensive research into news stories and historical sources in fields both related and unrelated to business.

In our research, we discovered converging themes in areas as diverse as biology, cybernetics, military operations, physics, behavioral finance, and national security, among others. Our inquiry into areas related to the natural and social sciences rested on the notion that the enterprise can be best understood as a living organism with two imperatives: to survive and to thrive.

Change and turbulence, whether they originate within the organism or enterprise or in the environment, typically present the greatest threats and the richest opportunities—provided adaptation occurs. Adaptation may be gradual or sudden, effective or ineffective, but adaptation typically occurs in unexpected ways and in response to unanticipated changes and events.

We have also dug deep into business-related disciplines such as quality and process improvement and scenario analysis to locate root causes of failure and to develop insights regarding success. However, this is no technical manual or treatise on risk. Rather it is a practical guide for directors and senior executives, as well as risk managers, business unit heads, and aspirants to these positions.

Given that directors and executives have cautioned us that a book of this type must provide compelling methods of successful application as well as a strong conceptual framework, we present numerous cases, examples, anecdotes, quotes, tools, and tactics within an overarching structure. Much in the way in which one must balance risk and reward, we have sought to balance often opposing factors, such as depth and breadth, theory and practice, and information and entertainment, in our effort to further the inquiry into risk and to foster optimal approaches to risk management.

The Structure of This Book

This book consists of seventeen chapters, organized into three parts, as follows:

Part I: When Risks Become Brutal Realities states the problems and challenges that leaders of large enterprises confront in managing risk and creating value. It details why conventional risk management and risk governance have failed and provides a new, more useful view of both of those key leadership activities.

Part II: Ten Essential Risk Intelligence Skills presents ten "fatal flaws" in conventional risk management and the corresponding skill required to correct and overcome each flaw. Each chapter in this part also contains tools for exercising that skill. Not every flaw or every tool will apply to every organization; however, collectively they amount to an intellectual approach, a mind-set, and a set of practical steps to improve risk management in your enterprise. These skills and tools address needs that repeatedly arose in our experience, our research, and our discussions with interviewees. These skills improve people's awareness of and responses to risks and opportunities, immediately and in the long term, at every level of the organization.

Part III: Creating the Risk Intelligent Enterprise describes the characteristics of the risk intelligent enterprise and provides a framework for developing such an organization. This part explains the roles of directors and executives and the leadership challenges they face in this endeavor. It also shows how to orchestrate people, processes, and systems toward that end. A risk intelligent enterprise incorporates risk intelligence into the ways it understands and manages the business. As result, it is better positioned to make superior decisions under conditions of uncertainty and turbulence and thus increases its chances of survival and competitive success.

Two additional features of this book warrant a mention. First, to reinforce specific points, we have presented verbatim views of our interviewees in sidebars titled Voice of Experience. These views illustrate the needs and concerns of these individuals as they pertain to the subject at hand (and not necessarily the views of their organizations, which many preferred not to have identified in these pages). Second, we have included Questions to Ask at the end of selected chapters. These questions, which are by no means exhaustive, are intended to focus discussion and prompt further inquiry into the related topic.

At this point in the development of business, of capitalism, and of the global economy, risk management presents the greatest challenges and opportunities for leaders in enterprises of every stripe. We trust that this book achieves our aim of inspiring leaders to accept those challenges and to pursue those opportunities, and to do so with greater effectiveness, efficiency, and enthusiasm.

Surviving and Thriving
in Uncertainty

When Risks Become Brutal Realities

CHAPTER 1

To Survive and Thrive
A Matter of Judgment

Life is short, art long, opportunity fleeting, experience misleading, judgment difficult.

—Hippocrates

The goal of every species is to survive and thrive, yet about 96 percent of all species that have ever lived on earth are now extinct.[1] Life is also short for individuals and—more to our point—for many of the enterprises they create. In 1997, the average life expectancy of a Fortune 500 company was about 45 years.[2] By now, it has likely become even shorter, as demonstrated most recently in the number of stressed and failed industrial and financial institutions in the crisis of 2007–08 and in the recession of 2008–09. While the events of that period have been well documented, a quick review of selected highlights will set the stage for our examination of risk and risk management in this part.

- Between the market highs of October 2007 and the final days of 2008, an estimated $8 trillion in value was lost, as measured by the Dow Jones Industrial Average, where every 500-point decline equals about $700 billion in losses.
- The U.K. hedge fund Peloton had been ranked the world's highest performing fund in 2007 with an 87 percent return on investment and $10 billion in assets. On March 5, 2008, Peloton was forced to dissolve when its liquidity dried up almost overnight.[3] That spring, the failure of 85-year-old Bear Stearns occurred in just over 20 days.[4]
- Within 20 months after the end of 2006, 274 major U.S. lending operations "imploded."[5] Between January 1 and the end of August 2008, nine

U.S. banks failed, and by September 2009 there were 552 on the Federal Deposit Insurance Corporation's troubled list.[6]

- General Motors and Chrysler underwent federally assisted bankruptcies, while thousands of retail stores, restaurants, travel, luxury goods, furniture, and other businesses that depend on consumer spending experienced severe decreases in revenue and pressure on profits.
- During 2008, U.S. residential mortgage foreclosure activity increased 81 percent over 2007 levels and 225 percent over 2006 levels.[7] Nationally, more than one in every 400 housing units was in some stage of foreclosure.[8]

Who is responsible? That question has been debated since the onset of the crisis, and it will be for years to come. Yet senior executives and boards of directors have clearly been held responsible in many quarters, representing a trend extending back to Sarbanes-Oxley in 2002, and it's a trend that we expect to continue.

The reasons should be obvious. People rightfully look to senior executives and boards to exercise judgment: to survey the environment, understand the organization, and make tough decisions in difficult and uncertain situations. The enterprise will either survive and thrive or wither and die on the quality and timeliness of its leaders' judgments.

We opened this chapter with a quote from Hippocrates, who spoke and taught with humility (to the point of choosing "First, do no harm" as the opening of his eponymous oath). He must have known how little physicians of his time knew about the unknown. Bacteria, brain chemistry, even various organ functions were yet to be discovered. Then, as now, physicians—and executives—must exercise judgment, and do so amid uncertainty.

We mentioned that 96 percent of all species that have appeared on the planet are now extinct. We implied that organizations aren't doing much better. Yet virtually all species except *Homo sapiens* operate mainly on genetics and instinct. Only we have judgment. We have what neuroscientists refer to as "executive functions" in our brains, the capacity to gather and process information and to make rational decisions and plans based on that information and on our wants and needs. Shouldn't our organizations—also equipped with "executive functions"—be doing better, exercising better judgment, even amid uncertainty and the difficulties it brings?

We think so, and we are not alone.

The Revolving Door to the Corner Office

The door to the corner office has been revolving at increasing speeds. In December 2008, National Public Radio (NPR) reported, "Corporate boards are holding chief executives accountable for falling stock prices as well as huge losses suffered in the credit and mortgage markets." According to the Corporate Library, the CEO turnover rate exceeded 18 percent in 2008. The NPR report noted, "CEOs are also spending less time at the helm—their median tenure is down to four years."[9]

In general, CEO turnover doubles in bad times, particularly when shareholder returns suffer. In 2008, 61 companies in the S&P 500 stock index changed CEOs. Boards typically oust CEOs a year or two after shareholder returns slip, and that "grace period" may decrease further.[10] (The average chief financial officer has 18 months to get the job done, according to *CFO Magazine*.[11])

The truth, however, is that a new CEO rarely reverses the losses. The shares of 30 companies at which chief executives were removed actually declined more than they gained.[12] More recently, CEOs in general have had their powers diminished, relative to their boards. According to a study by the University of Southern California (USC) Center for Effective Organizations and Heidrick & Struggles, 82 percent of directors believe that their "CEOs have less control over their boards, with 49 percent indicating this has happened to a great or very great extent."[13]

These trends may well affect management's view of risk. Jeff Cunningham, Chairman, CEO, and editorial director of *Directorship*, says, "There is no question that CEO power and prestige have fallen. The unintended consequence is that this can make the CEO overly risk averse. His or her decision making can become reflexive, conventional, and, from a business development point of view, unremarkable."[14] CEO tenure has been reduced to the point where leaders often cannot see significant initiatives through to completion, which can shift their focus to only short-term goals, since they won't be around to achieve long-term ones. Nor are CEOs the only leaders affected.

Broad Concerns about Boards

The business acumen of the board often fails to match the needs of the enterprise. Cunningham says, "A lot of people will dispute this, but CEOs complain they are just not getting the 'brain trust' and strategic counsel from their boards that they did years ago, although they are getting heaps of advice on the governance issues *du jour*—compensation, compliance, and succession."[15] A 2005 McKinsey survey of more than 1,000 directors reinforces these concerns:

- Only 11 percent of directors reported that they have a complete understanding of key enterprise strategies or risks.
- More than 50 percent have no clear sense of their companies' prospects five to ten years down the road.

- Just 8 percent of directors claim to have a complete understanding of long-term risks; 37 percent admit they have little or none.
- More than 50 percent of directors admit that they have no way of tracking changes in risks over time, leaving them vulnerable to unforeseen shifts.[16]

Note that these are directors' self-assessments. Moreover, the overall trends they identified seem to have continued. The above-noted USC/Heidrick & Struggles study found that 95 percent of directors rated themselves as highly effective in monitoring financial performance, representing shareholders' interests, and ensuring ethical behavior (compliance and monitoring).

However, they rated themselves much lower on shaping long-term strategy, identifying threats or opportunities, and planning for succession.[17] Those opinions square with reality. The *Wall Street Journal* reported on September 22, 2008, "Many U.S. boards don't cope well with a crisis." Consequently, "some directors are now ratcheting up efforts to anticipate, and avert, trouble." Going forward, boards need to "take a bigger role in risk management."[18]

Voice of Experience

"Even though there have always been challenges, they were on a different level. We are experiencing 'a perfect storm.' First, there is the economic environment—volatility in foreign exchange, raw material costs, oil, and other energy sources. Second, the general public is more vocal and more demanding. And third, public outcry is producing strong pressures for regulatory responses, which in turn create even more flux and unpredictability, not just in the United States but in the rest of the world as well. We are not used to this, and we are not trained or equipped to deal with it effectively.

"We have spent the past five years struggling with overkill of compliance and internal control issues, which are not always correlated with managing the uncertainties of a business. But we sort of took our eyes off the ball for what was on the horizon. That makes us even less prepared."

—Rolf Classon, Director

What's Reasonable to Expect of the Board?

The board's power emanates from the shareholders, whose interests the board represents, and its responsibilities center on governing, guiding, and when appropriate assisting management in protecting and increasing share-holder value. But how much actual responsibility for risk management can be laid upon directors? It's an open question. For instance, Jeff Cunningham says, "I think the public at large and, add for safe measure both politicians and regulators, may not understand how the board interrelates with the C-suite in the area of risk management, and so they lack some of the basic tools needed to understand the risk environment."[19]

Many boards and management teams also don't understand that interrelation, at least not fully and in practice. In fact, most conventional guidance on the board's governance role has far more to do with legal obligations, structures, and functions than with how key decisions are made.

For example, in *Corporate Governance*, Colley and colleagues state that the board is responsible for governance based on their articles of incorporation, bylaws, and shareholder agreements.[20] The authors go on to present three broad duties of the board: the fiduciary duty, the duty of fair dealing, and the duty to perform functions in good faith. Other standard expectations call upon directors to:

- Act as an ordinarily prudent person would reasonably believe to be in the best interests of the organization
- Fulfill the paramount duty of oversight, with the ability to delegate that authority
- Understand the corporation's operations, performance, and proper responses to problems
- Establish policies, such as specifying decisions requiring board approval, establishing codes of ethics and conduct, and ensuring accurate financial reporting

The vast majority of directors do their best to execute these responsibilities. However, they are often constrained by the limits of time and a lack of the right tools. In addition, a move toward increased director independence—a newfound priority for many shareholders and regulators—may have adverse, as well as positive, effects. While conflicts of interest and "coziness" with management may decrease, directors' insight into the business may also decrease.

Directors must understand the mechanisms by which the value of the enterprise is, and can be, created and destroyed, so they can provide sound governance and useful guidance. Absent understanding and processes that promote sound governance and useful guidance, the board will likely revert to the default setting of raising objections and roadblocks on the one hand, or, on the other, to rubber-stamping management's decisions and initiatives.

Indeed, many experts and enterprises preoccupy themselves with board structure. To their credit, Leblanc and Gillies note, "It is 'board effectiveness' not 'board structure' that must be analyzed, for it is the effectiveness of the board in the decision-making process that in the final analysis determines corporate performance."[21]

Unfortunately, many boards simply adopt a risk-averse posture rather than develop a decision-making process. Adopting a risk-averse posture in an attempt to protect shareholder value will hobble efforts to create value and, over time, actually erode value. Yet boards require time and certain tools if they are to improve their effectiveness and decision making.

Voice of Experience

"I can't emphasize enough the fact that continuing on a board is not an automatic entitlement. The board needs to take an inventory of the capabilities it needs to be a complete and an effective board, in terms of skills and experience. It needs to look at what it has relative to what it needs, because more often than not, there will be a historical mismatch. Your board's composition will reflect what you were in the past rather than what you need to be in the future. The board needs to manage that proactively."

—David Nierenberg, Director

Barriers to Board Effectiveness

In a Deloitte survey of 250 executives and board members,[22] respondents identified the two biggest barriers to effective risk governance systems as a lack of tools needed to analyze nonfinancial issues and skepticism that nonfinancial indicators relate directly to the bottom line:

- One-third of respondents said their companies' nonfinancial reporting measures were excellent or good, compared with 86 percent for financial reporting measures.
- Nearly half of respondents said nonfinancial reporting measures were ineffective or highly ineffective in helping the board and the CEO make long-term decisions (more than 12 months out).
- Nearly three-quarters of executives and directors were under pressure to measure nonfinancial performance indicators.

Three years later, the results were retested.[23] The majority of executives perceived a growing need to better understand the underlying drivers of their performance through nonfinancial measurements, but the available metrics remained inadequate. The study concluded that companies either did not have or were not sharing critical nonfinancial performance data with their boards. It is in this nonfinancial data that much of the information needed to formulate sound judgments resides.

Barriers to Improving Risk Oversight

Boards are certainly taking risk much more seriously. In 2004, just one in ten boards spent more than 10 percent of their time on formal risk management. By 2005, that number had risen to almost 40 percent. Yet this has not necessarily translated into greater expertise.[24]

In the 12 months prior to the Deloitte survey, one in five companies surveyed had suffered significant damage from a failure to manage risk and 56 percent had experienced at least one near miss (a serious threat to value that was averted or defused). Ten percent of respondents reported three near misses during the past year. However, despite increased discussion and awareness, adoption of risk management standards across the enterprise was limited. Only one-quarter of respondents set regular risk targets for managers, and less than one-third provided risk management training for managers and staff. This is an indicator of cultures in which risk management is considered "someone else's job."

It is the board's responsibility, in its role as steward of shareholder value, to exercise risk oversight. However, three key challenges must be addressed if the quality of directors' risk oversight is to be improved:

1. Limited time
2. Lack of industry-specific expertise
3. Different definitions of success

LIMITED TIME   Given that they are all part-timers, what time commitment is reasonable to expect of directors? Since the adoption of Sarbanes-Oxley in 2002, the average time spent by board members on their duties has increased by almost 30 percent. The USC/Heidrick & Struggles report noted, "On average, the directors indicated that they serve on 2.5 public boards. They report that during the last year, the average estimated time they spent on board matters—including preparation time, meetings, travel, and other activities—was 202 hours, up from 189 hours in 2004, 177 hours in 2003, and 156 hours in 2001."[25] Most boards meet from four to six times per year, although not always in person.

Given the available time, omniscience or even a highly detailed knowledge of operations cannot reasonably be expected. It may also be unreasonable to expect directors to spend significantly more time on those duties, in which case better use must be made of their available time.

LACK OF INDUSTRY-SPECIFIC EXPERTISE   While increased independence may have reduced potential conflicts of interest, it may also have deprived the CEO of sources of industry expertise and diminished the board's value as strategic partner. Professor Ray Reilly of the University of Michigan's Ross School of Business believes that board members should thoroughly understand the business and that companies should find ways to ensure that they do. He notes that because board members are involved in the business periodically rather than day to day, they often don't know which questions to ask.[26]

For example, before Lehman Brothers failed, only three directors had direct experience in the financial services industry. As a follow-up to the USC/Heidrick & Struggles study, authors Meyer and Rollo state that in their extensive informal conversations with CEOs, almost all confided that at most they have one or two "very effective directors who provide wise counsel, offer advice on key issues, and contribute both formally and informally to the direction of the company." A fortunate few CEOs say they have three or four such directors. Meyer and Rollo then extrapolate that "only about 10 to 20 percent of directors are seen by CEOs as effective." They add that CEOs also say their senior management team often regards "working with the board as a de-motivating experience."[27]

Such findings jibe with the views of directors themselves, as evidenced by the above-noted McKinsey Global Survey of directors in which only 11 percent described themselves as having a complete understanding of their company's strategy and risks.[28,29] It stands to reason that board members will have difficulty providing insight on strategy if they don't understand it. They may even be changing CEOs so frequently due to misperceptions regarding strategy, operations, and performance.

DIFFERENT DEFINITIONS OF SUCCESS   Meyer and Rollo[30] also report frequent disconnects between CEOs and their boards regarding expectations. CEOs want thought leaders who will partner with them on strategy. They want "independent directors who can help them make better, faster, and wiser decisions" but who let them run daily business operations. In contrast, "many directors define success in terms of committee work, fiduciary responsibility, and keeping the company in compliance with legal, regulatory, and other oversight requirements."[31]

This focus on the part of the board has generated an overemphasis on transparency, compliance, and governance ratings rather than on business strategy. If the board defines success as avoiding suits, fines, regulatory actions, or appearances before Congressional committees and if management defines it as growth in revenue, profits, and shareholder value, then disconnects between the two parties are inevitable.

Combine these three challenges with the potential for tighter regulation in many areas, and with boards perhaps being "gun-shy" after the events of the 2000s, which ranged from Sarbanes-Oxley through government bailouts, and you may have a recipe for even greater challenges. Meanwhile, the basic imperatives of the enterprise have not changed.

The Imperatives of the Enterprise

In Darwinian terms, the enterprise has two fundamental imperatives: to survive and to thrive. Accomplishing both requires resilience and agility. Resilience enables the enterprise to survive adversity and the impact of negative events. Agility enables it to evade or counter adversity and to adapt to seize opportunities.

According to the U.S. Council on Competitiveness, the potential for disruptions of "global transportation networks and supply chains, IT, and energy ... is rising in lock step with technological complexity, interdependency, terrorism, mutating viruses, and even weather phenomena ... For enterprises, communities and countries alike, resilience is becoming a competitive differentiator."[32] By definition, resilience is the ability to recover from a blow or, more technically, the ability to quickly resume a former shape and recover functionality following an adverse impact.

Impact is a function of the mass of whatever strikes the organism or entity and its velocity. A resilient enterprise can absorb or deflect an impact and still survive. It might possess that capacity by virtue of factors such as its size, capitalization, breadth of operations, or depth of experience, or it might develop it over time.

Agility is the ability—the coordination, speed, and strength—to change position quickly to avoid or mitigate the effect of an impact, to roll with the punches. Agility is also the ability to move quickly, even to assume a new configuration, to achieve a desired outcome. An agile enterprise can often avoid negative impact (e.g., by anticipating a competitor's move or a technology that could supersede its own) or take advantage of opportunities for growth (e.g., by moving from a centralized to a decentralized structure, acquiring another company, or changing its business model).

While resilience and agility in organisms have been developed through natural selection over millennia, those qualities develop—or fail to develop—in organizations through decisions made at the executive and board level. For instance, there are usually trade-offs between resilience and agility that require a decision to pursue one or the other or both in some combination.

Factors Affecting Resiliency and Agility

Esther Colwill, a partner in Deloitte's Calgary office in Canada, is one of perhaps 100 people ever to scale the Seven Summits—the highest peaks on each of the seven continents.[33] Colwill noted that when she climbed Mt. Everest, tough decisions had to be made about how much gear to carry. She and her team had to weigh the benefits of resilience to sudden changes in the weather against the agility and faster ascent enabled by small loads.

Likewise, enterprises must balance resilience and agility so they can withstand adverse impacts yet remain nimble enough to exploit opportunities. Jim Porter, retired chief engineer and vice president of Engineering and Operations at DuPont, says, "In the end resilience is about being able to cope successfully with the unexpected. It's about doing the right things in ways that allow you to remain sustainable."[34]

Resiliency and agility depend to a degree on size. The larger the entity, the more shock it can absorb and still return to its original shape or something approximating that shape. Obviously, there are limits, as major bankruptcies have repeatedly proven, and large size often undermines agility. Large organizations, particularly those that fail to survive, have a legendary lack of agility. Smaller enterprises are generally less resilient to adverse impacts (hence their high rate of failure) but are often better able to avoid them and to dodge threats and seize opportunities when they see them coming.

Resilience and agility must be designed into an entity. For instance, the Vendée Globe race is a solo, nonstop, around-the-world sailing race that includes passage through the tumultuous Southern Ocean, where waves up to 110 feet high have been recorded. In these waters, racers actually expect to be "knocked down," which means submersion of their vessels' masts. Vessels competing in the Vendée Globe are designed to self-right even when the mast is submerged up to 45 degrees. That is resilience.

Not only can an enterprise improve its resilience to specific known events through better preparation, response, and recovery, it can also improve its resilience to unknown and even to unknowable events. Take, for example, preparing for the outbreak of a pandemic. A pandemic can result in quarantine or loss of goods, facilities, or personnel and restrict activities and movements of workers, suppliers, and customers. But by addressing the known risks and effects of a pandemic, the enterprise can be better prepared for a range of unknown events with similar effects, including hurricanes, earthquakes, war, or bioterrorism.

Thus it is generally preferable to anticipate a risk—a specific event or development—and prepare for it rather than ignore it or simply hope for the best. Granted, anticipation and preparation are not always possible. When an event or development simply cannot be anticipated, an enterprise will be best served by improving its general resilience. In other words, the crisis that you prepare for may not be the one you experience, but that preparation will improve your resilience, come what may.

Voice of Experience

"The hardest thing to deal with is the board of a company that's doing really well. They tend to take an incremental view as opposed to looking at the environment and what's changing around them. Everything is good. The sun is shining.

"You might ask a board, 'So, how ready are you for the next downturn? Do you do simulations of what a downturn might look like, how fast it could happen, or how long it would last?' It seems like a waste of time and money and resources, and instead they're devoting their energy to increasing shareholder value and top line revenue.

"I think it goes back to whether this is simply a function of human nature that we'll never be able to change other than on an occasion, and it obviously depends on the leadership and the directors at the time."

—Suzanne Hopgood, Director

Agility requires awareness, speed, and flexibility, qualities rarely associated with large enterprises. Preparation can help an organization become more agile, but several structural and operational factors should also be considered. For instance, the level of centralization regarding management control and the degree to which responsibility, accountability, and authority are delegated down the line will affect agility. The more decentralized the approach, and the more middle managers and employees are able to make decisions and take action, the more nimble the organization will become.

It's also essential that the organization maintain a constant state of vigilance. Essentially, vigilance and its corollary, situational awareness, is the characteristic of being aware of the environment and changes in it, and of what the organization can do to respond effectively. It's harder than it sounds, and many enterprises fail to choose promontories from which to scan the horizon, fail to develop devices with which to detect changes, and fail to employ early-warning systems regarding threats and opportunities. (We discuss these matters in Chapter 5, "Maintain Constant Vigilance.")

Developing agility can itself expose an enterprise to risks, unless the right processes have also been developed. For example, delegating additional authority—even to middle management, let alone to sales reps and customer service reps—can present risks. So can allowing "skunk works" and other remote teams to perform research and develop business opportunities outside the bureaucracy. These are essential activities but must be properly managed. The Risk Intelligent Enterprise takes steps to inculcate knowledge of risk and risk management into people at all levels. It also establishes rigorous monitoring and reporting systems in order to control and flag risks when authority is delegated.

On that note, the enterprise must be resilient and agile in relation to both financial and nonfinancial events and developments. Our earlier point about executives' and board members' lack of focus on nonfinancial reporting measures has deep relevance here. In most organizations, transactions and accounts are monitored and reported that such financial effects are usually readily apparent.

Not so for nonfinancial effects, which include developments regarding organizational reputation, brand equity, stakeholder relations, legal and regulatory matters, and environment, health, and safety concerns. These are less quantifiable and measurable, not monitored or reported on as formally or rigorously (if at all) and thus far less apparent. However, nonfinancial effects can generate financial effects with rapid and severe consequences. So, resilience and agility demands an awareness of potential nonfinancial as well as financial developments and their potential impact.

The less prudence with which others conduct their affairs, the greater prudence with which we must conduct our own affairs.
—*Warren Buffett*[35]

To Adapt or Not to Adapt? That Is the Question

Like species, enterprises are subject to a process of natural selection that favors the resilient and the agile. Charles Darwin is often credited with saying, "It is not the strongest of the species that survives, nor the most intelligent that survives. It is the one that is the most adaptable to change." This remains true of enterprises despite occasional government interventions to prop up the slow-to-adapt. Actually, the interventions are intended to preserve jobs and stabilize the economy rather than to prop up the enterprises. Whether such interventions help or hurt the enterprise and the economy can be understood only over time.

Extending Darwin's thinking into the field of cybernetics, Ashby's Law of Requisite Variety[36] essentially states that it takes variety to deal with variety and complexity in the environment. The greater the variety and complexity and thus the uncertainty in the environment, the greater the variety required to survive and thrive in that environment.

Stated another way, the more finely adapted to a specific environment a species becomes, the more likely it is to be successful *as long as its environment does not change*. Conversely, such a species is more likely to fail if its environment changes suddenly. (Requisite variety is discussed further in Chapter 7, "Manage the Key Connections," as a means of dealing with complexity.) As a practical matter, the organism or organization is either fit to survive in the new environment or not. If it is not, it becomes extinct.

Unlike other species, individuals and the enterprises they create can choose how they adapt and evolve. Even so, individuals and enterprises often make choices that jeopardize their very existence. That may be their right, provided the laws permit it. However, in such cases the more interesting issue is whether those choices are conscious.

If the decision not to adapt is conscious, so be it. If it is not conscious and the individual or enterprise would prefer to adapt and survive, what can be done to improve the understanding of the situation, and thus improve the decisions and the chances of survival? An enterprise should be able to develop a sufficient variety of strategies to cope with a variety of changed environments. If companies are to improve their resilience and agility, then their ability to adapt to change must also improve.

The Darwin awards—"A Chronicle of Enterprising Demises: Honoring those who improve the species... by accidentally removing themselves from it!"[37]—document stories of individuals who made astonishingly bad choices and got themselves killed. No corporate version has yet been developed; however, if one ever is, there are many candidates awaiting their posthumous moment of glory.

Voice of Experience

"The real key in our view in many of our product lines is to think big, start small, and then scale fast. Crank it up, take a good look at it, and then if it looks right 'blow and go.' If, on the other hand, it doesn't appear as though it's likely going to be a winner, kill it quick and move on to the next opportunity."[38]

—Jim Porter, Retired Chief Engineer and Vice President, Engineering and Operations, DuPont

Risk Comes with the Territory

Enterprises regularly place themselves in the running for a Darwin Award by ignoring risks that could have been foreseen or by failing to manage risks they have foreseen. Equally frequent is failure to thrive due to extreme risk aversion, missed opportunities, and blindness to the risks inherent in specific initiatives. Those failures rest largely with senior management and the board of directors. It is up to senior management to protect existing value and to create new value within the enterprise; it is up to the board to govern and guide management in those activities. These amount to sacred duties (in business terms) and they are duties that too many boards and management teams have failed to carry out in recent years.

We maintain that one of the first tasks necessary in fulfilling these duties is for executives and directors to become aware of the need to exercise judgment in areas where they may have been operating on tradition, habit, or autopilot. In this context, the exercise of judgment will typically occur in areas fraught with uncertainty regarding threats and opportunities, often under turbulent conditions or circumstances.

To the extent that the leadership can anticipate and prepare for those conditions and circumstances and enhance the resilience and agility of the organization, they will also enhance its ability to survive and thrive. This is the sense in which risk intelligence is never actually attained, but rather is an ongoing way of making better decisions that enable the enterprise better to adapt. This represents a departure from many conventional management and board practices, and is certainly a departure from conventional risk management and its failures.

CHAPTER 2

Conventional Risk Management Has Failed

We seem to have a once-in-a-lifetime crisis every three or four years.
—Leslie Rahl, Capital Market Risk Advisors

In the global economic and business environment of the past 25 or 30 years, we have been living very full lives indeed. In fact, Ms. Rahl's statement appears to understate the case, as Exhibit 2.1 demonstrates.

The sheer frequency of these events reveals that they are neither rare nor isolated. They are the too-common products of complex, interconnected, even systemic developments. They often come about as unintended consequences of well-intentioned innovations, management practices, public policies, or cultural developments.

Most people persist in viewing crises as rare and unpredictable and as impossible or too expensive to prepare for. In some cases, those skeptics may be right, as they were about the Y2K "crisis" in 2000. But they are often wrong, and ignoring those who issue warnings (e.g., that home prices cannot rise indefinitely) jeopardizes their assets, careers, and enterprises.

To better protect their fortunes and their enterprises, leaders might adopt the watchwords "expect the unexpected" and always ensure that their enterprises and people will be ready to meet the challenges the unexpected can pose. For instance, Dr. Scott Parazynski, a NASA astronaut, undertook one of the most difficult spacewalks ever on November 3, 2007. A solar panel was torn, which put the entire International Space Station program at risk of failure. The spacewalk involved the repair of a jagged tangle of wires that could either burn or tear a hole in Parazynski's

EXHIBIT 2.1 "Once-in-a-Lifetime Crises," 1982–2008

South and Central American default 1982	Russian sovereign default 1998
U.S. Savings and Loan Crisis 1985	Long-Term Capital Management 1998
Space Shuttle Challenger 1986	Brazil 1998–1999
October Stock Market Crash 1987	Dot-com bubble bursts 2000
U.S. high-yield bond market collapse and demise of Drexel Burnham 1990	9/11 and payment system disruption 2001
Salomon Brothers 1991–92	Enron/Andersen 2001
Sterling Crisis 1992	Argentine crisis 2002
Metallgesellschaft 1993	German banking crisis 2002
U.S. bond market crash 1994	Space Shuttle Columbia 2003
Orange County, CA, bankruptcy 1994	Hurricane Katrina 2005
Mexico 1995	Amaranth 2006
Daiwa Bank 1995	Subprime mortgage crisis 2007
Barings Bank 1995	Credit bubble bursts 2007
Sumitomo 1996	Real estate bubble bursts 2007
Asian financial crisis 1997	Bernard Madoff investment fraud 2008
	The "Great Recession" 2008–09

suit, which would have led to his death. The walk was also the farthest ever from a command capsule, was of out the direct sight of the command capsule, and required a very delicate task while wearing cumbersome gloves.

Riding on a 90-foot robotic arm, Parazynski could just barely reach the damaged panel. It helped that at $6'2''$ he had a long reach and had 17 other spacewalks under his belt, including five from the current mission. Prior experience and a highly trained crew, combined with closely coordinated teamwork and quickly but carefully constructed plans, enabled a very dangerous but effective response to and recovery from an unanticipated near-disaster.

Corporate executives and astronauts dress for success quite differently and breathe in distinctly different atmospheres, but both can unexpectedly find themselves out on a limb. Yet even when attempting to consider the future, three factors—the herd mentality of human beings, the systemic nature of many crises, and the limits of conventional risk management—mitigate against crisis prevention and effective responses. These factors can, however, be addressed, as can others that make risk management so difficult.

This chapter examines some drivers of what has come to be known as the "Worst Financial Crisis since the Great Depression," and the "conventional wisdom" of the majority of homeowners, bankers, investors, and corporate and political leaders at the time. It also examines the theoretical underpinnings and development of conventional risk management, which also prevailed and generally continues. Our goal is to illuminate factors that generate financial crises and to set the stage for our discussion of an unconventional approach to risk management in Chapter 3.

What Goes Up Must Come Down

Financial meltdowns have become more frequent since the 1970s, which may, ironically, mark a return to normalcy. Panics, price swings, market meltdowns, and bank failures have characterized economies for centuries. Indeed, the roughly 25 years from 1945 to 1970 represent a time of unusual financial calm, with the post–World War II rebuilding of European and Japanese industries occupying much of the planet's economic resources and the blessing of fairly stable markets.

It is in the nature of markets to rise and fall, and occasionally to skyrocket and crash. Even *generally* orderly fiscal and monetary policies—particularly the Federal Reserve's attempts to engineer "soft landings" since the wrenching, inflation-fighting recession of the early 1980s—have failed to end the cycle of expansion and contraction that characterizes market economies. Today, however, policies may be overwhelmed by the global financial market's complexity, growth, and penchant for innovation (the latter giving rise to securitization, high-yield bonds, credit default swaps, and other often exotic instruments).

Paradoxically, policy measures designed to prevent the recurrence or to remedy the effects of past crises can trigger future ones. Similarly, even business strategies that aim to enhance resiliency and agility can expose enterprises to new risks. At a minimum, policy and strategic initiatives can breed the overconfidence that sets the stage for future crises and causes market participants to ignore those who actually do see trouble coming, as in the housing bubble and credit crisis of the 2000s.

Early Warnings Ignored, Again

Back in 2001, a U.S. recession in the wake of the 1990s dot-com boom and bust prompted the Federal Reserve to reduce the Fed Funds rate 11 times (from 6.5 percent to 1.75 percent) between May 2000 and December 2001.[1] This led to reduced mortgage rates, which in turn contributed to a surge in home prices. Perceiving endlessly rising housing prices and, given Fed policy, the prospect of continued low interest rates, many homeowners tapped their increased equity and used it and other borrowings to speculate on larger homes or on second or third properties, further inflating the housing bubble.

Subprime lending was identified as a concern as early as 1998. On June 23, 1998, Richard Spillenkothen, director of the Federal Reserve's Division of Banking Supervision, issued a supervisory letter to each Federal Reserve Bank and to each domestic and foreign banking organization supervised by the Federal Reserve.[2] The letter noted that banks had been easing their lending standards to remain competitive in the booming housing market. It went on to caution that if carried too far, the practice could "undermine a bank's financial health, especially if the economy weakens or the extraordinary recent performance of business profits and cash flows does not persist."

Spillenkothen also advised banks to "consider the potential impact of a wide range of borrower default rates and losses on the institution" and to "resist any tendency to assume in evaluating credits that the unusually favorable economic environment of the last few years will continue indefinitely." (Again, this was in *1998*.)

Similarly, in 2005, Yale economist Robert Shiller warned of "irrational exuberance" in the real estate market. At the time, it was reported that he believed the housing-price boom taking place in big metropolitan areas in the United States and around the world had no basis in economic fundamentals or precedent in real estate history.[3]

In 2006, the U.S. housing bubble burst, leaving many subprime borrowers unable to make their payments and many investors with mortgage-backed securities of little value. An international credit crisis, battered bank stocks, bank failures, financial institution bailouts, and the Great Recession followed. Analysts at Sanford C. Bernstein raised their 2008–10 total loss estimate for the banking industry by 11 percent to $420 billion, and said they remained cautious on the sector.[4]

In Black September 2008, the markets fluctuated by 2,000 points in a single week, beginning with the bailouts of Fannie Mae and Freddie Mac, followed by the collapse of Lehman Brothers, the fire sale of Merrill Lynch to Bank of America, and extensive efforts to rescue major insurer AIG. By then, public outrage over plummeting home prices, rising unemployment, and retirement fund losses triggered demands for massive regulatory reform. The proposed reforms ranged from caps on executive compensation to borrowing limits to restrictions on certain financial instruments.

On September 21, 2008, in a move that "fundamentally reshaped an era of high finance that defined the modern Gilded Age," the Federal Reserve announced that Morgan Stanley and Goldman Sachs, Wall Street's last major independent investment banks, would become bank holding companies and thus subject to far greater regulation.[5] The U.S. investment banking industry as we had known it had come to an end.

As usual in such situations, hindsight revealed early-warning signs that were missed or ignored. Former Fed Chairman Alan Greenspan admitted to missing riskier mortgage trends and rising home foreclosures despite Spillenkothen's 1998 and others' warnings. Lenders abandoned long-standing credit policies to pursue market share and loan portfolio growth based on unrealistic assumptions.

More cynically, "the greater fool" principle prevailed in many quarters. That principle states that even if you pay inflated prices for an asset in a bubble, a "greater fool" will pay a higher price and enable you to profit. More cynically still, a number of mortgage originators and lenders cheerfully abandoned their credit standards because they would be reselling the loans (presumably to "greater fools").

Some experts maintain that bank regulators lacked "counter-cyclical control mechanisms." According to Professors Charles Goodhart and Avinash Persaud, "Having foreseen the danger, the regulatory authorities did not have the instruments to do much about it. The Basel regime for capital adequacy does nothing to constrain credit booms. Its effect, if any, on the crunch will be to deepen it further."[6] Goodhart and Persaud maintain that market-based pricing and risk-sensitive models have their shortcomings. Specifically, the models tell banks that risks have fallen because the values of the underlying assets have risen and that capital is adequate for even more risk taking, when in fact the reverse is true.

This raises an important point and a key theme in this book—it was not financial institutions' models or math that got them into trouble. It was the assumptions underlying their models. Implicit in any model and its internal mathematical relationships are certain assumptions about the environment, the future, the motives of market participants, and a host of other unknowns that cannot, in fact, be accurately modeled or foretold.

Predictive models generally provide for the inclusion of "add factors." Add factors are variables that modelers can adjust according to their judgments about past and potential tendencies of the model to overpredict or underpredict whatever is being forecasted. According to economists Zvi Griliches and Michael D. Intriligator, "Experience indicates that such judgmental add factors can improve significantly on the accuracy of forecasts made with an econometric model."[7]

They can improve accuracy, but very often they do not. More broadly, it is up to executives and directors *not* to rely exclusively on models or any other substitutes for their judgment. John Maynard Keynes once said, "It is better to be roughly right than precisely wrong." That is particularly the case in decisions about value-creating endeavors undertaken in changing, unknown, or turbulent circumstances. As we noted earlier, conventional approaches to risk management as simply asset preservation tend to generate either risk aversion or unbridled risk taking in the pursuit of value.

The crisis of 2007–08 was, like most financial crises, ignited by executives prone to risk taking in the pursuit of value. Oddly, such risk taking is almost always accompanied by a failure to exercise good judgment. The excuse offered for this failure is usually overreliance on models, hedging strategies, risk-sharing schemes, and other devices that turn out to have been deeply flawed when inevitably the unexpected occurs. In other words in the pursuit of value, executives can be prone to abandon judgment in favor of models, strategies, and schemes that are in fact no substitute for judgment. Moreover, those devices are usually founded on incorrect, outmoded, or otherwise flawed assumptions.

As we will show, however, leadership teams that do exercise judgment, even to the point of overriding their models and established strategies, can enable their organizations to survive and thrive in challenging circumstances.

LESSONS LEARNED?   We review the foregoing facts to highlight three broad lessons:

1. Crises are inevitable given the business cycle, and the complexity of modern finance, the interconnectedness of markets, the motivations of market participants, and the optimism, politics, and limits of policymakers.
2. Warnings of crises typically occur and are just as typically ignored. Some people ignore what they see as pessimism, as when they dismiss the economist who has, as one wag put it, "correctly forecasted seven of the past three recessions." Others ignore warnings because they believe they can profit by doing so. But there is absolutely no reason to reject all warnings.
3. People survive and thrive even in crises. Many individuals and institutions made money in the housing bubble, exercising judgment to effect a timely exit and even reentry. Those who perished or suffered "near-death" experiences tended to hold highly leveraged positions in substandard markets. Some who survived accepted government assistance, which may or may not have been instrumental in their survival, but surely calmed the markets.

Equally important are lessons gleaned from those who experienced severe losses due to some or all of the "fatal flaws" in their approaches toward risk and risk management:

- Counting on false assumptions
- Failing to exercise vigilance
- Ignoring velocity and momentum

- Failing to make the key connections and manage complexity
- Failing to imagine failure
- Relying on unverified sources of information
- Maintaining inadequate margins of safety
- Focusing exclusively on the short term
- Taking the wrong—rather than right—risks
- Abandoning operational discipline

In certain circumstances, any one of these flaws can be fatal. In combination or during a crisis, they can kill an enterprise, send it to the brink of ruin, or push it into the government's arms. On a brighter note, the antitheses of these flaws constitute ten essential risk intelligence skills that enable an enterprise to survive and thrive in uncertain and turbulent times. We introduce those skills briefly in Chapter 3 and cover them in depth in Part 2.

Reimagining Risk Management

The foregoing prepares us for an examination of the foundations of conventional risk management. But before we proceed, three points ought to be made:

1. Conventional risk management, like any form of conventional thinking, rests upon a set of assumptions, an accepted understanding of how the world works.
2. Individuals and organizations tend to *automatically* reject notions that appear to contradict their assumptions and their understanding of how the world works.
3. There is a predictable process by which people come to accept new assumptions and a new understanding of how the world works: rejection, consideration, and acceptance.

That latter point has been expressed in various ways in the literature of persuasion and philosophy. The nineteenth-century German philosopher Schopenhauer stated, "All truth passes through three stages. First, it is ridiculed. Second, it is violently opposed. Third, it is accepted as being self-evident." Please bear this in mind if you are a board member or executive who wants to introduce a new approach to risk management to your organization.

Conventional risk management, like conventional wisdom, rests upon a set of assumptions. (The term "conventional wisdom" is usually not applied to known and proven facts. It is no longer conventional wisdom that the sun revolves around the earth. It is, in fact, the reverse. On the other hand, conventional wisdom states that low interest rates will stimulate business lending and economic growth—wisdom that did not apply to the U.S. economy in late 2008 and early 2009.) More broadly, the most elegant model, if built upon flawed assumptions, will have little applicability in the real world. So, to understand why conventional risk management is failing, one needs to understand its assumptions and how they have been applied.

The Evolution of Finance, Market, and Risk Management Theory

In the world of hard sciences, where variables can be controlled, certain assumptions are appropriate. In the rest of the world, they usually are not and any that have been made should be thoroughly checked. Thus, the assumptions underlying "conventional wisdom" describe how the world appears to be or should be and how people appear to behave or should behave. These assumptions tend to be normative, rather than descriptive, and often yield little insight regarding the world as it really is. Yet such assumptions are often very difficult to identify precisely because they become an implicit part of our worldview.

What if forecasts are unreliable, probabilities offer little guidance, and the unexpected occurs much more often than we assume? Turbulence is difficult (some would argue impossible) to predictively model, volatility is inevitable, and interactions are complex and tightly coupled. These three conditions generate high uncertainty and often huge and sudden losses for the unprepared. They also limit the value of conventional wisdom and of normative models, especially in uncertain and turbulent times.

Therefore, your greatest source of both risk and opportunity lies in constructively challenging what you regard as conventional wisdom. By that we mean the conventional wisdom regarding risk and value creation in general, and the assumptions every leader makes about the business risks and opportunities his or her enterprise faces. (Chapter 4, "Check Your Assumptions at the Door," discusses this topic in greater detail.) To the extent that you assume stability, predictability, and independence of events, your conventional wisdom may put you at great risk.

Challenging Conventional Wisdom

Conventional economic and finance theory and related risk management models have evolved based on the seminal work of Gauss, Bernoulli, de Moivre, Bachelier, Pearson, Knight, von Neumann and Morgenstern, Samuelson, Markowitz, Sharpe, Fama, Black, Scholes, Merton, and Malkiel, among others. Early studies of probability, beginning in the 1560s with Girolamo Cardano, were based on gambling.

According to Cardano, fair games of chance are founded on the notion of *ceteris paribus* or "all other things being equal." In *Liber de Ludo Aleae* (*The Book of Games and Chance*), Cardano wrote, "The most fundamental principle of all in gambling is simply equal conditions, of opponents, of bystanders, of money, of situation, of the dice box, and of the die itself. To the extent to which you depart from that equality, if it is in your opponent's favor, you are a fool, and if in your own, you are unjust." Despite the latter observation, Cardano also discussed effective methods of cheating.

Standard financial and economic analysis is built on the concept of *ceteris paribus*—that a situation is free from any influence other than the specific factors under consideration. However, Johann Carl Frederick Gauss noticed that measures of celestial mechanics were greatly affected by imperfections of measurement instruments, earth tremors, atmospheric conditions, and other uncontrollable factors. To account for these errors, Gauss developed a method known as "least squares," which minimizes the distance between a line or curve and a set of plotted data points or observations. This led to the "bell curve," and the so-called "normal" distribution.

The smoothness of Gauss's bell curve rests on the assumption that errors are random and "normally" distributed. Gauss thus leads us to conclude that extreme events are exceptionally rare and should be discarded as anomalies. (Nassim Taleb eloquently addresses the problems of Gaussian mathematics in *Fooled by Randomness*[8] and *The Black Swan*.[9]) *Ceteris paribus* and Gauss's assumptions formed the basis of modern risk management, which "assumes away" anomalous possibilities. In that context, business and investing terms such as sigma, standard deviation, variance, and correlation trace their lineage to Gauss's theories.

Because events in the conventional risk management model are evenly distributed, they are generally nonscalable. Scalability refers to the capacity of an entity, such as a company, process, or system, to grow in response to demand. Scalability also captures the distinction between an arithmetic and geometric scale. An arithmetic scale is composed of equal increments. A geometric (or logarithmic) scale is composed of increments an order of magnitude greater—usually ten times greater—than the preceding measure.

Standard deviation is built on an arithmetic scale. Arithmetic scales are useful for describing phenomena that follow a normal distribution. Data sets of the height and weight of people, the amount of annual rainfall in a locale, and even the width of rose petals fall into a normal distribution. But for phenomena such as stock market variation and volatility, one needs a logarithmic scale because an arithmetic scale cannot capture such variability and volatility. Logarithmic scales allow for extreme events. The Richter Scale for measuring earth tremors, for example, is built on a logarithmic scale.

The fair toss of a coin is often used as an example of smoothly distributed or arithmetic randomness. The coin has no emotion and no memory. Each toss of the coin is equal to the preceding one, and additional tosses won't change the distribution of the curve once a given point has been reached. There's no volatility, spiking, or off-the-scale event to consider. However, unlike coins, people have memories, albeit short ones, and they experience fear, greed, enthusiasm, and dread.

Rome wasn't built in a day. But Las Vegas was built on the bell curve. In a casino, Cardano's conditions are met. The rules are established, probabilities are known, conditions are stable, and outcomes are observable. Casinos can control limits and losses and hold certain conditions "equal," which is how they make money. They don't allow billion-dollar bets or card counting. They can stop a player's winning streak whenever they choose. They know that most people will lose, and they carefully control the winnings—all thanks to the normal curve.

CRACKS IN THE BELL CURVE   In the hard sciences, an experiment is an attempt to validate or falsify a hypothesis through observation of phenomena under controlled conditions. Experiments are designed so that all factors—except the one under study—are kept equal. Experimental errors such as measurement error and observer bias are eliminated or minimized. Even so, control of all variables can be extremely difficult, and errors still occur. For that reason, scientific procedure calls for results to be reproducible by others and externally validated.

As difficult as it is to achieve *ceteris paribus* and objectivity in the natural sciences, it's far more difficult in the social sciences, including economics, psychology, and organizational behavior. Indeed, it is literally impossible to achieve similar levels of control, validation, and predictability when it comes to human behavior in economies, markets, and enterprises.

Thus, history is replete with examples of probable events that failed to occur and improbable events that did occur. Rather than taking normal outcomes and mild randomness as its starting point, what might be called the turbulent model starts with what Benoit Mandelbrot[10] calls "wildly random" events characterized by high energy, instability, and lack of structure. These are events that the bell curve cannot predict. As Mandelbrot stated, "according to a normal distribution, from 1916 to 2003 the Daily Index of the Dow Jones Industrial Average should have moved more than 3.4 percent on 58 days. In fact, there were 1,001 such days."[11]

Taking a (Random) Walk

In 1828, Scottish botanist Robert Brown's observations of pollen particles suspended in water led to the theory of Brownian Motion, which states that particle movement has a continuous flow that is random, independent, and nonscalable. In Brownian Motion, dust particles are randomly bombarded by equally weighted water molecules and produce what has since been called the "random walk."

Building on Gauss's notion of random distribution, Karl Pearson introduced the "random walk" in 1905.[12] In his study of mosquito populations, Pearson developed a random formula to model how mosquitoes invaded cleared areas of the jungle. Pearson's "random walk," as he called it in *Nature* magazine, is central to probability theory.

The "random walk" was later adopted as financial theory, fostering conventional market models that assume a "random walk"—a series of small, unpredictable steps with no apparent pattern, resembling the path of a drunkard tottering from one foot to the other. But what if the market also runs, hops, skips, and jumps? Sometimes the market may take small steps, but at other times large ones. Again, it wasn't their models or math that got financial institutions into trouble. It was their assumption that extreme events, such as a huge spike in mortgage loan defaults, were extremely rare.

Are Extreme Events Extremely Rare?

Most modern risk-management models exclude the potential for wild, extreme, irrational, inefficient, and herdlike behavior because they are not "normal." They treat these events as anomalies, despite the ancient Greek warning "We must expect the unexpected often to happen." Worse, they do so despite evidence to the contrary, such as the list in Exhibit 2.1, and despite the findings of Eugene Fama, who noted, "If the population of price changes is strictly normal, on average for any stock ... an observation more than five standard deviations from the mean should be observed about once every 7,000 years. In fact, such observations seem to occur about once every three to four years."[13] No wonder we seem to experience "once in a lifetime" crises so often.

A conventional but potentially fatally flawed practice is to assess risk based on impact and likelihood. Of what use is such a practice when the likelihood of extreme events is underestimated to the degrees observed by Fama? According to Swiss Re, "predictions about the likelihood of multi-causal losses actually depend either on sound understanding of cause-and-effect relationships or on a detailed loss history, and the risks of the future have neither of the two."[14]

Take, for example, the Transportation Security Administration (TSA). According to a Government Accountability Office (GAO) report released in March 2009, "TSA officials said they do not believe that a traditional risk assessment methodology—such as that provided for in the National Infrastructure Protection Plan (NIPP)—provides a reliable method for determining the likelihood of terrorist attacks given the adaptive nature of terrorists. According to this view, unlike natural disasters, when one avenue of attack is deterred by a countermeasure, terrorists will find a new mode of attack, shifting their focus to other vulnerable areas of the transportation sector.

"Because terrorists adapt their tactics in response to countermeasures, TSA contends that *threat assessments that quantify the likelihood of a terrorism scenario have limited value because any numerical value assigned to threats could be invalid by the end of the day*" [italics added].

The GAO report goes on to say, "According to TSA officials, TSA's rejection of the NIPP's risk management framework in favor of an intelligence-driven approach is based in part on the assumption that risk assessment is intended to precisely predict terrorist threats. However, *this assumption is inconsistent with the purpose of risk assessment, which is to provide a tool for prioritizing which assets require greater protection relative to finite resources* [italics added]. As we reported in December 2005, although agencies may not have enough information to identify and characterize all threats related to their assets, known or imagined adverse events should be characterized in some detail based on an understanding of an adversary's capabilities and intentions.

"Additionally, TSA contends that the *traditional method of identifying terrorism scenarios is flawed because unlikely yet highly consequential threats that have never occurred cannot be anticipated and will not be included in a threat assessment* [italics added]. For example, prior to 9/11, an attack using a plane as a weapon would have been viewed as unlikely."

This "dialogue" between TSA and NIPP epitomizes the debate between conventional and unconventional risk management. As the GAO points out, NIPP's conventional approach was (a) mistakenly assumed to be a precise predictor of terrorist threats, when it is, (b) actually intended "to provide a tool for prioritizing which assets require greater protection relative to finite resources." Similar difficulties arise constantly in risk management. As the GAO points out, the TSA sees traditional risk assessment's inability to account for highly consequential events that have never occurred as a deep flaw. Hence the TSA's preference for an intelligence-driven approach, which, incidentally, is not mutually exclusive to NIPP's approach. In a sense, according to this GAO report, TSA is simply rejecting the notion that predictions have value. And that raises an important question.

Are Forecasts Meaningful?

The record of forecasting in business, investing, and economics is not good, particularly when it comes to crises, which are by definition improbable and, well, unpredictable. In *The Black Swan: The Impact of the Highly Improbable*, Nassim Taleb refers to rare, random, high-impact events as "black swans." (In

Europe, the notion that "all swans are white" was indisputable, by Europeans at least, until a black one was discovered in Australia in 1697.)

In the United States, forecasting is a $200 billion to $300 billion a year industry. In his book *The Fortune Sellers: The Big Business of Buying and Selling Predictions,*[15] William Sherden describes a "reign of error" created by the forecasting inabilities of economists, analysts, futurists, technologists, business planners, and other prognosticators. Sherden concludes that forecasts, beyond the very short term, are extremely unreliable with an error rate worse than chance.[16] For example, although the variables are very well known and precisely measured, weather forecasts remain unreliable. If we can't forecast the weather—a natural phenomenon with known and measured causes—how can we forecast economic conditions?

As Hurricane Katrina demonstrated, probabilities mean nothing when disasters strike. In September 2005, *BusinessWeek* noted, "In [the cases of] New Orleans, New York, *Challenger*, *Columbia*, and the blackout in the summer of 2003, the issue wasn't the lack of information [because the data existed] . . . Problems emerged because of deeply flawed organizations beset by poor management, siloed cultures, and inadequate communications. People could not deal with what they believed to be remote, low probability, high risk catastrophes even when confronted with irrefutable data."[17]

Interconnectedness is another complicating—and amplifying—factor. In *A Demon of Our Own Design*, Richard Bookstaber observes, "The cascade of failure that occurs in systems that share tight coupling and complexity gives rise to what are called normal accidents . . . that are to be expected; they are an unavoidable result of the structure of the process. The more complex and tightly coupled the system, the greater the frequency of normal accidents."[18]

Bookstaber states that the analysis of such accidents in airlines (the ValuJet crash) and in nuclear power plants (Three Mile Island and Chernobyl) reveals that because of the complex nature of the system, "the safety features themselves contributed to the accident"[19] and disaster was triggered by a simple, apparently innocent action that initiated a chain of increasingly problematic events. He also notes that attempts to prevent these disasters by layering on safety systems may have the opposite effect. "You never end up as safe as you think because there are inevitably points of interaction that can hide failures. And the more layers there are, the more obscured those points become."[20]

Many seemingly unrelated events can be better understood as tightly coupled. (The issue of coupling and complexity is covered in Chapter 7, "Manage the Key Connections.") In that vein, Bookstaber describes how the breakdown of basic market physics during enormous sell-offs such as in 1987 means that all stocks moved together. He states in such cases, "the huge volatility of the market broke down all but the most fundamental relationships between the market securities. The usual day-to-day world where investors cared about subtleties like corporate earnings or analyst forecasts dissolved as the energy of the market was turned up. All stocks moved together; if it was a stock, it was sold ... It was like plasma physics: as matter becomes hotter, it becomes less differentiated ... The high-energy in the financial markets created a world where securities were no more differentiable than that they contained risk."[21]

The market can remain irrational longer than you can remain solvent.

—*John Maynard Keynes*

Are Markets Efficient and Rational?

Markets actually do not appear to be rational, as the crash of 2008 and many other past crashes have demonstrated. As Warren Buffet reportedly said, "I'd be a bum on the street with a tin cup if the markets were always efficient." If you still think the market is rational, consider that September 29, 2008, saw the worst market drop ever, of 778 points in the Dow Jones Industrial Average and 106.85 in the S&P 500. Consider further that Benoit Mandelbrot estimated that according to conventional financial theory the chance of the prior worst drop, Black Monday, October 19, 1987, was less than 1 in 10 to the 50th power. As Mandelbrot pointed out, "Odds so small have no meaning."[22]

By December 2008, the markets were on track for the worst losses since 1931. Emotions shifted from the irrational exuberance and utter disregard for risk that had led to the bubble to the irrational fear and risk aversion that followed it.

Fear came to dominate the markets so much that even though governments around the globe were pulling every economic lever they could to kick-start the economy, banks and consumers remained on the sidelines as unemployment continued to rise and home prices continued to fall. Few businesses escaped unscathed.

And that's the point. When it comes to a crisis, forecasts and probabilities have limited value. Conventional risk assessment and management cannot really account for events that have never—or only rarely—occurred. For these reasons, conventional risk management fails due to flawed assumptions.

Conventional theories of finance, markets, and risk describe the world as it "ought to be" rather than as it is. Conventional assumptions—that factors are equal, randomness is mild, extreme events are rare, forecasts are meaningful, events are independent of one another, and markets are rational—have outlived their usefulness. To survive and thrive in uncertainty, we need an unconventional approach.

CHAPTER 3

An Unconventional Approach
to Risk Management

> *The logical, competent decisions of management that are critical to the success of their companies are also the reasons why they lose their positions of leadership.*
>
> —Clayton M. Christensen, *The Innovator's Dilemma*[1]

From our brief tour of conventional views of risk and their historical development, we return to the responsibilities of enterprise leaders in this very uncertain world. The events of the recent past, and of the past 25 years, have surely made the case for reevaluating approaches to risk. Exhibit 3.1 sums up that case with a point-by-point comparison of conventional wisdom and unconventional truths regarding approaches to risk in finance theory and business management.

Despite its omnipresence, risk is rarely well understood, as reflected in the linguistic wrestling match of numerous attempts to define it. The Latin word *riscus* was derived from the Greek navigation term *rhizikon,* meaning "root, stone, cut of the firm land," which designated "a difficulty to avoid in the sea."[2] In this sense, risk meant literally running into danger. The French may have adopted their word "hazard," used to express risk or exposure to danger, from the Arabic *al zahr,* referring to dice, a game the Crusaders brought back to Europe. Hence, risk is associated with the potential for loss or harm.

In his challenging but seminal 1921 book, *Risk, Uncertainty and Profit,* Frank Knight proudly declared his work to be one of pure theory and condemned the "pragmatic and philistine tendencies of the present age." As we noted in the preface to this book, Knight separated the definitions of

EXHIBIT 3.1 Conventional Wisdom versus Unconventional Realities

Conventional Wisdom *A random walk*	Unconventional Realities *A random walk with hops, skips, and jumps*
Factors affecting events will remain equal	Factors affecting events will change
Events are mildly random	Events can be wildly random
Extreme events are rare and should be treated as anomalies	Extreme events are more common than we think and should be treated as such
Forecasts are accurate and reliable	Forecasts are inaccurate and unreliable
Events are independent of one another	Events interact
Markets are efficient and rational	Markets are neither efficient nor rational

risk and uncertainty. He defined risk as measurable uncertainty, where the probability of an outcome is known or knowable, and defined uncertainty as unmeasurable and unknowable.

Given his definition, perhaps enterprise risk management (ERM) might be more usefully viewed as enterprise uncertainty management. Conventional risk management has also tended to separate the discussion of value and risk. Yet whenever you are talking about protecting existing assets or creating future growth, you must also talk about risks to those existing assets and the risks that must be undertaken and managed to successfully create and sustain future growth.

The discussion of value and risk cannot be separated. For this reason, it would be best to speak of enterprise management rather than enterprise risk management. Risk intelligent enterprise management properly incorporates risk intelligence into every decision, practice, and initiative that management undertakes.

Frankly, the concept of ERM has been misunderstood, misrepresented, and misused to a point at which it has little real meaning. Too often, it is seen by operating management as a complex, bureaucratic burden on the business separate from the realities that they must understand and manage every day. And the more separately it is perceived, the less successful it is likely to be. Neither does ERM usually capture the imagination of most senior executives or board members. Nor does it provide a proper framework—from either the conceptual or practical standpoint—for our approach to risk. Hence, the term "risk intelligence" or "risk intelligent enterprise management."

Broadly defined, risk management is the discipline of improving your chances of survival and success, particularly in uncertainty and turbulence. In this context, we define risk as the potential for failure in terms of loss or harm *or* missed opportunity. Forensic engineers define failure as an unacceptable difference between actual and expected performance.[3] That definition also applies very well in unconventional risk management.

The loss or harm may be financial or nonfinancial. It could be loss of money, or harm to life, limb, health, real property, intellectual property, equipment, brand equity, or reputation. Opportunity cost—the cost of missed opportunities, of gains foregone because scarce resources were put to another, less productive use—results from failure to seize opportunity or from failure to correctly prioritize opportunities. Opportunity cost also arises from decisions and activities that suboptimize gain and thus fail to achieve all that could have otherwise been achieved.

Failure should never become a "dirty word" in an enterprise. Only by considering and managing the potential for failure—that is, considering and managing risk—can an enterprise succeed in optimizing its value and success.

Success is going from failure to failure without losing your enthusiasm.

—Winston Churchill

Calculated Risk Taking Creates Value

There's much to learn from failure (provided, of course, the individual or enterprise survives it). To promote someone who has never failed may be to promote someone who has never taken a risk. To invest in a company that has never weathered a new product failure or a failed market initiative may be to invest in mediocre returns. Success demands a degree of risk taking and tolerance of failure.

Henry Ford once said, "Failure to learn from your mistakes is the only real failure." What is your level of risk taking and what is your tolerance for failure? How much risk taking and failure is too much? How much is too little? While one can learn from failure, it can easily be overdone. While it is important to learn from your own mistakes, it is preferable to learn from the mistakes of others. That is, it is better to be "leading edge" rather than "bleeding edge." When is it necessary to learn from failure, as Thomas

Edison did so many times before inventing the light bulb? When it is best to learn from others' mistakes, as IBM did when in the 1950s it saw the computer's market potential, which Sperry-Rand missed in its commitment to government work?

Such questions are the proper line of risk intelligent inquiry for boards and senior managers. Risk management must be woven into the decision-making and business processes of the enterprise and cannot be viewed as an ancillary activity, afterthought, or necessary evil. Nor should it be viewed only as compliance, hedging, insurance, and loss prevention.

Securing and sustaining competitive advantage calls for calculated risk taking, a dash of daring, a soupçon of caution, and great discipline, which may be why many leaders have difficulty developing and using a workable risk management scheme for their enterprise. It requires a sense of balance. In the 2000s housing bubble, many financial institutions and individual decision makers bet the ranch (or at least ranch houses) on endlessly rising home prices—a huge risk given the levels of speculative buying recognized at the time—yet failed to develop a system of calculated risk taking.

Voice of Experience

"I always called what I was facing calculated risk. The calculated part is that you prepare. You test. You try to simulate what your race space can be to understand what you can sustain without crashing."[4]

—Mario Andretti, race car driver and entrepreneur

Whether you are Mario Andretti or the CEO of an enterprise, if you know the risk you face and determine that risk is worth the potential reward, then it is a matter of your judgment whether to accept or reject it. This would be informed and calculated risk taking—that is, if you know your capabilities and determine that you can manage the risk within your limits.

Did those who lost hundreds of billions in the aftermath of the subprime crisis really understand the risk they were taking? Not according to the Senior Supervisors Group, composed of the regulators from France, Germany, Switzerland, the United Kingdom, and the United States.[5] In March 2008, they noted in their report[6] that, among many factors, "exposures far exceeded their [banking and securities firms'] understanding of inherent risks."

Under uncertain and turbulent conditions, the challenges to judgment can be enormous. Critical decisions must be made with incomplete and sometimes conflicting information as well as with conflicting advice about the best course of action. Often such decisions must be made with little time to spare.

Risk, it seems, has developed a bad reputation. Through an unprecedented and relentless series of events—business scandals, natural disasters, subprime meltdown, and geopolitical upheaval—"risk" has become a pejorative term in certain circles, something to be avoided at all cost.

Companies vary markedly in their orientation toward risk, their willingness to assume risk, and their determination to avoid it. A single company, apparently comfortable with and skilled at risk taking, can display mastery in one decade and stumble years later. For instance, in the late 1970s, Citibank introduced the automatic teller machine (ATM) at great expense despite market research telling them unequivocally that their customers would never use "cash machines" given their desire to interact with tellers, concerns about errors, and fear of muggers. The bank took a calculated risk and its "bet" on the ATM paid off handsomely. However, Citi's bets on the mortgage market of the 2000s did not pay off.

What constitutes sound risk governance on the part of a board and effective risk management by executives? It begins with a basic understanding of the mission of the enterprise and of the reasons that it exists in relation to shareholders, customers, employees, suppliers, and all other stakeholders, including the community, society, and economy. From that starting point, directors and senior executives can develop and select strategies and initiatives by which the enterprise can deploy its resources to create and preserve value in ways that are consonant with its mission.

In the realm of board governance, this includes everything from hiring and compensating senior executives to examining and approving mergers and acquisitions to setting dividend distribution policy. In the realm of senior executive responsibilities, it includes everything from selecting and developing new products and markets to outsourcing operations to raising funds through loans, leases, and investments and allocating the proceeds.

The reality is that risk—or more precisely, the intelligent and ethical pursuit of rewarded risk—forms the foundation of any successful business enterprise. Try to avoid all risks, and you'll avoid success too. Disregard risks that may destroy value, and you may destroy the enterprise.

Risk is in the eye of the beholder and is unique to individuals based on their experiences, their education, their values, and how they are or believe they are affected by the outcome.[7] In the post-bubble environment, it might appear that businesses were being asked to become more risk averse, rather than take rewarded risks. Yet successful enterprise management is as much about optimizing opportunities for competitive advantage as it is about minimizing risks to existing assets. Risk—the potential for some form of failure—is inherent in all board and management activities. Moreover, risk takes many forms, and among the most basic are unrewarded and rewarded risk. Understanding risk in these terms can lend clarity to leaders' views of and approach to risk management.

Unrewarded versus Rewarded Risk

For every enterprise, the challenge is twofold: First, protect the value you already have, and second, create new value. To create value, enterprises must be able to identify and seize opportunities by taking calculated risks that have the potential to be rewarded. Peter Drucker summed it up well: "The best way to predict the future is to create it."

Such risk taking lies at the heart of capitalism and, despite some theories to the contrary, sustainable success is more than mere luck. Some enterprises and executives will get lucky for a while, but luck cannot be viewed as a sustainable resource, nor as a business strategy. So, in the long run, being smarter about managing risks to the success of the enterprise will help you first protect what you've got by being more resilient, and then create new value by being more agile. Clearly, loss or harm comes to those who fail to understand and manage risks intelligently. They're unprepared, and they get blindsided by the sudden and unexpected.

Value protection and value creation both depend on the enterprise's ability to avoid unrewarded risks and to pursue rewarded risks successfully. In turn, this ability depends on the skill with which leaders identify and distinguish between these two different risks and their sources. In general, unrewarded risks present only a downside. Unrewarded risks expose the enterprise to the potential for loss, failure, or even punishment without the prospect of gain. In contrast, rewarded risk presents the opportunity for gain, along with a downside. Rewarded risk almost always accompanies decisions involving value creation and the pursuit of new value.

As shown in Exhibit 3.2, in terms of board and executive responsibilities, unrewarded risks typically emanate from decisions and activities related to operations, reporting, and compliance, while rewarded risks emanate from decisions and activities related to strategy and execution. For (a very basic) example, a public company that fails to file its annual 10-K with the Securities and Exchange Commission (SEC) incurs a completely unrewarded risk. One could argue that the company's accountants could have been busy with more remunerative duties, but that's hardly persuasive.

In contrast, rewarded risks accompany decisions and activities related to strategy and execution of strategy. Product development or new market entry provide clear examples. Yes, there's the potential for failure, loss,

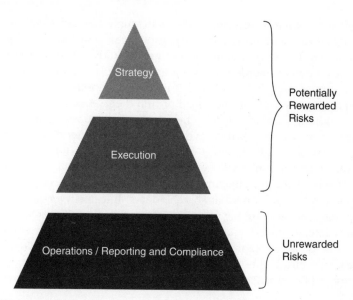

EXHIBIT 3.2 Rewarded versus Unrewarded Risk

and opportunity cost, but that downside potential accompanies the upside potential for growth in revenue, profit, market share, and shareholder value. Both unrewarded and rewarded risk warrant further discussion.

UNREWARDED RISK Conventional risk management focuses primarily on protecting existing assets. When people think about conventional risk management, they tend to think of insurance, security, loss prevention, or business continuity. These are necessary for the enterprise but insufficient to achieve or sustain competitive advantage. Conventional risk management aims to reduce or eliminate variability in performance caused by people, processes, systems, and external factors. It also aims to protect or insure against known hazards such as fire, theft, and fraud. While it's essential to protect existing assets, and enterprises are punished if they fail to do so, they are not rewarded for doing so. That is, no increase in shareholder value arises from simply protecting existing assets.

Unrewarded risks include lack of integrity in financial statements or business conduct, operational failure, and legal or regulatory noncompliance. Protecting existing assets represents "table stakes" in business. In effect, investors say, "If you can't even protect what you have (i.e., our assets), why should we invest in your enterprise?"

Deloitte's own research clearly shows the real value killers are problems with strategy and operations, not with compliance.[8] Compliance is necessary but it's not sufficient for sustainable competitive advantage. Unfortunately, companies are not rewarded for being exceptionally compliant. This is not in any way to imply that compliance is unimportant or that related penalties are trivial. Nobody wants to go to jail or ruin their reputation.

Yet, although compliance is the conventional domain of risk management, it is an area where we consistently find companies do not manage as well as they could. Consider, for example, the backdating of employee stock options. A 2006 study by Bernile, Jarrell, and Mulcahey of the effects of the ensuing scandal on 110 companies accused of backdating option grants found that shareholders "suffer on average significant stock-price declines, ranging between 20 percent and 50 percent [which] translates into total dollar losses of well over $100 billion ... to approximately one-quarter trillion dollars of lost shareholder value. There is no evidence that this decline is driven by temporary overreaction, judging by the average performance of these 110 companies over a nearly two-year period."[9]

Unrewarded risks and failure to preserve value amount to far more than pocket change. A 2003 report by the New York State Office of the Comptroller described the "Impact of the Corporate Scandals on New York State." During this period, "the Standard and Poor's 500 stock index declined by almost 28 percent ... the scandals reduced the national economy by $35 billion in the first year after they were revealed.[10]

Numerous executives from Marc Rich to Bernard Madoff—and thousands of lower-profile individuals—have found themselves undergoing investigation, prosecution, conviction, civil penalties, or imprisonment, and, almost invariably, professional ruination. But not all unrewarded risks relate to noncompliance or to illegal or unethical behavior. Operational failures such as poor product quality, supply chain disruption, or compromised customer data also hold unrewarded risks. Companies win no points and receive no premium for incurring these types of risks, which must therefore be very well managed.

For instance, a 2005 study by Hendricks and Singhal[11] based on 800 incidents of supply chain disruption over a three-year period revealed that companies that suffer a supply chain disruption also, compared with the previous year, experience:

- 33 to 40 percent lower stock returns
- 13.5 percent higher share-price volatility
- 107 percent lower operating income
- 7 percent lower sales growth
- 11 percent growth in cost

The study also noted that performance continues to deteriorate for at least two years after the disruption. These effects were found to be independent of the cause, the industry, or the time of occurrence.

In the case of data breaches, the Identity Theft Resource Center of San Diego reported that in 2007, 446 U.S. businesses, government agencies, and universities reported a loss or theft of consumer data potentially affecting more than 127 million consumer records.[12] For example, in August 2007, TJX reported that its costs from the largest computer data breach in corporate history had ballooned to $256 million, a more than tenfold increase from just three months prior. The breach involved more than 45 million customer debit and credit cards. The costs of recovering from the theft included those of litigation, claims, and investigations as well as fixes to the company's computer systems.[13]

Without question, unrewarded risk holds the potential for serious downside effects, with little to no upside potential, particularly in comparison to rewarded risk.

REWARDED RISK Rewarded risk presents the potential for an upside, a premium, or a positive return. Risks that hold the potential for reward include entry into new markets, development and introduction of new products and services, development and adoption of new processes and business models, and alliances, mergers, and acquisitions. These essential entrepreneurial activities create value and generate growth. In fact, the ethical pursuit of rewarded risk forms the foundation of any successful business enterprise.

Although unethical and irresponsible behavior has often been "rewarded" in the short term, it can never be condoned or tolerated. Not only is it morally wrong, it's bad business: Sustainable growth depends on ethical and responsible behavior, as many an indictment, fine, and lawsuit has proven. Unethical, irresponsible, or illegal decisions and activities must be "off the table" even if the short-term "rewards" are perceived by some as extraordinarily high.

What is "on the table" for a specific enterprise? That question must be answered at two levels—at the strategic level and at the day-to-day operating level. At the strategic level, the board and management must answer questions such as:

- What business are we in, and how do we remain competitive in it?
- How can we create new value for our customers and shareholders?
- How do we optimize the value that we bring to, and derive from, customer (and all other) relationships?
- What is our overall posture regarding the rewarded risks we will assume?
- What is our risk appetite?
- What risks are we willing or unwilling to assume?

- How much risk are we willing to take? How much are we willing to lose?
- How much can we afford to lose?
- How capable are we in managing this type of risk?
- What are the risks of inaction?
- Who is responsible for managing the risks inherent in our decisions and activities?

At the operating level, the questions for the specific enterprise involve procedures and processes that enable people in each function and position to understand the risks they encounter in creating value in their roles. These procedures and processes pertain to reporting standards in finance and accounting, to quality standards in production, to product claims in marketing, to commitments made to customers by sales, to credit standards in the credit department, to handling of customer complaints by service, and so on.

As employees go about creating value, they must not only know how to minimize unrewarded risks but also understand limits regarding the rewarded risks that they encounter. They need not actually distinguish between unrewarded and rewarded risk in a technical sense (although that could be useful), but they should do their jobs in ways that enable them to better manage both types of risk.

Implications for Directors and Executives

A board and an executive team taking a risk intelligent approach to enterprise management will ensure there are established systems and processes that minimize unrewarded risks. These systems and processes usually focus on conforming decisions and activities to corporate policies and procedures and on achieving compliance with regulatory and statutory requirements. To the extent practicable, they should employ technology, training, and supervisory systems such that they are built into the ways of doing business like a form of autopilot. This occurs when the enterprise has developed reliable control, testing, and exception-reporting processes and embedded them into the fabric of decisions and behaviors at departmental and individual levels.

This is *not* to imply that the "autopilot" setting on such processes and systems is permanent or that all unrewarded risk can be managed on an exception basis. First, over time, processes and systems deteriorate, go out of kilter, or break down. They require routine maintenance as well as rigorous periodic examination and occasional overhaul. Second, business realities and regulatory and statutory requirements change; therefore, corporate policies and procedures also must change. Processes and systems must be flexible enough to accommodate such changes and be updated as needed. Third, unrewarded risk may emanate from new, unexpected quarters, not only due to changes in regulatory or statutory requirements but to changes in the operations or needs of a customer, supplier, or participant in an alliance, as well as from other sources.

To the extent that management of unrewarded risk can be automated and built in, management time, attention, and expertise can be directed toward managing rewarded risk. That, of course, is where the big money is. While rewarded risk sounds like it's more fun to deal with, the potential downside can also threaten the survival of the enterprise. The sources of those threats can be more difficult to identify than those of unrewarded risks.

For example, consider all the sources of risk that a company exposes itself to when, say, entering the consumer products market in China (to pursue rewards) versus those of, say, adhering to anti-money laundering laws (to avoid unrewarded risk). Also, the sheer enthusiasm that accompanies many value creation initiatives generates risks, including that of quelling contrarian positions or ignoring the potential for loss or harm or blindly pursuing revenue growth at the expense of operating margin.

Although processes and systems for managing rewarded risks can be more challenging to develop, it is essential to do so. For example, product development can and should call for rigorous concept testing, prototype design and testing, product testing, environmental impact assessment, legal review, and market testing. Decisions to do business with a new vendor or new alliance participant can be guided by selection criteria, due diligence guidelines, and contract development and review procedures.

Yet the complexity of value creation and the pursuit of rewards often far outstrip the ability of automated processes and systems to manage their risks. In fact, attempts to "automate" or even to standardize decisions about value creation can themselves create risks. This occurs, for instance, when companies become overreliant on models or scenario planning. Although these tools certainly have their uses, overreliance can lead executives to ignore unexpected or seemingly "impossible" outcomes or scenarios that hold remote but potentially serious risks. (Note our earlier comments regarding financial or economic models and judgment.)

The basic task in altering a leadership team's or enterprise's approach to risk is to use language and make distinctions that enable people to improve their decision making and ability to achieve their goals. One distinction concerns unrewarded and rewarded risk. Another is that between calculated risk taking and risk aversion.

Calculated Risk Taking and Risk Aversion

Voice of Experience

"In many of my missions there has been an inherent risk. The question is: Am I managing it? Or, how well am I managing that inherent risk to get you to an acceptable level of exposure? The problem is that risk aversion will lead you to inaction, which is probably the worst thing you can do. The biggest risk is inaction.

"Being risk averse really should mean being very thorough in picking a business action. It shouldn't have a value judgment associated with the word. Calculated risk doesn't mean 'let's not do anything'. But being risk averse does and that's the problem. That's why you need to differentiate between risk aversion and active risk management. I wouldn't have ever thought that I shouldn't be taking calculated risks in my missions. That's what kept me alive and my missions successful."

—William O. McCabe, Former B-52 pilot, Pentagon official, and DuPont executive

To varying degrees, individuals and enterprises can be considered on a continuum from risk taker to risk averse. Individuals' choices regarding habits and diet, profession and hobbies, sports and vacations, and spending patterns and investments affect mainly them and those close to them. However, an enterprise's decisions can have ramifications for entire stakeholder groups and affect tens or hundreds of thousands, or millions, of individuals. (Little wonder some leadership teams become overly risk averse.)

Individuals and enterprises must find a workable balance between the two extremes of risk taking and risk aversion. For individuals, it's a matter of balancing the urge to live a full life (however one defines it) with health, safety, relationship, professional, and financial concerns. For enterprises, it's a matter of balancing value creation (which occurs through innovation, competitive marketing, acquisitions, and other aggressive strategies) with value preservation (which involves tending to current businesses and customers, guarding market share, pricing effectively, and executing proven strategies).

However, just as unbridled risk taking can get a person or company killed, severe risk aversion can result in stunted growth, atrophy, degeneration, or extinction. For an individual, the latter can mean a dull or perhaps "unlived" life. For an enterprise, risk aversion can mean a death as sure, if not as swift, as that resulting from unwise risk taking. An organization actually cannot choose stability in today's business environment, nor can it develop resilience based on size alone. (On that latter point, even being "too big to fail" cannot sustain an enterprise indefinitely, nor is it a strategy for optimizing shareholder value.) An organization must take some risks or it will be outpaced by more agile competitors.

When it comes to risk, some people are adrenaline junkies and gravitate toward high-risk activities, such as skydiving, base jumping, cave diving, and mountain climbing. Risk-averse individuals are less likely to engage in dangerous recreational activities or adopt unhealthy behaviors. These individuals are less likely to smoke, drink, be overweight, or drive over the speed limit, and are more likely to use a seat belt.[14]

But extreme risk aversion can result in phobias and paralyzing fear. Some argue that as a result of the many dangers facing children, parents and teachers have become risk averse to the point of restricting children's play in ways that constrain their exploration of physical, social, and virtual worlds. (The image of a child wearing a helmet as she jumps on the bed—if allowed to jump on the bed—springs to mind.) Most parents seek a balance between protecting children from genuine threats and providing interesting and enjoyable learning and growth opportunities.

To be successful, an enterprise must find the optimal level of risk taking for itself and its stakeholders—the appropriate balance—remembering that the definition of enterprise is to be bold and willing to undertake new initiatives that involve risk. That point of balance rests where the organization is aware of risks and cautious enough to avoid trouble, but encourages innovation and pursues profitable, competitive, and even aggressive investment opportunities.

Voice of Experience

"There's no doubt about it, particularly for the business development guys. They have never seen a prospect that isn't great. So you've got this very good and very healthy push and pull and tug between the guys wanting to grow the business on the top line, and the folks who want to take intelligent risks and make intelligent profit.

"Saying no and walking away is a very difficult position to take because you're probably going to ruin a client relationship for a long time when you do, but you gotta do what you gotta do."

—Richard Slater, Director

Extreme risk aversion can result in an unwillingness to take even reasonable risks, such as lending money so that creditworthy businesses can function in their day-to-day operations. During the financial crisis, risk aversion at times caused otherwise viable companies to become illiquid because they couldn't obtain necessary operating capital in the credit markets. Perhaps a more rational, less emotional approach by market participants would have yielded better results.

Risk Intelligence: An Unconventional Approach

Conventional risk management separates risk from most strategic decisions and tends to view it in isolation. It also concerns itself mainly with the potential for financial loss and tends to ignore risks to brand and reputation. This has caused more than a few management teams to make the wrong call during a public relations crisis. Conventional risk management therefore tends to be episodic, specialized, isolated in "silos," and lacking in integration across the enterprise and across strategy, execution, and operations.

An unconventional, risk intelligent approach understands that factors affecting events will change and that outside of the laboratory or a casino, all things are not equal. While events may be mildly random, they can also be "wildly" random. Again, there is not just a random walk, but also hops, skips, and jumps. Extreme events are more common than we think and should be treated as such.

Risk intelligence generates awareness of risk at all levels within an integrated framework to obtain the best intelligence available under the circumstance. The goal is to achieve decision superiority and competitive success.

In essence, the risk intelligent enterprise:

- Understands that discussions of value and risk are inseparable from enterprise management
- Understands that risk management must be built into the core ways of protecting existing assets and of creating future value
- Assumes that turbulence (and thus the extreme) is inevitable and therefore emphasizes prevention and preparedness
- Is vigilant for a broad range of opportunities and risks across the enterprise, including industry, strategic, compliance, competitive, financial, security, reporting, operational, environmental, country, and political
- Acknowledges the need for specialization by business function, as well as the need to harmonize, synchronize, and rationalize risk management and controls
- Considers interactions among multiple risks rather than focusing on a single risk or event, and considers the impacts that could result from multiple threats

- Creates a common language and set of metrics for value and risk, and a culture in which people account for value and risk in every key decision and activity
- Encourages risk taking for reward and value creation, rather than pure risk avoidance, by driving out fear of failure

Risk intelligent practices generate a rationalized approach to identifying, discussing, measuring, and managing all the vital opportunities and risks the enterprise faces. By coordinating the activities of the board, senior management, risk managers, business managers, and employees, this approach combines multiple views into better insights and intelligence about the risks the enterprise faces. It then enables leaders to prioritize those risks for mitigation and management, and to allocate risk management resources accordingly.

Ten Essential Risk Intelligence Skills

Enterprise risk intelligence comprises ten skills essential to the art and discipline of robust enterprise management:

1. Check your assumptions at the door.
2. Maintain constant vigilance.
3. Factor in velocity and momentum.
4. Manage the key connections.
5. Anticipate causes of failure.
6. Verify sources and corroborate information.
7. Maintain a margin of safety.
8. Set your enterprise time horizons.
9. Take enough of the right risks.
10. Sustain operational discipline.

We find that a number of directors and senior executives practice some of these skills some of the time, if only intuitively. However, very few boards and executive teams practice them consciously, consistently, and concertedly. These skills form the core of enterprise risk intelligence and inform each of its tenets and practices.

We have consciously chosen the terms "risk intelligent" and "risk intelligence" for their connotations. "Intelligence" is the ability to anticipate, understand, act, and then learn from experience. An intelligence unit is responsible for gathering and interpreting information and producing essential insights for decision makers. Thus, intelligence is both a process and a capability.

We are not implying that other approaches are unintelligent; however, an intelligent approach to risk does decrease the likelihood that the organization will receive a nomination for a corporate Darwin Award. We also recognize there is no such thing as perfect prevention.

Risk intelligence applies in general and specific ways to every level and function in the enterprise—from the board of directors and senior executive team to production workers and customer service reps, and from finance and accounting to warehousing and distribution. Here are five quick examples of how risk intelligent practices apply in specific areas and aspects of today's major enterprise:

1. *Board risk governance.* Risk intelligence can help the board to understand the full range of risks that management must consider and address in protecting assets and pursuing value, and management's proper roles vis-à-vis risk. Risk intelligence helps the board to develop awareness of risks to value and to foster a productive conversation with management (e.g., by asking the right questions and persisting in getting credible and reliable answers). Finally, risk intelligence leads the board to develop the governance structures (e.g., a risk committee on the order of the audit committee, if needed) and oversight processes and decision-making mechanisms to improve risk governance.

2. *Regulatory demands.* The overall burden of U.S. regulatory demands rose with Sarbanes-Oxley in 2002 and shows no sign of letting up. Certain industries, notably financial services, pharmaceuticals, and healthcare, traditionally face high regulatory demands, which will probably increase. In providing a durable but flexible risk management framework, risk intelligence brings new levels of order, consistency, continuity, and control to risk management at all levels.

3. *Third-party relationships.* Increased use of outsourcing, off-shoring, strategic alliances, and other third-party relationships that extend the enterprise have provided many benefits. These include reduced costs, access to new technologies and markets, greater flexibility in resource allocation, and increased responsiveness to variances in customer demands.

   However, such relationships can expose an enterprise to a broad range of risks having to do with cost controls, quality controls, service levels, and liabilities. When risk intelligence informs efforts such as contract risk and compliance programs, the usage and performance of those programs increases dramatically.

4. *Risk management cost controls.* One of the greatest challenges in risk management is that of controlling costs. Risk intelligence prompts management to identify and consider the full range of risks the enterprise

faces, unrewarded and rewarded, political, financial, strategic, operational, regulatory, legal, and reputational, among others.

In doing so, senior executives and risk managers can explicitly weigh risks and rewards, prioritize risks, and allocate resources to those risks that warrant them. Also, risk intelligence enables management to rationalize and harmonize controls and reporting mechanisms to eliminate duplicates and to institute new ones where needed.

5. *Return on investment.* Risk intelligent approaches are often self-funding investments. Prevention is intuitively less expensive than response and recovery (a topic discussed in more detail in Chapter 14, "Risk Intelligence is Free"). Further, many modern enterprises have multiple functions responsible for managing specific aspects of risk which, although necessary, increase costs and burden the business.

A solid contract risk and compliance program improves vendor performance and enables you to measure the true costs and benefits of outsourcing. Avoiding unrewarded risks—and associated regulatory actions—saves money, as does revisiting the costs of existing policies and procedures.

Risk intelligence can improve relations with regulators by enabling the enterprise to respond readily to requests and even to anticipate—and at times to help shape—new regulations.

Finally, risk intelligence is inclusive. It recognizes the need for specific expertise and traditional tools, such as currency hedging, insurance, performance bonds, IT security, and ERM systems. It also provides a framework in which expertise and tools can be considered in an enterprise-wide context, with risks prioritized for evaluation and action and addressed with the right tool and optimal resources. Other approaches to risk management and other tools and skills have value. Yet the best of them can be "downloaded" to risk intelligent enterprise management. It is within that framework that they will usually work most efficiently and effectively and for the greatest good of the enterprise.

Part II describes the ten skills of enterprise risk intelligence in detail and in the context of instances drawn from diverse areas of life and business. Part III describes risk intelligent approaches to enterprise management and discusses ways of creating a risk intelligent enterprise.

Ten Essential Risk Intelligence Skills

CHAPTER 4

Check Your Assumptions
at the Door

*Sooner or later, something fundamental in your business world
will change.*
—Andrew Grove, former chairman and CEO, Intel Corporation[1]

This chapter presents the first of ten skills that can better inform leaders' thinking and conduct in surviving and thriving in uncertainty. It is the skill of challenging your most basic assumptions so you can identify risks and opportunities, and manage the former and leverage the latter. We present this as the first skill because you must challenge your assumptions in order to even begin improving your approach to risk management. Your assumptions dictate your point of view, and your experience informs your assumptions.

Neuroscientists now tell us that from the cognitive standpoint, human beings largely construct their own realities, individually and collectively. Call it a mind-set, tunnel vision, groupthink, or culture but whatever you call it, your assumptions dictate—and limit—your thinking, decisions, and responses to events, and those of your enterprise.

There's another vital aspect and benefit to challenging your assumptions. Doing so enables you not only to identify the risks *to* the strategy under consideration but also the risks *of* the strategy. In executive decision making, most analyses focus on identifying and managing the risks *to* a strategy—the factors and circumstances that could cause it to fail. Indeed, conventional risk management focuses almost exclusively on that realm of risk, on defining and addressing obstacles to successful implementation of a strategy. But that assumes that the chosen strategy is the correct strategy and that it will work as long as the risks to the strategy are identified and managed.

Many conventional approaches to risk management incorrectly assume that the strategy or the objective being pursued is the right one. For example, in their efforts to grow revenues, many lending institutions chose to expand into subprime markets. In that effort, some of them did away with verification of income and creditworthiness. Such relaxations of due diligence paved the way for a general economic collapse. Thus, the enterprise must challenge the appropriateness of an objective and strategy as well as the risks to carrying it out.

Simply identifying risk *to* the strategy ignores the risks *of* the strategy, and thus most strategic risks. It fails to address the question, what if the strategy itself is flawed or incorrect for the enterprise because circumstances have changed? Equally important, it also fails to identify risks that the strategy itself can create within the unit that is implementing it and across the larger organization. Strategic risks generally far outweigh operational risks, financial risks, and external risks in terms of their danger to enterprise value.

Once they choose a strategy, leaders tend to assume that the strategy they've chosen is solid and correct. They and the organization work from that assumption going forward. That strategy and that assumption provide the context in which key decisions are made and actions are taken. This can lead to those all-too-common situations in which a team "redoubles its efforts after losing sight of the objective."

The superordinate objective is to create new value and protect existing value; a strategy is only a means of doing that, one of a number from which management could choose. Only by challenging all assumptions—including the correctness, validity, and fit of a strategy before it is adopted and even thereafter—can relevant strategic risks be identified.

Challenging one's own assumptions, let alone someone else's, isn't easy. We cherish our assumptions and rely on them to help us order everything from our universe to our sock drawer. Certain assumptions have extremely practical uses. We assume that our spouses are faithful, our biopsies are accurate, and our fellow motorists are reasonably sane, just to get through the day. Nonetheless, it is still risky, as the number of divorces, inaccurate diagnoses, and traffic fatalities clearly demonstrate. Yet assuming that our business environment will remain (or become) stable, that our industry will endure forever, and that our enterprises will remain competitive can be extremely risky. We must regularly challenge those assumptions and remain constantly vigilant to changes in our environment.

Therefore, this chapter will show why you should, and how you can, constructively challenge your assumptions. Only by doing so can you identify extraordinary risks and opportunities, prepare your enterprise to address them, and perhaps survive and even thrive.

Voice of Experience

"We've tried to deal with the risks in our assumptions, but I'd just add that you should check your ego at the door also because the ego's an assumption, and sometimes you're clouded. I've seen situations where very large egos can create chaos, particularly if the egos are so large they just refuse to admit they don't know something. So the assumptions and the ego are all part of the optimism and the hubris that goes along with, 'I haven't been wrong before, so why would I be wrong now?'

"It's still shocking to me that people are defending the indefensible, giving excuses for why these things happen, and saying, 'It's not my fault.' Basic business assumptions, what if we're wrong, what it would look like if we were? How do we actually set up early-warning systems to detect evidence that we're wrong because all of the existing systems are really only designed to tell you that you're right? A lot of times there's a bias in even setting up the systems in order to arrive at the conclusion that you want."

—Tom O'Neill, Principal, Sandler O'Neill + Partners L.P.

Fatal Flaw #1: Failing to Challenge Your Assumptions

Given how much depends on leaders' assumptions about the environment, the industry, and the enterprise, at a minimum these assumptions must be made explicit and understood. Understanding leaders' assumptions yields insight into the risks and opportunities in the environment and within the enterprise and into the risks of its strategies.

The process begins with challenging the basic assumptions of the enterprise's business and mental models (the conventional wisdom), then envisioning their destruction in order to identify threats and opportunities. For an individual or an enterprise to challenge their assumptions, the assumptions must first be made explicit.

This can be difficult because assumptions are usually deeply embedded in leaders' psyches and in the organization's business model, processes, and culture. However, it's generally preferable to challenge your own assumptions rather than to wait until they are invalidated by events.

Indeed, we can rely on events to invalidate our assumptions, given two realities that have repeatedly asserted themselves in the business environment:

1. Economic and industry cyclicality
2. Technology shift

Economic and industry cyclicality has been so well documented and so often demonstrated that it's hard to believe any of us could deny it, forget it, or ignore it. Yet we often do. The recurring, periodic mismatch between supply and demand that characterizes virtually all economies and markets occurred most recently in the U.S. and European housing industries and in the recession of the 2000s. This chapter will present an analysis of boom and bust cycles and help you to challenge any remaining assumptions you may hold about continued stability.

Shifts in technologies will occur quite regularly, but this is difficult for leaders to accept, particularly leaders of highly successful organizations. Whether it is the automobile displacing the horse, the process-controlled production techniques of Toyota displacing those of Detroit's Big Three, or the personal computer and the Internet displacing everything from the typewriter to the television, disruptive innovation and new technologies regularly redraw the competitive landscape. And just as regularly, leaders in the industries being displaced find themselves shocked to learn their assumptions about their everlasting dominance have been wrong.

These forces relate to managing risk in a capitalist economy (not that centrally planned economies have a better risk management record). In *Capitalism, Socialism and Democracy*, Joseph Schumpeter introduced the term "creative destruction" to describe the "process of industrial mutation . . . that incessantly revolutionizes the economic structure *from within*, incessantly destroying the old one, incessantly creating a new one."[2]

Cyclicality and technology shifts are the two main drivers of creative destruction but they are not the only ones. Schumpeter believed that capitalism is, by its nature, always dynamic, never static. We believe that risk in business can be understood in the context of Schumpeter's "perennial gale of creative destruction." *Major* risks and opportunities typically come from new customer needs and desires, new competitors and new technologies, rather than from incremental change. Schumpeter describes a history of competitive revolutions ranging from horse-drawn carts to the locomotive and the automobile, from the water wheel to the generating station, and from the mail coach to the airplane. Creative destruction is here to stay. It can be delayed but it cannot be denied.

Economic Cycles: Déjà Vu Again

Although it was exacerbated by easy money and madcap lending policies, the recession of 2008–09 occurred as part of the business cycle and was just one of many downturns. Even the financial crisis was one of many, as evidenced by our list in Exhibit 2.1 in Chapter 2. Bank regulation authority Jean-Charles Rochet cites in his book *Why Are There So Many Banking Crises?* a 1997 IMF study stating that between 1975 and 1995 there were 112 systemic banking crises in 93 countries and 51 borderline crises in 46 countries.[3]

Similarly, Charles Kindleberger's *Manias, Panics and Crashes,* first published in 1978, described financial crisis as a "hardy perennial" and defined a financial crisis as "a sharp, brief, ultra-cyclical deterioration of all or most of a group of financial indicators."[4] He argued that although details may vary, the underlying structure of financial boom-and-bust crises remains the same and comprises five stages:

1. Displacement
2. Overtrading
3. Monetary expansion
4. Revulsion
5. Discredit

The first stage, *displacement,* occurs when a positive or negative event "shocks" or changes the macroeconomic outlook. In *Irrational Exuberance,* Robert Shiller describes a number of structural or precipitating factors in the 2000s financial crisis, including the Internet, the decline of foreign economic rivals, the baby boom, expanded reporting of business news, analysts' optimistic forecasts, and 24-hour trading.

Second, *overtrading* occurs amid speculation. Shiller[5] identifies what he calls "amplification mechanisms," such as high investor confidence, undiminished expectations (in spite of market highs), public attention to the market, and the feedback theory of bubbles in which "perceived long-term risk is down but expected returns are not down and emotions and heightened attention increase desire to get into the game."[6]

In such an environment, people jump on what they see as profit opportunities and fuel further speculation. Increased demand leads to increased prices and attracts more "investors" in an upwardly spiraling cycle.

The third stage, *monetary expansion,* feeds the boom by easing interest rates and increasing the money supply. This includes, Kindleberger notes, "the development of new credit instruments and the expansion of personal credit outside of banks."[7]

A 1986 report of the Bank for International Settlements stated that financial innovations are "often under-priced and hence overused." In the late-2000s crisis, many failures were associated with the misuse and abuse of derivatives. Although originally designed as instruments of risk management, they quickly become instruments of highly leveraged speculation and what Warren Buffett labeled "weapons of mass financial destruction."

The fourth stage, *revulsion,* begins with profit taking, a leveling of prices followed by a period of "financial distress" in which the possibility of insolvency looms. A rapid rush to liquidity may ignite a panic, crisis, or crash. This can be triggered by a bankruptcy or loan default caused by sudden demand for liquidity, which essentially caused the collapse of Bear Stearns and Lehman Brothers and the larger "meltdown" in the credit markets.

The final stage, *discredit,* follows the rush to liquidity and marks a period of falling prices and rising bankruptcies. Banks cease lending against assets that formerly served as collateral, and prices can be driven so low that some people are tempted to move back into the market.[8] This seems to have happened in January 2009, when housing prices had declined by 18.2 percent according to the S&P/Case-Shiller Index and sales increased 6.5 percent compared with December 2008.

Similar analysis has been applied to other markets and events. During the 1990s dot-com bubble, many of us knew that the inmates had taken over the asylum when venture capitalists, once among the most sober and cautious of investors, held "gong shows" in Silicon Valley for entrepreneurs presenting business plans.

According to Russel and Torbey, "Evidence in the psychology literature reveals that individuals have limited information processing capabilities, exhibit systematic bias in processing information, are prone to making mistakes, and often tend to rely on the opinion of others."[9] Indeed, the sane and sober can begin to appear foolish for sitting on the sidelines. This predominant short-term bias during bubbles and booms undermines long-term focus and strategy, and constitutes a dangerous approach to risk. (Chapter 11, "Set Your Enterprise Time Horizons," discusses antidotes.)

Shift Happens

New business models, new competitors, new regulatory regimes, rapid changes in customer preferences, and purchasing behaviors and economic conditions can all result from technology shift. Surviving and thriving amid such change demands adaptation, which in turn demands a clear understanding of the risks *of* a business strategy and the risks *to* a business strategy.

The process begins with challenging the most fundamental assumptions of the enterprise's business and mental models (the conventional wisdom), and then envisioning their destruction to identify both threats and opportunities. For an individual or an enterprise to challenge their assumptions, the assumptions must first be made explicit—often a very difficult task. Sometimes assumptions are so implicit, both in the way people see the world and in their enterprise business models, that those assumptions go unrecognized.

Different cultures can have very different views and biases about the way the world operates. These views become ingrained and intuitive.

Experience can create misleading biases. People can be optimistic or pessimistic. A strong tendency toward optimism can be constructive, but not when people avoid the unpleasant, deny reality, and reject the extreme as implausible. Too many enterprises tend to "assume away" the challenges inherent in their corporate conventional wisdom. David James, a professional crisis manager, notes, "Companies do not necessarily go wrong because they are in chronically difficult industries. Nor is it that their managers are hasty or overconfident in making decisions or cannot obtain capital on reasonable terms. Most of the failures I have dealt with occurred at companies with a track record of success, whose managers had detailed business plans and where capital was available at low rates."[10]

That accounts for why even highly successful companies may fail to take advantage of their own inventions or fail to see the "killer" shift in their business environment. Whenever a disruptive technology occurs, leaders of established enterprises typically make three assumptions that often damage their businesses:

1. They assume that the new technology is no threat and tend to ignore it.
2. They assume that conventional responses to the threat will counter it.
3. They assume they can move later, when the technology is proven and the market is established.

Assuming that the technology is no threat is a huge and common mistake and often causes leaders in established companies to do nothing in response until it's too late. Sometimes they assume the innovation is a fad and dismiss it. Sometimes they assume that customer "loyalty" will carry the day or that customers won't spend the time or effort to adopt the technology. These are dangerous assumptions.

Assuming that conventional responses will counter an unconventional threat is equally dangerous. Price reductions, product extensions, service enhancements, or improved warranties will usually not counter a truly disruptive technology. What, really, could the recorded music industry, with a business model based on hardcopy manufacturing and distribution, do about online music distribution? Lawsuits, price cuts, and even new distribution channels (Walmart, Amazon) won't save the CD, which now sells to a demographic that resembles that of newspapers (discussed below).

Assuming that there is ample time to wait and act, say, after the pioneers have died off, can be overly optimistic. IBM legendarily developed its personal computer in a dramatic push conducted away from headquarters, but the company had by then dismissed early microcomputers as toys and games, which some of them actually were. IBM still pays royalties to Microsoft, which saw the potential in a disc operating system, developed DOS, and had the wit to license—rather than sell—it to IBM.

BAD NEWS FOR PAPERS   The popularity of printed newspapers has declined sharply as readers have increasingly turned to the Internet for news. U.S. newspaper circulation declined by 16 percent in two decades, from a peak of 63 million in the 1980s to 53 million in 2007.[11] The number of U.S. dailies also fell from its peak of about 1,600 titles in 1984 to some 1,450 in 2007.[12] Among young readers, the Internet has almost fully replaced print as a news source. Only 19 percent of Americans aged 18 to 34 claim to look at a daily newspaper; the average age of readers is 55 and rising.[13]

The newspapers' future depends on their ability to address changes wrought by digital media. Readership of some papers has even increased through online editions.[14,15] Some newspapers' Web sites have benefited from the growth of online advertising, but the resulting revenue amounts to far less than the circulation and ad revenue lost.[16]

Sites like Craigslist.com and Monster.com grabbed classified and help-wanted ads. Social networks, such as Facebook, YouTube, and Twitter, have added still more competition. The Institute of Practitioners in Advertising forecasts that social network sites could reduce traditional advertising growth to as low as 1.2 percent a year by 2016.[17] Social networks enable friends to share recommendations, which carry more weight than advertising.

Publishers have cut costs aggressively and 9 percent of U.S. papers have closed or merged.[18] The *New York Times* cut jobs, with its parent consolidating New York–area printing plants and seeking investors.[19] The Washington Post Company repositioned itself as an "education and media company." Its exam-preparation company, Kaplan, now generates a significant portion of the company's revenue.[20] The 150-year-old Hearst-owned *Seattle Post-Intelligencer* published its last paper edition on March 17, 2009, and became the first sizable city paper to go completely online for written news.

Given the changes, it is all that even a news organization can do to keep pace. In an April 2009 speech to the Newspaper Association of America, Eric Schmidt, CEO of Google, Inc., called on industry executives to work with Google to create a new format of online journalism with more personalized content. "We think we can build a business with you," Mr. Schmidt said. "That is the only solution we can see." He envisions a revenue model based on micro-payments similar to that of Apple's iTunes, with readers paying a nominal amount for each online article.

Newspapers became vulnerable when they failed to challenge their assumptions about readership, revenue sources, cost structures, format preferences, and media mobility. They failed to grasp the ability of online media to disrupt their business. Similar changes are occurring in recorded music, filmed entertainment, and book and magazine publishing. Even retailers must reexamine their assumptions in the face of online stores' huge selection, low overhead, and user reviews. In any business, whenever a disruptive technology erupts, questions arise: How quickly is it developing and being adopted? What will be the applications? What are the risks? Where are the opportunities? The answers largely depend on leadership's assumptions, and what it does about them.

Sacred cows make the best hamburger.

—Mark Twain

Risk Intelligence Skill #1: Check Your Assumptions at the Door

The greatest source of risk and opportunity lies in your assumptions. The skill of challenging assumptions is the necessary starting point in considering value and risks and ways of addressing them. Its importance is underscored by the fact that even when assumptions have been proven false—as in the case of "the economy will only continue to expand" or "nothing can supersede our technology"—people can still continue to think and act as if they are true. You can never assume that a cycle will move in one direction, either upward or downward. By definition, it cannot. During a cycle, particularly one marked by high emotion, overinvestment, unrealistic prices, unsustainable demand, and new, inexperienced participants, question others' assumptions as well as your own. Similarly, you can never assume that your technology will never be superseded. After all, the technology that your enterprise currently produces or uses superseded other technologies, didn't it?

Also, make use of the two tools examined in the rest of this chapter. These tools will help you to identify and challenge the assumptions your leadership team may bring to governance and risk management. The first tool is Thesis-Antithesis-Synthesis (TAS), a tool from the world of logic and philosophy that helps people to challenge their assumptions and develop new ideas. The second tool is scenario planning, a conventional method of anticipating risks in the military and in business, whose effectiveness depends on the assumptions one chooses.

Tool #1: Thesis-Antithesis-Synthesis (TAS)

TAS is useful for challenging assumptions, revealing flaws in conventional risk management approaches, and fostering evolution in ideas. Essentially, TAS calls for the statement of a thesis—an intellectual or (apparently) factual proposition or assumption, such as "Man cannot reach the moon"—and the statement of its opposite, the antithesis—"Man can reach the moon." The

EXHIBIT 4.1 Challenge Your Assumptions

Thesis	Antithesis
Fatal Flaw: Failure to challenge basic assumptions	Risk Intelligence Skill: Check your assumptions at the door
Our assumptions are sound.	Our assumptions could be wrong.
Linear thinking works.	Sometimes things are nonlinear.
We don't know what we don't know.	We can know what we don't know or at least better prepare for it.
Challenging certain assumptions is taboo.	Every assumption should be constructively challenged.
We can consider only the plausible.	We can imagine the unimaginable.

Synthesis
1. Assume cyclicality, disruption, and extreme events.
2. Integrate linear and nonlinear thinking.
3. Ask "*What if* our revenue sources, cost structure, or customer base fell apart?"
4. Some previously unchallengeable assumptions will stand and some will fall.
5. Anticipate extreme events along with potential risks and opportunities.

third step is to develop a statement that reconciles the two propositions, the synthesis—"Man can build a vehicle to take him to the moon."

TAS makes an excellent organizing device for identifying your current assumptions and constructively challenging them, as shown in Exhibit 4.1.

FINDING THE BLACK SWAN BEFORE IT FINDS YOU In *The Black Swan,* Nassim Taleb describes the impact of highly improbable events.[21] He uses the example of the black swan, which, as noted in Chapter 2, Europeans once thought to be nonexistent. Taleb argues that just because events are improbable doesn't mean they can't happen.

Taleb's thesis supports what Hippocrates said nearly 2,400 years ago: Experience can be misleading. Just because you've never seen a black swan doesn't mean there is no such thing. Experience leads people to form assumptions about what is probable or improbable, and possible or impossible. Unfortunately, when these assumptions are wrong, the consequences can be fatal for those who are unprepared. Taleb describes how assumptions about probability, or rather improbability, have led to disaster.

Apart from experience there are many sources of assumptions, and it is management's job to identify them and the board's to make sure that they have. TAS can be quite useful in that effort. Also, placed in the context of TAS, the search for black swans enables you to challenge your most basic assumptions, including the assumptions that underlie the strategy itself. Thus the search for black swans assists your efforts to identify the risks *of* a strategy as well as the risks *to* a strategy.

TAS encourages you to contradict the enterprise's current assumptions or your white swans. These antitheses will often be extreme, but they can point to heretofore unseen threats or opportunities, and to "black swan events." That's because TAS calls for nonlinear thinking, rather than incremental extrapolation from the current state. Most businesses can adapt to incremental change but find a shift that obviates basic assumptions far more difficult to address. The Pony Express had halved the delivery time of transcontinental mail carried by stagecoach, but it ended on October 24, 1861—the very day the Pacific Telegraph line was completed.

Apparent opposites—good/evil, love/hate, masculine/feminine, profit/loss, risk/reward, boom/bust, black/white—animate our entire world. Georg Wilhelm Hegel, often credited with originating the basis of TAS, said, "Contradiction in nature is the root of all motion and of all life." The tension between opposing forces and its resolution underlie all drama and comedy, as well as sporting, political, and legal contests. Without delving into philosophy, we can say that TAS—Thesis-Antithesis-Synthesis—can help you to understand and perhaps even harness the forces of creative destruction.

How to Use TAS

Directors and executives want to identify the next big risk or opportunity before it occurs. They want to simplify complexity, reduce uncertainty, and prepare their enterprises for the unexpected future. TAS can help, and it works as follows:

Thesis is the starting point, a statement of current business assumptions, values, concepts, or practices that can be expressed positively or negatively. The thesis represents conventional wisdom—the white swans, the "already seen"—or what you believe to be true.

Antithesis is the opposite of the thesis. The antithesis represents the unconventional view—the black swan. What if you are wrong?

Synthesis is the combination of thesis and antithesis that produces a new, unified approach. The synthesis takes the best of both worlds to create an optimum, not maximum, solution.

This approach can be applied to any enterprise in any sector by use of these three steps.

STEP 1: THESIS—EXPLICITLY STATE YOUR FUNDAMENTAL ASSUMPTIONS In stating assumptions explicitly, pay particular attention to those that are essential to the survival and success of the company—the "vital few" versus the "trivial many":

- What are the most fundamental assumptions, which, if they were wrong, could cause the company to fail?
- Conversely, what conventional assumptions could be challenged to gain competitive advantage?

Before answering these questions, be sure there's a common understanding of how the enterprise creates value, and of the major underlying business assumptions. These include assumptions about the industry, the market, the operating environment, the regulatory environment, interest rates, and key employees, suppliers, or customers. According to Professor Ray Reilly of the University of Michigan's Ross School of Business, depending on the industry and business model, the key assumptions could relate to:

- Industry structure
- Business strategy
- Market segment served
- Product positioning
- Customer value proposition
- Competitive forces
- Growth potential and drivers
- Value chain, resource requirements, costs, and investment structure
- Talent assessment, retention, and management
- Investor value proposition
- Other assumptions specific to your business

STEP 2: ANTITHESIS—CHALLENGE EACH ASSUMPTION The next step is to describe the exact opposite of each assumption or the black swan. Take care not to think incrementally or narrowly. Challenging basic assumptions can identify potential sources of competitive advantage. For example, Toyota achieved huge productivity gains by challenging the conventional assumption that it took about eight hours to change the stamping tools on a blanking press (which shapes sheet metal into the required profile). As a result, Toyota eventually reduced the required time to just over one minute.

Applying this kind of thought process to the entire value chain can deliver significant rewards. But it must be part of a broader approach to a system of management rather than a single element. For instance, Southwest Airlines achieved 39 consecutive years of profitability, thanks largely to its business model, which was originated as the antithesis of the conventional airline as shown in Exhibit 4.2.

EXHIBIT 4.2 TAS Southwest Airlines

Thesis *Conventional Airline Wisdom*	Antithesis *Southwest's Unconventional Wisdom*
Customer Focus	
National/international	Regional
Primary markets	Secondary markets
Assigned seats	No assigned seats (boarding groups)
Premium service provider	Low-cost provider
Fee for reservation changes	No fees
People	
Organizational hierarchy (command and control)	Inverted pyramid (management exists to support personnel serving customers)
Formal/stiff	Informal/fun
Salaries and wages	First to introduce profit sharing
Equipment	
Multiple types of aircraft	Single type (Boeing 737)
Process	
No fuel price hedging	Fuel price hedging
Conventional media	One of the first to have a Web site
Long turnarounds	High-speed turnarounds (20 min. avg.)
Hub and spoke	Point to point
Primary airports (high cost/traffic)	Secondary airports (lower cost/lower traffic)
Multiple sources of ticket issuance	Direct by Southwest (phone or online)

You get the idea. Developing a business model that is the antithesis of the conventional model can be a significant source of competitive advantage.

STEP 3: SYNTHESIS—OPTIMIZE THE SOLUTION An optimizing strategy is designed to succeed under a variety of scenarios, not a single scenario. A singular strategy may be the best way to maximize returns in the short run, but it comes with a lot of "ifs." A maximizing strategy can work *if* all things are equal, events are independent, forecasts are meaningful, extreme events are extremely rare, and markets are rational and efficient. If all those conditions are met, a single strategy can be effective and may even maximize returns in the short-run. But if business conditions change significantly and quickly, the very survival of the enterprise may be at stake. Given the forces of creative destruction, it is more prudent to assume that cycles, disruptions, and shifts will occur.

The optimal, synthesized strategy can combine the best of the theses and the antitheses and avoid reliance on probabilities to determine which strategy to adopt. It is a means to equip the enterprise with a viable set of options if the antithesis (one or more of the alternate futures) becomes reality. Because the future is unknowable, the enterprise should have options that it can exercise as alternate futures materialize.

Options can be arrayed in a hierarchy according to the resilience and agility they yield, compared with the cost, resources, time, and difficulty required for implementation. The enterprise can also array its options from the least it could do under the circumstances to the most it could do. The least it could do might be to monitor the situation for changes. The most it could do might be to divest its existing businesses and make acquisitions to reposition itself. Optimizing often means having more than one strategy. This may cost more, but it improves the chances of survival and success. (Recall that an organism or organization requires variety in order to cope with variety and complexity in the environment.)

Case Example: The Encyclopedia Business   In the 1990s, companies publishing printed encyclopedias found that their basic assumptions no longer held. First, portable CD-ROMs made lengthy, bound volumes nearly obsolete. Then the Internet made comprehensive, updated coverage instantly available, usually for free, and hand-held devices made remote access possible. An encyclopedia publisher's TAS exercise might have looked like Exhibit 4.3.

EXHIBIT 4.3 TAS for an Encyclopedia Publisher

Thesis *Key Business Assumptions*	Antithesis *The Opposite*
All reference knowledge will be communicated in printed form in nice leather-bound volumes.	Reference knowledge will be communicated in other media.
Knowledge will be updated periodically in more nice leather-bound volumes.	Knowledge will be updated instantly.
A subscription fee will be charged to the user.	Content will be free to the user and revenue will come from other sources.
Because of the weight and number of volumes, the reference knowledge will be housed in a library or office (i.e., it will be stationary).	Access will be mobile.

Synthesis
1. Corroborated knowledge tailored to specific audiences
2. Constantly refreshed and available online
3. Blend of user fees and advertising
4. Stationary and mobile access

What would these new assumptions mean for the company's business model? It could ignore them, perceive them as threats, or see them as opportunities. But what would be the shape of those opportunities and how would the company avoid threats? What early-warning signs might signal that the antitheses were afoot? What could be done to better position the business? What distribution model should it use? What revenue model? What synthesized strategy might enable it to survive and thrive?

Perhaps the company could sell paid-search capabilities, customized information products, or information updating services. Perhaps it could gain a competitive advantage in quality of information by having expert input and corroboration, verification by second and third sources, or more frequent and reliable updating. Distribution options might include partnering with manufacturers of devices or software, using aggressive Web-based marketing, and perhaps unbundling and reconfiguring its product offerings (e.g., into the "archeology store," "space store," "ancient history store," and others).

The main point is that the company could have synthesized several alternative strategies into a playbook of responses as soon as the personal computer, CD-ROM, and Internet emerged as potentially disruptive technologies. These would be identified as such by maintaining constant vigilance and situational awareness, as recommended in Chapter 5. Then the company could have established mechanisms that trigger an alert regarding the opportunity or threat and the need to exercise an option.

Case Example: Thomson Reuters Corporation Thomson Reuters Corporation (TRI) evolved from a family-controlled company into one of the premier information purveyors in the world. The company has transformed itself from publishing newspapers to meeting technical, financial, legal, and other specialized information needs. In the 1980s and 1990s, Thomson began its shift toward professional publishing while shedding unrelated assets, including some newspapers. The transformation accelerated under Richard Harrington, who became chief executive officer in 1997. Harrington saw two potential threats: the disappearance of the company's traditional small retail advertisers, which were being gobbled up by large store chains, and the loss of classified-advertising revenue to the Internet.[22]

Thomson sold off about $15 billion in assets and dismantled its North American newspaper operation. The company also embarked on a roughly $30 billion acquisition spree, including the purchase of Reuters, and the financial division acquired companies to bolster its product line and improve its appeal to bond traders.[23] Most of the company's purchases provided information that influential professionals were willing to pay a premium for, although it was becoming increasingly available for free online.[24]

As the amount of information on the Internet has exploded, its quality has, Harrington says, gone through an "information devolution."[25] Because Internet search engines do not differentiate and prioritize the billions of documents they locate, they have been unable to deliver reliable, high-quality, specialized technical and professional information. Harrington believed that TRI could take the lead in meeting the needs of its targeted professional users—or else get out of the way of players such as Bloomberg and NewsCorp.[26]

He and the TRI board decided to invest in building domain expertise with a staff of almost 2,000 professionals who vet and assure the quality of the information they provide. Realizing that such expertise was useless without the infrastructure to distribute the information, TRI acquired software and application tools and the ability to deliver information in immediately useable forms. Content is key, Harrington has said, but the competitive battle will be primarily in the areas of workflow solutions and services.[27,28]

Although other corporations might have seen these moves as incredibly risky, especially given the profitability of the mature units that were sold, Harrington saw the risk as minimal.[29] He said, "There was a need for a Google for the high end user—one which provided an inch-wide but mile long hose of information with a nozzle that could finely tune the spray of information, as opposed to one segment of sewer pipe holding vast amounts of murky and oblique information."[30]

Tool # 2: Scenario Planning

First developed for military use, scenario planning is often used to model alternative futures and to develop the flexibility to survive and thrive in them. Many organizations use it in their strategic planning processes, but its actual value depends on the underlying assumptions one brings to the exercise. For example, in 2005 the CEO of a midcap company was asked about major risks to the company. He said, "Our business is very cyclical." When asked how prepared the company was for the next downturn, he replied, "Not very." Those simple questions and candid answers triggered an in-depth analysis of the possible effects of the downturn on the company. A number of scenarios were generated to portray effects of differing magnitude and duration. Some examples are shown in Exhibit 4.4.

The sensitivity of factors affecting earnings to these scenarios was also tested. For example, Exhibit 4.5 shows the potential adverse impact of changes on volume and price in 5 percent increments.

Of course, the analysis could have been extended to further price and volume decreases, but on the basis of these calculations alone, the company faced significant exposure. Such analyses usually do not require high degrees of precision—something that critics often forget. The senior

EXHIBIT 4.4 Scenario Analysis

Scenario Description	Detailed Assumptions	EBIT* Impact ($MM)
1. Currency changes impact competitive landscape	15% volume decrease 20% price decrease Sustained for 9 months Recovery takes additional 9 months	− $500
2. Natural gas prices increase	$5/MM Btu increase Sustained for 12 months No ability to pass through increase	− $150
3. Crude oil prices increase	100% increase Sustained for 3 months Pass thru 25% of cost increase	− $15
4. Technology shift	15% volume decrease/year 15% price decrease/year $2MM less in R&D expenditures	− $275
5. Competitive pressure	10% price decrease Sustained for 24 months	− $200
6. Supply chain disruption	10% volume decrease Sustained for 6 months	− $175

*Earnings before interest & taxes.

executives readily recognized similarities to effects that were experienced in the previous downturn.

That recognition triggered an analysis of two ways to improve resilience and agility. The first was to identify potential cost reductions. This led to efforts to reduce selling, general, and administrative expenses by more than $100 million. The second was to improve the quality of the revenue stream. This meant identifying customers and suppliers most likely to survive a downturn and measuring their creditworthiness. The company focused

EXHIBIT 4.5 Sensitivity Analysis

Sensitivity Analysis: Scenario 1 (currency changes)

EBIT Impact ($MM)		Volume Decrease		
		5%	10%	15%
Price Decrease	5%	$200	$225	$250
	10%	$250	$275	$300
	15%	$325	$350	$400
	20%	$400	$450	$500

on developing longer-term contracts with the most desirable ones while culling its less profitable and thus less desirable customers. When the downturn occurred, the company was better prepared and, in the interim, more profitable.

Voice of Experience

"The financial institutions played a high-risk game thinking it was a low-risk game, all because their assumptions on losses and volatility were too low. We'd be watching an entirely different picture if only they'd said, 'This stuff is potentially risky. Since home prices have gone up so much, and mortgages have been available so easily, there might be widespread declines in home prices this time. So we're only going to lever up half as much as past performance might suggest.'"[31]

—Howard Marks, Chairman, Oaktree Capital Management

STRENGTHS AND WEAKNESSES OF SCENARIO PLANNING Scenario planning enables management to identify the likely direction and relative (though usually not precise) magnitude of the effects of changes that affect the drivers of the enterprise's revenues, costs, profits, and market share. It can also open people's minds while helping them to structure their thinking. Also, according to Raspin and Terjesen,[32] scenario planning can help the enterprise to:

- Challenge expectations
- Pose "what if" questions
- Clarify sensitivities to environmental factors
- Enable the development of contingency plans
- Reinforce the need for strategic change

However, scenario planning also has its weaknesses. First, it depends on assumptions not only about the drivers of revenue, costs, and other performance metrics, but also about the number, nature, direction, and magnitude of changes in those drivers. Again, however, tremendous precision is not the goal. Second, the mathematical nature of the tool can give some analysts and executives a false sense of security. People must realize that while numbers may seem precise, they can be incorrect. Third, scenario planning can generate many possibilities, but it can be difficult to distinguish the "vital few" from the "trivial many," so the key is to focus on the key risks. Fourth, scenarios may be linear and incremental and thus fail to portray discontinuity. Fifth, executives may dismiss extreme scenarios as implausible or see the entire effort as an academic exercise. Finally, management must provide meaningful input to the analysis.

On the latter point, in March 2008, the Senior Supervisors Group (SSG)—financial institution regulators from France, Germany, the United Kingdom, Switzerland, and the United States—issued a report on the effectiveness of banks in addressing the financial crisis. The report highlighted the impact of risk management practices on performance as of December 31, 2007.

In the more successful banks, senior executives were more involved in scenario analyses and stress testing. In less successful ones, they were less involved and "the larger the shock imposed, the less plausible were the stress tests or scenarios in the eyes of business units and senior management."[33] The SSG also found that "knowledge of how business areas made money helped risk managers identify relevant stress scenarios or provide warning when the assumptions underlying single-factor stress tests were inaccurate."[34]

Voice of Experience

"You always have different scenarios, but the board should say, 'Let's look at what the business drivers are here, what makes this successful, what's the value proposition, and then what's going to destroy that value?' You need to have skeptical people with imagination because many times, it's hard to step out of the current culture and business model and ask, 'What is the opposite of this?'"

—David Meuse, Director

Don't Make an Ass of U and Me (Assume)

An enterprise's greatest competitive risks and opportunities stem from the assumptions under which it formulates and executes strategy, conducts operations, and manages risk. These assumptions can be a source of competitive advantage or, if left unchallenged, can become a cause of disadvantage, failure, and extinction. The skill of challenging assumptions thus represents a starting point for leaders contemplating value, and risk, and intelligent risk management.

The risk intelligent enterprise checks its assumptions at the doors of the boardroom and the executive suite. Two tools—Thesis-Antithesis-Synthesis (TAS) and scenario planning—can be particularly useful in exercising this skill. This is especially the case when TAS is combined with a search for "black swans," to borrow Nassim Taleb's metaphor. TAS enables management to make fundamental assumptions explicit (the theses) and then to define the opposites (the antitheses). Then management is positioned to either develop and pursue an antithetical strategy or strategies or resolve the two propositions into an optimal, synthesized strategy or set of strategic options.

With TAS, boards and senior executive teams can better understand the potential forces and events that will affect and determine the ability of the enterprise to survive and thrive. TAS can also produce clearer views of opportunities and risks of the enterprise strategy itself. This challenge to basic assumptions is, as noted at the beginning of this chapter, necessary to identify risks *of* a strategy, which can be even more dangerous than risks *to* a strategy.

A more common tool, scenario planning is widely used by organizations in planning and risk management, but its utility and success depend on the assumptions underlying the analysis. Used properly, scenario planning can help test the effects of various assumptions and the sensitivity of enterprise performance under various conditions or should various events occur. But without rigorous challenge of assumptions, open minds, and senior management involvement, the tool will reveal little about either potential risks and opportunities or about the effects of various decisions or responses.

We close this chapter with questions designed to help you constructively challenge your business assumptions.

Questions to Ask about Assumptions

- Have the fundamental underlying assumptions (theses) of the industry and our enterprise been made explicit?
- Have we identified the opposites (the antitheses) of these assumptions?
- What are the implications of the antitheses for our business model?
- How can we synthesize the theses and antitheses?
- Are there signals or evidence of the antitheses occurring?
- Can we gain competitive advantage by adopting the antitheses or syntheses?
- What are the options for doing this?
- Will we challenge convention successfully or allow a competitor to do so?

CHAPTER 5

Maintain Constant Vigilance

*Organizational structures often divert, delay, or distort the upward
flow of negative information.*
—Senior Supervisors Group Report, March 2008

To respond to a change, either within the organization or in the external
environment, the enterprise—and not just a few individuals in it—must
be aware of the change, understand what is happening and what may happen, and grasp the potential implications. This calls for constant vigilance,
the second of our ten skills. Developing this skill is difficult enough for individuals and an enormous challenge for the enterprise. However, it's a key
determinant of an organization's resilience and agility and thus its ability to
survive and thrive.

A number of factors mitigate against vigilance. Success tends to breed
complacency and resistance to changing that which has produced success.
In large, hierachical organizations this is compounded by multidivisional
or silo-style structures, bureaucracy, and centralization; in flat, decentralized organizations, it is compounded by lack of effective communication.
In other words, there is no simple structural solution that will automatically lead to vigilance, but it is possible—and necessary—to develop such
awareness.

Fatal Flaw #2: Lack of Vigilance

Eighty percent of accidents are caused by operator error, and almost
80 percent of operator errors are caused by lack of vigilance or situational awareness.[1] Surviving and thriving amid turbulence and uncertainty
demands situational awareness—the ability to perceive, comprehend, and

anticipate the effects of important changes in the environment. Without well-developed "sensory" capabilities and a "central nervous system" to connect them, an organization or even a nation will find itself blindsided by competitors, developments, events, and attacks, as recent history has proven:

- Before and during the 9/11 tragedy, multiple and disastrous breakdowns in communications were linked to the inability—or unwillingness—of various agencies to share information; the central nervous system failed.
- The subprime mortgage crisis can be attributed, in part, to banks' failure to recognize the nature and extent of the risks they were taking and to their faulty sensory capabilities. However, a few were much better than most and have experienced significant competitive advantage as a result.
- In Hurricane Katrina, the equipment breakdowns, mobilization difficulties, and power failures were exacerbated by human resource, communication, and command-and-control failures—a combination of dysfunctional sensory and response systems.

These examples were dramatic and far-reaching in their consequences. Yet, before these disasters, most people who were to be affected—and even many of those responsible for preventing or addressing them—were moving along in business-as-usual mode, unaware of what lay ahead. Yes, with the benefit of hindsight we can see what happened; however, there were signals from various quarters, which were ignored, minimized, or lost in the shuffle of "normal operations."

Three Failures in Vigilance

In general, major unpleasant surprises can be traced to one or more of the three types of failures that characterize lack of vigilance:

1. Failure to see a shift coming
2. Failure to grasp the implications of the shift
3. Failure to anticipate the future path of the shift

This chapter first discusses these three failures and then introduces the skill and tools that will help boards, executives, and risk managers to anticipate and manage them. In employing these tools, the enterprise and its leadership will improve vigilance and situational awareness and thus improve resilience and agility—resilience because, usually, the sooner and more clearly a threat is identified, the more efficient and effective the response, and agility because, generally, the sooner and more precisely an opportunity is analyzed, the better the organization's chances of capitalizing on it. In many situations, the first organization to detect a shift can secure first-mover advantage.

Voice of Experience

"I see a complete and total lack of understanding and awareness, and with that, a complete lack of action. Recently, a company brought me in just to take a look at where they stood. At the end of the meeting, they asked, 'What do you think?' I said, 'I think you're going to file for bankruptcy in about six weeks.' I thought they were going to fall over. I haven't heard from them since."

—Suzanne Hopgood, Director

FAILURE TO SEE A SHIFT COMING Five factors can render directors and executives unaware of threats, opportunities, or other changes in the enterprise or the environment:

1. Overload of information and tasks
2. Lack of common sensors and a "central nervous system"
3. Organizational silos
4. Incomplete integration following mergers and acquisitions
5. Perceptual blind spots

The following sections briefly discuss each of these factors.

Overload of Information and Tasks Executives must make tough decisions in the face of excessive workloads, extraordinary pressures to excel (especially in the short term), competing priorities, incomplete information, conflicting opinions, and high stress. Such common conditions go a long way to explaining why many who have experienced catastrophic loss simply didn't see disaster looming, understand what it meant, or respond quickly enough. Yet those who have the best chances to survive and thrive under adverse conditions are constantly vigilant.

Too much information can create as many problems as too little information. Information technology (IT) enables the production of new information, access to huge amounts of historical data, and communication over an ever-increasing array of channels and devices. But in doing so, IT can generate overload and an inability to identify inaccuracies and to evaluate the reliability of information.

Task overload produces stress and associated psychological effects. Ceaseless interruptions—phone calls, e-mails, and instant messages—generate still more information, leaving less time to devote to a given task, and for thinking, let alone reflection. This can break down mental focus on the task at hand and leave one unaware of one's situation and its implications.

Voice of Experience

"In my experience, there is an issue of how much detail reporting you should get from the director of risk management or the treasurer or CFO or whoever has the overall responsibility for risk.

"In the case of one board, even though there was a separate risk committee, the full board was getting a huge deck of slides every meeting on all kinds of detailed things we were measuring. Frankly, one of the concerns I had was separating the forest from the trees.

"There's so much detail that it's really hard to understand what the most important risks were. So you start asking for some improvement to highlight the things that we need to know more about. Then bring exceptions to the risk management committee or the audit committee or the full board ... My point is that a lot of information was being provided, but it wasn't necessarily understandable or insightful."

—Denny Beresford, Director and Professor, J.M. Tull School of Accounting

---

LACK OF SENSORS AND A "NERVOUS SYSTEM"   Enterprises don't naturally possess a well-developed central nervous system. They are not hard-wired from the outset to recognize threats or opportunities or to transmit key signals. If anything, certain structural and political characteristics of enterprises mitigate against development of such a nervous system. Therefore, the board and management must actively establish and then maintain appropriate sensors, processes, and communication channels that amount to an organizational nervous system.

In many enterprises those sensors, processes, and channels either don't exist or have proven inadequate. In fact, such organizations often have management layers that, instead of sensing changes and expediting information, actually filter out changes and divert, delay, or dilute information—especially negative information.

Organizational Silos   Enterprises require specialization to deal with complexity and diversity within and across functions, markets, product lines, distribution channels, supply chains, and stakeholder relationships. As the enterprise develops increasingly specialized functions, it develops functional silos that all too often either fail to communicate with one another, or fail to understand one another when they do. Worse, incentives in these silos may not promote mutual goals and interests and may work against collaboration across silos. This can produce unhealthy competition and lack of coordinated responses to larger threats and opportunities.

That's why, for example, information about a customer relations problem or a data breach, which ought to quickly travel up and across the chain of command, may be left to develop into a public relations nightmare or a legal issue. Managers are rarely trained to recognize, much less handle, issues that transcend their specialties or organizational boundaries. Many believe it's in their interests to hoard or conceal information—even information about opportunities.

In addition to their narrow interests, specialists speak jargon and can find communicating across specialties difficult. Absent a common language, signals may be picked up by one area—say customer service, quality control, or finance—but not be communicated, or communicated but dismissed as irrelevant, or communicated and recognized, but never reach a high enough level to effect a coordinated response.

Inadequate Postmerger Integration   Mergers and acquisitions have long been a popular path to growth, despite a historical failure rate of about 70 to 80 percent (i.e., failure to fully achieve the intended synergies). Rather than growing organically, many enterprises might as well have been assembled by Dr. Frankenstein, with the corporate equivalent of bolted-on capabilities and stitched together policies, processes, and cultures. The result? Cumbersome enterprises lurching about the landscape, with ineffective sensory capabilities, garbled communications, and uncoordinated appendages.

When a company's mergers and acquisitions go global, national as well as organizational cultures create further disarray. For instance, the Corruption Perception Index reveals startling national differences in perceived levels of corruption, to the extent that "corruption" appears to be the national pastime in some cultures. Yet to locals, the practices in question may constitute accepted, centuries-old business methods. Cultures also exhibit marked differences toward risk taking, initiative, innovation, and hierarchy. These characteristics, biases, and relationships must be well understood and well managed if anything like a "central nervous system" is to be developed.

Voice of Experience

As one director put it, "Most companies do not manage their 'internal' relationships all that well. Different subsidiaries do their own thing. They don't even get together very frequently to talk about how they could interact better. I'm not sure that those issues are specific to risk management, but they certainly affect how companies drive the overall business strategy."

Perceptual Blind Spots   Add to the foregoing the human tendencies to per-ceive the environment in highly selective ways, to filter out seemingly irrelevant input or to become distracted by it, and to fall into boredom, habit, or somnambulance, and it's a wonder anyone is ever aware of any but the most immediate and personally relevant threat or opportunity. As you may imagine, group modes of perception make matters worse. These include mental models that generate preconceived notions, blind optimism due to commitment to certain goals, and groupthink stemming from pressure to conform.

Individually or collectively, people paying close attention can develop tunnel vision by hyper-focusing on their objective, such as revenue growth or cost reduction. In a study of what the researchers called "unintentional blindness," subjects were asked to view a 30-second video and count the number of times players passed a basketball back and forth. Most subjects focused so intensely on the assigned task that they failed to notice when an actor in a gorilla suit entered stage right, beat his chest, and exited stage left.[2]

Other visual awareness studies consistently reveal that even when people are looking for it, they have difficulty noticing a gradual change. When just one feature in a simple scene changes, many people do not perceive it. Detecting gradual changes in a complex scene can be quite dif-ficult, as often occurs when the business environment changes slowly and the enterprise perceives the change too late.

One of the major biases in risky decision making is optimism. Optimism is a source of high-risk thinking.
                                    —*Daniel Kahneman, Nobel Laureate*

FAILURE TO GRASP THE IMPLICATIONS OF THE SHIFT   If you see a change com-ing, what does it mean—especially to your organization? In being vigilant, when an individual or enterprise perceives a change, one must identify it as a threat or an opportunity and assess its implications. An enterprise may fail to grasp the nature, meaning, or implications of a change for any of many reasons. Three very common ones are:

1. Overconfidence
2. Unwillingness to listen and denial
3. Preexisting mental models and biases

Overconfidence   Overconfidence leads an enterprise to underestimate or dismiss risk and fosters lack of preparedness. It is perhaps the major reason that established enterprises are consistently undone by new, disruptive technologies. They not only fail to preemptively develop the technologies that could potentially undo them, but they then fail to recognize the risks—and opportunities—that the technologies may hold when another organization develops them.

Given the oft-cited dangers of hubris, organizational overconfidence can reach almost comical (or tragic) proportions. Consider some remarks of former AIG executive Joseph Cassano, quoted in the *New York Times*, September 28, 2008: "It is hard for us, without being flippant, to even see a scenario within any kind of realm of reason that would see us losing one dollar in any of those transactions. We're sitting on a great balance sheet, a strong investment portfolio and a global trading platform where we can take advantage of the market in any variety of places."[3] As of March 2009, at least one count had AIG receiving up to $180 billion in federal "bailout" money.[4]

Overconfidence causes boards and executives not only to fail to perceive threats and opportunities, but also to misjudge their nature and magnitude when they do perceive them.

Unwillingness to Listen and Denial Even when a message concerning a threat does get through, it may simply be unwelcome. Recall that most people display an *automatic* tendency to reject new information that contradicts their assumptions. In many organizations, overconfidence, fear, *esprit de corps*, or executive egos create an atmosphere in which the truth cannot be spoken. The killing of messengers bearing bad news is age-old. Experts citing risks are routinely ignored as cranks, Cassandras, or criers of wolf, and organizations are just as routinely blindsided.

In this respect, as in most, tone-at-the-top determines organizational culture. One chairman confided, "The biggest single factor in the demise of the bank was that the CEO was not willing to listen and accept other points of view." An unwillingness to listen to calls for change may follow when CEOs become superstars.

In fact, company performance has been shown to decline after CEOs win awards. Researchers Malmendier and Tate[5] found that award-winning CEOs often underperform compared with their own previous performance and with a matched sample of non-award winning CEOs. They conclude that the effects on shareholder value are negative when a CEO attains superstar status. Too often, where imperial CEOs prevail, sycophants are promoted and bad news doesn't travel at all.

Extreme enthusiasm and inflated egos can generate unbridled determination to win at all costs or to simply refuse to change with the times. Leaders with such determination often consciously decide to deflect or deny intelligence that contradicts their decision or even to deny that failure may be imminent.

Take, for example, Operation Market Garden, a World War II Allied operation designed to secure a series of bridges in German-occupied territory in the Netherlands. Senior officers ignored intelligence about German Panzer divisions already in the area. Staff were afraid to voice their concerns about whether their radios would work, and there were no contingencies should the expected armored divisions be delayed. At the end of the war, British Field Marshal Bernard Montgomery partly blamed himself but couldn't fully contain his ego and laid a large portion of the blame on U.S. General Dwight D. Eisenhower.[6]

Even when a key shift has been identified and the implications understood, without a receptive leadership the enterprise will inevitably be blindsided by these events. Such blindness, willful or not, and statements of "it can't happen to us, we are too smart or too big to fail" will be heard repeatedly because leadership is deaf to internal and external signals.

For example, before Bernard Madoff admitted he defrauded people of almost $50 billion, Harry Markopoulos and Dan diBartolomeo believed he was cheating investors. Markopoulos waged a remarkable battle to flag fraud at Madoff's operation, sounding the alarm as far back as 1999 and continuing into the 2000s. Similarly, the *Wall Street Journal* reported that Union Bancaire Privée (UBP) invested hundreds of millions of dollars with Madoff despite in-house warnings. The Swiss bank's own research team raised concerns in early 2007. UBP's then-deputy head of research, Gideon Nieuwouldt, listed several worries, including lack of basic information, and recommended that Madoff be removed from UBP's list of approved funds.[7] His warnings went unheeded.

Voice of Experience

"The hardest job I've had in the last six to eight months is convincing people how bad things could get. Now the organization has certainly come around to it and is planning properly, but people just don't want to even contemplate the good times stopping. You have to do worst-case-scenario planning."

—Eric Krasnoff, Chairman and CEO, Pall Corporation

Preexisting Mental Models and Biases   Leaders often refuse even to listen to news of a development or event and its potential implications. But sometimes they listen and fail to grasp the implications due to their mental models and biases. One of the most interesting cases of this occurred when Louis

Pasteur discovered that doctors were risking transmission of disease through the transfer of germs among their patients, and could avoid doing so by washing their hands. When Pasteur presented his findings, the overwhelming majority of physicians vigorously rejected them. The reason? They were healers. How could they possibly be doing something that would make their patients sicker?

In fact, most comprehension errors can be attributed to incorrect mental models.[8] People see what they expect to see and want to see. That's why writers should not edit their own work, programmers should not review their own code, and a lawyer who represents herself has a fool for a client. Mental models—and resolution of cognitive dissonance—explain why once people have made up their minds, they are unlikely to change.

Resolution of cognitive dissonance occurs when one makes a decision or commits to a line of thinking or course of action and then filters out or misinterprets any new information that runs counter to his or her position. Perception (cognition) of the new, contradictory information generates dissonance in their minds, which is uncomfortable. To rid themselves of that feeling they must resolve the cognitive dissonance. Most people do so by filtering out the new information, dismissing it as unreliable, or impugning its source. Most people aren't rational; they are rationalizers.

FAILURE TO ANTICIPATE THE PATH OF THE SHIFT   Two factors can contribute to the inability to anticipate the direction of a shift:

1. Loss of long-term memory
2. Failure of foresight

After all, most business people understand that there's an economic cycle of expansion and contraction and that a downturn follows an upturn and vice versa. Some even know when they are taking risks that they haven't adequately understood or prepared for, and simply hope for the best. Others see bad situations develop and do almost nothing or at least nothing very effective.

Loss of Long-Term Memory   For an organization, long-term institutional memory represents a storehouse of knowledge and experience. While people should not feel constricted by the past, there's not much to support the practice of ignoring it. However, organizational long-term memory becomes compromised in the face of management and employee turnover, or when new leadership teams rewrite history to foster change, paper over the past, or blame predecessors. People retire, pursue new opportunities, or get downsized. Henry Petroski, professor of civil engineering at Duke University, found that major bridge failures are projected to occur at 30-year intervals. Why? Because that is the average length of the career of an engineer.

A company may not see where it's going because people have forgotten where they've been. A new generation forgets what the prior one learned, and many companies fail to record and disseminate experience within the company. If they did, they might avoid repeating disastrous mistakes. In the larger society—and in families—oral history as well as traditions help cultures retain memories of important events.

But when a culture or a company loses its institutional memory—say, by being conquered or assimilated in the case of a culture or being merged or acquired in the case of a company—it is less able to predict the path of events and to cope with change. The enterprise forgets what happened in the last major downturn, the previous cost-cutting spree, or the successful product introduction ten years ago. It becomes less able to avoid risky behavior or events, and "winging it" becomes the order of the day when the unexpected occurs.

Failures of Foresight   Failures of foresight often stem from an enterprise's inability to learn the right lessons from the past and to incorporate them into its collective consciousness. For example, the Columbia Accident Investigation Board (CAIB), convened by NASA to investigate the *Columbia* Space Shuttle disaster in 2003, concluded, "Both accidents" [the *Columbia* and the earlier destruction of the *Challenger* Space Shuttle in 1986] were "failures of foresight"' and the parallels between them demonstrate that "the causes of the institutional failure responsible for *Challenger* have not been fixed." In addition, the CAIB stated, "if these persistent, systemic flaws are not resolved, the scene is set for another accident." Furthermore, "NASA's problems cannot be solved simply by retirements, resignations, or transferring personnel."[9]

We are not suggesting that forecasting the future is easy or even possible. Instead, we are recommending close examination and analysis of potential events and outcomes once a nascent shift has been identified. Such a shift might be signaled by a turning point in the economic cycle or in a housing boom, for example, or by the entry of a new participant with a potentially disruptive technology in your market.

TAS, scenario planning, sensitivity analysis, other forms of modeling, and standard forecasts of interest rates, inflation, consumer spending, and economic growth all have their uses. But by far the most critical factor is the board's and management's willingness and ability to consider the ways in which future developments might affect the enterprise. That's because only when the board and management recognize a threat or an opportunity can the enterprise do anything to respond. For that reason, constant vigilance represents a key component of risk intelligence.

We now turn to tools for developing and maintaining constant vigilance.

Risk Intelligence Skill #2: Maintain Constant Vigilance

Vigilance, or situational awareness, can be developed and exercised by people in an enterprise with the help of three broad sets of tools:

1. Signal detection capabilities
2. Signal interpretation methodology
3. Signal communication system

Tool #1: Signal Detection Capabilities

Signal detection capabilities enable someone at some level of the enterprise to perceive a potentially relevant change when it occurs. This tool forms the foundation of situational awareness because if you don't perceive a signal—whether it be a change within the enterprise, or out in the environment—then you cannot interpret, communicate, or formulate a response to the potential threat or opportunity.

Signal detection capabilities combine scanning and sensing capabilities to form the eyes, ears, and other senses of the "central nervous system" of the risk intelligent enterprise. Such a system requires active sensory mechanisms for detecting signs of change—however faint—in the enterprise and especially in the environment. We say "especially in the environment" because the typical organization has—or can readily develop—fairly reliable internal systems for monitoring product and service quality, transaction size and volume, costs and changes in costs, employee conduct (at least on the job), and similar "signals." Monitoring the external environment is more difficult because it is far larger and more unpredictable. It is also where most rewarded risks tend to originate.

So, to develop superb signal scanning capabilities, management at senior, functional, and business unit levels must focus on developing and maintaining:

- Internal monitoring capabilities and skills
- External monitoring capabilities and skills

Internal monitoring includes the full range of accounting, financial, security, inventory, regulatory compliance, internal audit, IT security, and other monitoring processes particular to the industry and the enterprise. Keys to success in these activities, which rely upon exception reporting and statistical process control systems, and regular and spot audits, include making the processes and systems as automatic as possible while maintaining vigilance. That means not only employing technology to the extent possible, but also promulgating other mechanisms to encourage vigilance in work processes and procedures and in training and supervisory practices. Thus, internal monitoring aims to detect variability from expected performance.

External monitoring depends on the skills discussed in detail earlier: paying attention, listening, and minimizing the effects of overconfidence, biases, and existing mental models. That's because, as has been well documented, the signals of change are usually perceptible but people either filter them out or they communicate them only to be ignored. For example, when the costs of homeownership reach a historically high multiple of the costs of renting, home prices may be peaking. When something fundamentally different like the automobile, television, or Internet is invented, your business model probably needs to change.

To improve your enterprise's ability to detect external changes, continually develop people's awareness of the environment. Teach them to scan the horizon for changes in their areas—and to report them. Develop mechanisms to identify early signs of emerging black swans. Have them look beyond the obvious by asking about your customers' customers, your suppliers' suppliers, and your investors' and lenders' sources of funds. Have people develop reliable information sources by nurturing relationships and sharing information.

Also, locate "promontories" from which to scan the environment—specialized journals, venture capitalists, young experts, even small, highly focused conferences, user groups, or associations. Make sure that when people attend conferences they gather information on longer-term industry problems and opportunities and not just the issue *du jour*. Whether or not you do business globally, scan the international environment and developing economies for threats and opportunities.

Enterprises must develop the ability to detect weak signals amid background noise if they are to survive and thrive in uncertainty. Igor Ansoff introduced the theory of weak signals in the mid-1970s to improve strategic planning models. Ansoff argued that signals of change are often inexact and difficult to observe and understand. He has said that corporations therefore need to develop better weak-signal detection capabilities.[10, 11] Similarly, Wharton marketing professor Paul Schoemaker found that companies that used feedback from scanning for weak signals to adjust their strategies were better able to develop markets beyond their core capabilities. He cites the following examples:

- Abbot Laboratories had traditionally defined its core business as ethical pharmaceuticals but expanded to a broad range of products that lower health care costs. Abbott now produces hospital nutritional products, diagnostics, and supplies.
- FedEx had defined its core business as the overnight delivery of small packages but, after studying the impact of electronic commerce on

global sourcing, became a leading provider of end-to-end logistics services.

- Pitney Bowes had defined its core as postage meters and mail handling but considered a wide range of related back-office trends and now makes systems and provides services that support workflow, document, and mail-center management.

How do you detect something when you don't know what you are looking for? Most companies have "intelligence" gathering processes for market and product development, but not for other strategic concerns. Part of the problem is not knowing which signals to look for or being unable to detect them due to noise in the system. However, TAS and scenario planning can help hone weak signal detection capabilities.

Case Example: Royal Dutch Shell Scenario Planning   Kees van der Heijden tells the now well-known story of scenario planning at Shell Oil.[12] Prior to 1973, Shell's planners had defined a number of scenarios about developments in the Middle East. One scenario was an energy crisis triggered by rising militarism of the oil producing states. By being alert to signals of a range of scenarios, including the crisis scenario, the company was able to quickly recognize when the energy crisis scenario was materializing and it began to reprioritize its investments.

Based on alternatives already developed, Shell quickly shifted from further development of primary refining capacity to improvements in refining outputs. The remainder of the oil industry took years to recognize this shift and continued to build refining capacity, resulting in significant overcapacity and reduced profitability—and a competitive advantage for Shell for almost two decades.

"What the scenarios did was to enable Shell's manufacturing people to be more perceptive, recognize events for what they were, a part of a pattern, and on this basis realize their implications."[13] (Interestingly, Shell's Marine Transport division did not adopt the same process and continued to build overcapacity.)

Voice of Experience

"How do you look at the changing paradigms or potentially changing paradigms ahead of time and get a leg up to make the enterprise more maneuverable?

"Every company falls in love with itself and its strategy. Of course, everyone believes they have a winning policy, but we also know that
(Continued)

(*Continued*)

many of the great companies are no longer around. Eventually, most of them will not be around ... or no longer be great. Strategy may work for 10 or 15 years. It may even work for 100 years, but eventually, it wears out.

"The key is that you never know when it's going to wear out. Your strategy could be terrific today and not be any good tomorrow, or you could have a 50-year run. But you have to think about alternatives, and it can't come with a cookbook of, 'Here are your standard risks. I'm going to leave you with this template and everything will be lovely.' It takes a lot of thought on a regular basis and the willingness and ability to quickly adjust."

—Eric Krasnoff, Chairman and CEO, Pall Corporation

One way to counter senior management's tendency to disregard extreme cases as implausible is to identify major threats to the business model and then look for evidence of those threats. Forward-looking sensors and pathways need to be created and maintained. One way to improve signal detection is to set up mechanisms that specifically challenge mental models and then scan for threats and opportunities.

TAS: A TOOL FOR IMPROVING VIGILANCE   We've noted the importance of making management's assumptions about enterprise risk and value creation explicit, and then challenging that "conventional wisdom." Most management information takes a "white swan" view of the world, which makes it hard for leaders to detect changes in the business environment. By describing the antitheses of the white swans, the enterprise can ready itself to detect the approach of black swans. People can become more alert to signals that may contradict their worldview.

Once a key assumption has been made explicit—the thesis statement—you describe its antithesis or opposite. Then you are better positioned to detect and interpret the signal. Moreover, once you recognize and record the signal, as shown in Exhibit 5.1, which references the hardcopy encyclopedia publisher discussed in Chapter 4, you can establish metrics that will help you monitor future developments for threats and opportunities.

By definition, the antithesis should include the worst-case scenario, regardless of plausibility, so you can seek evidence of its occurrence. This TAS analysis can amplify sensitivity even to weak signals. By developing sensors for signals relating to the antitheses, the encyclopedia company might have detected early warnings of a disruptive technology and a seismic shift

EXHIBIT 5.1 Signal Detection Scheme

Hardcopy Encyclopedia Publisher Examples for Establishing Signal Detection			
Thesis White Swan	Antithesis Black Swan	Signal	Metric
All reference knowledge will be communicated in printed form.	Reference knowledge will be communicated in media other than print.	Alternatives to print for storage and delivery media Growth of nonprint media as a source of reference knowledge	Internet usage rates In-home computers
It will be updated periodically.	It will be updated instantly.	Refresh rate	Instant, hourly, daily, weekly, monthly, annual rates
A subscription fee will be charged to the end user.	It will be free to the end user.	Cost to end user	User behavior; Alternative revenue sources (e.g., advertising)
The reference base will be stationary.	The reference base will be mobile.	Use in home or in office vs. mobile	Growth rate of mobile devices

in its business and then developed strategic options. To become attuned to signals and to sort through them, and weigh their relative importance, enterprises can develop metrics related to each of the antitheses on its TAS chart. This can help to reduce information overload and focus attention on the "vital few" rather than the "trivial many" developments.

Voice of Experience

"If you really want to learn what is going on in a company, spend time in the employee cafeteria. That's where the truth is. It's not at the top floor in the corner office."

—Bob Eckert, Chairman and CEO Mattel, Inc.[14]

Robust Dialogue Turns Up the Volume   In March 2008, the Senior Supervisors Group (SSG), mentioned in Chapter 4, reported that the banking and securities firms that had more success in dealing with the market turbulence by the end of 2007 also had a more complete understanding of their exposures. These firms had used enterprise-wide intelligence to adapt their business strategy and risk management practices more quickly. The SSG also found that robust dialogue among senior executives and risk management functions at all levels had enabled more effective and timely sharing of risk information. In other words, it had turned up the volume on a relatively weak signal.

The report notes, "Some firms were consequently able to identify the sources of significant risk as early as mid-2006; they had as much as a year to evaluate the magnitude of those risks and to implement plans to reduce exposures or hedge risks while it was still practical and not prohibitively expensive."[15] The SSG also reported that in firms with greater success in addressing market turbulence, "Senior management undertook to surmount organizational structures that tended to delay, divert, or distort the flow of information up the management chain of the firm."[16]

At the time, one of those successful companies was Goldman Sachs. According to a January 4, 2009, *New York Times* article by Joe Nocera,[17] in December 2006 a number of indicators had begun to emit weak signals that something was amiss. Goldman Sachs, which reviewed its profit and loss statement daily, had found that the company's mortgage arm had lost money every day for ten consecutive days. The chief financial officer, David Viniar, convened a meeting of risk managers and traders to pinpoint the problem.

While they used a number of models, including Value at Risk (VaR), it was their collective judgment that determined that the situation was likely to deteriorate further. They therefore reduced their exposure to collateralized debt obligations by disposing of them or hedging their positions and tightening credit. When management had seen unanticipated losses they decided to take action, regardless of what the conventional risk models indicated. Judgment, rather than any single tool or set of tools, must be the deciding factor.

Voice of Experience

"The key to survival is not just to recognize when you make a mistake—everybody does—but to recognize it quickly. Let me give you a personal example. I started on Wall Street as a municipal bond underwriter in 1972. It was six or seven months before they allowed me to

> commit any money. My first trade was Garland ISD Texas, while my boss was on vacation. Then the market weakened, and I wanted to sell. So I took a $40,000 loss, no small amount at the time. I literally thought I'd be fired from my $10,000 a year job.
>
> "When my boss got back, he said, 'Great sale.' I thought he was being sarcastic, and shot back, 'What are you talking about? I lost $40,000.' He said, 'Yeah, but if you'd waited, it would've been $140,000.'"
>
> —Tom O'Neill, Principal, Sandler O'Neill + Partners L.P.

Recognize Mistakes Quickly Even the best scanning and intelligence development will be useless if people are afraid to bring issues forward. This is a cultural issue in which management must lead by example. If you shoot messengers and don't tolerate dissent, you will not find many messengers or dissenters in your organization. When problems are discovered, do you seek someone to blame and punish or do you focus on fixing the problem? Instead, you may consider punishing those who bury bad news and hide problems, and recognizing those who have the courage to speak the truth as they see it.

Tool #2: Signal Interpretation Methodology

Most signals of threats and opportunities are noticed by someone, somewhere in a large organization, but not interpreted properly. The company "scanners" must create enterprise radar in their ability not only to spot but also to interpret risks, as air traffic controllers do. Air traffic controllers use radar and other technologies to detect the position of aircraft in their airspace, and to identify the type, owner, and even purpose of the craft. The latest technology gathers a great deal of data, but the basic concept dates to World War II technology for IFF—identify friend or foe.

Enterprises need similar sensors in their "airspace" to detect signals that may indicate a threat or an opportunity. In addition, people—particularly senior executives—must be able to judge the nature and magnitude of the threat or opportunity, and the likely path of events. Elite athletes usually have a highly developed ability to anticipate events in their "airspace." Hockey great Wayne Gretsky seemed to know where the puck was going to be, rather than just where the puck was. To hone this ability, Gretsky's father, Walter, had taught Wayne to watch a game and draw the movements of the puck.[18]

Voice of Experience

"Being situationally aware can come from the wisdom of experience. Failure is failure. I don't care how you paint it, that's what you're trying to minimize. You minimize mistakes; you minimize failure. How do you do that? By anticipating. You have to anticipate."

—Mario Andretti, race car driver and entrepreneur

Case Example: General Electric   General Electric (GE) provides an example of how an enterprise "central nervous system" with common sensors can escalate significant risks to key decision makers. GE's Policy 6.0 requires that risk be assessed at both the product level and the portfolio level. The board reviews the strategic portfolio, risk assessments, and emerging issues. The business CEO level conducts a portfolio risk assessment and reviews key risk metrics and emerging issues. The product level conducts reviews for each product.

Each level of review is based on GE's Six Sigma disciplines and analytic tools. The GE process has five major steps:

1. *Define*. Determine the product/program characteristics matrix and identify the "critical few" performance drivers.
2. *Measure*. Collect data and baseline performance and define performance standards, including external benchmarks plus the business leader's maximum allowable loss.
3. *Analyze*. Isolate root causes of loss including use of statistical analysis to determine significant loss drivers and establish tolerance levels of allowable losses with trigger levels or "smoke detectors."
4. *Improve*. Establish levels of acceptable variability to yield better performance and monitor results using established feedback loops.
5. *Control*. Establish a control-monitoring plane and take corrective action when triggers are breached.[19]

Note that these parallel the Six Sigma steps known as DMAIC (*da may' ic*), which stands for define, measure, analyze, improve, and control. In the DMAIC approach, you define a quality problem, measure data that evidences the problem, analyze the cause or causes of the problem, improve quality by solving the problem in the process, and then control the process thereafter to maintain the new level of quality.

Tool #3: Signal Communication System

To overcome the communication obstacles inherent in their diverse, siloed structures, large enterprises require a common understanding of risk, threats, opportunities, and communication protocols. That understanding, together with established pathways, enables rapid communication up the chain of command and across the enterprise to alert people who need risk-related information that pertains to them.

This means developing the following commonalities:

- Language of risk
- Tolerance for specific types and levels of risk
- Criteria for risk assessment
- Triggers for escalating threats and opportunities
- Reporting pathways and mechanisms
- Response mechanisms for key types of incidents

Chapter 16, "Risk Intelligent Enterprise Management," discusses ways of developing these commonalities in greater detail from a management perspective. We note them at this point because they are integral to developing vigilance, a key skill in the risk intelligent enterprise.

ALIVE, ALERT, AND ADAPTABLE Although they are like living organisms, most organizations lack what might be termed common senses. As noted earlier, enterprises are not hard-wired to detect changes in their environment, to evaluate them quickly, and to communicate about them effectively. As a result, they may act in ways that appear to be irrational or counter to their interests.

Senior management must consciously develop the organization's central nervous system to overcome these shortcomings. This begins by establishing specific capabilities and processes for sensing, evaluating, and communicating threats and opportunities. To avoid being blindsided or overtaken by unexpected events, an enterprise needs sensors to detect even weak signals of the antithesis of key assumptions and a central nervous system to communicate them up the line—a topic we take up in greater detail in Part III.

Risk intelligent enterprises understand their fundamental assumptions or theses (white swans) and develop their antitheses (black swans). They develop scenarios and playbooks in advance to enable rapid detection of black swans and have prepared coordinated responses to inevitable but unpredictable threats and opportunities. They have explored the range of options that using tools like TAS and scenario planning can identify.

Another essential is having reliable, current information on the environment, which requires verifying the credibility of sources and then corroborating their information. Chapter 9 discusses the necessity and the challenges of conducting these activities *before* acting on such information.

Questions to Ask about Maintaining Constant Vigilance

Re: Signal Detection Capabilities

- What are the life and death assumptions of the business (the white swans)?
- If these change, what would be the impact on the enterprise?
- What would be our chances of surviving and thriving?
- Has the enterprise identified the antitheses of its fundamental business assumptions (the black swans)?
- Are there mechanisms to detect significant changes (black swans) in the environment that may change our fundamental assumptions and impact our business model?

Re: Signal Interpretation Methodology

- Is there a common understanding of risk and opportunity? Do we have common definitions of common risks? Is there a common language that bridges different risk and business silos?
- Does the enterprise have common sensors to alert leadership to changes? Is there an effective escalation procedure?
- Does bad news travel fast or have there been delays in escalating negative issues?
- Are there meaningful signal detection processes, metrics, and dashboards?

Re: Signal Communication System

- Is there a meaningful dialogue between directors and officers based on signals from key metrics and dashboards?
- Have we defined our strategic options and our response if a black swan were to emerge?
- Is there any evidence of those changes beginning to occur?
- How could we be among the first to detect those changes?

CHAPTER 6

Factor in Velocity and Momentum

Reputation is gained in inches per year and lost in feet per second.
—Anonymous

The speeds at which events occur can be deceptive. While an enterprise's reputation can unravel in minutes or days, and the global economy can melt down in weeks, such events are usually longer in the making. Nevertheless, accidents, crimes, and natural disasters—not to mention attacks—often emerge with little or no warning. Risk intelligence demands readiness for such events, regardless of their likelihood, provided they are relevant to the survival and success of the enterprise. Consider the following events, all worthy of the label crisis, all of which unfolded in different ways:

- *9/11 attack on the World Trade Center.* The destruction of the World Trade Center in Manhattan in 2001 shocked many people in its suddenness, belligerence, and loss of innocent lives. However, the same building had been attacked by Muslim extremists planting a bomb in the basement in 1993, and 2001 intelligence reports cited the possibility of an attack by means of airplanes. So, it should not have come as a complete surprise. Still, the event triggered massive change in a matter of hours and a long succession of follow-on effects.
- *Oil price shocks of the 1970s.* In the early 1970s Arab oil-exporting nations placed an embargo on oil exports to the United States, in response to its support for Israel. This quadrupled the price of oil and created long lines at gas pumps, when supply suddenly fell short of demand. This provided a market opportunity for foreign automakers who built smaller, more fuel-efficient cars, and they seized it. Then a second oil shock came in the late 1970s after Iranian "revolutionaries"

took 66 Americans hostage at the U.S. embassy in Tehran. Fast-forward
to the spike in oil prices in 2007 and the recession of 2008 when we
saw dealerships full of unsold SUVs.

- *Hurricane Katrina.* If you live in a hurricane zone, hurricanes
  should come as no surprise, but Katrina hit the Louisiana Gulf Coast
  with unexpected force. Still, the response of government at various
  levels—particularly that of the Federal Emergency Management Agency
  (FEMA)—was woefully inadequate. Various political explanations have
  been put forth for FEMA's slow response, but whatever the reason, it
  was clearly a case of poor preparedness and risk management.
- *Credit crisis of 2008.* Although it was a few years in the making,
  given that the housing bubble ran from about 2002 to 2007, the actual
  credit crisis—the evaporation of liquidity in 2008—occurred extremely
  quickly. As an example of a crisis's range of complex effects, this
  one is hard to beat. Essentially, banks and investors lost confidence in
  mortgage-backed securities, which had seemingly infiltrated every loan
  and investment portfolio in the world.

In this chapter, we focus on the velocity and momentum of events that
generate risks and opportunities. The above-noted events, though different in character and origin, all happened fairly rapidly and with lasting
effects. The oil price shocks bracketed a decade of "stagflation" (stagnant
economic growth coupled with inflation) and signaled the end of the U.S.
auto market as we knew it. The 9/11 WTC attack brought about a crisis in
the payments system, stock market shutdown, spikes in oil and other commodity prices, and revamping of U.S. intelligence agencies. The credit crisis
triggered a recession, stressed many financial institutions, and prompted
global government involvement in banking and business not seen since the
1930s.

Some of these events were not completely unforeseen, but even
observers not taken completely by surprise marveled at their velocity and
momentum (the tendency for movement in an established direction to continue). Velocity is important and must be addressed. However, the risks
of many, perhaps most, fast-breaking events—natural disasters and other
such crises—can be addressed by means of disaster planning and insurance.
Events with strong momentum can be more difficult to address through crisis
planning and traditional risk management.

For example, consider the difference between a factory burning down
overnight and the oil price shocks of the 1970s. The fire produces sudden,
rapid, but localized impact, covered by insurance and with effects addressable by means of extra shifts at other locations or temporary outsourcing.
The oil price shocks occurred more slowly, but they were not covered by
insurance or addressable through quick responses or existing strategies.

So this chapter examines velocity and momentum, and it discusses ways to consider and address these factors in a risk intelligent manner. Although risk intelligence focuses on upside opportunities as much as downside risks, this chapter focuses more on the latter—that is, on potential crises. It also presents ways of factoring velocity and momentum into your enterprise's risk management efforts. As you read this chapter, please bear in mind the following two points, which we will develop more fully in this chapter:

1. The enterprise must gauge the speed of the event, threat, or opportunity and match or exceed its speed of onset when it would be useful and possible to do so.
2. The enterprise must also properly gauge the momentum and impact of the event and match the strength of its response to that momentum and impact; that is, the strength of the response must be proportionate to that of the event.

The speed and quality of the enterprise's response to a crisis will determine the speed and quality of its recovery, or even whether recovery is possible. Rapid response to sudden events depends upon the enterprise's crisis management capabilities. In cases of events with strong momentum or long-term impact, strategic response capabilities also come into play.

Overall, the watchword is preparation. Checking your assumptions at the door and maintaining constant vigilance are important skills. But in this case, the Boy Scout motto—"Be prepared"—and the Rule of Five Ps—proper planning prevents poor performance—will enable the enterprise to address rapidly unfolding, high-momentum, potentially high-impact threats.

Sometimes bad things start happening faster and faster, and then all of a sudden it blows up. If you're not prepared for it, you can find yourself in a lot of trouble.
> —*Mario Andretti, race car driver and entrepreneur*

Fatal Flaw # 3: Failure to Consider Velocity and Momentum

Conventional risk management assesses the severity of potential negative events and the likelihood that they will happen. Yet unlikely events occur all too often, and many likely events don't come to pass. Worse, unlikely events often occur with astonishing speed. So instead of asking, "How likely is it that this event—good or bad—will happen?" ask instead, "How good or bad can it get, and how fast can it get that way?" Recall that speed is a distinguishing characteristic of turbulence.

Those questions will help you consider what your organization must do to develop resilience and agility. By gauging how good or bad something could get, you can develop a picture of your needs. When you gauge how quickly it could happen, you understand the need for agility and rapid adaptation. Those two factors—the magnitude of the event and the speed at which it can reach that magnitude—will dictate the degree of resilience and agility required.

In the credit crisis of 2008, investors lost faith in mortgage-backed securities (MBS) when large banks wrote off tens of billions of dollars worth of subprime loans. Those write-offs and rising subprime delinquencies and foreclosures placed all MBSs under suspicion. MBSs were widely held, and their lack of transparency made it impossible to judge their risk. A given MBS may or may not have included tranches of subprime loans or Alt-A loans (no income verification and "teaser-rate" loans). Add to that the risky nature of many large banks' funding strategies, in which they funded long-term assets (loans) with short-term liabilities (commercial paper) *and* the specter of credit default swaps—complex, opaque, hard-to-value, off-balance-sheet contracts—*and* a slowing economy. In retrospect, we can see that such conditions signaled that credit and liquidity could quickly dry up. And they did, with the commercial paper market freezing and banks' liquidity evaporating in a matter of days.

A Rolling Stone Gathers Momentum

In common parlance, momentum refers to the force of movement, the tendency of an object, event, or trend to keep moving in the established direction. We speak of the momentum of a basketball or football team's scoring run, or the momentum of a sales trend, or the momentum of a political candidate's campaign. Momentum is not just velocity, which indicates speed, or acceleration, which indicates increasing speed. It also considers the mass of the object, event, or trend.

In classical mechanics, which applies to physical objects, momentum is the product (P) of an object's mass (m) and its velocity (v). The equation is written: $P = mv$. As the equation indicates, the greater the mass, the greater the momentum; and the less the mass, the less the momentum. Similarly, the greater the velocity, the greater the momentum; and the lower the velocity, the lower the momentum.

Volatility is yet another consideration. In common parlance, volatile means highly or unpredictably changeable or even explosive (as in a volatile temper). In physics, volatility is a measure of a substance's tendency to vaporize at a given temperature. When applied to an event, phenomenon, or trend, volatility designates the degree, frequency, and unpredictability of changes. Volatility also means unexpected changes in accelerations or decelerations—that is, changes in velocity. In the market, volatility was once (incorrectly) assumed to be relatively constant. It's not, which is why volatility increases the challenges of risk management.

VELOCITY Because velocity has direction—up or down, forward or reverse—in any given instance it can be either positive or negative. On the Internet, positive or negative velocity can produce a network effect. For example, (Robert) Metcalf's law says that the value of a telecommunications network is proportional to the square of the number of people connected to the system.[1] Essentially, this produces the network effect, in which the value of something increases with each additional user. A positive network effect occurs for many technologies and products, such as the telephone—the more people who have a phone, the more value a phone has to any individual user. Negative network effects also occur, as when too many users create congestion, for instance, on a highway or when market turbulence creates fear and severe risk aversion.

In a positive network effect, once a critical mass of connectivity is achieved, the benefits of the network grow faster than its costs. This has certainly been the case with social networking sites. Social networks form around common interests or "affinities." For each affinity, there is a critical mass at which the network expands rapidly because of the effect that one user of a product has on other users. As more people use the product, it gains positive momentum as a result of both mass (the number of users) and velocity (the speed of adoption) producing a network effect.

But networks are vulnerable and the more people who are on one, the more vulnerable it becomes and the more widespread the effects if something bad happens. Richard Bookstaber notes that in a tightly coupled and interactively complex system, "We cannot prepare for every thread of causality through every interaction; in the speed of the event we find there is no time to make adjustments."[2]

Generally, it makes sense to ride the momentum when it's in your favor, and to get off the ride, so to speak, when it works against you. When dealing with strong momentum or volatility, it may be inadvisable to do nothing. As William O. McCabe, former B-52 vice wing commander, says, "One of the biggest risks you can create for yourself and your crew, when you're right in the middle of everything, going 400 miles per hour, facing a critical decision, is to do nothing."[3]

SUDDEN HITS, SNOWBALLS, AND SPOTLIGHTS   The ways in which crises and their effects develop vary with their velocity and momentum. Thus crises demand different risk management approaches before they occur and different crisis management approaches when they occur. It's not just velocity that drives a crisis, but also its mass and the way in which it accumulates momentum, which can be considered in three basic ways:

1. *The sudden hit.* A single, catastrophic, overwhelming event occurs, such as a natural disaster, fire, or accident, or widespread product problem or failure.
2. *The snowball effect.* A series of related or unrelated events pile up, gather mass and momentum, and produce one or more strong cumulative effects; the credit crisis and economic recession are excellent examples.
3. *The spotlight effect.* One single event draws attention or scrutiny and then triggers still other events and consequences.

The Sudden Hit: Prepare, then Execute   Most sudden hits are of the "expected" variety. Certain types of natural disasters tend to occur in certain geographic locales, as do certain man-made disasters. Areas prone to natural disasters should be better prepared, whether they be earthquakes, hurricanes, tsunamis, or wildfires. Likewise, man-made disasters can be anticipated, though not predicted, including terrorism or problems with specific products, such as malfunction, misuse, tainted ingredients, and tampering.

The way to deal with sudden hits is to anticipate them—even if you see them as remote possibilities—and to prepare a feasible, cost-effective plan to respond and recover. Again, preparing for one type of event tends to prepare the enterprise for others because of their common outcomes: loss of life or injury, breakdowns in communication and transportation systems, disrupted supply chains, food and water shortages, plumbing and electrical problems, fires, perhaps looting, and so on.

In the case of product problems, limiting harm to affected individuals, customers and other downstream and upstream parties and the public must be the top priority. The classic case of superb handling of a product problem remains the 1982 Tylenol tampering case, which prompted the company to remove all product from stores, reassure the public, and adopt tamper-proof packaging. Examples of less adroit handling of such cases abound. A disaster, accident, or incident usually puts stress on management resources and emotions, so it's essential to have a plan in place beforehand—and, of course, to take every reasonable step to avoid such occurrences.

Waiting until disaster strikes is not good risk management. For instance, seismic activity occurs often in Indonesia, which straddles active fault lines.

In early 2008, about a year after the devastating tsunami in the Indian Ocean, a series of earthquakes in the 5.0 to 7.0 range on the Richter scale struck the nation. But these smaller—yet still sizable quakes—instilled little panic. Some residents fled, but most failed to heed the warnings that accompanied the tremors, and they paid dearly for not doing so.

The Snowball Effect: Get Ahead of It, and Stay There It's not just major, rapid-onset disasters that cause failure and extinction, but also series of often small and common incidents that can do so. In recounting her successful ascent of Mt. Everest, Esther Colwill recalls, "Before the ascent, any good team practices crisis management so we all know how to rescue someone if they fall in a crevasse. Because everyone knows things can happen very quickly, we plan for an avalanche or falling in a crevasse or falling and breaking a leg. But climbers typically don't think about some of the things that can happen slowly and can add up to a disaster as well.

"There were twelve of us but only four went to the summit. Probably the reason the other eight didn't make it was all the little things they didn't do to look after themselves. At that altitude, it's really hard to eat or exercise. All those little day-to-day things can be easy to just let go because everything takes so much effort. If you end up letting them go too much, after six weeks you can be very, very weakened, and you actually can't recover from it. I think most of them were just too weak. When it came time for the ascent, they ended up saying, 'No, we don't feel we're strong enough to go.' So it wasn't the avalanche or falling into a crevasse that ended the expedition for them. It was a combination of these tiny little things, little decisions that they made along the way, and in the end, they just weren't strong enough to succeed."

The home-price bubble, subprime crisis, credit crisis, financial institution stresses and failures, and recession of the 2000s represented a true snowballing crisis. Various parties issued warnings. Sound public- and private-sector policies (particularly credit and risk management policies) were ignored or abandoned. Funding policies and high leverage created risks. The cyclical nature of the real estate industry and the economy was ignored.

Snowballs gain momentum as their mass accumulates. Even if their speed does not increase—and it usually does—they become extremely difficult to stop once they reach critical mass. As a crisis snowballs, it develops massive force that can bring down all but the most well prepared and resilient enterprises, as we saw in the 2000s.

The Spotlight Effect: What Have We Here? Very often it is the discovery of an issue, incident, or indiscretion—and the way in which the discovery is handled—that launches a crisis. This happens often in politics, where leaders are exposed to close public scrutiny, and often handle discoveries badly. President Clinton's handling of the Monica Lewinski affair and President Nixon's handling of the Watergate break-in are two classic cases.

By failing to handle the discovery or disclosure of a negative event or even a rumor, management can draw further scrutiny or publicity, which can trigger other events and consequences. The speed at which such a crisis can gain momentum has astonished many an executive team and board. One major reason for this speed is the rabid nature of the media, and—now, thanks to the Internet—the ubiquity of amateur as well as actual "reporters" and the speed at which they can transmit their messages. The effects range from justified or unjustified negative word of mouth for a movie or a product to character assassination to the destruction of an enterprise.

Suzanne Hopgood and Michael Tankersley advise, "At the early stages, experience has shown that it is highly likely that things are much worse than they appear; you just don't know it yet!"[4] As with the snowball effect, if the crisis is local, simply getting out in front of it can prevent it from growing into a full-fledged disaster. Major errors at this stage are failing to admit a mistake, failing to apologize for it, and failing to correct it.

It often doesn't even matter if any wrongdoing occurred. In the 1970s and 1980s, the Ford Motor Company experienced a number of lawsuits after it was alleged that the company continued to sell the Pinto after it had learned that the fuel tank could explode during a rear-end collision. Years later, a law review article maintained that the Pinto was no more unsafe than similar cars in this respect, but the damage to the brand had long since been done.

In cases of the spotlight effect, crisis management calls for rapid response and effective communication aimed at damage control. As Director Norm Augustine advises, "Tell the truth and tell it fast." This means getting the factual story out, avoiding cover-ups (which typically become larger problems than the one they aim to conceal), apologizing when appropriate and useful, and correcting the problem and announcing that you did. It may also call for reprimand or punishment of certain parties or termination of certain relationships.

In any crisis, management must gauge the velocity, mass, momentum, and consequences of the crisis itself and of the likely follow-on effects, and manage them accordingly. This stands as a key component of risk intelligent risk management and involves steps taken in anticipation of, during, and after the crisis.

Voice of Experience

"We used to have time to think about things, but now we're so interconnected in the global economy and markets. Things happen so quickly you have to be ready to seize opportunities."

—David Meuse, Director

Risk Intelligence Skill #3: Factor in Velocity and Momentum

The concepts of velocity and momentum can help boards and executive teams to think usefully about crises both prospectively and as a crisis develops. Note too that while we've focused on crises, velocity and momentum also characterize opportunities. Indeed, a crisis can itself present opportunities, in the form of new needs for certain products and services and chances to exploit competitors' weaknesses.

Also, market developments and product needs can either develop or fail to develop momentum. For example, the momentum for growth in the U.S. market for small cars decreased as the price of oil moderated. In fact, that moderation and the U.S. preference for large vehicles—coupled with the baby boomers starting families—fueled the market for minivans and SUVs from the 1980s until 2008. At that point, recession hit, oil prices increased, and dealers and manufacturers wound up with unsold inventories of large vehicles.

So when your enterprise is on the offensive, gauging the speed at which a market is developing, the strength of its momentum (and the position of competitors) can confer a competitive advantage—provided you are prepared to act. When your enterprise is on the defensive, avoiding, precluding, or deflecting the threat is the preferred response, but it's not always possible. When prevention fails or is not possible, as is most often the case with external threats, early detection and rapid response are required for the organization to be both resilient and agile.

Lead time varies with the type of event. For instance, residents in hurricane-prone areas have some advance warning before a major storm, but their preparations should have begun long before an actual warning. Tornadoes may come with some warning, but fires and earthquakes provide next to none. In such cases, survival depends (sometimes literally) on readiness and on reaction times, which can be developed in drills and by raising awareness. Fire and evacuation drills not only tell people what to do when a crisis strikes but enable them to rehearse their response. Rehearsal improves response times and helps people further anticipate needs and problems.

Thus the key things for management to do in factoring in velocity and momentum are (1) to improve preparation so that speed of response equals or exceeds speed of onset and development, and (2) to improve planning and crisis management to increase the quality of response. It can be done, even in established, capital-intensive industries.

For instance, speed of response isn't a virtue most people would associate with a basic industry like steel. But with a continuing decline in the demand for steel, the price per ton dropped precipitously from $1,160 in July 2008 to a low of $676 in early December of that year. In response, China rapidly cut production.[5] John Lichtenstein, head of the metals industry group at Accenture, states, "The speed and decisiveness of the cutbacks in production [by big steelmakers] have been unprecedented, which means profitability in this downturn for the steel industry is likely to hold up better than in other comparable periods." Quick responses to changing conditions can mean continued profitability.

Crisis: A Turning Point, for Better or Worse

Crises, the most severe manifestation of risk, often represent turning points. They often cause confusion and a "reshuffling of the deck." In that reshuffling, basic assumptions as well as links among factors and forces can be altered, often radically. During the crisis itself, the shape of that change and its potential effects and consequences may be unclear. Lack of access to current, updated, accurate information becomes a major problem—one that risk intelligent enterprises do their best to address.

Crises run the risk of escalating in intensity, falling under close media or government scrutiny, interfering in normal business operations, jeopardizing the safety or freedom of employees, or damaging the company's credibility, reputation, or financial performance. Some risks become crises when they can no longer be managed in "silos," occur simultaneously, or overflow into silos that were assumed to be watertight. An infinite range of events could precipitate a crisis anywhere in the world. Exhibit 6.1 provides examples of the types of events that can precipitate a crisis.

Exhibit 6.2 identifies some of the typical consequences of crises.

Speed of Response Affects Speed of Recovery

The costs of a crisis can be extreme. So can the cost of recovery. Obvious costs include expenses associated with addressing the crisis; sales or profits lost through damage to products, reputation, or channels; decreases in the

EXHIBIT 6.1 Causes of Crises

People	Employee sabotage/violence
	Corporate malfeasance
Process	Product recalls
	Health violations
External Factors	Natural disasters
	Hostile takeover
	Act of war
	Economic downturn
	Patent/trade secret infringement
	Terrorism/bomb threats
	Hostage situations
	Civil unrest
	Strikes/boycotts
	Nuclear attack
	Air strikes
	Guerrilla force invasion
	Cyber terrorism/Internet rumors/computer viruses
	Power outages
	Environmental pollution
	Regulatory inspections
	Lawsuits

EXHIBIT 6.2 Consequences of Crises

Financial	Loss of market share
	Decreased sales
	Lower stock prices
	Decreased operating margin
Non-financial	Eroded brand equity
	Difficulties in attracting and retaining people
	Dissatisfied and vocal investors
	Damaged reputation and/or negative media coverage
	Increased potential for government investigation and/or regulatory scrutiny
	Dissatisfied customers
	Business interruption
	▪ Building unusable
	▪ Internet disabled
	▪ Telecommunication systems down
	▪ Transportation disrupted
	▪ Power disruptions
	▪ Data center destruction

company's market value or equity; and legal costs, fines, settlements, or judgments. Most companies in major crises take a 5 to 50 percent hit on stock prices. According to the Conference Board, organizations prepared for a crisis recover two to three times faster, with significantly less financial and human cost, than unprepared organizations.[6]

In 2001, Dr. Deborah Pretty of Oxford Metrica[7] reported that the speed and quality of management's response are key determinants of the difference between those who recover quickly and survive and those who don't. Pretty concludes:

- Catastrophe insurance alone will not protect shareholder value.
- Recovery appears to be a function of managerial ability.
- Share price is an effective measure of postcatastrophe management performance.

Subsequent research by Oxford Metrica[8] examined the effects of extreme, negative events on firms' share prices and differences in management's ability to lead the enterprise to recovery. The research supported earlier findings.[9]

The appropriate speed of response relates directly to the nature of the threat or event. In specific contexts, speed of response can be thought of as "requisite reaction time." Chapter 7, "Manage the Key Connections," discusses the importance of identifying your critical dependencies: key suppliers, key inputs, key people, processes and systems, key outputs, and key customers (SIPOC). That's an essential step in any response and recovery plan. Factoring in speed of response requires an understanding of requisite *reaction times* for these critical dependencies. The requisite reaction time depends on the answers to several questions:

- How long can the enterprise go without those key dependencies and with what consequences?
- What are the options for replacing or restoring those capabilities?
- What are the costs—both out of pocket and opportunity cost—of the various options for replacement or restoration?
- How fast can replacement or restoration occur?
- What are the fully loaded costs and benefits of various options of restoring the needed capabilities?

For example, a cyber attack requires mechanisms for prevention but also for rapid detection and correction. The requisite reaction time can be measured in nanoseconds. In other instances, the circumstances are different but the consequences nonetheless dire. Consider a manufacturing enterprise that depends on a JIT—just-in-time—supply chain. Any disruption in the availability of a critical component can bring the entire operation to a halt. These examples highlight the fact that the skills presented here work best in concert. For instance, in many cases, requisite reaction time relates directly to the level of situational awareness or the knowledge of interconnections (again, to be covered in Chapter 7), and the effects may relate to the margin of safety the enterprise maintains (as we discuss in Chapter 10, "Maintain a Margin of Safety").

Voice of Experience

"We've learned two very painful but valuable lessons about the rapidity of problem propagation and the slowness and expense of recovery. First, we came to understand, in no uncertain terms, how rapidly delays in one part of the system can spread throughout the network when you are operating at or near your design capacity. Second, we learned how difficult it is to undo a disruption once the congestion has spread. Fundamentally, everything stops and nothing moves.

"You have to start by moving the chess pieces around. First, you free up space somewhere in a terminal and then you move cars from congested areas to that open space. Then you repeat the process over and over across the network until traffic begins to flow freely on its own. It's a long, drawn-out, and very costly process, not only in terms of the expense but in terms of your commercial position."

—Charley Eisele, SVP Strategic Planning, Union Pacific

Planning for the Inevitable, but Unpredictable

Crisis preparedness tells you what to do if a crisis occurs. Consider the possibilities, understand the implications, and decide how to deal with them. Although the benefits of crisis planning are well documented, many organizations lack a plan to deal with cyber attacks, natural disasters, and other crises. Preparation for crisis management demands training, scenario planning, and disaster and recovery planning. These all cost money and management must decide whether and how much to spend to prepare for a given crisis or set of crises. (We discuss this issue in Part III.)

Crisis management aims to prevent risks from gathering momentum and escalating and to contain and, when possible, reverse damage. Crisis management programs improve overall preparedness by coordinating responses, establishing crisis management teams, promulgating communication protocols, and creating a culture that demonstrates proactive concern for all stakeholders. For example, by building in excess capacity, a company becomes better able to respond quickly to sudden surges in demand. By having contingency plans in place, it can more quickly redeploy capacity. As a result, one company reduced its reaction and recovery times by more than 50 percent.

Voice of Experience

"The toy business is very fast-moving—a little bit of rock 'n' roll. We produce 8,000 new toys and about three-quarters of a billion products every year, and it all has to clear the market by Christmas.

"So, as a general rule, we at Mattel have to be very thoughtful. When you're in the heat of the moment, it's not the best time to start being thoughtful about your options.

"We try to consider all the options in advance so that when the moment of truth or a problem comes, we've done our thinking in advance and we're better prepared to deal with whatever it is."

—Bob Eckert, Chairman and CEO, Mattel, Inc.[10]

Building a capable crisis management team thus stands among management's most important responsibilities, and it's the board's responsibility to see that one has been established. It is certainly a basic element in protecting assets and shareholder value, as well as a matter of positioning the enterprise to thrive after (and even during) a crisis. People in the crisis management team must be well-vetted senior executives, have clear roles and responsibilities, and be able to exercise good judgment under stress. The team should receive crisis management training, be prepared to evaluate crises situations, and be able to make strategic as well as tactical decisions. At DuPont, for example, there are 17 crisis response teams composed of specific executives based on their areas of responsibility, and these teams can be mobilized within 30 minutes.

Tool for Rapid Response to Crises: ICS

Organizations typically exercise preparedness when it comes to physical disasters or acts of terrorism. For instance, first-responders constantly train and rehearse emergency procedures. Why don't enterprises do the same thing when it comes to other potential crises? We have suggested that the risk intelligent enterprise can adapt tools from quality and process improvement to risk management purposes. Here is another borrowed tool, this one originally developed by California wildfire fighters—the Incident Command

System (ICS)—which provides a valuable lesson in speed of response and crisis management.

ICS can be a valuable tool for planning, organizing, and managing an enterprise's response to a crisis. It is a special-purpose, temporary hierarchical system of command and control for coordinating interdependent but autonomous groups of first-responders, including, for example, local, state, and federal agencies and firefighters, police, emergency medical crews, National Guard, and volunteers.

Since its development, ICS has seen widespread use elsewhere, for instance, in the Oklahoma City bombings and later by the Department of Homeland Security, which mandated its use by all first-responders. ICS was also used in response to Hurricane Katrina with questionable success, due to lack of training and clear chains of command. Any large enterprise can learn from ICS and adopt certain elements, some of which have been adapted in this book as risk intelligent enterprise management skills.

The following list presents the 14 basic elements of an ICS:[11]

1. Common terminology to enable communication and understanding
2. Modular organization that can expand to fit the incident yet remain under a single area command
3. Management by objectives with regular, written incident action plans
4. Reliance on an incident action plan to ensure overall coordinated response strategy
5. Manageable span of control to ensure supervision of appropriate number of subordinates
6. Predesignated locations and facilities for ICS operations
7. Comprehensive resource management with processes for categorizing, ordering, dispatching, tracking, and recovering resources, and timely resource utilization reports
8. Integrated communications facilitated through development and use of a common communications plan
9. A process for establishing and transferring command by the primary authority
10. Chain and unity of command with clear lines of authority to ensure everyone has a designated supervisor
11. Unified command, including for shared jurisdiction where multiple incident commanders work as a single team
12. Accountability of resources and personnel to ensure adherence to the incident action plan
13. Deployment that ensures personnel and equipment respond only when requested or dispatched
14. Information and intelligence management for gathering and sharing incident-related intelligence

You can learn more about ICS at www.training.fema.gov/EMIWeb/IS/ICSResource/TrainingMaterials.htm. In fact, one of the most popular courses offered by FEMA's Emergency Management Institute (EMI) as of this writing is "G402 Incident Command System (ICS) Overview for Executives/Senior Officials." The two-hour course is not a self-study course but one designed to be delivered by a trainer. Nonetheless, its popularity speaks to organizations' recognition of the importance of preparedness and of the potential of ICS.

Voice of Experience

"I've been delivering the message—as softly as possible over the past couple of years—that companies need a person experienced in crisis management on the board. Not all people can manage a crisis. But there's another much more important reason: That kind of experienced individual sees things very differently. They actually know that the light you see coming at you really is a train."

—Suzanne Hopgood, Director

Be Prepared

The majority of conventional risk assessments are based on impact and likelihood and neglect velocity and momentum. However, the latter factors can dictate whether a potential or unfolding event is a crisis or just an incident. They also dictate the speed and force with which the enterprise should respond to the risk.

Keys to addressing velocity and momentum, and thus crises in general include:

- Planning well in advance, rather than waiting until a crisis forces action and limits options
- Matching the speed of response with the speed of onset of the crisis
- Matching the strength of the response with the momentum of the crisis
- Developing a process for responding *before* the crisis occurs
- Establishing protocols and rehearsing responses in drills
- Monitoring early-warning signs and mobilizing crisis management teams per protocols and drills

Crisis management represents a fundamental element in preserving assets and shareholder value, and it is the responsibility of management to prepare the enterprise for crises and the responsibility of the board to see that management fulfills that responsibility. At all levels, recognition of the complexities and interconnections within the organization and in its environment will help people to anticipate, recognize, and respond to the effects of crises. We take up those complexities and interconnections in Chapter 7.

Questions to Ask about Velocity and Momentum

- How good or bad can it get?
- How fast can it get that way?
- How fast can we respond or recover?
- How much lead time do we need?
- How much delay or downtime can we tolerate? How fast do our reaction times need to be?
- What resources should we and can we devote to overall preparedness and to preparedness for specific crises?
- How can we apply all of these questions to potential opportunities?

CHAPTER 7

Manage the Key Connections

Systems thinking is a discipline for seeing wholes. It is a framework for seeing interrelationships rather than things, for seeing patterns of change rather than static "snapshots" ... the subtle interconnectedness that gives living systems their unique character.
—Peter Senge, *The Fifth Discipline*

Complexity is a relative term, but it usually applies to a situation or system—and we'll concern ourselves mainly with systems here—characterized by multiple factors, facets, and forces. Complexity arises from the number of these characteristics and from their levels of intricacy, interdependence, and interactivity. Unfortunately, these characteristics can be difficult to identify, gauge, and understand. Only close observation, patient analysis, and firsthand experience makes complexity comprehensible—and even then, not always.

In general, systems can be classified as either linear or nonlinear. Linear systems can be complex, but they are characteristically sequential, unidirectional, proportional in terms of input and output, and transparent. An assembly line is a linear system. It moves step by step in a defined direction, output is predictably proportional to input, and the process can be readily observed. Failures in linear systems typically allow people enough time to anticipate or to quickly identify problems and to respond before they become catastrophic.

In contrast, nonlinear systems are chaotic. Factors and forces can function independently of one another, output is disproportionate to input, and small changes in one area can produce large changes elsewhere in the system. Such systems are opaque rather than transparent. The global economy is an example of a nonlinear system; it is turbulent, impossible to predict, and very difficult if not impossible to control.

Because enterprises are to an extent nonlinear and operate in a non-linear environment, leaders must identify, understand, and (to the extent possible) manage the key connections and dependencies that enable the enterprise to protect and create value. Risks arise when those connections and dependencies experience disruption, breakdown, or failure.

Chapter 4, "Check Your Assumptions at the Door," described how an understanding of the underlying assumptions of value creation is essential to risk intelligence. Chapter 5, "Maintain Constant Vigilance," examined the need for and ways to develop sensing capabilities regarding the enterprise and its environment. This chapter builds on those two by exploring the interconnectedness of the elements in a system.

The cliché "connect the dots" became popular after 9/11 and continued in use because that is what so many of us so often fail to do. We have the dots—the data points—but we fail to make the connections that portray their relatedness and the potential effects arising from those relationships. So this chapter examines complexity and why it exists, how key connections and dependencies are formed, and how they generate both risk and opportunity. The second half of this chapter offers tools to promote an understanding of interconnectedness and to assist you in managing complexity in nonlinear systems.

Voice of Experience

"When I've made big mistakes, it's been because I've had too much going on, had too many complex deals happening. I found myself operating from the gut only and not being very analytical about it or collaborative. What I'm trying to do now is look at the upside and the downside. There is going to be a recovery but where should we be and where is the greatest reward and lowest risk? And boy, it's hard to figure out in this market."

—David Meuse, Director

Fatal Flaw #4: Failure to Make Key Connections and Manage Complexity

The complexity of a nonlinear system arises from the number, significance, and interrelatedness of the factors in it and their potential and actual effects. For any sizable enterprise, these factors can include energy and natural resources, climate and pollution, transportation and distribution, labor supplies and human rights, demographic patterns and immigration policies, regulation and taxation, trade volume and currency issues, funding sources and financial markets, safety and health care, war and terrorism. Even the relatively linear structure of a supply chain must function within the larger environment subject to these factors.

In the Industrial Age and for much of the past century, linkages were looser; in the Information Age, they are becoming tighter, with implications that are continuing to emerge. Complexity and interrelatedness are the key reasons that risks are multiplying, broadening, and rippling in more directions. When subprime defaults in California can bring Iceland to bankruptcy, you know that the "butterfly effect" has truly taken hold.

How do you make sense of this? How can you determine the potential risks to your organization? You could pore over prices, scrutinize stocks, and study statistics. Or you could just order a beer. Your tab at your local pub may tell you more about complexity and connections than the metrics employed in boardrooms, legislatures, and academe.

Drink Up

The cost of a liter of beer at the 2007 Oktoberfest in Munich had increased by 5.5 percent over the prior year.[1] A wide array of seemingly unrelated factors and scenarios may have contributed to this rise:

- *Pricey beer, scenario 1.* Climate change alters worldwide weather patterns. A lengthy drought in Australia and heavy rains in Europe depress barley production and spur a spike in barley prices.[2] The higher cost of barley leads to higher beer prices.
- *Pricey beer, scenario 2.* Biofuel is promoted as an energy source that will (1) reduce dependence on pipelines and shipping channels vulnerable to war and terrorism, (2) counter the rise of petro-states and dependence on OPEC, and (3) reduce global warming and help meet "green" goals. Strong demand for biofuels combined with government incentives encourage farmers to plant crops like rapeseed and corn, which can be turned into ethanol or bio-diesel, instead of barley.[3] The decreased supply of barley increases its price—and the cost of beer.
- *Pricey beer, scenario 3.* People in some emerging countries evolve toward a U.S.-style diet emphasizing meat and animal products.[4] Meat consumption rises. Barley production is diverted from malting barley (used to make beer) to feed barley (used to fatten livestock).[5] The reduced supply of malting barley increases costs for brewers, who pass them along to the pub patron.

While beer drinkers dig deeper into their pockets, the diversion of North American food crops to biofuel causes a spike in corn prices, which raises prices for consumers in Mexico, for whom corn is a diet staple and who take to the streets in protest.[6] Some associations may be tangential, others may come into play, and certain factors may be in dispute. But our point is not to show direct cause and effect but to show that an invisible web of unanticipated risks and opportunities can lead to unexpected results.

Tight Coupling and Complexity

In *A Demon of Our Own Design*, Richard Bookstaber states, "The greatest dangers arise when there is both interactive complexity and a tightly coupled system that does not provide the time to intervene."[7] Systems engineers define a tightly coupled system as one in which the parts are interdependent *and* difficult to separate. In such a system, once events are set in motion, they can be difficult or impossible to stop—or manage.

Tight coupling and nonlinearity set the stage for inevitable "accidents" resulting from the structure of the system. Bookstaber notes that financial derivatives produce nonlinear results relative to the prices of the underlying securities. He cites examples such as the failure of Long-Term Capital Management (LTCM) and broader, nonfinancial events like nuclear power plant accidents and the ValuJet crash. Each disaster began with an incident that triggered a complex chain reaction. Bookstaber also raises concerns that attempts to regulate a complex, tightly coupled system may worsen the problem by further increasing the complexity and opacity of the system.

Voice of Experience

"I was having lunch with top management of the bank, one level below the chairman. I asked him, 'Do you guys have any clue how close you had these dominoes stacked? Were you so close to the forest that you couldn't see the trees?'

"His answer was, 'You know what? It turns out we didn't really realize how closely they were stacked.'

"I'm not sure I buy that answer. I think these people decided that the money was too great to pass up and took an undue risk."

—James Hambrick, Chairman and CEO, The Lubrizol Corporation

A 2004 study of major North American electrical blackouts found that they occur in a nonlinear manner. The report says, "Mitigation of blackout risk should take care to account for counterintuitive effects in complex self-organized critical systems. For example, suppressing small blackouts could lead the system to be operated closer to the edge and ultimately increase the risk of large blackouts."[8] In other words, amid tight coupling, what might appear to be a reasonable solution may have devastating consequences. The same can be said of suppressing small brush fires that later result in large-scale disasters, such as the San Diego, California, wildfires of October 2007.

Coupling and complexity also arises from multipurpose tools, products, and processes. Henry Petroski notes, in *Success through Failure: The Paradox of Design*, that multiple purposes complicate not only how a thing is designed, but also how it can fail.[9] The more complicated the design problem, the more difficult the solution and the more likely that some details may be overlooked, only to create problems when the item is put to use.

Travelers flying though London experienced such a situation on March 27, 2008, when the new Heathrow Airport Terminal 5 opened. A series of events disrupted baggage handling and dealt a blow to British Airways' image and stock price. Staff had difficulty logging into the new baggage system, which resulted in passengers waiting around for their bags. The biometric fingerprint security system was pulled from service because of data protection and privacy concerns. And airport staff complained of insufficient parking. Between March 27 and April 3, British Airways cancelled 381 flights and amassed a backlog of 20,000 lost bags. The airline even brought in FedEx to help expedite baggage handling and delivery.

Paul Ormerod, in *Why Most Things Fail*, asserts that companies have difficulty confronting and dealing with complexity.[10] Nevertheless, firms should not concede defeat but instead aim to understand the limitations that uncertainty imposes as well as their systems' key connections.

Voice of Experience

"I think companies are responding to risk, but they're still responding as they have historically. It's not a very sophisticated response. The areas of risk that they understand well and recognize well, they respond to well. Their ability to respond to cascading risk, linkages among risks, and catastrophic-event risk is still in its infancy."

—Richard Slater, Director

Complexity Exemplified: Abuse of Derivatives

High leverage and low liquidity can be a lethal combination, particularly when the financial instruments known as derivatives are involved.

Derivatives are financial instruments whose value is derived from that of the underlying assets on which they are based. The assets may be securities, commodities, mortgages, or credit in the form of loans secured by assets. Derivatives were developed as a tool to hedge or mitigate risk. However, derivatives can also be used for speculative purposes by creating highly leveraged "bets" that an asset's value will move in a particular direction.

This is what happened when credit default swaps (CDS) were used by speculators (who did not hold the underlying bonds) to "bet" on the bonds' default potential. In that way, CDSs multiplied risk and spread it to parties who were often unaware of it, such as customers of financial institutions that held CDSs.

Derivatives can be extremely complex, volatile, and difficult to model or value. They are also interconnected, nonlinear, and opaque. Many of the "Once-in-a-Lifetime Crises" listed in Exhibit 2.1 were related to the derivatives used for speculative purposes. Indeed, derivatives have been associated with many of the major financial meltdowns over the past 25 years. They're a great example of how the interconnectedness of risks that cannot always be identified will often undo the very strategies, tactics, and instruments that people use to manage risks.

Information: The Biggest Connection of Them All

In a complex and connected world, nothing is more ubiquitous than the Internet. Its integrity is essential both to global commerce and to security. Yet this is not usually well understood.

In the twenty-first century, rapid access to reliable information is essential. According to the Network Centric Operations Industry Consortium (NCOIC), which comprises leaders in the aerospace, defense, information technology, large-scale integrator, and services industries, "The deciding factor in any military conflict is not the weaponry, it is the network. The missing link in today's disaster recovery efforts is a working network. And the key to emergency response is accurate information that enables first-responders to know what happened, who's responded, and what is still required. From the warrior to emergency personnel to the modern day consumer, access to all information, without regard to hardware, software, or location of the user, is no longer attractive, it is imperative."[11]

General Harry Raduege (ret), co-chairman of the Commission on Cybersecurity for the Forty-Fourth Presidency and former director of the Defense Information Systems Agency, says:

> "In cyber security, we must first recognize that the risk is global in nature. The Internet is breaking down barriers in communicating and sharing information. This, of course, provides a great opportunity for global economies to grow but because of its openness, there will be vulnerabilities.

"Risk-intelligent decision making is right at the core of everything controlling, caring for and protecting the critical information that lies within all of our business operations today. Within an organization, you generally know who is authorized to have and to share specific information. The problem is there are folks also operating in cyberspace who, for competitive advantage, criminal activity, or for espionage, are trying to break into those networks and are being increasingly successful in doing so.

"In the world of cyber-crime, anyone can become a world player. All you need is a person who is smart about computer technology, an inexpensive computer, and a connection to the Internet. All of a sudden, you're a player on the world stage from the sanctuary of your nation, from your criminal connections, or from the confines of your basement. There's no limit to the level and type of activity in which you can engage."

Events since General Raduege spoke have underscored both the need for and the importance of improved responsiveness to cyber-crime by the government and the private sector. For example, in April 2009, sophisticated penetrations of the U.S. electric grid[12] and key defense systems were reported, including the hacking of the $300 billion Joint Strike Fighter program and the theft of data.[13]

Risk Intelligence Skill #4: Manage Your Key Connections

Enterprises have increasingly adopted more virtual, extended, fluid, global structures. This is both a response to and a factor in increased complexity. As enterprises become more fluid and interconnected, they themselves become more complex, less transparent, and more exposed to threats as well as better able (at least in theory) to exploit opportunities. Boards, executives, risk managers, and business unit heads must understand—to the extent necessary and possible—how factors, forces, and entities connect, how effects can be generated by and transmitted through connections, and how to manage risks by identifying and managing these connections.

Voice of Experience

"One of Nassim Taleb's arguments about black swans is that people have what he calls 'retroactive predictability' or 'retrospective predictability.' So people see things happen and they think they understand why. They

(Continued)

(Continued)

think that means that they understand how they're going to happen in the future, and that they can predict them.

"But things happen for much more complex reasons than the simple explanations that they come up with after the fact. There's usually a set of circumstances and a process which either could have produced other outcomes or for which you simply can't see all the moving parts. People overestimate their understanding of how things work."

—Howard Marks, Chairman, Oaktree Capital Management

Chapter 4, "Check Your Assumptions at the Door," notes that the assumption that events are independent and linear is dangerous. Like wildfires, risks do not recognize the boundaries of organizational silos. Yet most siloed systems treat risks as independent and employ models that may prove useless when some risks inevitably cross boundaries.

Voice of Experience

"Managing complexity is really a question of whether you have the right quality of management, infrastructure, and process in place to deal with the breadth, depth, and structure of the business.

"Complexity itself isn't necessarily bad with the right management team. In fact, rather than being a problem, it can be a diversification strategy that if managed right can actually be a plus. But it's got to be managed right."

—Dennis Chookasian, Director

The skill of managing complexity begins with recognizing its existence and the fact that complexity itself is not necessarily bad. Indeed, thinking back to Darwin and Ashby, it is the very variety of life forms that enable life to exist in so many environments on earth. The wide variety of responses that humans have developed to threats and opportunities has sustained us in changing environments and against innumerable threats since we first appeared on the planet. Thus the responses of the enterprise must evolve to match the complexity of the situation.

Daryl Wyckoff, author of *Organizational Formality and Performance in the Motor Carrier Industry*, noticed an odd pattern when studying the profitability of trucking enterprises. Large and small enterprises were often quite profitable, but medium-sized enterprises struggled.

Why?

As it turns out, the profitable small trucking enterprises were run by strong, often hands-on entrepreneurs. As the companies grew, those owners found tracking myriad activities, routes, and centers increasingly difficult. Some realized they needed a new approach and delegated authority to those who could develop and manage that approach, for instance, via sophisticated planning-and-control systems. Those enterprises became profitable and large. Owners who couldn't relinquish control, even when activities became too complex to handle, typically oversaw companies that achieved less profitability and stopped growing at midsize. Others in this group scaled back to captain profitable, smaller enterprises.[14]

Voice of Experience

"I've been attempting to find tools to deal with complexity, but I haven't been very successful. Not many exist right now. We must begin to look at the enterprise as a system—as interconnected assets or activities—and the complicated way of dealing with these elements, understanding that it is a complex system. We have recognized that we need to look at interdependencies, but we don't have as good a tool set as one would want in order to manage those very well, particularly ones that scale out or that entail uncertainty."

—Spiros Dimolitsas, Vice President, Georgetown University

Requisite Variety

The more specifically attuned an organism or enterprise is to its environment, the more vulnerable it is when its environment suddenly changes. Just as highly adapted species have failed when quick and adverse changes occur in their habitats, enterprises have been crippled by swift market changes.

In 1956, W. Ross Ashby developed the Law of Requisite Variety to deal with complexity in computational controls. Ashby argued, "Only variety can destroy variety."[15] Essentially, survival in complex, tightly coupled environments requires specialization and control *equal to* the variety in the environment. Thus, the enterprise requires a variety—or rather the right variety—of strategies, structures, and skills. Variety itself is insufficient for survival. It must be the requisite variety, which enables the resilience required to withstand unexpected adversity and the agility to seize unexpected opportunity.

Because the future is unknowable, the requisite variety of strengths and strategies must be developed before a crisis. Then, regardless of the specific form of the crisis, the entity will be better able to survive, and even thrive, during it. In the 2007–08 credit crisis, companies and some countries (such as China) with strong cash positions were more resilient and even able to exploit competitors' distress. They acquired businesses, won markets, and hired talents that competitors had to abandon. An enterprise must also develop requisite variety in processes, products, and services. In some cases—utilities, for example—requisite variety may be limited (to, say, variety in types and sources of fuel). In other industries, companies benefit from a larger repertoire.

In *The Strategy Paradox*, Michael Raynor makes a similar point about strategic flexibility. The more committed an enterprise is to a particular strategy, the more likely it is to *either* succeed or to fail. He argues for developing options that increase strategic flexibility and deferring firm commitments until uncertainty is reduced. As noted in Chapter 4, wholehearted commitment to a strategy keyed to a specific environment can bring success as long as the environment remains unchanged. Unfortunately, such commitment leaves the organization less able to adapt to sudden environmental change, which occurs quite frequently. Raynor says, "The downside of commitment is that if you happen to make the wrong commitments, it can take a long time to undo them and make new ones."[16]

The need for variety extends to organizational design, which presents its own set of challenges. A chief characteristic of organizational design in this regard is how tightly or loosely coupled it is in terms of hierarchy, delegation, response, and other aspects of structure and management.

TIGHTLY VERSUS LOOSELY COUPLED ORGANIZATIONS Responses to changing circumstances should be contextual and situational. Certain circumstances may require a tightly coupled response, others a loosely coupled one. Regulatory compliance and quality control may require tight coupling, innovation loose coupling, and crisis-response a hybrid of tight and loose coupling. Tight and loose coupling each have their advantages and disadvantages, and neither is always going to be the best approach; however, loose coupling will tend to provide greater variety and flexibility of response.

University of Michigan professor Karl Weick described the conventional wisdom of organizations as they try to move forward through goal-setting, planning, and instituting processes and procedures such as cost-benefit analysis, division of labor, delegation of authority, job descriptions, and performance appraisal systems. He noted that doing this well and thoroughly is rare.[17] When it is done well, the result is a tightly coupled organization. Weick also described the characteristics of loosely coupled organizations, which are less hierarchical and more decentralized. Exhibit 7.1 provides a summary of the *organizational characteristics* of tightly coupled and

EXHIBIT 7.1 Organizational Characteristics

Tightly vs. Loosely Coupled Organizations		
Organizational Characteristics	Tightly Coupled	Loosely Coupled
Hierarchy	High control	Low control
Supervision, regulation, and inspection	High	Low
Autonomy	Low	High
Ceremony	High	Low
Alternatives	Few	Many
Response to problems	Structural	Procedural
Feedback loop	Fast	Slow

loosely coupled organizations. The corresponding Exhibit 7.2 compares the *performance characteristics* of tight and loose organizations.

As you can see, there are trade-offs between tight and loose coupling. The management goal and skill would be to combine the best of both forms of coupling. Achieving this is not easy and represents something of a Holy Grail for executives who want the adaptability and innovativeness of a loosely coupled organization combined with the control and orderliness of a tightly coupled one. Various ways of achieving this have been tried, including flatter organizations with strong reporting systems and strategic alliances

EXHIBIT 7.2 Performance Characteristics

Tightly vs. Loosely Coupled Organizations		
Performance Characteristics	Tight	Loose
Sensitivity to changes in the environment	Low	High
Local adaptation	Low	High
Vulnerability to fads	Low	High
Insulation from problems elsewhere in the system	Low	High
Time to intervene and recover	Low	High
Innovation	Low	High
Coordination	High	Low
Sharing of best practices	High	Low
Simultaneous adaptation to conflicting demands	Low	High
Stability in rapidly changing circumstances	Low	High
Control costs	High	Low
Time, difficulty, and cost of systemic change	Low	High
Coupling mechanism	Authority	Values
Slack in the system	Low/None	High
Orderliness	High	Low

between large enterprises with market access and smaller ones with innovative technologies. For the purposes of risk management, the enterprise must analyze the environment(s) in which it operates, understand the pros and cons of each degree of coupling, and improve its risk intelligent enterprise management.

Tools for Making and Managing the Key Connections

The following tools will also help management to make and manage the connections that characterize complex enterprises and environments.

TOOL #1: DIAGRAMS AND PROCESS MAPS Visual diagrams and process maps can assist management in identifying the parts of the enterprise, the value they create, and their interconnections, vulnerabilities, and risks. Here we summarize two such tools: the enterprise value chain and the business interaction model.

Enterprise Value Chain (EVC) The enterprise value chain (EVC) should summarize the entire life cycle of value creation, including the extended enterprise. The latter includes outsourced service providers and other vendors as well as sales channels, strategic alliance participants, licensors and licensees (e.g., of brands or patents), and other external parties that contribute value to the enterprise. Essentially the EVC portrays the end-to-end process of value creation as shown in Exhibit 7.3, that is, from research and development through delivery to the customer and postsale service.

Exhibit 7.3 presents a graphic view of a high-level EVC for a manufacturing enterprise process. Whatever the industry, enterprise, or process, a graphic description can help directors and executives more precisely understand how value is created. With that understanding, they can begin to more precisely identify how value can be destroyed.

This tool can help management make assumptions about value creation explicit and identify related dependencies. It can also help management answer questions related to each value creation activity, such as:

- *R&D*. What would happen if we cut back or lost our R&D capabilities?
- *Source and ship*. What assumptions are we making about our vendors and participants in strategic alliances?

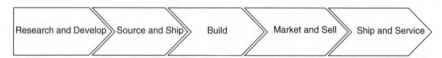

EXHIBIT 7.3 High-Level Enterprise Value Chain: Manufacturing Company

- *Build.* How vulnerable are our production facilities to various risks?
- *Market and sell.* What opportunities to market our products—such as other sales channels, product line extensions, and new market development—might we be overlooking?
- *Ship and service.* How can we use our service capabilities to help our customers to identify risks and to assist them if they encounter a crisis that affects our products and relationship?

Many of the benefits of the EVC and similar diagrams come from the exercise of creating them. The diagram is not to be created by a single individual but by a team composed of representatives from various functions, preferably in the same room at the same time, at least for some of the effort. In creating the visual representation, the group will examine and explore the ways in which their areas create value and are connected, and in doing so develop a greater understanding of how their activities are interrelated. Also, Deloitte has developed a Risk Intelligence Map, available through deloitte.com, which categorizes and identifies highly specific risks that an enterprise may face and links them to the drivers of value.

Business Interaction Model (BIM) In similar ways, a business interaction model (BIM) can help define how the enterprise creates value. Sometimes referred to as a relationship map, BIM is a tool for modeling the internal and external interactions of a business. The concept was first developed by Terry Winograd and Fernando Flores in 1983.[18] Exhibit 7.4 shows a

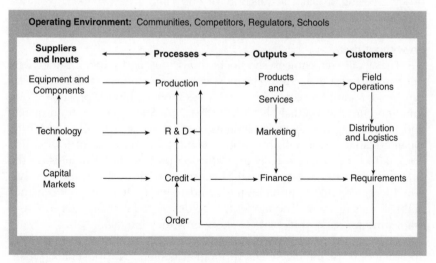

EXHIBIT 7.4 Sample Business Interaction Model

simplified, high-level BIM that describes the relationships, workflow, and feedback channels among internal and external suppliers and their respective customers in the context of their operating environment. Mapping such interactions can yield considerable insight about interdependencies that otherwise might escape notice.

As with the EVC, creating the diagram yields many of the benefits. Both tools represent starting points for further analysis. In other words, the team or specific team members should drill down into specific areas to identify unrewarded and rewarded risks, prioritize such risks, and examine potential effects on related areas. The group can then examine assumptions and develop methods of scanning for, recognizing, and communicating risks. This can also be of value in improving conventional risk management mechanisms, which are typically in need of harmonization, synchronization, and rationalization.

TOOL #2: SIPOC ANALYSIS There are three essential elements of human survival—air, water, and food. Humans can survive about three minutes without air, three days without water, and three weeks without food. (Typically, the organizational equivalent of air is cash.) We recommend that you define the basic elements of survival for your enterprise. What essentials does the organization depend on for its survival? How long can it survive without them? What exposures can the board and management accept? What level of contingency should they plan for?

It resembles the analysis you would conduct in planning any highly risky endeavor, whether it be a transoceanic sail, a mountaineering expedition, a desert crossing, a major acquisition, or entry into a new market. What are the essentials needed for survival if you were stranded on the proverbial desert island? What are your critical dependencies and how long can you go without them?

These difficult choices should be conscious and explicit rather than unconscious and unspoken. For most enterprises, these key dependencies can be identified by means of a SIPOC—suppliers, inputs, processes, output, and customers—analysis (see Exhibit 7.5). SIPOC comes from quality and process improvement disciplines, such as Six Sigma, Lean, and Total Quality Management, which use it to identify the universe of factors that could affect a process, usually a production process. SIPOC builds on the BIM and generates another visual representation of the enterprise as a system. Identifying SIPOC provides the foundation for integrating performance and risk management. The model can be developed for the enterprise as a whole and for each of its parts to show how they interact.

Widely used in process improvement initiatives, SIPOC has excellent application to risk intelligent enterprise management. The tool enables management to identify key value drivers as they relate to suppliers, inputs

Key Suppliers

← Upstream ─────

- Commodities
- Capital
- Components
- Stakeholders
- Other

Key Inputs

- Energy
- Water
- Materials
- Equipment
- People
- Capital
- Ratings
- Other

Key Processes

Midstream ─────

- Business operations
- People
- Process
- Systems
- Facilities
- Other

Key Outputs

- Products
- Services
- Other

Key Customers

Downstream →

- Internal
- External
- Stakeholders
- Other

EXHIBIT 7.5 Sample SIPOC

125

to processes, business processes, outputs of processes, and internal and external customers.

SIPOC analysis can pinpoint areas that may be subject to breakdown, degradation, or threat. It can help you to identify specific vulnerabilities and gauge the potential effects upstream and downstream in the process—and in other related or seemingly unrelated processes. Finally, it can help the board, senior management, risk managers, and business unit heads to see how specific processes and outputs relate to other processes and outputs and to see how disruptions or failures would ripple through the system.

To develop a SIPOC analysis for risk management purposes:

1. Describe the enterprise's key dependencies.
    a. Who are the critical suppliers? What do they supply?
        i. Capital
        ii. Components
        iii. Infrastructure
        iv. Commodities
        v. Expertise
        vi. Other?
    b. Who are the key people?
    c. What are the critical processes, systems, and facilities?
    d. What are the key outputs, products, and services?
    e. Who are the key customers—internal and external—for each output?
2. How long can the enterprise survive without this critical dependency or dependencies? For example, how long can it survive without:
    a. Lines of credit? Working capital? Current credit rating?
    b. Key components/commodities?
    c. Key personnel?
    d. Key facilities?
    e. Key systems?
    f. Key products or services?
    g. Key customers?

Will survival be measured in seconds, minutes, hours, days, weeks, months, or years?

Answering these questions sets the stage for deeper examination of the dimensions and implications of each area and connection. For example:

- Which suppliers do we depend on for essential inputs? What mechanisms do we have that signal risks—for example, upstream from the supplier or in the supplier's financial condition—that could affect us? How long could we survive without that supplier?

- At what concentration of revenue in any one customer does our business become a potential hostage to that customer? Ten percent? Fifteen percent? Twenty? What happens if a key customer goes elsewhere or goes bankrupt?
- At every stage of the process, what would be the implications of a shortage, disruption, or quality problem in an input or output? Which inputs or outputs are essential? What mechanisms do we have for scanning, recognizing, and communicating threats and opportunities?
- At every point, how to we monitor the supplier's supplier and the customer's customers? What early-warning systems are in place?
- What unrewarded risks are being incurred? How are people pursuing rewarded risks at each point in the process?

Business continuity plans and measures became an area of increasing focus after 9/11. Many companies, particularly in manufacturing, have had well-developed programs for quite some time.

Case Example: Aerospace and Defense Manufacturing The manufacture of aerospace and defense equipment is both complex and interconnected. These products require large numbers of components and multiple suppliers, many of which are sole sourced. Steady production depends on these suppliers for timely receipt of quality components. Some of these components require a complex path of production with much processing and long distances to travel to reach the final assembly point.

A certain manufacturer has developed and begun to use a process to assist in determining the most critical suppliers. The process uses manifold factors to determine the potential for failure to produce the components needed. Factors other than the usual financial condition, quality, and timeliness measures are reviewed to determine the potential for a production disruption. Some of these factors are workforce stability, supplier fabrication location (and susceptibility to natural disasters), length and complexity of transportation routes, and government stability.

In addition, the company implemented its business continuity program specifically to mitigate risks identified as a result of ERM. The company recognized that it could reduce downtime at its production facilities in the event of a disruption from a natural disaster or other events by developing a business continuity plan. Development of the continuity plans is prioritized by the amount of risk impact on the enterprise, as determined by the ERM assessment. Plan effectiveness is measured by the reduction in impact, usually in faster resumption of work resulting in a smaller loss in production.

The company has found several instances where a risk event from one business unit will affect one or more business units (usually downstream in a supply chain process). They call these "correlated" risks because they affect multiple business units. For example, Business Unit A supplies parts used in products produced by Business Units B and C. A risk event at Business Unit A that stops production would also stop production at Business Units B and C.

These risk assessments are coordinated through the ERM group to define the scenario and risk assumptions so that all assessments have the same basis, which allows all the impacts to be aggregated. This shows the company the true and full impact of a risk event at Business Unit A. With that perspective, risk mitigation for a potential event at Business Unit A can accurately consider the larger impact on the entire enterprise.

Make the Key Connections

Both the environment and major enterprises are characterized by interactive complexity and tightly coupled factors and forces. Because the future is unknown, the enterprise must have the requisite variety of strategies, skills, responses, products, services, and markets to survive and thrive amid turbulence and uncertainty. This implies having the right level and mix of tightly and loosely coupled structures and capabilities. Loosely coupled organizational forms are characterized by strong values, high self-control and autonomy, low ceremony, and rapid response to local opportunities and threats. These advantages need to be balanced with the need for tightly coupled hierarchies that can determine enterprise priorities and provide coordination in times of crisis.

Managing key connections requires an in-depth understanding of the enterprise. It involves knowing where vulnerabilities lie and making conscious decisions about which vulnerabilities to accept and which to mitigate, and to what extent. Every effort should be made to understand key dependencies and interdependencies of the enterprise. Without the resulting transparency, the enterprise may be unprepared for profound disruption and dislocation or for opportunity.

The enterprise needs to determine where it makes sense to have common processes and systems. This is discussed further in Chapter 16, "Risk Intelligent Enterprise Management." The enterprise also needs to determine the margin of safety it requires. This is discussed further in Chapter 10, "Maintain a Margin of Safety." Before establishing common systems and determining the margin of safety, leaders must acknowledge the possibility of failure and anticipate its causes. This is discussed in the following chapter.

Questions to Ask about Managing Key Connections

- How is value created?
- How can value be destroyed?
- What are the key dependencies and interdependencies of the extended enterprise?
- How long can the enterprise survive without these dependencies?
- What are the alternatives?

CHAPTER 8

Anticipate Causes of Failure

*Never in all history have we harnessed such formidable technology.
Every scientific advancement known to man has been incorporated
into its design. The operational controls are sound and foolproof!*
—E. J. Smith, captain of the *Titanic*

When shots from Confederate sharpshooters sent troops ducking for cover at the Battle of Spotsylvania in 1864, Union Army General John Sedgwick chided one of his troops, "Why, my man, I am ashamed of you, dodging that way. They couldn't hit an elephant at this distance." Those were General Sedgwick's final words: A bullet struck him in the head moments later.[1]

In business, last words are rarely as accurately recorded, but they are often equally inaccurate. For instance, in February 2008, Federal Reserve Chairman Ben Bernanke said of smaller banks, "I expect there will be some failures," then added, "Among the largest banks, the capital ratios remain good and I don't anticipate any serious problems of that sort among the large, internationally active banks that make up a very substantial part of our banking system."[2]

Then, in July 2008, IndyMac Bank failed with $32 billion in assets. In September 2008, Washington Mutual failed with $307 billion in assets—constituting the largest bank failure thus far at the time. In October that same year, Wachovia was sold to Wells Fargo amid concerns about its financial health, and in spring 2009, Citigroup was still struggling. At least Bernanke recognized his forecasting error a few months after making it and instituted broadly expanded Federal Reserve loan facilities and other measures to assist stressed banks. Would that all such errors were addressed as quickly and vigorously.

However, most are not, nor do leaders of enterprises always learn from the failures that they do recognize. Hence, we've included this essential skill of risk intelligence—anticipating causes of failure. Chapter 4 noted that we can never assume success. This chapter discusses ways to identify specific causes of failure. Here we focus on the need to *systematically* consider the possibility of failure. To do that, of course, leaders must first recognize the potential for failure (i.e., risk) and then analyze its causes so that they can take steps to avoid, or at least manage, the risk of failure in the future.

Fatal Flaw #5: Failure to Anticipate Failure

It's not enough to say, "We failed, we see that, we'll do better next time," nor even to recognize *a* cause of failure and to avoid it in the future. What's needed are methods of understanding why and how failure occurred—and tools that support those methods—so that failure can be examined in an orderly way, people can agree upon causes and ways to mitigate the risk of failure in the future, and, when appropriate, agree on an acceptable versus an unacceptable level of failure.

We begin with a definition of failure and an examination of why most people shy away from even mentioning failure, much less discussing it as a possibility. Then we move to methods and tools for identifying causes of failure and anticipating the potential for future failure in systematic ways.

Voice of Experience

"Confusing as it may seem, failure and getting results are not mutually exclusive. When driving experimental discovery within a company, failures should be expected. It is important to recognize that today's positive results may be derived from yesterday's lessons learned from failure.

"To be clear, our organization does not reward failure. Although we expect it on occasion, we strive to avoid it. In addition to learning from our failures, we must recognize whether the failure resulted from poorly thought-out or impulsive actions, or belongs to that percentage of failures to be expected from prudent risk-taking, such as well-designed experiments or bets."[3]

—Charles Koch, CEO, Koch Industries

Defining Failure

The Technical Council on Forensic Engineering defines failure as an "unacceptable difference between actual and expected performance."[4] This definition covers everything from a spacecraft disaster to a bankruptcy. But we need to know more about the many faces of failure if we are to anticipate its causes.

In risk management terms, failure is when the risk of a potential loss, harm, or missed opportunity becomes reality. Risk management is about improving the chances of survival and success, particularly under extreme and uncertain conditions.

More specifically, common types of failure include:

- *Falling short of individual or collective goals.* This, the most common definition of failure, jibes with that of the forensic engineers quoted above.
- *Being bested or overcome by a competitor.* This is failure to prevail in the win-lose arenas of sports, elective politics, and other competitions. While it may be true that "nobody remembers who came in second," it's also true that failure to win is not always true failure.
- *Undergoing a natural or planned demise.* Doctors speak of kidney failure; engineers calculate mean time to failure for components to determine their life span and maintenance schedule. Some enterprises come to a natural end, but fail to understand it.
- *Failing to act.* Choosing to "sit it out" is failure when it's incumbent upon the person or organization to set and pursue a goal. Imagine if the Fed "failed to act" during the 2008 credit crisis. As hockey great Wayne Gretzky said, "You miss 100 percent of the shots you don't take."

As you can see, the definition of failure is related to the cause of failure and vice versa. But as we examine the skill of anticipating failure in this chapter, we will focus mainly on the first definition: failure to reach a goal, failure to achieve the intended level of performance, failure to produce the intended results. This places us firmly in the world of enterprises, which all aim to create value by meeting customers' desires and needs for their products and services.

Leaders in every sphere must recognize that failure walks arm in arm with success. The late political operative Lee Atwater was fond of saying, "In every victory is the seed of defeat, and in every defeat is the seed of victory." Although he was talking about political campaigns, Atwater recognized the intertwined nature of success and failure, and how one can find valuable lessons in moments of either glory or agony and learn how to handle things better next time. Thus, we can and should imagine failure as well as success.

In the aftermath of the financial crisis, Howard Marks, chairman of Oaktree Capital Management, said, "Risk management matters most when risk is extreme. Failure to imagine failure is the belief that things can only get better. These false assumptions are very important. I think false assumptions about the low likelihood of failure gave rise to a lot of the pain we're feeling now."[5] Only by anticipating failure and understanding how it can happen can leadership prepare to prevent, manage, and recover from it.

Voice of Experience

"It's the emotional aspect of optimism that seems so difficult to change. The greatest risk is when you're on top; the lowest is when you're at the bottom. But nobody ever seems to believe that. That's why I'm seeing management teams again and again and again presenting budgets or setting expectations for the coming year that are outrageous.

"You'd think they hadn't read a newspaper for the last six months. They're on a path they've been on for years. If they had read the news, it's just human nature to say, 'This doesn't apply to me.'"

—Suzanne Hopgood, Director

Seeking Success

In *The Strategy Paradox*, Michael E. Raynor writes of the need to balance commitment to a specific strategy against the reality of an uncertain and unknowable future. The more committed an enterprise is to a specific strategy, the more likely it is *either* to succeed or to fail. But this is not the only paradox leaders face.

Military historians have noted that the best military commanders understand and manage the paradox of command—that they must simultaneously care deeply about their troops and yet still send them into deadly battles. In carrying out that most difficult duty, commanders must analyze their strengths and weaknesses, understand potential causes of failure, and not fall prey to "analysis paralysis." On a less dangerous level, this is a challenge for every executive: being honest about facts, acting constructively on that knowledge, and rallying the troops to exert their best efforts.

General George S. Patton, known for his victories but no stranger to defeat, said, "The time to take counsel of your fears is before you make an important battle decision. That is the time to listen to every fear you can imagine! When you have collected all of the facts and fears, make your decision. After you make your decision, forget all of your fears and go full steam ahead."

To be sure, confidence and optimism—or at least consistent displays of same—are essential leadership traits, instrumental to boosting morale and motivating people. In *The Endurance: The Story of Shackleton's Legendary Antarctic Expedition*, author Caroline Alexander discusses

Sir Ernest Shackleton's ability to maintain optimism among his men by having them put on plays, stay busy with their work, and play games.[6]

However, blind optimism—usually based on erroneous assumptions—is no virtue. The blindly optimistic believe that bad things happen only to others, which means they are more likely to make riskier decisions. As noted in Chapters 4 and 5, in March of 2008, the Senior Supervisors Group submitted a report on how various risk management practices in banking and securities firms affected their success or failure in the subprime crises. In many cases, they found that the managers of companies that experienced catastrophic failure had simply refused to consider worst-case scenarios.[7]

Voice of Experience

"Executives typically believe that most risk management programs deal with asset protection, not with risks to future growth. That's part of the disconnect with executives.

"In almost every board I have served on, when somebody says 'risk management,' the first thing that comes to mind is the person who buys insurance. And the second thing they think is 'How do we make sure that if there's a fire in the data center, we've done something about business interruption?'

"It's hard to find somebody who doesn't respond that way, when in fact most don't have an effective risk management process. Very few firms have a crisis management and disaster response program in place. To get them to understand the problem, you say, 'Okay, you've got the disaster recovery plan for the data center, but what if short-term interest rates go to 20 percent like they did in 1980? Or what if oil goes to $120 and you're an airline. Or worse yet, what if oil goes to $220? What do you do then?'

"There's hardly a corporation that does anything to prepare for the very unlikely event. It's all part of the failure to imagine failure, to think the unthinkable. In the end result, this is the root cause of most corporate failures—you were standing on the railroad tracks in front of the oncoming train and did not know it."

—Dennis Chookasian, Director

Underestimating the Potential for Failure

We've all often heard and perhaps uttered the phrase "Failure is not an option." Maybe so, but it's always a possibility. People who feel invulnerable to cancer, emphysema, sexually transmitted disease, and diabetes often engage in corresponding harmful behaviors.[8] Drivers underestimate the likelihood they will be in an automobile accident.[9] Financial analysts tend to overestimate corporate earnings. And business school students are overly optimistic about the number of job offers and the starting salaries they will receive.[10] Every day, many such individuals find themselves deeply disappointed.

Then there are those who have been somehow insured against risk and fall into moral hazard. While, as *Boston Globe* columnist Ellen Goodman noted, moral hazard sounds like "the name of a country-western singer,"[11] economists use the term to explain certain people's behavior.

Moral hazard occurs when people disregard the consequences of their actions because they are somehow insulated from those consequences. The term has its roots in the insurance industry, where underwriters may fear that people will, for instance, park their unlocked cars in places where they might be stolen because they have auto theft insurance. While most people are honest and take due care, we have all heard (and perhaps uttered) the phrase, "Don't worry, the insurance will pay for it." That's moral hazard in action.

Moral hazard is a major concern of people who worry about the skills and motives of executives of enterprises deemed "too big to fail." If an implied promise of a government bailout insulates executives from the effects of their own bad decisions, why should they worry about making the best decisions, particularly if they can profit from either good or bad ones? In fact, many opposed the U.S. government's bank bailouts under the Troubled Asset Relief Program in 2008 on that very basis. Additional regulatory efforts to prevent the reoccurrence of a financial crisis may also contribute to moral hazard by eliminating fear of failure.

Similarly, Chapter 11 of the U.S. Bankruptcy Code enables directors and executives to remain in control—despite their failures. Critics argue that by protecting an enterprise from its creditors as it continues to operate, Chapter 11 puts the competition at a disadvantage and undermines market forces and potentially the entire industry.[12] In contrast, Sweden conducts "bankruptcy auctions," where the highest bidder gains ownership of an enterprise on the brink of bankruptcy. Faster than Chapter 11 proceedings, which can last two years or more, these auctions typically require about two months and are cheaper due to lower legal fees and other costs.[13]

As one director put it "When the executives worry about business, I feel a little better about it. The ones who are cavalier and casual and say, 'We're going to kick the stuffing out of the competition. Just give us another year and they're going to be dead.' Those are the people I worry about."

Risk Intelligence Skill #5: Anticipate Causes of Failure

How can an organization overcome blind optimism and examine and learn from failure? With apologies to Dr. Norman Vincent Peale, by embracing the power of *negative* thinking, by making the examination and discussion of failure systematic and integrating it into the fabric of the organization. This isn't easy, given the egos of many leaders, the enthusiasm that accompanies most initiatives, and the barbs that can be directed toward "naysayers" in an organization. When people raise the possibility of something going wrong, they can be seen as weak, nervous, or "not with the program."

A CFO of a major enterprise, who asked to remain anonymous, explains the plight: "I always seem to be the skeptic. The one who asks, 'What about this risk or what about that risk?' It gets really tiring—for me and for others, I sense—if you're always the one who points out the problem."

Voice of Experience

"The toughest thing to say at the board today is, 'Time out, guys. This isn't going to last. What happens when it doesn't last? What happens when it goes south?'

"Getting people to take that conversation seriously, to really sink their teeth into it, is terribly difficult. People will tell you, 'Come on, you're being a worry monger. Why are you worried about that? Let's go have a beer.'

"The potential for failure is just not a topic that many directors want to spend much time talking about. And yet, we all know, sooner or later, it's going to come to an end."

—Richard Slater, Director

Even regarding concerns about possible illegal or unethical behavior, people need a lot of encouragement and guarantees of protection to get them to come forward. Whistle-blower hot lines and legal protections from retaliation have varying degrees of success. How much more difficult does it become for an individual, regardless of whether they are a director, an executive, or a front-line employee, to raise concerns about the CEO's strategy?

Risk Intelligent Methods for Identifying Causes of Failure

But what if the emperor has no clothes? Shouldn't someone point it out before the shortcoming is exposed? Wouldn't it be easier and less painful if companies had a more systematic and impersonal way of understanding how they could fail?

We believe so. There are three steps management can take to begin changing the culture and its processes in order to recognize the potential for failure and to identify its potential causes:

1. Legitimize constructive discussion of failure
2. Attack your own position
3. Employ process improvement approaches

LEGITIMIZE DISCUSSION OF FAILURE   Getting people to report potential problems takes deliberate effort. Chinese nuclear power plants pay bonuses to employees who identify problems. In Japan, and subsequently elsewhere, discussions of quality occur among the people involved in the processes in forums called quality circles. Process improvement experts recognize the need for systematic examination and discussion of problems and risks. They know that people fear being labeled tattletales or negativists.

As W. Edwards Deming, a founding father of quality improvement, said in the eighth of his 14 Points for Management, "Drive out fear, so that everyone can work effectively for the company." When people feel less afraid and more secure, they will hopefully be less reluctant to raise concerns, ask questions, or report problems.[14]

The key is to legitimize a constructive discussion of failure. That means building a systematic discussion of possible causes of failure—that is, risk—into analytical and decision-making processes.

Voice of Experience

"One CEO would say to his risk advisors, 'Given my goals, don't just tell me what could go wrong; be proactive and tell me what we *can* do to reach these goals, while minimizing risks. I need "can do" advisors, not "can't do." ' He was looking for the smartest ethical way to go forward, which would allow him to determine whether the reward was worth the risk and then to set his priorities."[15]

—Lynn Krominga, Director

If you have questioned your assumptions, developed situational awareness, factored in velocity and momentum, and recognized key dependencies, you are ready for a discussion of potential causes of failure. At every level, from the board of directors to hourly employees, to get this discussion going you must ask:

- What resources does the success of this decision, initiative, or process depend on?
- Who does success depend on?
- What could in any way interfere with the resources or people that success depends upon?

Voice of Experience

"The greater the risk, the greater the likelihood that you're going to have a failure. Not all risks or potential failures are created equally. Some are more important than others. We all recognize the need to prioritize. A key worry of ours is what methodology do we use to try to make sure we get that right."

—James Hambrick, Chairman and CEO, The Lubrizol Corporation

Also, it often helps to quote Murphy's Law in its entirety: "Everything will cost more than you think it will. Everything will take longer than you think it will. And if anything can go wrong, it will." Then ask: What could possibly add to our costs? What could make this take longer than we've projected? What could go wrong? Then, make sure you get the answers to those questions.

ATTACK YOUR OWN POSITION By "attacking your own position," you set out to locate the vulnerabilities in your own plan, unit, or organization. In *The Godforsaken Sea*, Derek Lundy cautions, "the sea, among its many qualities, is an unerring discoverer of weakness."[16] So are turbulent times and creative destruction. The risk intelligent enterprise finds and addresses its vulnerabilities before they manifest themselves as full-blown failures. To identify potential sources of failure, it's not enough to just look for them from your own perspective. You need to step outside of it or, better yet, find someone who stands outside of it and ask that person to find the vulnerabilities.

One way is to "think like a perp." For example, approaches such as the manner in which SAS 99 is applied could be useful. (SAS 99 is the Statement on Auditing Standards issued by the American Institute of Certified Public Accountants that deals with fraud detection.) When asked to brainstorm ways to commit accounting fraud, experienced CPAs, given their knowledge of internal controls, can often come up with a wide array of schemes that might otherwise be undetectable using traditional checklists.

Attack-your-position exercises are not new. The military has for decades used "Red Teams" to find vulnerabilities before the enemy did. The first was a U.S. Navy Seal team created to test national security, particularly military bases and installations sensitive to national interests. In another exercise, a Red Team fleet was given the task of attacking the Blue Team's fleet in a harbor after the anchored team took every defensive precaution. The Red Team won when they deployed underwater divers to secure (dummy) limpet mines to the Blue Team's hulls, when the Blue Team had planned only for artillery fire or torpedoes.

Similarly, "White Hats" are ethical hackers who attack computer systems or networks to help the owners to discover weaknesses before they are attacked. "Black Hat" hackers, on the other hand, are those who illegally exploit weaknesses in networked systems. The U.S. Department of Homeland Security oversaw Cyber Storms 1 and 2 in which "White Hat" hackers tried to compromise the nation's defenses against digital espionage.

The exercises simulated major attacks on digital infrastructure supporting communications, transportation, and energy production. The exercises identified gaps in cyber defenses and raised concerns that the relatively modest resources allocated to defense would be inadequate. In that same vein, DuPont draws on internal and external resources to form Red Teams to "attack" key business proposals. Once the vulnerabilities are understood, informed "go" or "no go" decisions can be made.

Enterprises can take a lesson from Red Teams and White Hats by searching for—and addressing—their own vulnerabilities. For example, the Web Application Security Consortium has identified 24 classes of Internet-related vulnerabilities. Also, internal resources and third parties can provide customized services to conduct such assessments at the enterprise level.

Voice of Experience

"We call it a Red Team like the Navy Seal team. If you're on the receiving end, it feels like a wrestling tag team. We go to a team and ask, 'What's your recommendation?' It's usually 'Do this project or don't do this type of project.' Sometimes there are some modifications.

"We ask each individual what their recommendation is, so they take it very seriously because they know they're held accountable. The only problem we find is it's too easy to vote no because there are no guarantees. It's tougher to vote yes on these teams so we have a lot of them come back and say, 'Don't do it.'

"We have to determine, of course, what risks we are willing to take despite the potential for loss. We can always go back to the team and tell them whether or not we decided to do it, or that we did it without this or that requirement. Or sometimes we just say, 'No, we don't want to take that risk. We understand but we don't want to take the risk.' "

—Charles O. Holliday, Jr., Chairman and former CEO, DuPont

EMPLOY PROCESS IMPROVEMENT APPROACHES   One great benefit of formal quality and process improvement methodologies, such as Six Sigma, Lean, and Total Quality Management, is that they *assume imperfection* in a process as their starting point. Process improvement professionals assume that failure will occur and that each failure (or "defect," to use their term) has one or more causes. They also assume that the causes of failure can be identified and corrected. The decision about whether to correct them depends on whether it makes sense based on the cost to the company and the benefit to the customer. What a wonderfully rational, systematic, and scientific approach to failure!

You're probably aware that many of the world's most successful companies, and most of the world's largest manufacturers, including Motorola (where Six Sigma was initially developed), Toyota (where Lean manufacturing was developed), IBM, Xerox, Allied Signal, Texas Instruments, and General Electric, have used one or more formal process improvement methodologies. Explaining these approaches is beyond the scope of this book, although two good primers on the topic include *The Six Sigma Way* by Peter S. Pande and colleagues and *The Machine That Changed the World: The Story of Lean Production* by James P. Womack and Daniel T. Jones.

Incidentally, the term "Six Sigma" refers not only to the methodology but to a statistical measure of variation, similar to standard deviation in the normal bell curve, in which the higher the sigma value, the less the variation in whatever is being measured. Six Sigma, the measure, translates to 3.4 defects per million, or 99.999 percent defect free. Such performance is usually attained only in narrowly defined processes and products, but it shows how seriously Six Sigma professionals take variability and failure. (Six Sigma may be most applicable in situations where a normal distribution, linear process, or other narrowly defined process exists and thus the principles of Gaussian mathematics do apply; our earlier caveats about applying them to strategic risk analyses still stand.)

The relevance of process improvement methodologies to anticipating causes of failure is threefold:

1. Those methodologies all aim to reduce error, failure, and waste in business processes by rigorously analyzing cause and effect. Once a quality goal is defined and measured—tensile strength of a material, mean time to failure for a motor, purity of a food product—then variations can be detected. That variation is caused by something. Find that something and fix it, and you've eliminated the variation and thus the risk of error or waste. Might this mind-set help management better anticipate and mitigate other risks? Yes!
2. Speaking of management, even in companies or units that have employed quality and process improvement, executives fail to anticipate causes of failure. They see the methodologies and cause-and-effect

analysis and other tools as applying only to production processes. However, both the mind-set and a number of the tools have much broader applicability.

3. Some specific tools from process improvement can be used to anticipate potential causes of failure in a risk management context. We're not suggesting that the sophisticated statistical analysis employed in Six Sigma should be applied to every decision. We are suggesting that the cause-and-effect mind-set and certain related tools can help you anticipate and then mitigate potential causes of failure.

We cover two of those tools in the remainder of this chapter.

Tools for Anticipating Causes of Failure

The causes of failure of a strategy, plan, decision, or initiative are as varied as the suppliers, processes, inputs, outputs, and customers involved in or affected by it. In general, however, failures occur for a finite (but not always predictable) number of reasons. They may be failures in design, materials, transport, storage, handling, assembly, delivery, set up, communication, expectation setting, or service—among others. The good news is that, as discussed in Chapter 1, in preparing for known causes of failure we also often prepare for unknown ones.

There are many risk identification techniques. Most are retrospective; some are prospective. Here we examine Root Cause Analysis (RCA), a retrospective technique, and Failure Modes and Effects Analysis (FMEA), a prospective technique.

WHAT HAPPENED AND WHY? ROOT CAUSE ANALYSIS Retrospective techniques are useful for analyzing how a risk or near-miss occurred and identifying ways to prevent, prepare for, or respond to a risk event. Acknowledging that perfect prevention is impossible, enterprises must prepare response and recovery plans for significant potential problems, subject to costs and benefits. Thus, they analyze failures after they occur to determine ways to improve preparedness. The military conducts After-Action Reviews (AARs) following every engagement or exercise to identify lessons learned about what worked well and what can be improved. Environmental and occupational health and safety regulations often demand similar reviews after an incident.

Root Cause Analysis (RCA) aims to locate the fundamental cause of the defect, error, or failure. The root cause is, by definition, the one that when eliminated results in the elimination of the defect, error, or failure. RCA is used to find and correct root causes, instead of addressing symptoms.

For example, tracing down the root causes of quality problems in automobile production often led manufacturers backward to designs and to suppliers of materials and components. The manufacturer's quality assurance and production teams then met with suppliers to clarify the specifications, assembly processes, product applications, handling, transport, and storage procedures and other aspects of the end-to-end process in which the suppliers' materials and components were used by the manufacturers.

Opening up in this way and engaging suppliers as partners in the design and production process enabled the auto companies to demand better quality *and* to assist suppliers' efforts to deliver that quality. The manufacturers also provided incentives for the suppliers to hit quality targets consistently, including "preferred supplier" designation and larger orders.

RCA is not a single methodology but rather the term for different tools and approaches for identifying causes of defects and failures. One useful RCA tool is a visual brainstorming device called a fishbone diagram (or Ishikawa diagram, after its designer, Kaoru Ishikawa). Creating a cause-and-effect diagram helps to identify and categorize potential root causes (see Exhibit 8.1). This is related to the technique called "Five Whys," which is simply asking, "Why?" five times to get to the root cause of the problem.

Again, RCA is a retrospective tool, but it has its limits. For instance, if people feel they don't have direct control over the causes, they stop worrying about the effects. A similar dynamic occurs when something may happen so

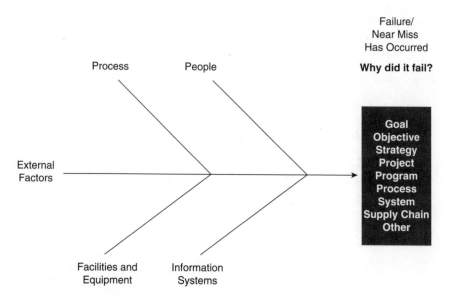

EXHIBIT 8.1 Root Cause Analysis

far in the future that they won't be around to feel the effects or to be held accountable. Such thinking can lead to serious consequences. Also, even RCA cannot always clarify which factors created which outcome, but that's no reason to stop trying. Most major problems in business are solvable given enough time, effort, and resources. The main question to be addressed is "What are the most important things we can do something about?"

WHAT COULD HAPPEN? FAILURE MODES AND EFFECTS ANALYSIS (FMEA)   Another tool of quality and process improvement, Failure Modes and Effects Analysis (FMEA), can be used prospectively to identify how failure might occur. The U.S. Armed Forces have been using FMEA since the late 1940s in planning. It was used extensively in the aerospace industry to find errors at a stage when the costs and consequences of failure would be lower. Now used extensively in manufacturing, FMEA helps to identify possible causes of failure throughout product development, production, and use. Ideally, it begins in the earliest concept stages and continues through design, engineering, and manufacturing, and throughout the product or service lifecycle.

Enterprises can apply FMEA to a broad range of issues, functions, and endeavors, as the open-ended template in Exhibit 8.2 illustrates. The FMEA model and its forward-looking questions can help to locate spots that present risks, or, in the case of an opportunity, the possibility of missed or suboptimized gains.

At the strategic level, a "starter set" of FMEA questions could include:

- How could we fail to achieve our strategy, goals, and objectives?
- What would cause us to fail?

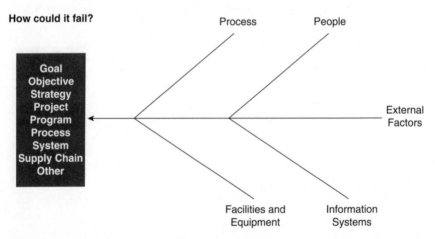

EXHIBIT 8.2 Failure Modes and Effects Analysis

- What would be the effects of the failure?
- How bad could it get? What is the worst case?
- What are we currently doing to prevent, detect, correct, or escalate attention to such failure?
- What is our remaining vulnerability or exposure to such failure?
- What further actions must we take to mitigate this potential failure in a cost-effective manner?

Voice of Experience

"We've never actually made what I would call the intellectual leap to take failure modes and effects analysis up to the strategic level. We've always kept it at the operating level, because it lends itself there. We've never really done the hard work on some of these larger strategic issues, so that will be a challenge for us.

"We need to look at how we could fail, what could cause us to fail, and what the effects would be without trying to assign a probability to them because of the uncertain nature of things."

—James Hambrick, Chairman and CEO, The Lubrizol Corporation

One private equity firm learned the hard way that FMEA could have helped identify problems in advance of several acquisitions. When acquiring a well-established family business, they did not anticipate that family tradition would preclude rapid responses to market changes. In another, they did not anticipate the disintermediating effect of the Internet. They now apply FMEA to every proposal to better anticipate factors that could cause failure. Once they have identified these factors, they can choose whether to proceed and, if they do, what can be done to mitigate potential sources of loss.

Risk Intelligent Decisions: A Case in Point

Consider a company with multiple U.S. locations and key foreign facilities in areas prone to natural disasters. Using SIPOC, described in Chapter 7, the company has identified multiple critical dependencies, including sole-source suppliers and reliance on regional energy and transportation infrastructures. A FMEA exercise identified that a disruption in any one of these dependencies could shut down key facilities and disrupt revenue flows. With this knowledge, senior management asked whether the enterprise should develop business continuity plans for each location. This would require investments, some major, some smaller. The company had several options, each with its pros and cons, two of which were:

1. *Option 1: Decide to accept the risk.* Some executives argued that since disruption can come from so many sources, preparing for all of them would be impossible and unaffordable and, therefore, nothing further should be done. The company should hope for the best and keep a positive attitude. After all, everyone else in the region will be similarly affected.
2. *Option 2: Decide to mitigate the risks.* Other executives argued that some improvement would be better than nothing. While addressing all sources of disruption would be impractical, addressing a number of key factors could have multiple benefits. Some level of preparedness would surely be better than none. As part of this decision, for example, they chose to increase inventory buffers of critical components in the event of a disruption in supply.

The key here is that management understood the exposure and the cost of mitigation and then made a conscious, calculated, informed decision about whether or not to accept that level of risk. In this context, the option the company chose is secondary to the approach it used.

CASE EXAMPLE: A SIX SIGMA MANUFACTURER   As part of its Six Sigma program, one manufacturer identified some initial risks as part of the piloting process to test ERM tools and processes. One of these early risks was the potential for a facility disruption from a hurricane at the company's location on the Louisiana coast. This risk was initially assessed as a $1 million impact (ERM risk impacts are measured in monetary loss potential) because the company had insurance with a deductible of $1 million and had the usual hurricane preparation plan for Gulf Coast businesses.

On August 29, 2005, Hurricane Katrina struck the coast near New Orleans, causing widespread damage to the city, homes, businesses, and infrastructure. The company's production was severely affected, with approximately 18 feet of water in one facility. With heroic efforts on the part of employees, some production resumed two months later. However, the cost of the storm far exceeded the $1 million in the initial ERM risk assessment.

In early 2006, the ERM assessment for the facility's hurricane risk was revised to indicate an impact of $100 million. With an anticipated disruption of four months, a business continuity plan was being implemented to reduce the disruption time to about one month. An extensive effort was underway to prepare the facilities for another hurricane. Upon completion of all business continuity activities, another ERM risk assessment was performed that now indicated the impact to be $14 million with a one-month anticipated disruption of business.

On September 1, 2008, Hurricane Gustav, with wind speeds just below the category 3 level, struck the Louisiana coast just a few miles west of where Hurricane Katrina had struck three years earlier. The same facilities were again severely affected, with several feet of water in the buildings. This time, thanks to the advance preparations, the business was disrupted for only three days. The cost of this storm was much less than the $14 million anticipated in the ERM assessment.

Finding Causes of Future Failures

The saying goes, "Only a fool trips twice over the same stone." An enterprise can avoid repeating the same mistakes only if it knows what caused the mistakes. Anticipating the causes of failures that haven't yet occurred represents an even greater challenge. Meeting that challenge begins with first admitting that failure can occur, setting aside blind optimism, listening to your own and others' fears, and imagining what could go wrong.

Management must set the tone and the example for such activities. It can do so by legitimizing discussion of failure, attacking their own position, and adopting the mind-set and a few tools from quality and process improvement methodologies. The two such tools we covered in this chapter were Root Cause Analysis and Failure Modes and Effects Analysis. Both enable analysts and managers to systematically approach, examine, and anticipate and thus better manage potential causes of failure.

With that information, boards and executives can make conscious, calculated choices about whether to accept specific risks and, if they choose, how best to mitigate them.

Questions to Ask about Anticipating Causes of Failure

General Questions

- What are the major exposures for the enterprise?
- What can—and should—we do about these exposures?
- What is the least we could do? What is the most we could do?
- How can we reduce our exposure to an acceptable level?
- How will this affect our total cost of risk? (See Chapter 14, "Risk Intelligence Is Free.")

(Continued)

(*Continued*)

Retrospective Questions

- For events that have already occurred, how can we use root cause analysis (RCA) to identify and correct causal factors?
- Are we conducting root cause analyses after every direct hit or near miss?
- Are the relevant lessons communicated appropriately across the enterprise?
- Have these lessons been incorporated into actual practice?

Prospective Questions

- Given our goals and strategies to achieve them, what could cause us to fail?
- What would be the effects of such failure?
- Which failures have the potential to ruin the enterprise?
- For the "killer" failures, what are we doing to prevent, detect, and quickly respond and recover?

CHAPTER 9

Verify Sources and Corroborate Information

In God we trust; all others must bring data.
—W. Edwards Deming[1]

In November 1999, Rafid Ahmed Alwan defected from Iraq and requested asylum at a refugee center near Nuremburg, Germany. A chemical engineer, Alwan informed German intelligence he had been employed at a seed purification plant outside Baghdad that was secretly producing mobile biological weapons of mass destruction. German intelligence informed CIA Director George Tenet that Alwan's story was "plausible and believable" but "attempts to verify the information have been unsuccessful."[2]

Despite the caveat, the U.S. government used Alwan's report as part of its rationale for invading Iraq. Both President George W. Bush, in his 2003 State of the Union address, and later Secretary of State Colin Powell, in addressing the United Nations Security Council, referred to the intelligence. Three days after the latter presentation, UN inspectors visited the suspected weapons site in Iraq and found no evidence that biological weapons had been manufactured there. Another search 20 days later again revealed nothing.

The CIA made numerous unsuccessful attempts to corroborate Alwan's allegations. However, accurate or not, a case had been made, and the war in Iraq began on March 20, 2003. After a two-year investigation, the CBS television show *60 Minutes* found that many of Alwan's claims had been fabricated. The CIA finally acknowledged that Alwan—code named "Curve Ball"—was a fraud. Alwan really just wanted the German equivalent of a green card.

The story holds a valuable lesson about the importance of verifying the credibility of sources and corroborating the accuracy of their information. Credible does not mean true; it means believable. Accurate can mean true, or it can mean "true based upon the facts available at this time as we understand them." Given that the discipline of risk management aims to develop the best intelligence available to support superior decision making, having credible sources and accurate information for making judgments represents an essential skill.

Trust, but verify.

—Ronald Reagan

Fatal Flaw #6: Failure to Verify Sources and Corroborate Information

Enterprises that depend on imperfect, disparate sources of information must verify the credibility of their sources and then corroborate the information they provide. Chapters 4 and 8 discussed ways in which failing to challenge your own assumptions and failing to imagine failure can undermine an enterprise. Unbridled optimism, biases, and groupthink can also hinder verification and corroboration.

This chapter helps you to address the effects of those flaws by providing practical guidance on verifying sources and corroborating the information they supply. The term "sources" here refers to internal and external numerical and textual written reports, statements made by people in informal and formal meetings or in conversations or in passing, and information from newspapers, Web sites, blogs, government reports, and various experts. This chapter also examines challenges in verification and offers tools for verifying the credibility of sources and the accuracy of their information and in acquiring the most useful information for risk-related decision making. And finally, in this chapter you will find insight into one of the most commonly used risk assessment tools, Risk Control and Self-Assessment (RCSA).

Says Who? A Question of Credibility

If the modern enterprise runs on information, how can it better ensure the credibility of the information on which it bases important decisions?

Typically, two characteristics determine the credibility of a source: expertise and trustworthiness. The difficulty lies in determining who is an expert and whom you can trust. For instance, consider the following situations:

- The Internet provides virtually unlimited access to huge amounts of information, which can range from the worthless ravings of clinically psychotic individuals, to opinion masquerading as fact, to highly researched, objective analyses from serious, ethical experts.
- In a court of law, jurors give great credence to eyewitness testimony, but in reality it is the leading cause of wrongful conviction in the United States. According to the Innocence Project, eyewitness misidentification led to more than 75 percent of convictions that were later overturned through DNA testing.[3]
- People in positions of high authority all too often succumb to the corruption that such power can create and can override controls. According to a 1999 Committee of Sponsoring Organizations (COSO) study of 300 cases of fraud over an 11-year period, CEOs were involved 72 percent of the time and CFOs in 43 percent of cases.[4]
- The parade of unethical individuals in the investment business stretches back to Charles Ponzi and beyond, up to the more recent example of Bernard Madoff, who, in history's largest financial fraud yet, bilked investors of an estimated $50 billion by means of a Ponzi scheme. (In a Ponzi scheme money from new investors is used to pay what appear to be extraordinary returns to existing investors.)

It is incumbent upon anyone depending in any meaningful way on the information supplied to verify the source and to corroborate the information itself. While it has always been important to verify sources and corroborate information, it is particularly important at this time in the development of technology and the culture. Technology has created an environment in which reporters, editors, and traditional news intermediaries have in many areas—and most Web sites—been cut out of the information gathering, corroboration, and transmission process.

While many cheer the "democratic" nature of this development, it is in many ways akin to everyone having his own soapbox in Hyde Park. Not all opinions are created equal. Also, perhaps due to cultural relativism or to entertainment values overtaking journalistic values, hosts of "news programs"—often entertainers posing as journalists—report all information as if it had equal credence and value. Press releases, whether from the White House or foreign dictators, are passed on with little analysis to viewers and readers who often cannot point out on a map the countries in which their troops are fighting.

In more serious venues, such as boardrooms and executive suites, the pace of business and the pressure to hit the next quarter's earnings estimates work against deliberation. Those forces even work against adequate information and intelligence gathering and analysis—let alone verification of sources and accuracy. However, too much is riding on risk management efforts to rely on bad information. Also, as some of the facts cited in this chapter so far indicate, the world can exact serious penalties for acting on erroneous information.

Diligent or Gullible?

Features of the Bernard Madoff fraud give pause to anyone who trusts what most of us consider to be reliable ways of judging sources and information. Madoff had excellent credentials. He had helped develop the National Association of Securities Dealers Automated Quotations (NASDAQ) and served as its chairman. He was a prominent philanthropist and sat on the boards of several nonprofit organizations. He involved himself in the social networks surrounding these charities, especially in the Jewish community.

Madoff's investment fund was very exclusive and initially available only through prestigious feeder networks. He maintained steady annual returns of 12 to 13 percent every year, with only five down months in 1996.[5] The returns of just above 10 percent and those down months increased his allure, for if returns had been truly outlandish, they would have raised alarms. Thus, the fund survived despite strong concerns being raised by some, and it may well have continued if not for the market meltdown of 2008.

Madoff told investors that his method was too complicated for outsiders to understand, and he was highly secretive about the business. Yet lack of transparency is not uncommon among hedge funds. Madoff had been investigated sixteen times by the SEC,[6] but nothing substantive was ever detected. Any questions raised were answered swiftly and apparently satisfactorily. Some investors who requested early on that their money be returned were repaid and fines were paid when levied.

Yet there were contrary indications. In 2001, *Barron's* magazine wrote that Madoff's strategy was not sound. Analysts performing due diligence were unable to replicate his fund's past returns. Madoff's company avoided filing disclosures of its holdings with the SEC and sold its holdings for cash at the end of each period.[7] He used a two-person auditing firm and served as his own broker-dealer, contrary to the practice of most hedge funds.[8] Even though he pioneered electronic trading, Madoff refused to allow his clients access to their accounts online. Account statements were always sent by mail.

Two features of the Madoff fraud have particular relevance to this chapter. First, his victims did not behave foolishly, but rather relied on the usual earmarks of credibility, such as experience, expertise, reputation, and referrals. They were a bit too taken with those things, perhaps, and ignored the few warnings that may have reached them. But by and large they were swindled by a skilled professional. Second, the fraud was not uncovered by audits, government investigations, or internal whistle-blowers. It surfaced when Madoff's investors were forced to liquidate their holdings during the economic collapse, forcing a run on Madoff's funds that he could not cover. In sum, Madoff was credible, respected, and successful, although his strategy was highly opaque and secretive

Professor Stephen Greenspan cites four key factors in a successful scam in which people are "going ahead with socially or physically risky behavior in spite of danger signs or unresolved questions"—situation, cognition, personality, and emotion. Different factors have different weights depending on the circumstances and, according to Greenspan, the Madoff case had elements of all four. In addition, Greenspan defines "gullibility" as a type of foolish behavior that "always occurs in the presence of pressure or deception by other people."

The Madoff case demonstrates gullibility to an extent, but also the difficulty of determining when a source is credible. If a fund with solid returns, being run by an investment manager who helped develop NASDAQ and served as its chairman, sits on boards of charitable organizations to which he also donates money, and is recommended by other people whom you respect, isn't a safe place to put your money, then what is?

Show Me! A Question of Corroboration

Verification of sources is one side of establishing credibility—corroboration of the information is the other. Defined as the act of confirming facts or statements, corroboration is a vital step required in disciplines ranging from national security and military intelligence to medical diagnoses and scientific experiments to legal proceedings and journalism. It makes sense that directors and executives dealing with risk management in major enterprises would exercise a similar level of care, skepticism, and discipline.

Indeed, the stakes run high in publicly held companies. A 2001 study by professor Mark Beasley and colleagues identified the top ten audit deficiencies that resulted in an SEC enforcement action, as shown in Exhibit 9.1. Of those, seven can be considered related to failure to corroborate or lack of professional skepticism, and we have underlined them in the exhibit.[9]

Note that these items can be addressed by—and only by—gathering additional information, maintaining professional objectivity and skepticism, and being persistent. This list implies, in a sense, that auditors should take nothing at face value, confirm every item of importance or potential importance, and "see for themselves" when possible.

EXHIBIT 9.1 Top Audit Deficiencies in SEC Enforcement Actions: 1987–1997

Problem area	Percentage (Number) of Cases
1. Gathering sufficient audit evidence	80% (36 cases)
2. Exercising due professional care	71% (32)
3. Demonstrating appropriate level of professional skepticism	60% (27)
4. Interpreting or applying requirements of GAAP.	49% (22)
5. Designing audit programs and planning the engagement (overlooking risk issues and nonroutine transactions)	44% (20)
6. Using inquiry as form of evidence (relying too much on this method)	40% (18)
7. Obtaining adequate evidence related to the evaluation of significant management estimates (failing to gather sufficient evidence)	36% (16)
8. Confirming accounts receivable	29% (13)
9. Recognizing/disclosing key related parties	27% (12)
10. Relying on internal controls (relying too much on, or failing to react to, known control weaknesses)	24% (11)

Source: Mark S. Beasly, Joseph V. Carcello, and Dana R. Hermanson, "Top Ten Audit Deficiencies," 13 May 2003, *Journal of Accounting*, www.accountancy.com.pk/articles.asp?id=70 (Accessed 1 June 2009).

The first U.S. Secretary of Homeland Security, Tom Ridge, stated that his department approached corroboration by getting "as much awareness as you possibly can … Have we had information from that source or sources before that proved to be accurate? Did they tell us something six months ago or a year ago that turned out to be right? Can we corroborate from another source? Do we hear other sources talking about the same thing? Is it credible; is it corroborated?"[10]

When It's Too Good to Be True

Whether you are a director, an officer, an investor, or an auditor, be particularly skeptical of claims that seem too good to be true. Always strive to understand how results are being achieved operationally and financially, and what, if anything, has changed in the environment—and obtain corroborating information or evidence whenever possible.

Voice of Experience

"Some time ago, I was a director at an automotive finance company. Things were going great, and then all of a sudden the industry started to deteriorate. The board asked the CEO, 'How come we're still doing great, and everybody else is in trouble. How are you doing it?'

"He said, 'Oh, I'm tough. I go out and visit the offices and meet with the managers.' We had 500 offices at the time. He said, 'I beat 'em up and I tell 'em to run it tight. I'm also very tough on repos (repossessed cars).' He gave us a number of detailed operating explanations, and the board accepted them.

"Another quarter went by and the industry was doing even worse, and our results were still very strong. The board said, 'Wow, this is terrific. How are you doing this? Let us see what's really happening in the repo inventory (a key indicator of default trends), and let's drill down on this because it's just hard to understand how we can be doing that much better than our competitors.'

"The following board meeting the CEO presented the repo inventory and provided an operating review. At the time, $25 million was the normal level of the inventory, and sure enough, the CEO showed the board a one-page computer report that stated that the inventory was still $25 million. It later turned out that there was a second page of the report, which he didn't give us, that showed the repo inventory was actually $50 million. If the board had known that the repo inventory had grown to $50 million, warning bells would have gone off, and we would have set reserves up and taken other actions.

"So this was a case where the board actually asked the CEO the right questions and also to produce information to validate the facts, and he did. But the board didn't corroborate the information independently by asking either the internal audit or external audit function to verify the information.

"The fraud was discovered in the following quarter when some reconciliations pointed out the problem. Even the external auditors missed it entirely in two prior year-end audits. The moral of this story is that when it's too good to be true, it probably is, and you have to perform a thorough check on it."

—Dennis Chookasian, Director

According to the Activity Based Risk Evaluation Model of Auditing (ABREMA), this means not simply accepting answers at face value. "There should be professional doubt as to whether:

- The evidence may be misleading
- The evidence may be incomplete
- The person providing the evidence may be either incompetent or motivated to provide evidence that is misleading or incomplete
- The possibility of fraud exists"[11]

Although this applies to auditors, from the risk management perspective, "professional doubt" would be a good attitude for any board member or executive to cultivate in regard to external recommendations and credit ratings. The Senior Supervisors Group found that in financial institutions that performed relatively well in the credit crisis management had, before the crisis occurred, established "rigorous internal processes requiring critical judgment and discipline in the valuation of holdings of complex or potentially illiquid securities."[12]

"These firms were skeptical of rating agencies' assessments of complex structured credit securities and consequently had developed in-house expertise to conduct independent assessments of the credit quality of assets underlying the complex securities to help value their exposures appropriately. Finally, when they reached decisions on values, they sought to use those values consistently across the firm, including for their own and their counterparties' positions." The report also stated, "Subsequent to the onset of the turmoil, these firms were also more likely to test their valuation estimates by selling a small percentage of relevant assets to observe a price or by looking for other clues, such as disputes over the value of collateral, to assess the accuracy of their valuations of the same or similar assets."

By comparison, firms that experienced larger losses hadn't challenged those valuations. They made no changes to their pricing of the super-senior tranches of collateralized debt obligations (CDOs) even though there had been clear declines in the performance of the underlying collateral and decreasing market liquidity. "Management did not exercise sufficient discipline over the valuation process: Those firms generally lacked relevant internal valuation models and sometimes relied too passively on external views of credit risk from rating agencies and pricing services to determine values for their exposures . . . Furthermore, when considering how the value of their exposures would behave in the future, they often continued to rely on estimates of asset correlation that reflected more favorable market conditions."[13]

Checking sources is particularly important if different signals are coming from different parts of the market. Goldman Sachs did this with its models.

As noted in Chapter 5, when it found it had experienced ten consecutive days of loss, it pulled back, even though its VaR models weren't indicating a problem.[14]

A SENSE OF SECURITY: TRUE OR FALSE?   Without corroboration, a false sense of security can become the norm. In 2004, America Online (AOL) and the National Cyber Security Alliance joined forces to find out how well people are protected from Internet attacks—and how well they think they're protected. Of the 329 people surveyed, only 85 percent were running antivirus software. Seventy-one percent of those running antivirus software thought that they were updating their protection on a weekly basis, when less than half actually were (and one in five reported that their computers were infected with a virus). Eighty percent of those surveyed had spyware on their systems, only about 30 percent were using a firewall, and many had unencrypted wireless networks.[15] Most surprising was the finding that the average survey respondents considered themselves intermediate or expert users and had been online for about seven years.

Drawing a parallel, the enterprise should examine the robustness and effectiveness of its risk management and controls. When it comes to both information and physical security, senior executives need to see security as a necessary component of key business processes and decision making. Therefore, interrelated risks and controls across the enterprise must be tested and corroborated.

Voice of Experience

"Being on a board has changed an awful lot over the last several years, because people are much more aware that they have to be skeptical, and they have to share in a straightforward way what's on their minds or they aren't doing their job as a board member.

"That wasn't the case for many, many years, and it may still not be the case on a lot of boards, but it's very important to speak up. I'm old enough where I don't worry about whether people agree or disagree with me, or whether they think I'm asking a stupid question. I just ask it because it's going to elicit a conversation. I may be wrong and that would be fine. But at least I brought it to the table so that we can discuss it and analyze it and take it apart. Unless we do that on a board, we're going to miss something."

—David Meuse, Director

Risk Intelligence Skill # 6: Verify Sources and Corroborate Information

While the board is ultimately responsible for governance, management is responsible for managing the business. That means management must identify key risks and then avoid them or accept and mitigate them, while providing reasonable assurance to the board that the risks are within the appetite of the enterprise. It's also management's role to provide reasonable assurance that controls exist to prevent, detect, correct, or escalate a risk.

The organizational culture either will or will not enable ideas, opinions, and assertions about the level of risk to be constructively challenged. Independent reassurance can also confirm or challenge the reliability of reports, controls, and measures of exposure. Internal and external audit performs this role with respect to financial statements. As in the case of second medical opinions, some companies go beyond the audit functions to secure corroboration and use third parties, especially in highly technical areas, such as systems controls or advanced engineering. Other companies form special internal teams to make the challenge (such as those discussed in "Attack Your Own Position" in Chapter 8).

Voice of Experience

"Corroboration of risk and data is so important that we have folks whose job it is to corroborate, be the check and balance, ask the off-the-wall questions. But they should not just be auditors or quality types. These should be line people who are your best, brightest, and most experienced managers, staff who are in empowered, line organizations to check on other line organizations.

"One such organization reports directly to the president, and they carry his clout. It has very senior people who vet and evaluate and have an equal vote with the divisional presidents in deciding what business we take or don't take on, whether it's an acquisition, a project, or whatever. That's number one. This is not just a staff function."

— Richard Slater, Director

Audits = Reassurance

Internal audit, of course, plays an important role in assurance. But how does internal audit's assurance responsibility differ from management's? We find it helpful to describe internal audit's role as providing reasonable "reassurance" to executive management and to the board that management's reports on the effectiveness and efficiency of mitigation and control for all key risks are reliable. In a sense, reassurance better describes internal audit's role, given that management provides assurance. However, there are, as always, some challenges to be addressed.

Even though internal audit typically has a dotted line relationship to the audit committee, internal audit is not really as independent of management as one might hope. After all, internal audit is still part of the management structure that determines their compensation and their career path.

Some directors of internal audit find they must navigate a political minefield in order to express their "independent" opinions. Especially in times of constraint and cost reductions, the costs of internal audit are rarely exempt. Thus, the monitoring of the effectiveness of internal controls may be diminished at precisely the time when others, due to similar constraints and downsizing, may be taking shortcuts to streamline the workloads of those that survived the restructuring. (See Chapter 14, "Risk Intelligence Is Free," for further discussion of this topic.)

Thus, while improving effectiveness is important, many enterprises (particularly in highly regulated industries) also need to improve efficiencies and reduce governance, compliance, and risk-management costs. Internal audit can support those goals by broadening the scope of its activity to include facilitating the identification and evaluation of all relevant risks and the costs of risk management across the enterprise. Internal audit can also help by coaching management in responses to risks, including redeployment of resources to higher priorities, and reporting on consolidated risks and management's responses. In this way internal audit can champion more risk intelligent practices.

External auditors perform the public accounting function of providing objective audits and opinions of financial statements. However, executives can additionally benefit from the business insights that auditors often develop based on experience gleaned from exposure to an array of enterprises, industries, and approaches. Again, however, it is worth emphasizing that management always remains responsible for risk management and for developing and providing sound information on the organization's operations, finances, and risks.

Self-Assessment: Can the Enterprise Assess Itself?

The story of Alwan that opened this chapter demonstrates that reports from confidential informants, defectors, and other potentially compromised or conflicted sources must be corroborated, even if they've proven reliable in the past. But what about the reliability of sources within the enterprise? In many enterprises, self-assessment is the predominant mode of risk measurement. As much as half or more of corporate risk assessments are developed in the form of self-assessments.[16]

If a business's greatest risks lie in its basic assumptions, we must acknowledge the danger in assuming that internal sources are always reliable. To avoid making that assumption, information from internal sources should be corroborated, particularly in sensitive or high-risk areas, such as security, financial systems, and IT and operational integrity.

A multidisciplinary, multiview approach to risk self-assessment is desirable, but it also presents difficulties. Usually, various internal sources are trustworthy, but do they understand risk? Do they understand their bias? Should all involved parties "get a vote" on a risk, or should the enterprise rely on expert opinion?

ASSESSING RISK AND CONTROL SELF-ASSESSMENT (RCSA)   Risk and Control Self-Assessment (RCSA) is a facilitated method for bringing staff from a unit or several related units together to identify strengths and weaknesses in an enterprise's risk and control approach, and to develop action plans to address identified weaknesses. As a facilitated approach, RCSA uses various techniques to produce information, including brainstorming, multidisciplinary workshops, and a democratic group process of identifying and ranking issues. Similar methods have been used in quality circles to identify opportunities to improve processes.

Although popular, RCSA has strengths and weaknesses that are seldom discussed. Among the benefits, according to the Institute of Internal Auditors, RCSAs raise "red flags" for emerging issues, monitor and assess risk across the enterprise, improve the quantity and quality of risk-management practices, reduce time and cost of internal audits, target audit work, clarify management responsibility for risk management and control, and capture and share best practices.

The primary weakness? You don't know what you don't know. Or in the words of Donald Rumsfeld, former U.S. Secretary of Defense: "As we know, there are known knowns. There are things we know we know. We also know there are known unknowns. That is to say, we know there are some things we do not know. But there are also unknown unknowns, the ones we don't know we don't know."[17]

There are also things we don't know about ourselves, which affect group problem-solving exercises. In their work in relationships and communications, Joseph Luft and Harry Ingham discovered that, in general, those who are incompetent at a skill don't recognize their incompetence because they are unable to assess their own performance.[18] So if people don't know that they are incompetent in an area in which they are trying to solve a problem, their solution is likely to be suboptimal. Moreover, any self-assessment by such people is bound to be flawed.

Another weakness of RCSA is its democratic nature and potential to promote groupthink. Even groups of experts fall prey to social dynamics and pressures. Because not all participants will be equally knowledgeable about a topic, the group's results might be "averaged down," like the statistician who drowned in a river with an average depth of three feet. According to social psychologists, within a group, the pressures to minimize conflict and maximize consensus can weaken processes, which can result in bad decisions, with individual questions or doubts never vocalized and conclusions made too hastily.[19]

In his 1972 book, *Victims of Groupthink*, Irving Janis described the problems that can lead groups of experts to reach incorrect conclusions. Janis observed that experts are often overconfident in their ability to estimate accurately from small data samples. Of greater concern, using a number of experts, rather than one, to estimate risks does not necessarily lead to better estimates because groupthink can lead them to make completely wrong, but agreed upon, conclusions.

Based on his analysis of failures such as Pearl Harbor, the invasion of North Korea, the Bay of Pigs invasion of Cuba, the Vietnam War, and Watergate, among others, Janis concluded that groups that are highly cohesive, insulated, under high stress, and characterized by strong directive leadership can fail because of poor decision-making processes and pressures to conform. Janis defined groupthink as "a mode of thinking that people engage in when they are deeply involved in a cohesive in-group, when the members' strivings for unanimity override their motivation to realistically appraise alternative courses of action."[20]

Janis identified eight characteristics of groupthink:[21]

1. *Illusions of invulnerability* that create excessive optimism and promote risk taking
2. *Rationalizing warnings* that might challenge the group's assumptions
3. *Unquestioned belief* in the morality of the group, causing members to ignore the consequences of their actions
4. *Stereotyping* those who are opposed to the group as weak, evil, disfigured, impotent, or stupid
5. *Direct pressure* to conform placed on any member who questions the group, couched in terms of "disloyalty"
6. *Self-censorship* of ideas that deviate from the apparent group consensus
7. *Illusions of unanimity* among group members and interpreting silence as agreement
8. *"Mindguards,"* self-appointed members who shield the group from dissenting information

In contrast, mountaineer Esther Colwill recounts that the most successful teams are often composed of dissimilar individuals. In such situations, team members cannot assume they have a common frame of reference or understanding about a problem or risk. That means they must develop their own common language and shared understandings of their assumptions in order to accomplish their goals. The process of developing that shared understanding, acceptance, and commitment (although time consuming) aligns the members in ways that more initially homogeneous teams might not be able to achieve.

Finally, there is insufficient data to support the ultimate value of self-assessment or to demonstrate its benefits. Therefore, any RCSA initiative must ensure that those participating are the most knowledgeable about the specific risk, have responsibility for day-to-day management of the risk, and have sufficient experience with the risk in its extreme forms. A tall order perhaps, but one that must be filled.

While RCSAs have a useful role to play in any enterprise, results must be interpreted cautiously in the absence of corroboration and actual evidence. They are quite useful for stimulating dialogue and improving risk awareness. But compiling a comprehensive list of threats can produce an unwieldy "risk universe." RCSAs can also help to narrow the focus to the "vital few versus the trivial many" by helping to decide what needs to be quantified and prioritized.

Voice of Experience

"After our initial risk self-assessment, we have gone back and challenged and probed the various risk assumptions. Now that we've got some maturity around what we're doing here, we can go back to those initial assumptions and say, 'You know what, guys? You did a really nice job on that initial assumption, but we've learned some other things and we think it may be different. Can we recalibrate here?'

"We also recalibrate after every risk experience. What was our initial estimate of the exposure and how accurate were we? So far, we've been accurate within 10 percent."

— ERM director

Tools for Verifying Sources and Corroborating Information

Several tools for verifying sources and corroborating information come from journalism, a profession that relies on gathering, verifying, and reporting accurate information. Journalists—true, professional journalists with training and a commitment to the profession and to the public—follow practices aimed at ensuring the reliability of sources and information. As the Pew Research Center's Project for Excellence in Journalism states:

> *Journalism does not pursue truth in an absolute or philosophical sense, but it can—and must—pursue it in a practical sense. This "journalistic truth" is a process that begins with the professional discipline of assembling and verifying facts. Then journalists try to convey a fair and reliable account of their meaning, valid for now, subject to further investigation. Journalists should be as transparent as possible about sources and methods so audiences can make their own assessment of the information.*[22]

Journalists cultivate a process for gathering reliable information and presenting it with objectivity. They recognize that they are biased, so they employ a method, which good editors insist upon and enforce, that will ensure or at least maximize objectivity. We have adapted some of these tools to our purposes here.

SOURCE VERIFICATION TOOLS

To gather reliable information:

- Cultivate good sources, but recognize that if you get too emotionally close to a live source, your objectivity can be compromised.
- Develop trusted sources by being trustworthy and using information as you have agreed to use it (e.g., not quoting statements given "on background" and not quoting sources who have not spoken for attribution).
- Assess sources' objectivity and consider their motives, potential conflicts of interest, and ability to know what they claim to know; be skeptical.

INFORMATION CORROBORATION TOOLS

To corroborate information:

- Locate and check second sources and don't rely on a sole source for important information.
- Seek expert opinion, which can be quite valuable, particularly when the expert has firsthand experience, research results, and a record of reliability.
- Use statistical and numerical evidence, but know that just because a number is precise does not mean it is accurate.

Also, be persistent when gathering or verifying information. Ask and then ask again. When a source seems unsure of his or her facts, ask for evidence and examples. Ask for another source. It often takes a detective's instincts and methods to gather and verify information.

You'll Never Regret Double-Checking

So, verify that sources are reliable and credible, and that their biases are acknowledged. Be sure decision-making teams reflect diversity of opinion to avoid groupthink and allow time for them to do their work and formulate their findings. Assign an executive with overall responsibility for the end-to-end assessment of specific risks across the enterprise. The executive responsible for a specific type of risk should provide assurance to the leadership team that he or she understands the risks to the enterprise. That person should also ascertain that there are appropriate controls in place to manage the risk, such that the exposure remains within the enterprise's risk appetite.

Corroborate important information with second sources, written or verbal, and maintain professional objectivity and skepticism. Even credible, historically reliable sources should be corroborated when the situation warrants it, for instance, when results are exceptionally good or bad or risks are high. Understand the reassurance function of internal auditors, and the resources available from external auditors, and deploy and employ those resources accordingly.

Be aware of the strengths and weaknesses of RCSAs and use data to corroborate the findings of such self-assessments. Boards should obtain assurance from management that appropriate risk mitigation is in place, and validate the reliability of management's reports through independent reassurance.

This chapter has described the importance of verifying sources and corroborating information. The next chapter describes the importance of establishing an acceptable margin of safety in the event your assessment of risk—or your information—turns out to be wrong.

Questions to Ask about Verification and Corroboration

- What is the source of the information?
- Is the source credible? How reliable has it been in the past?
- Who is performing the risk assessment?
- Is the assessment or report entirely subjective? If not, what data was used to reach these conclusions?
- Are other sources saying the same thing? Can those sources be corroborated?
- Has the assessment or report been tested independently?
- What is the level of confidence?
- What if we are wrong?

CHAPTER 10

Maintain a Margin of Safety

To distill the secret of sound investment into three words, we venture the following motto, Margin of Safety.
— Benjamin Graham, *The Intelligent Investor*[1]

Warren Buffett certainly agreed with his mentor, Ben Graham, an economist and investor and the originator of value investing. The credit crisis of 2008 starkly demonstrated the dangers of high leverage, low liquidity, and inadequate margins of safety. Banks, companies, and households that lacked cash or some other margin of safety found their survival threatened.

Overextended enterprises in a wide range of industries, and particularly in the finance, retail, real estate, restaurant, and automotive industries, lost money, market share, creditworthiness, and even their futures. Major and regional banks required government assistance, as did General Motors and Chrysler, both in an industry with significant overcapacity and both of which went into Chapter 11 reorganizations. Hundreds of thousands of households went into foreclosure.

In early 2009, as some major companies struggled to survive, the "super-major" oil companies, such as ExxonMobil and Chevron, faced the enviable task of figuring out how to capitalize on their strength. Analysts were expecting them to buy smaller, weaker competitors, as they did when oil prices nosedived in 1998 and Exxon acquired Mobil. After a year of record oil company profits in 2008, analysts believed ExxonMobil's large cash reserve positioned the company to make another large acquisition in the near future.

That's partly because despite a run-up in oil prices that peaked at around $147 in July 2008, ExxonMobil, unlike other oil companies, did not purchase assets at what it saw as inflated prices. The company also resisted short-term political pressures to increase production. As a result, ExxonMobil proved resilient and was well positioned to seize opportunities.

There are, of course, a number of ways to establish and maintain a margin of safety in business apart from having copious amounts of cash on hand. We will examine a number of them in this chapter and discuss the fatal flaw of failing to maintain a margin of safety, as well as the skills and tools required to address that flaw.

Voice of Experience

"Maintaining a margin of safety is certainly a good idea. Companies try, but it's very hard to actually accomplish. It ties back to assumptions. Companies can think they're building in a margin of safety, but plans can change dramatically, and assumptions they thought sounded reasonable at the time later proved not to be. At one company, because of the risk of a particular investment situation, we built in an extra-large margin of safety, but even that has been used up dramatically.

"Another company presented its latest estimates at each board meeting, including a base case and a worst case. At every single meeting for about six months or so, the previous worst case became the new base case, and still another worst case was presented. Clearly, things were changing much more quickly than the estimation process could handle."

—Denny Beresford, Director and Professor, J.M. Tull School of Accounting

Fatal Flaw #7: Failing to Maintain a Margin of Safety

As noted, executives and enterprises can become overconfident in their success, believe they are too smart or too big to fail, take the wrong risks, or become overly leveraged. While leaders must maintain confidence in their abilities, they must also grasp their limitations. Automobile racing legend Mario Andretti says, "Knowing your limits is a matter of survival. My career spanned eras where the mortality rate in our sport was just unbelievable because we didn't have the safety nets we do today. I would ask certain drivers, 'What's the matter with you? Why are you taking these risks? Sooner or later it's gonna bite you.'"[2]

Individuals and enterprises can be blinded to their limitations when they focus on a competitor and try to match them step-for-step or become involved in quick-fix schemes. Mountaineer Esther Colwill recalls that her journey just to get to Mount Elbrus in the western Caucasus was so arduous that she determined she would reach the peak on her first try. "I pushed too hard through some potentially dangerous weather, just because I really wanted to get it done, and I made some wrong decisions. I was so focused on that particular mountain that I didn't think about my values or why I was doing it." She calls herself "very lucky" to have reached the summit and come back safely.[3]

An incident from NASA's Apollo lunar landing program of the 1960s illustrates the value of maintaining a margin of safety. During the design and construction of the lunar lander, the weight of the craft continued to increase, yet development of the rockets that would deliver the lunar lander continued pretty much according to the original designs. That was possible thanks only to the experience and foresight of Wernher von Braun.

Early on, von Braun, the director of NASA's rocket development center, had met with the capsule team to determine how much the Apollo spacecraft was going to weigh. They told him that the final number, including all margins and "fudge-factors," was 75,000 pounds (34 tons). The Apollo spacecraft definitely would weigh no more than that.

Quietly and without confrontation, von Braun decided they were wrong. He had seen past weight estimates increase and did not believe that this one would be an exception. He told his rocket development team that the *real* requirement was 85,000 pounds (39 tons), which he later increased even more. At liftoff, the Apollo 11 spacecraft weighed roughly 100,000 pounds (45 tons) and it flew on schedule only because von Braun had been so cautious about the margin of safety.

When Lean Becomes Anorexic

Maintaining a margin of safety may seem at odds with certain notions of effective management. For instance, while disciplines of process improvement like lean manufacturing have much to offer, including certain tools that are of value in risk management, those disciplines can present risks of their own. For instance, lean manufacturing and other lean processes aim to remove all waste and all needless materials, activities, and resource demands from a process. The goal is to get the process to deliver what the internal or external customer wants and needs when they want and need it through just-in-time manufacturing, just-in-time inventory management, and related efforts.

Yet management must ask, at what point does "lean" become anorexic? How can we be efficient yet still maintain an acceptable margin of safety?

Lean techniques aim to improve profits by using less of everything—from human effort and manufacturing space to engineering and retooling time. These techniques certainly can lower costs by shortening setup times, improving workflows, reducing inventories, and smoothing production levels. But there's an inverse relationship between being lean and being resilient: The leaner the enterprise, the less resilient it is to disruptive shocks. Just-in-time processes have no materials or finished-goods inventory buffers. Each element of the supply chain depends on having the right part at the right place at the right time—and depends on every other element. This increases the interconnectedness that we identified as a cause of vulnerability in Chapter 7. A problem at any point in the system can profoundly affect the entire system.

By the same token, while sole-source suppliers may provide a cost advantage, they also create critical dependencies. If they fail to provide the right components at the right time and place, production can come to a full stop. Relationships can become complicated and wind up creating major delays in their own ways. For instance, some manufacturers have had to sue suppliers to obtain release of proprietary tooling in order to resume production.

Because sole-source suppliers can also pose intellectual property protection risks, manufacturers may decide to selectively distribute the intellectual property needed for component production and assembly. They may also act, legally and contractually, to protect their ownership of and access to that intellectual property to provide an adequate margin of safety. In fact, margins of safety are required in a huge range of business activities and situations and come in various forms.

Voice of Experience

"The key to successful investing in the long run is an adequate margin for safety. But when you're competing in a heated environment, it's hard to get that margin for safety, especially if a 'lend-or-lose-market-share' mentality is widespread."

—Howard Marks, Chairman, Oaktree Capital Management

Types of Margins of Safety

Margin of safety can be defined in various ways, depending on the situation and risk being considered and the expert doing the defining. In some cases it can be defined in numerical terms, but in others the calculation must be more intuitive.

- In management accounting, margin of safety is the amount by which actual or budgeted sales exceed the breakeven point. (The breakeven point is where sales revenue equals total production costs, including fixed and variable production costs.) After the breakeven point, fixed costs are covered and the company starts making money on every incremental unit it sells. The higher the revenue—or the lower the fixed or variable costs—the higher the margin of safety.
- In investing, the margin of safety is the difference between a stock's intrinsic value and its market price. Intrinsic value is calculated by discounting the future earnings of the company to their present value per share (there are various methods of doing so) and comparing that value to the share price. If the share price is lower and you are a value investor, you buy the stock, unless there are stocks you like with higher margins of safety. Graham's idea of margin of safety states that investors will never know everything about a given company and, even if all company-specific risks are accounted for, a multitude of economic factors could still trigger failure.
- From a medical perspective, margin of safety may describe the difference between a drug's effective dose and a lethal dose. Naturally, wider margins of safety are preferred, but in the absence of other treatment options or if the condition is critical, physicians and patients often accept narrower margins of safety.
- In mountain climbing, margin of safety considers the climbers' level of ability, the peak they are climbing, and the conditions of the climb. On Mount Everest, for example, the margin of safety, even for experienced climbers, is razor thin. Factors such as oxygen deprivation, avalanches, storms, and hidden crevasses are all beyond a climber's control, so factors that can be controlled, such as route, time of year, gear, and climber's skills, count for a lot.

In business, many decisions lend themselves to considerations and calculations regarding a required or desired margin of safety. Inventory levels and order quantities depend on transportation and carrying costs and on the potential for supply disruption. Investment decisions must factor in the costs of capital, interest rate movements, and currency fluctuations as well as competitors' likely strategies and responses. Data backup and IT system requirements must factor in costs, reliability, and the need for speedy recovery from potential disruptions.

Shaving margins of safety too thin and leaving little or no room for errors or for the unforeseen exposes the enterprise to risks with severe consequences, even to the point of jeopardizing its survival. One of the most common and recent cases of this was the out-of-balance leverage-to-liquidity positions many financial institutions adopted during the 2000s.

Indeed, failed companies in any industry often share the characteristics of high leverage and low liquidity.

Voice of Experience

"Really good departments or companies are very disciplined, and rarely do they ever take huge risks. It just doesn't make any sense to them. They wouldn't even go close to that. It's so amazing to me that the Wall Street firms were leveraged 30 or 40 to 1. It's just unbelievable.

"If we were taking risks, we made sure we had good reserves. The greater your reserves, the more you can be creative. There's a discipline in creating the margin of safety and yet still expanding the boundaries and creating a space for people to be highly creative, imaginative, and take risks, but they must be measured risks.

"The entrepreneurs I've seen rarely bet the farm unless they had no choice. But once they've got something up and going, and they are profitable, they take some off the table and put it aside. Then they can take a little bit bigger risk, and if they profit then they take some off the table. They're always ratcheting and never betting the whole farm."

— David Meuse, Director

Risk Intelligence Skill #7: Maintain a Margin of Safety

The skill of maintaining a margin of safety comes down to knowing your management's and enterprise's limits, working within them, and allowing for or creating a buffer for situations in which you might have gauged limits or the situation incorrectly or when a completely unexpected event occurs. Chapter 7 examined ways to identify key connections and critical dependencies, the equivalents to the human needs for air, water, and food. Chapter 8 discussed failure to anticipate failure.

The enterprise equivalent of air is cash. Illiquidity (lack of cash) and insolvency (inability to pay obligations as they become due) are precursors to bankruptcy. One dependency that many banks failed to fully consider and factor into their decisions in the 2000s was the consequence of their widespread shift from asset-based liquidity strategies (which maintain pools of marketable securities and other highly liquid assets to meet unexpected funding needs) to liability-based or off-balance sheet strategies (which rely at least partly on funding through securitization, brokered deposits, Internet deposits, borrowings, and purchased liabilities). Liability-based funding strategies increase liquidity risk. As the FDIC stated—or perhaps understated—in its Financial Institutions Letter dated August 26, 2008, "Some institutions have underestimated the difficulty of obtaining or retaining funding sources during times of financial stress."[4]

The FDIC added, "Funding decisions can be influenced by unplanned events. Such events include, but are not limited to, the inability to fund asset growth; difficulty renewing or replacing funding as it matures; the exercise of options by customers to withdraw deposits or to draw down lines of credit; legal or operational risks; the demise of a business line; and market disruptions." The letter went on to recommend that each institution create a contingency funding plan to:

- Define responsibilities, decision-making authority, and roles in problematic funding situations
- Assess possible liquidity events the institution might encounter
- Detail how management will monitor for liquidity events, typically through stress testing various scenarios with pro forma cash flows
- Assess the potential for triggering restrictions on the bank's access to brokered and high-cost deposits
- Identify and assess the adequacy of contingent funding sources
- Identify any backup facilities (lines of credit), the conditions and limitations to their use, and circumstances where the institution might use such facilities

The letter also said, "The FDIC expects institutions to use liquidity measurement tools that match their funds' management strategies and that provide a comprehensive view of an institution's liquidity risk. Risk limits should be approved by an institution's board of directors and should be consistent with the measurement tools used." In other words, the FDIC advised institutions to understand their limits, work within them, and plan for contingencies.

By the time of the FDIC's August 26, 2008, letter, many banks had already failed to adjust to the new liquidity risk profiles they had developed through the use of liability-based liquidity strategies. As a result, cash became king once again, as banks monitored their cash flows daily, if not hourly, to gauge their chances of survival. While such monitoring occurs during times of crisis, a similar process should always be in place to determine the margin of safety based on the liquidity of enterprise assets. The less liquid the assets, the greater the reserves ought to be. Pro forma cash flow analyses can help monitor cash flows under various scenarios and time horizons to identify vulnerabilities, so contingency plans can be activated as soon as they are needed.

Voice of Experience

"The healthiest looking companies are often the most likely to get into trouble. The dynamic usually unfolds this way. Delighted with the company's results, shareholders press management to grow by increasing production capacity, moving into new markets, or even making acquisitions, often backing up their demands with offers to fund more equity. At the same time, the company's banks are eager to lend to what they perceive as a sure credit risk."[5]

— David N. James, Crisis manager

The right time to determine margin of safety is when times are good. What margin of safety or level of cash flow is required to repay the debt the company is considering in its expansion plans? What are the underlying assumptions? What if they are wrong?

Complexity in the banking system and in the global economy demands excellent liquidity risk management. In June 2008, the Basel Committee on Banking Supervision (BCBS) issued a draft of its Principles for Sound Liquidity Risk Management and Supervision.[6] The draft expands on its earlier guidance from 2000 and especially on the following issues:

- Importance of establishing a liquidity risk tolerance
- Maintenance of adequate liquidity, including a cushion of liquid assets
- Necessity of allocating liquidity costs, benefits, and risks to all significant business activities
- Identification and measurement of the full range of liquidity risks, including contingent liquidity risks
- Design and use of severe stress test scenarios
- Need for a ready and robust contingency funding plan
- Management of intraday liquidity risk and collateral
- Public disclosure in promoting market discipline

While these principles were developed for banks, nonfinancial institutions may also benefit by determining margins of safety for each critical dependency by asking:

- How much buffer do we have?
- How much do we need?
- How much lead time do we have? How much do we need before our survival is threatened?
- When does lean become anorexic?

- How thinly stretched are our supply lines?
- How fast can they be disrupted or recovered?

Key factors and dependencies for all enterprises to consider include:

- Liquidity and cash flow requirements
- Inputs, such as lines of credit and long-term debt facilities
- Supply chain dependencies, such as sole-source suppliers
- People, including retention of critical competencies or succession planning for key executives
- Operations, equipment, facilities, and inventory buffers
- Information needs fulfilled by key systems
- Customers, who and how stable, resilient, and loyal they are

The question every enterprise needs to answer is, how close to the edge do we want to run? NASCAR drivers run entire races close to the edge. They are trained to do so, and conditions require it. But NASCAR drivers cannot race 100 percent of the time—only during actual events.

Case Example: Union Pacific Railroad

Union Pacific is one of America's leading transportation companies. Its principal operating company, Union Pacific Railroad (UPR), is the largest railroad in North America, covering 23 states across two-thirds of the United States.

During the economic expansion following the 2001 recession, the rate of growth for U.S. industrial production and GDP more than doubled from the second to the third quarter of 2003. UNP found it could not respond fast enough to the unprecedented increase in demand for rail transport. They had hit their theoretical capacity ceiling, which meant that any disruption had a prolonged, negative effect on operations and service throughout entire system.

Realizing they needed to get smarter about risks that affected the resilience of the railway network, Union Pacific challenged their basic assumptions about five critical resources:

1. People (engineers and crew)
2. Locomotives
3. Railcars
4. Line capacity
5. Terminal capacity

The senior vice president for strategic planning, Charley Eisele, notes that the company looked closely at the basic assumptions underlying demand for these resources and then asked, "What if we are wrong on the high or low side? What are our contingency plans in the event we are wrong? What if there is a sudden surge or unexpected decline in demand?"

Eisele says, "We have driven an awareness of risk in a very real and meaningful way down through the organization to the point where every assumption that is made with respect to all the critical planning processes that drive our operations are all now made in the context of, 'What if we're wrong?' or 'What can go wrong?'"

He cites the example of training locomotive engineers, one of the five critical resources. "We look at volume levels and the demand for engineers that those drive. Then we look at projected attrition and we decide on how much hiring we need to do and where. This in turn determines how full the training pipeline needs to be at each critical stage of training.

"Then we sit back and we say, 'What if we're wrong on the high side because we've overestimated business volumes or attrition, and we end up with more people than we need? Alternatively, what if we're wrong on the low side because demand or attrition exceeds our estimates?"

The next step, says Eisele, is to put a contingency plan in place for both. The high-side plan describes how the company can "work off a bubble in three to six months through attrition or by moving people around from areas of excess to areas of shortage." Eisele also notes that the company has specific contingency plans in place for a scenario that could result in a shortage of train crew personnel.

Eisele says the company looks at all five critical resources in the same way. "We look at locomotives, freight cars, terminal capacity, and mainline capacity. In all those instances we're always asking the same questions: What if we're wrong on the high side? What if we're wrong on the low side? What if we're right, but something else goes wrong?"

In this way, Union Pacific analyzes its needs in the face of various contingencies and maintains a margin of safety.

Leverage Can Create Losses

Maintaining a margin of safety represents a key component of resiliency and the organization's ability to "take a punch" without losing its footing. Therefore, maintaining and—up to a point—increasing the margin of safety enhances an enterprise's resiliency. We emphasize "up to a point" because there are costs associated with maintaining a margin of safety, and, as is always the case in risk intelligent enterprise management, the goal is to find the proper balance between costs and benefits, risk and reward.

For example, despite what anyone might think in the wake of the 2000s, leverage is not in itself a bad thing. It is simply an investing strategy for raising (as a lever does) the rate of return on an investment by borrowing funds and then investing them at a higher rate of return than the rate you pay on the borrowed funds. It tends to work extremely effectively, except when it doesn't. It doesn't work when the rate of return on the investment falls below the rate that must be paid on the borrowed funds. And then there's the fact that the principal must be repaid as well, which is where a lot of highly leveraged deals fall apart.

Leverage can also result from situations in which parties enter—for financial consideration, of course—a contract, such as a credit default swap, that obligates them to pay a certain sum to a certain party if a certain event, such as nonpayment of the interest or principal due on a bond, occurs and then they cannot make that payment. Writ large and multiplied across thousands of credit default swaps, that is how insurance giant AIG found itself in deep trouble in 2008, and required some $180 billion at last count in various forms of government assistance.

When an enterprise is leveraged highly enough and is placing "bets" on the directional movement of asset prices, insolvency and bankruptcy can be the risks that management and the board are choosing to incur. One must wonder whether such a choice represents a strategy for running a business or an outright gamble.

Indeed, as Michael Lewis entertainingly pointed out in his article "The End" in the November 2008 issue of now defunct Condé Naste *Portfolio*, it was the transformation of Wall Street investment banking firms from partnerships, in which the partners' capital was put at risk, into public companies with wider access to the capital markets and the ability to put shareholders' money at risk, that brought about "the end" of investment banking as we knew it.[7]

As it turned out, partners putting their own money at risk were wont to maintain a higher margin of safety than managers putting OPM (other people's money) at risk. Incidentally, the term OPM originated in the 1980s when it was applied to money raised in the high-yield-debt (aka "junk bond") market to finance leveraged buyouts, which were instrumental in the demise of Drexel Burnham Lambert.

So perhaps one of the best ways for an enterprise—and its board—to maintain a margin of safety is not a tool or a mechanism but rather the simple, sensible act of making sure that decision makers have some meaningful stake in the outcome. Compensation systems based on the pursuit of bonuses based on investing (or gambling, if that be the case) OPM do not encourage decision makers to maintain a margin of safety.

Margins Can Be Moved

A mountain climber wants to pack the absolute minimum amount of gear needed to make the ascent and descent safely. That minimum varies from person to person and from mountain to mountain and with the weather and other factors. Climbers must understand what gear provides an acceptable margin of safety. During the climb they constantly assess and reassess margins of safety as conditions—including their physical and mental states—change. They must understand their own limitations and recognize when it's time to pack it in and try another day.

Similarly, an enterprise must constantly evaluate and reassess margins of safety. Other than margins related to employee and public safety, enterprises will likely need to adjust margins of safety either up or down.

For instance, conserving cash and increasing liquidity during a downturn may mean reducing inventory buffers and incurring increased risk of stock-outs, deferring capital expenditures and preventive maintenance, renegotiating purchasing and supplier agreements, increasing the number of suppliers to reduce sole-source dependencies, and decreasing customer credit limits even at the risk of reducing sales. Strategies for retaining key personnel may require adjustment and provide opportunities to attract talent from stressed competitors. In an upturn, the emphasis in these positions will likely shift or even reverse.

Voice of Experience

"Limits are very difficult to quantify. Most people don't really know because they've never practiced pushing themselves to their limits. The only way to know yours is to frequently go there.

"From a physical perspective, part of your training is to understand, when you max out—when your body shuts down and you fall to the ground and black out. Knowing how long you can go without food and water and how your body responds to extreme cold and wind. The only way that you can learn those limits is by actually pushing to them in a controlled environment.

"I train in a controlled environment and push myself right to the edge. I've always got a buddy there to pour me into the car, or access to a taxi, or I can get on the gondola in ten minutes. When I'm in the field, I never push myself to that point because I always need a little reserve.

"I think of it like a little box I'm holding inside my chest that's going to give me another three hours of top-level performance. I never want to tap into that in the field when there is no margin. But how do I know where my limit is? How do I know that point? I have to go to it in a controlled place.

"In the Canadian Rockies there's a mountain called Sulfur Mountain. Above the pass is a gondola so we're five minutes away from the town of Banff. I'll get on that mountain, and I'll put a heavy load in my backpack.

I will grind myself up and down that trail for 12 hours to the point where I literally cannot stand up anymore and I have to abandon my pack in the trees and crawl down, and get to my hotel.

"I can do that there because I've got a safety network. I've got a buddy who's been riding his bike while I've been doing it. Then I can understand how my body behaves when it's about to come apart. I can understand what's going on psychologically and physiologically.

"I'm gaining experience with the crazy mind games that go on when you are reaching or exceeding your limits. You can be tempted with weird decision making, this sense that you don't have to walk, that you can just jump off a cliff and fly down the mountain. That's the crazy shit that goes on in your head. As a result of having been to my limit, I know now in the field when the stakes are higher, when the telltale signs come up.

"Knowing your limits is enormously important, but it takes a lot of exercise, in terms of planning and preparation to understand the experience."

—Jamie Clarke, mountaineer and entrepreneur

THE COSTS OF SAFETY MARGINS The most significant costs of maintaining a margin of safety are the out-of-pocket costs—for instance, the costs of carrying a large enough inventory of materials or finished goods so you don't run out during shortages or disruptions, the costs of insurance policies (an obvious and traditional way to buy safety), and the costs of maintaining certain relationships. Also included are opportunity costs, such as earnings foregone because money was tied up in inventory or used to pay for insurance and because the enterprise chose low-leverage rather than high-leverage strategies.

Given that risk intelligence aims to position an enterprise to take the right risks, we are not recommending that management seek a margin of safety in every area of the operation, but rather consciously consider the risks and rewards and then decide which areas demand what margins of safety. There are certain resources and capabilities that the company simply cannot afford to do without for any length of time and others that are less essential or addressable by means of substitute sources or capabilities.

For example, every hospital has a backup generator, but not every restaurant does. Every member bank of the Federal Reserve system has access to certain Federal Reserve lending facilities, but not every bank chooses to be a member. Few major organizations could survive long without their IT capabilities, but those in consumer financial services could not function for an hour without them—as major credit card companies such as American Express and MBNA, which *were* able to function after the 9/11 attack, found. These are only examples of the kinds of decisions that management and the board must make when it comes to deciding how wide a margin of safety the enterprise requires in a given area.

Opportunity costs—the initiatives and activities not pursued because money and other resources were dedicated to maintaining safety or because management chose to use less leverage—can be substantial. It can be galling to a management team to see the "hares" of the corporate world racking up huge profits by employing risky strategies while they, in "tortoise" fashion, stick with safer strategies.

However, as discussed in detail in the next two chapters, respectively, management must set time horizons that work for the enterprise and its stakeholders and, in keeping with the scope of its mission, take enough of the right risks to optimize shareholder value and the survival of the enterprise. So management and the board must always consider opportunity cost but also find a strategy and a risk appetite that works for the enterprise and its stakeholders.

That said, there are several tools available to enterprises that want to maintain a margin of safety.

Tools for Maintaining a Margin of Safety

The following tools, among others, will generally help an enterprise to establish and maintain a margin of safety in various business and financial situations:

- *Buffer levels of resources and assets.* Maintaining more of a resource than required for immediate operations represents a buffer, and you almost always want some buffer (despite what lean manufacturing and just-in-time inventory management have promulgated). How large a buffer you need will vary with the resource being considered and its relation to the risks in the current and future situation. As noted, although cash is always a good thing, sometimes inventories should be increased or decreased. Sometimes less leverage will produce better buffers and better longer-term results than more leverage.
- *Reserve capabilities.* Similar to buffer levels of resources are reserve capabilities. It's generally best, especially in turbulent times, for an organization not to be running flat-out at all times. Of course, excessive capacity holds its own risks. Yet access to additional in-house or outsourced capacity and to additional suppliers, borrowings, and expertise—as well as alternatives to too much surplus capacity (such as spinning off or winding down the business in question)—can enhance the margin of safety for an enterprise.

- *Insurance policies.* These are the traditional tools of risk management, in which an insurer prices risks on an actuarial and case-by-case basis and the insured purchases a certain amount of coverage. In the event of a loss, that coverage indemnifies the insured against the loss, replaces that which is lost, or otherwise makes the insured whole. We are not suggesting that the "margin of safety" provided by insurance should generate moral hazard but that traditional forms of insurance should always be considered as ways of achieving a margin of safety.
- *Contracts and hedging strategies.* Contracts and hedging are another form of insurance, but they offset or limit a loss rather than indemnify the insured against loss or damage (although indemnification—compensation paid by the insurer—also offsets or limits loss).

For instance, a hedge against inflation is an investment in an asset that will appreciate faster than the rate of inflation and thus offset value lost to inflation. An option to purchase a currency in a certain amount at a certain price by a certain date helps to offset the risk that the currency will rise to a level that presents unacceptable cost, risk, or loss.

When used properly for their intended purpose, a credit default swap and other swaps enable investors to exchange ("swap") various types of risks, such as inflation, credit, or foreign exchange risk, even over various time horizons, to suit their situations, needs, and risk appetites.

Voice of Experience

"Presupposed in my prescription for improving the margin of safety is that strong CEOs are willing to communicate candidly to investors, and that boards back them because the investor—particularly one with short-term horizons—may be misinformed or misaligned with the majority of stockholders.

"Consider an automotive company developing an electric car before its time. It's really a hedging strategy. At the time of the investment, there's no clear market for the car, but it would be a hedge against a downturn in the mainstream gasoline-fueled auto market. Whether you're Toyota or a financial institution hedging currencies, the cost of the hedge has to be sufficiently low—therefore, you either move into a market early or you wait and pay up once it has proven its value, or else you don't hedge. That's risk management."

—Jeff Cunningham, Chairman, CEO, and editorial director of *Directorship*

Better Safe than Extinct

In the end, a margin of safety will rarely cost an enterprise too dearly, and maintaining one is a skill in that most basic activity of risk management—asset preservation. Even when you believe you have a sure thing, you may not, as investors in Bernard Madoff's funds found. On that subject, in his book "Annals of Gullibility," professor Stephen Greenspan said of his own investment strategy, "The skeptical course of action would have been not to avoid a Madoff investment entirely, but to ensure that one maintained a sufficient safety net in the event (however low a probability it might have seemed) that Mr. Madoff turned out to be not the Messiah, but Satan. As I avoided drinking a full glass of Madoff Kool-Aid—I had invested 30 percent of my retirement savings in the fund—maybe I'm not as lacking in wisdom as I thought."[8]

How well an enterprise manages risk depends in part, and sometimes completely, on the margins of safety it builds into strategies, decisions, activities, and initiatives. The margin of safety should be established based on an understanding not only of the relevant risks but also of the relevant capabilities and limits. How resilient is the enterprise to adversity? How agile is it when opportunities arise?

In general, critical risks will require higher margins of safety, as will those involving health, safety, and the environment. With regard to these and all risks, the enterprise should periodically or continually evaluate and adjust margins of safety as circumstances demand.

Questions to Ask about Margin of Safety

- What margin of safety do we require for specific resources in given situations?
- What is our liquidity risk tolerance?
- What are the specific liquidity risk limits that are appropriate for our enterprise and our industry?
- How liquid are our assets?
- Have we tested that liquidity, for instance, with small test-sales of the supposedly liquid asset?
- What are our contingent liquidity risks (quantitatively and qualitatively)?
- How effective is the enterprise in maintaining discipline and control in order to stay within approved liquidity limits?

- How closely aligned is our treasury function with other risk management functions?
- Have we established early-warning indicators?
- How dynamic are our models for establishing and monitoring buffers?
- Can the underlying assumptions be readily changed to assess sensitivities?

CHAPTER 11

Set Your Enterprise Time Horizons

Our favorite holding period is forever.

—Warren Buffett

To thrive in the long term, enterprises must survive in the short term. These competing imperatives can give rise to difficult choices. When enterprises choose to maximize short-term gains in ways that jeopardize their chances of long-term survival, it's called short-termism. The *Economist* defines short-termism as "doing things that make you better off in the short-run but worse off in the end."[1] Many enterprises, particularly U.S. publicly held companies, have adopted short-termism as their primary decision-making and operating model, and many of them suffered for it in the 2000s, as did the U.S. and global economies.

The key question regarding short-termism in enterprises is, what can boards and senior executives do about it? This chapter answers that question. This chapter acknowledges that only the board, which represents the shareholders and sets executive compensation policies, and senior executives, who actually manage the enterprise, can change an organization's orientation from short term to long term. However, they must also bring the analysts and investors around to a longer-term way of thinking. This chapter first examines the nature and effects of short-termism and then presents ways of addressing it by refocusing the enterprise on the longer-term.

Fatal Flaw #8: Short-Termism

Instant gratification takes too long.
—Carrie Fisher, American actress and writer

Short-termism can damage long-term corporate growth, jeopardize an organization's survival, and produce other deleterious effects. When shareholders invest with an eye only on the short term, they may be less active in monitoring management or corporate governance. To the extent that they affect management's behavior, such shareholders tend to encourage only decisions that boost the near-term stock price.

For instance, the investment community has pressured management to meet short-term quarterly earnings expectations. That can cause enterprises to lose sight of strategic considerations and potentially to compromise their global competitiveness and their willingness and ability to invest in R&D, environmental controls, and other long-term needs.[2] If everyone—from analysts to investors to boards and executives—is interested only in quick hits, no one will stick around to see how it all turns out.

David Blood, former CEO of Goldman Sachs Asset Management, thinks that "short-termism" in the marketplace is "detrimental to economies, detrimental to value creation, detrimental to capital markets, and a bad investment strategy." He also says that it's common knowledge in corporate finance that "something on the order of 60 to 80 percent of the value of a business lies in its long-term cash flows. And if you're investing with a short-term horizon you're giving up the value creation of a business."[3] Favoring fast profits over performance down the road leads to an enterprise—and to an economy—that cannot create or sustain long-term growth.

Our current environment also encourages other forms of short-term thinking among executives, such as:

- Why consider long-term investments when the enterprise might be sold or taken over by a private equity firm in three years?
- Why invest in employees who might just leave anyway?
- Why invest in branding?
- Why invest in or build anything that can be outsourced?

With its emphasis on immediate profit rather than sustainability and growth, short-termism is a characteristic of our times. In the 1960s, investors held onto stocks for more than 10 years; today, it's closer to six months.[4]

At one time, mortgages were originated and perhaps resold once or twice rather than divided, repackaged into securities, and repeatedly resold. In the 2000s housing bubble, real estate, once a long-term investment, became instead a speculative asset to be "flipped." In addition to investors, it is analysts, fund managers, directors, and executives who bear responsibility for short-termism.

Voice of Experience

"The arrival of new investment vehicles, along with other changes in the capital markets, has created pressure on boards to focus on the short-term movement of stock prices. For example, activist hedge funds may urge boards to raise the stock price in the short term through a stock buyback, a special dividend, or the sale of an asset.

"Private equity may offer to buy out management and public shareholders at a premium over the current market price, with the hope of exiting their investment profitably, over time. Boards, in order to deter or improve such private equity 'deals,' may seek to boost share prices in the short term, often sacrificing long-term achievable strategies for the company.

"Moreover, these pressures may trigger the adoption of takeover defenses (poison pills, staggered boards) and pay plans (golden parachutes) designed for such 'just in case' events... The adoption of these plans by the board, with the interest of giving management time to fulfill its long-term plans, are often viewed by shareholders as an anti-shareholder stance.

"Such potential conflicts of interests among shareholder groups affect decision making by boards. Diverging interests and agendas raise questions about whether these changes in patterns of share ownership alter the board's fiduciary duty."[5]

— Ira Millstein, Senior Partner, Weil, Gotshal and Manges LLP

Downsides of Short-Termism

Short-termism creates numerous problems, with wide-ranging consequences, which include:

- Excessive risk taking for short-term paybacks, and aversion to risk taking for long-term returns
- Lack of continuity in leadership and strategic direction

- Emphasis on tactics rather than strategy, resulting in vulnerability to shifts in the environment
- Failure to invest in R&D and to develop product pipelines
- Loss of employees with essential knowledge and skills
- Failure to maintain and upgrade plant and equipment
- Lack of social responsibility, and failure to adopt sustainable technologies and to develop renewable resources
- High leverage, low liquidity, and increased vulnerability to bankruptcy

What makes short-termism so irresistible in the face of these consequences? Three major factors seem to contribute, each of which is explored in more detail here:

1. Undue pressures to meet short-term earnings expectations
2. Misalignment of executive compensation
3. Complacency toward long-term risks

UNDUE PRESSURES TO MEET SHORT-TERM EARNINGS EXPECTATIONS One CEO said, "A lot of shareholders only care what your stock's going to do in the next 15 minutes. For some, it's a week or a month, and for most, it's a quarter." He laments that too many enterprises focus on such investors rather than those who want long-term growth, and he's right. A March 2007 survey conducted by *CFO* magazine and Duke University revealed that 78 percent of chief financial officers would sacrifice long-term investments to meet quarterly earnings expectations.[6] This focus on quarterly expectations can lead to a fork in the road: Some executives may take the path of risk avoidance; others may try to "hit it out of the ballpark," and still others may engage in misleading or even fraudulent practices to boost short-term profits.

Voice of Experience

"A friend of mine invented something called First Call, which is the 'consensus number.' There's not a CEO, CFO, or member of senior management around who doesn't know what the consensus number is. Therefore, everything is geared to making your number. And making it, of course, isn't good enough. You've got to beat it by a penny or two, but not by not too much, though.

"What kind of way is that to run a company? The reality is, the investment community, the mutual funds, the hedge funds, all play the numbers game. And the game is making the number. Frankly, we ought to find a way to do away with the number. It was much healthier when there were eight, ten, twelve, fifteen different views, and somebody didn't just add them all up and divide it to get the number, which is what happens now.

"Unfortunately, the primary determinant of how most people value a company is by the share price. That's one of the reasons you find people going through contortions to maneuver the activities of the corporation for one single purpose—making the number. We need to address that issue. The current system is not working. It has become a sacred cow and it needs to be slaughtered."

—Jules Kroll, Director and founder of Kroll Inc.

In *Putting Investors First*, Scott Newquist maintains that corporate executives may spend more time managing earnings than building long-term value. He also points out that although it may start out well intentioned, "unchecked, those good intentions can become the proverbial paving stones to a far more sinister place."[7]

Meanwhile, the debate over whether or not to provide earnings guidance rages in boardrooms, but movement against doing so may be increasing. In late 2008 and early 2009, a number of companies, such as Intel, Microsoft, and General Electric, joined the ranks of Coca-Cola and McDonald's, among others, in ceasing to provide formal earnings guidance. If that trend continues, analysts' expectations will probably vary more widely as they will interpret circumstances differently.

Voice of Experience

"There's a push and pull among corporate decision makers about whether they're really entitled to think long term if they've got significant short-term profit opportunities that could benefit shareholders. The most extreme form of short-termism is managing to the quarter, which is really the wrong way to manage a company.

"That's why guidance can be such a bad thing. Failing to meet guidance can have disproportionately negative results on a company. There really isn't much upside. Even if companies make or sometimes exceed overall expectations, by missing guidance they can be deemed volatile or lose credibility with the market and the stock goes down."

—Lynn Krominga, Director

Resistance to these short-term pressures requires a strong alliance between directors and executives regarding long-term strategy and the associated risks. Once upon a time, investors put money into a business and counted on the dividends and long-term price appreciation. Now, many large corporations don't pay dividends, and investors try to make their money by buying and selling at a profit.

Warren Buffett knows how to say no to short-term pressures. He said no to the dot-com bubble and was widely criticized for "not getting it" and being too old-fashioned. He agreed and stated he wouldn't invest in a business model he didn't understand and he was proven right. While 2008 was Berkshire Hathaway's worst year since 1965, with almost a 10 percent decline, that significantly bested the S&P 500's decline of over 37 percent.

Whether, after the meltdown of the 2000s, investors will continue the pressure for short-term performance remains to be seen; however, we don't see such pressure easing in the near future. Part of the problem is that institutional, hedge fund, and individual investors don't necessarily have the same investment objectives. The lack of alignment among these key shareholders and other stakeholders contributes to short-termism.

Voice of Experience

"If there have been so many booms and busts, why don't companies see them coming? I think Alan Greenspan was right; maybe bubbles can't be avoided. To an extent, stakeholder activism has affected the ability of companies to discriminate between stakeholder objectives by forcing them to appease everyone and satisfying no one.

"Take the housing that boom started in the 1980s. Everyone was aware of it by the mid-'90s. It continued in every market, in every state, in every region for ten years. I think to conclude that it was a predictable boom/bust cycle is sophomoric. For ten years you would have bet wrong. Of course, the eleventh year proved you right. How does a rational person place odds on that bet?

"Take mortgage origination as an example. Loans were made and then sold to investors who were demanding the highest-yielding loans, specifically, subprime. Those were the loans those investors asked for, which we now refer to as toxic.

"Add to the mix politicians and community groups demanding loans so that home ownership would increase among high-risk groups, economically speaking. Originators could not simply reject the loan products; either they would be targeted by the activist groups, or they would suffer market share erosion. So there was plenty of pressure to make those kinds of loans from everywhere—marketplace, political, social.

"Then, finally, you have the rating agencies guaranteeing tranches of the loans as AAA! You tell me what CEO is going to turn to his people and say, 'We are out of this market because somewhere in the next eleven years it is going to fall apart.' You can't expect that. We're all so correlated."

—Jeff Cunningham, Chairman, CEO, and editorial director of *Directorship*

Misalignment of Executive Compensation

The discrepancy between executive compensation and corporate goals can be partially attributed to project life cycles that rarely map to fiscal calendars. Former U.S. Vice President Al Gore asked, "If you want management according to long-term horizons, but you incentivize on a quarterly basis, will you be surprised if performance is maximized on a quarterly basis, and if there is a tension between meeting targets and long-term objectives?"[8] Similarly, the *CFO* magazine/Duke University survey cited earlier also found, "An overwhelming majority—87.6 percent—of finance chiefs reported that enterprises have shortened the payoff horizons of their investment decisions to coincide with the shorter tenure of executives."[9]

Evidence of misaligned executive compensation can be found in the use of employee stock options. Originally intended to align to compensation with performance and shareholders' interests, employee stock options often fail to achieve that goal because their design assigns relatively heavy weight to short-term performance. In fact, the use of options is questionable if raising the stock price is the primary objective. Scott Newquist notes, "It makes little sense to provide incentive to change behavior to focus only on increasing stock price instead of long-term value, and options have been structured to do just that."[10]

COMPLACENCY TOWARD LONG-TERM RISKS Even when people know they face risks, they can become complacent, fail to be vigilant, and allow operational discipline to break down. Apart from obvious differences in extremity, another key difference between the risks encountered in the military, motor sports, and mountaineering, on the one hand, and in business organizations, on the other, is the time horizon. It's hard to get people excited about prevention unless failure has an immediate and serious consequence.

The less imminent the threat, the harder it is to mobilize people to deal with it. However, given that livelihoods, health benefits, retirement income, and billions of dollars are at stake, prevailing levels of corporate complacency seem unwarranted. In fact, it's usually not an overwhelming near-term threat that brings an enterprise down, but other longer-term risks that finally come to pass. Only a longer-term approach can address such risks.

Voice of Experience

"DuPont is 206 years old, so we very naturally have a long-term view and don't have to put a lot of emphasis on it internally. I think some organizations probably need to. I find other companies are very short-term and don't really know it."

—Charles O. Holliday Jr., Chairman and former CEO, DuPont

Risk Intelligence Skill #8: Set Your Enterprise Time Horizons

Addressing short-termism represents a major challenge because it involves a complex, tightly linked set of forces. The key stakeholders—directors, executives, employees, investors, analysts, and regulators—all need to be aligned, and that begins with the enterprise and its directors and executives. That means that the board and the CEO must agree on the long-term performance goals of the company and on the strategies for achieving them. Without that, how can the board and management better understand the risks of key decisions, consider the long-term implications, and thus make superior decisions?

Risk Intelligent Innovation

In February 2009, Intel announced plans to invest $7 billion in wafer fabrication for its next generation of 32 nanometer processors. The company did this when others were cutting back and its main rival, AMD, had announced plans to spin off its fabrication operations. (Despite a 90 percent drop in fourth-quarter net income, by the end of 2008, Intel had nearly $12 billion in cash and investments.)

That kind of long-term strategic decision making requires strong alignment with the board, particularly as it goes against the conventional trend toward cash conservation. Any long-term decision requires alignment between directors and executives on short- and long-term goals and on the strategies to achieve them. Such alignment enables them to make tough decisions about the future that demand the "kind of bold management initiatives that can only be undertaken in consultation with the board."[11]

In a similar vein, in fiscal 2009, Microsoft planned to spend about $9 billion on R&D. This might be a problem for investors with short-term horizons. However, Craig Mundie, Microsoft's chief research and strategy officer, publicly stated his belief that these R&D investments are critical to Microsoft's "long-term survivability . . . Particularly in times like this, the disparity between the relatively short-term view of the investment community and what the management view is of what it takes to have the company succeed for the long term stands in the starkest contrast."[12] Microsoft CEO Steve Ballmer cited RCA Corporation's decision to continue to invest in R&D during the Great Depression, which enabled the company to emerge as the dominant force in TV technology.[13]

Establish Requisite Time Horizons

The board, in concert with management, bears responsibility for setting appropriate strategic time horizons for the enterprise. In *The Requisite Organization*,[14] organizational psychologist Elliott Jaques laid out a framework for organizational structure that matched the time-spans and complexity of positions at various organizational levels to the capabilities of the employees who fill the positions. The time-span reflects the level of complexity and abstraction that someone at a given managerial level must understand and address.

According to Jaques, depending on the size of the enterprise, a CEO, for example, should have a time-span of 10 years to as long as 50 years—far from the current reality in most organizations. Explicit consideration of long-term consequences must be intrinsic to the decision-making process. Exhibit 11.1 depicts Jaques's views of the domains to be overseen, the position, the related stratum or strata (level or levels) in the organization, and their respective time-spans.

While Jaques describes a framework for a very tightly coupled organizational structure, he does not consider the benefits or challenges associated with the networked or loosely coupled enterprise of the 21st century. He

EXHIBIT 11.1 Time-Spans and Organizational Structure

Domain	Position	Stratum	Time-Spans
Corporate	CEO	VI & VII	10 to 20+ years
General	BU president	IV & V	2 to 10 years
Operations	Operational managers	II & III	3 months to 2 years
Direct hands-on work	Operators/clerks	I	1 day to 3 months

Source: Elliott Jaques, *The Requisite Organization* (Cason Hall & Co Publishers), 1989.

also makes no mention of the time-span of the board in his treatise (but he may have assumed this was addressed in the corporate stratum).

Nevertheless, the board clearly should be thinking long term and explicitly determining its time horizon and that of senior management—particularly when it comes to risk management. On that subject, Michael Raynor, in *The Strategy Paradox*, builds on Jaques's work to formulate the notion of requisite uncertainty to integrate risk and uncertainty into considerations of organizational levels and responsibilities.[15] Raynor points out that the higher the level of the position, the more the person in it must deal with uncertainty as well as with longer time horizons and greater complexity.

Of course, the three are bound up together—longer time horizons clearly create greater uncertainty and risk, and greater complexity. Indeed, the "strategy paradox" centers on the need for management to commit to a course of action while remaining flexible enough to address uncertainty. As Raynor puts it, "under requisite uncertainty, a well-functioning hierarchy is *differentiated* by the degree of *strategic* uncertainty addressed at each level and *integrated* through a cascading series of strategic commitments as those uncertainties are resolved." [Raynor's italics]

We'll look more deeply into these concepts in Part III, but we wanted to raise them at this point because they relate to setting time horizons and to the levels at which risk is managed. Everyone at every level, from directors contemplating an acquisition to a customer service rep trying to solve an angry customer's problem, manages uncertainty and risk. But it is up to the board (and to senior management) to manage strategic uncertainty, which Raynor defines as uncertainty that "has implications for the basic elements of how a company creates and captures value." Strategic uncertainty increases as the time horizon lengthens.

The time horizons relevant to lower levels should also be integrated, or "rolled up," into those of higher levels. For example, the CEO of a food company should be concerned that in day-to-day operations, the food chain is not contaminated and that policies and procedures prevent contamination. The board of that company should be concerned that policies and procedures reflect any applicable regulations, such as food purity or content laws. The board does not actually manage food-borne risks, but it is responsible for knowing that capable people, processes, and systems are in place to do so.

The board should focus on longer-term, strategic risks—especially the risks of the strategy itself. Responsibility for long-term strategies and risks—and all strategies and risks—starts with the board and its committees. The board, through management, delegates responsibility and authority for implementing the strategies and managing the risks. Each enterprise must determine its time horizons for various positions at various organizational levels. They also must establish criteria to ensure that issues with potentially strategic consequences are quickly escalated up the chain of command.

When an issue, decision, or concern is escalated, it should be addressed at the lowest level at which it can be effectively addressed. This is, of course, a basic tenet of delegation—that decisions and tasks should be delegated to the lowest level of the organization at which they can be effectively completed (or to a machine, where appropriate).

However, in our experience the delegation—and communication—of issues, decisions, and concerns related to risks is less well developed than it is for the delegation of operating decisions, tasks, and concerns. The risk intelligent enterprise understands this to be a problem and addresses it.

Aligning the Enterprise

In general, directors and executives can improve their management of risk—and management in general—by thinking of the longer-term consequences of their decisions, especially regarding potential unintended consequences. They should ask: What are the requisite horizons we need to consider? Who is specifically charged with keeping these horizons in mind? What is the optimum strategy for long-term success under a variety of alternative futures?

But what good does "thinking long term" do unless the board and the enterprise act on that thinking? How can the board and enterprise translate thought into action?

That requires alignment among various stakeholders, which calls first for internal alignment. An enterprise that achieves internal alignment in this regard positions itself to resist undue short-term pressures and to maintain reasonable, sustainable, long-term performance expectations. Such alignment also helps the organization improve communication and increase transparency among key stakeholder groups, especially investors, analysts, and regulators.

To initiate the alignment process, directors and executives can develop policies and communications that:

- Define enterprise criteria for success and failure in ways that consider long-term as well as near-term horizons
- Define how value is created and how it can be destroyed
- Describe the strategy for value creation and asset and capital preservation
- Identify metrics to evaluate and reward financial *and* nonfinancial performance
- Establish requisite time horizons for various types of decisions as part of its monitoring, review, and approval processes
- Identify the unintended consequences of short-term decision making
- Define and employ financial and nonfinancial performance measures

- Establish the relative costs of action, inaction, failure, and risk management

Such policies should provide meaningful guidance and disclosure affecting long-term valuation and include criteria for evaluating the business model based on longevity and sustainability, financial and nonfinancial performance, and risk management capabilities. Notice that these policies concern themselves with broader and more basic issues than do management's efforts to provide analysts and investors with the "earnings guidance" that has contributed to short-termism.

Voice of Experience

"The board needs to have structured time to deliberate its long-term strategy, which ought to, in turn, drive a set of financial statements. It ought to include a discussion about the optimal capital strategy for the company.

"From that discussion should emerge an idealized model for what we might like the share price to be and the return for everybody involved. If you don't do that, it's going to be very hard to understand the economic value of the stock options and the restricted stock that you're giving to board members and management. All of that needs to be addressed on a regular basis in an integrated way. An excessively short-term orientation is a waste of everybody's time."

—David Nierenberg, Director

THE CASE AGAINST EARNINGS GUIDANCE   Demand for changes on earnings guidance is coming from pension funds, the U.S. Chamber of Commerce, the Business Roundtable Institute for Corporate Ethics, and from other quarters. The Aspen Institute, a leadership think tank, completed a four-year study in 2007 and as a result issued the Aspen Principles.[16]

These principles begin by urging enterprise leaders to define metrics of value creation that aim "to maximize future value (even at the expense of lower near-term earnings) and to provide the investment community and other key stakeholders the information they need to make better decisions about long-term value." Those principles also call upon boards and executives to:

- Discontinue the practice of providing quarterly earnings guidance to analysts

- Focus corporate-investor communication on long-term metrics
- Align company and investor compensation policies with long-term metrics
- Have stock-related rewards for senior executives extend beyond their tenure
- Ban senior executives from hedging the risk of long-term oriented stock options
- Recoup (via "clawbacks") compensation that later proves to have been undeserved[17]

Whether or not one agrees with these recommendations, concern continued to mount amid regulatory reforms following public outrage over executive compensation. The enterprise, therefore, should view its guidance policy as a key governance issue, and one that will strongly affect the decisions and behaviors of senior executives. That said, the overall trend remains uncertain. A 2004 National Investor Relations Institute (NIRI) study found that companies providing earnings guidance had declined from 77 to 71 percent. The number of companies providing guidance decreased after Sarbanes-Oxley, but that trend may be reversing itself.

A 2007 NIRI survey found that about two-thirds of companies were providing earnings guidance—well above the 51 percent that did so in 2006. About 70 percent were providing broader financial guidance, and about 60 percent provided nonfinancial guidance. A study of Chartered Financial Analysts Institute (CFAI) members concurrently reported that the majority of its respondents supported yearly, rather than quarterly, earnings guidance.

Potential loss of focus on long-term performance is the main reason that NIRI (74 percent) and CFAI (91 percent) members choose not to provide guidance. Of those who provided financial guidance (excluding earnings), the majority did so annually and, in some cases, for even longer horizons.

Analysts receiving guidance preferred that companies also provide it on a broad range of financial measures, especially revenue and capital expenditures. In terms of nonfinancial metrics, information about trends that may affect the company and the industry sector were most valued.[18]

Voice of Experience

"Communication on nonfinancial metrics is one of the things that sometimes gets lost because it's not as quantifiable and maybe not as familiar to investors as compensation structure, metrics, and earnings guidance. It gets dropped a lot between boards, management, and investors because

(Continued)

(*Continued*)

there's too much fear about stepping over the line with Regulation FD."[19] [*Note:* Introduced in 2000, Regulation FD (Fair Disclosure) requires that public companies must disclose material information to all investors at the same time. More information and more transparency is to be encouraged, as long as it is shared with everyone equally.]

"Too many companies don't listen to their investors and the people who are following them. Regulation FD is a rationale that companies use to be quiet about long-term strategy, their key performance indicators, and environmental, social, and governance issues because those metrics can be fuzzy and they don't want to get in trouble. They feel they have had to run everything by their lawyers before they talk about anything in a long-term context that isn't especially quantifiable, and they don't want to mention potential things that may be cited down the road as inaccurate statements or misrepresentations.

"We'd like to see more discussion and communication on both short-term and longer-term strategy issues so we can get an understanding of a company's long-term goals, their strategies, and how incentives are being aligned. We just don't see enough of that."[20]

— Matt Orsagh, Senior Policy Analyst, CFA Institute

ALIGNING INSTITUTIONAL INVESTORS   Many institutional investors have been monitoring management more closely than ever and demanding greater accountability, asserting shareholders' rights, and seeking higher ethical standards. Some are considering longer-term horizons and encouraging more balanced compensation schemes. They are also paying attention to the international convergence of accounting principles, corporate reporting based on true value-drivers, and the linkage between corporate social responsibility and share prices.

While aligning the needs of individual investors is beyond the ability of any enterprise, institutional investment funds certainly have both the opportunity and a critical role to play in aligning their own interests. Although many issues remain the subject of heated debate, directors and officers of institutional investment funds should evaluate their policy positions on the following list of starter questions:

- Is the compensation system for fund managers too focused on the short term?
- Is there adequate transparency and communication on the part of institutional investors?
- Does the composition and skills of pension fund boards of trustees match their responsibility to oversee investment strategies?

- Within each institutional investor, is there an effective dialogue between those concerned about governance and those who manage funds?
- Are governance policies consistent with a long-term investment outlook and fund management approach?
- Given limited resources, how much time and energy can be devoted to monitoring governance and risk management practices of portfolio companies?

Enterprise leaders should communicate with institutional investors regarding their long-term strategic directions and garner support and tolerance of short-term price fluctuations. Because the investment objectives and horizons of shareholders and institutional investors can differ widely, companies should understand the motives of activist hedge funds and other activist interests, as well as the motives of more traditional investors and speculators in their stock.

Voice of Experience

"There are issues and risks that are short term, and then there are issues and risks that are longer term. A company needs to define a risk horizon and a benefit horizon. We've done this now for several years.

"We present our five-year plan to investors and say, 'These are the very specific goals that we expect to meet, these are the business drivers, and here are the reasons why we currently believe we can meet our long-range goals.' And we regularly review and update our plan.

"This gives us a road map and the drivers for long-term success. The alternative is to manage just for the short term, have a great year, and destroy the company's future. We are not going to do that."

—Eric Krasnoff, Chairman and CEO, Pall Corporation

If the enterprise can align itself internally, it's in a much stronger position to say no to undue short-term pressures and to maintain reasonable, long-term performance expectations. Such alignment helps improve communication and meaningful disclosure with key stakeholder groups, especially investors, analysts, and regulators.

To initiate the alignment process, directors and officers can develop a guidance policy that:

- Defines enterprise criteria for success and failure
- Defines how value is created and how it can be destroyed
- Describes the strategy for value creation and capital preservation

- Identifies the most appropriate metrics to evaluate and reward both financial and nonfinancial performance (the matter of executive compensation is discussed further in Chapter 15, "Risk Intelligent Governance")
- Establishes requisite time horizons for various types of enterprise decisions as part of the review, approval, and monitoring of the long-term course of action
- Pays increased attention to the unintended consequences of short-term decision making
- Determines the key milestones (financial and nonfinancial) and assesses performance based on them
- Establishes the relative costs of action/inaction, failure, and risk management (see Chapter 14, "Risk Intelligence Is Free," for more)

Such a policy should aim to provide meaningful guidance and disclosure affecting long-term valuation and including criteria for evaluating the quality and viability of a business model. Those criteria should include, for example, longevity and sustainability, key financial and nonfinancial metrics, and, not least, risk management capabilities.

Corporate Social Responsibility and Risk Intelligence

The divide between short-termism and long-term sustainability becomes apparent when one considers issues of corporate social responsibility and the environment. In addition to undermining long-term capital investments, short-term views of corporate responsibility and profit maximization may also result in waste, pollution, depletion of resources, and destruction of wildlife habitat. In contrast, optimization takes a long-term, environmentally responsible, and sustainable approach.

Corporate social responsibility and sustainability go by a number of terms—enterprise sustainability, environmentally friendly, eco-friendly, green policies, greening, conservation, and good corporate citizenship. While the terms vary, they all generally refer to activities and approaches that strategically manage the social, environmental, and ethical risks and opportunities of business. In general, they make good business sense.

In October 2005, Lee Scott, Walmart's CEO, announced the company's goal to be a "good steward for the environment" by reducing waste and greenhouse gases and by improving energy efficiency. Acknowledging that Walmart had been criticized for, among other things, its size, Scott said, "To better understand our critics and Walmart's impact on the world and society, we spent a year meeting with and listening to customers, associates, citizen groups, government leaders, non-profit and non-government organizations, and other concerned individuals. You might be surprised about what we heard. Many of these individuals and groups see things differently than we do, but they also have ideas. In fact many of our most vocal critics do not want us to stop doing business, but they feel business needs to change, not just our company, but all companies."[21]

Scott described how the appreciation that Walmart received for its response in the aftermath of Katrina caused the company to consider the potential contribution it could make. He announced that Walmart's "environmental goals are simple and straightforward: to be supplied 100 percent by renewable energy, to create zero waste, and to sell products that sustain our natural resources and the environment."[22] Scott sees being a good environmental steward as compatible with being an efficient and profitable business.

His announcement produced mixed reactions, with some dismissing it as pure public relations. Yet Walmart has since informed its suppliers it would begin to evaluate them on the environmental sustainability of their packaging. This has driven more innovation, reduced waste, and lowered shipping costs. Walmart's objective is to reduce packaging by 5 percent from 2006 to 2013.

Optimizing versus Maximizing

The classic goal of executive management has been typically described as "to maximize long-term shareholder value." That definition captures the notion of creating *and* sustaining value for the owners of the enterprise and precludes sacrificing long-term value for short-term gain. However, that goal has been largely (though not completely) elbowed aside by short-termism in today's environment. Indeed, the goal itself may be confusing or in need of updating.

We propose that a more realistic and useful goal may be to optimize, not maximize, value. Optimization is a process of determining the trade-offs that need to be made to ensure both the short- and long-term survival and success of the enterprise. From the practical standpoint, maximization tends to be viewed as a short-term strategy, as reflected in compensation systems. Maximization—more, bigger, faster, sooner—can encourage unethical or socially irresponsible behavior and ultimately unsustainable strategies, such as extracting the greatest possible profit from an operation with little thought for safety or the environment. Yet in certain cases, such as when there is a takeover bid, the courts have ruled that the board must maximize value for the shareholders.

Why optimize? For starters, investors have become increasingly interested in companies' corporate social responsibility factors as a means of managing risk. A *Financial Times* article of November 3, 2008, titled "Investing in Doing Good Can Be Good Risk Management," notes that

"Investing the old-fashioned way, just by looking at a company's financial statements and deciding how the current share price relates to the fair value of the stock, is so last year."

The article continues, "The most hard-headed commercially minded asset managers are talking about a new form of investment process, including a checklist more usually associated with Greenpeace or Oxfam. Climate change, corporate responsibility, human rights—all these come under the banner of sustainable investment, and a broad range of industry participants have simultaneously come to the conclusion this is the way forward... In the current environment, where everything seems terrifyingly unpredictable, anything that helps pin down what is going on is welcome."[23]

If enterprises and the economy are founded on long-term growth and stability, and the private sector is to continue to generate wealth as only the private sector can, short-termism cannot continue. To create and sustain value, investment strategies and corporate initiatives must embody long-term horizons, planning, and execution.

Voice of Experience

"A private company builds itself for future markets. A public company does not have that luxury generally, especially against a quarterly earnings bar to beat, and so it builds for the current market. Short-termism is a product of that. I don't know that it's anyone's fault. I do know that if everyone thinks short term but lends and invests long, you end up with a credit crisis. If a public company CEO thinks long term and has the backing of the board, then you have a chance of success. We also refer to that as Warren Buffett."

—Jeff Cunningham, Chairman, CEO, and editorial director of *Directorship*

Looking Ahead

An enterprise cannot generate long-term value by compensating executives and employees and focusing investors primarily on short-term strategies and results. Without an understanding of and alignment around long-term goals and strategies, an enterprise will find itself to be unsustainable (at least without government assistance). The board holds the primary responsibility for thinking long term and compensating senior management accordingly.

Yet it is simplistic as well as ineffective simply to admonish directors and executives to "just say no" to short-termism. Ultimately, the market and investors will speak most forcefully. In the meantime, a review of investor relations and communications and a policy of greater engagement with key stakeholders and closer alignment of goals and strategies would benefit most enterprises. That review, along with compensation policies focused on long-term performance metrics, represent excellent first steps toward setting more useful time horizons.

Questions to Ask about Setting Enterprise Time Horizons

- What requisite horizons should we consider? Who is charged with focusing on these horizons from the strategic and operational stand-points?
- What time horizon should we use to evaluate various decisions and their impact?
- Which financial and nonfinancial measures should we use to gauge success or failure? Over what periods of time?
- What kind of decisions and behavior will our compensation scheme drive?
- Are those decisions and behaviors aligned with the long-term goals of the enterprise?
- Will the proposed R&D budget be sufficient to drive innovation?
- What is the optimum strategy for long-term success under various future scenarios?
- What might be the unintended long-term consequences of major decisions?
- What are the signals of the unintended consequences? How will these signals be detected and escalated?
- What kind of earnings guidance, if any, should we provide to investors and analysts? What will be the effects of providing, or not providing, it?

CHAPTER 12

Take Enough of the Right Risks

There are risks and costs to a program of action. But they are far less than the long-range risks and costs of comfortable inaction.
— John F. Kennedy[1]

C apitalism depends on calculated risk taking for reward, both as its animating principle and as its mechanism for achieving economic growth. Sometimes risk-taking becomes excessive, as does risk aversion, in ways that mimic capitalist economies' periodic swings between expansion and recession. In fact, risk taking and risk aversion can exhibit the same pendulum-like swings that characterize the business cycle. In the business cycle, expansion can lead to boom and then to bust, rather than to a gentle contraction or a "soft landing."

Similarly, risk-taking behavior can overreach, create a bubble that bursts, and conditions that then lead to risk aversion. The recession of 2008–09 was doubtlessly ignited, exacerbated, and lengthened by the housing bubble, subprime lending, financial innovation, and excessive risk taking. And this much we all know: Risk taking and risk aversion will continue their uneasy dance in developed and emerging economies and within enterprises and individuals.

This chapter examines risk aversion and, more to the point, risk taking for reward. As noted in Chapter 3, such risk taking is a core principle of risk intelligence and of value creation. Conventional risk management typically emphasizes asset preservation and risk avoidance, which is important in risk intelligence as well. Yet risk intelligence always recognizes that risk taking and value creation are inseparable. Thus, taking risks intelligently is the focus of this chapter.

We begin with a discussion of risk taking for reward and of the fatal flaw of failing to do so—that is, of indiscriminate risk aversion. We then move to the skill of daring to take enough of the right risks, and to a few tools that are useful in identifying such risks.

This chapter also touches on the matter of risk appetite, the enterprise's overall and multilevel posture toward risk. That appetite both derives from and accommodates the forces favoring risk-taking and risk aversion within the organization. Risk appetite varies from enterprise to enterprise and can vary over time within a given enterprise. For instance, as many enterprises grow larger, they become more risk averse. By the same token, even a large company may find that at times it must "bet the farm" on a strategy or decision. However, if you're always betting the farm, sooner or later you will lose your farm.

Voice of Experience

"Individuals, financial institutions, and companies of every type have become excessively risk averse. Everyone is hoarding cash to prevent a liquidity crisis. Now we find ourselves in a very interesting situation where the objective of avoiding serious financial risk putting the company in peril is actually causing it to happen.

"This country was the envy of the world economically because of our willingness to take calculated or measured risks. Clearly we have to be intelligent about risk, but we must also still be willing to take risk.

"We must be very, very careful that we don't so overburden the system with risk management that we make the entire system risk averse and susceptible to failure. We have to get focused again on competitiveness, otherwise we're going to risk manage our way right out of business completely."

—Tom Donohue, CEO, U.S. Chamber of Commerce

Fatal Flaw #9: Failure to Take Enough of the Right Risks

Indiscriminate risk aversion can just as surely lead to downfall as can indiscriminate risk taking. The real issue to consider is the true nature of the risk in question and whether it has potential for reward that is at least commensurate with the potential for loss. Also, risk aversion makes complete sense under certain circumstances. For instance, unsafe business practices, and of course unethical and fraudulent behavior, must be avoided on the grounds of the potential for loss as well as moral grounds. But as a strategic option and as business policy, risk aversion will almost inevitably generate suboptimal growth, competitive disadvantage, and eventual extinction.

A respected board member of a Fortune 100 technology enterprise said, "Our biggest risk is failure to innovate. Every time we come up with a new idea, the 'risk antibodies' come out and kill it." That director is not alone. In many organizations, risk aversion flourishes and as a result companies fail to adopt new technologies quickly enough, fail to protect their markets from upstarts, and fail to meet customers' needs proactively. Of course, many companies take too much of the wrong risks, expanding too quickly, leveraging themselves too highly, overextending themselves in various initiatives, and failing to maintain a margin of safety.

Some observers fear that the excesses of the 2000s and government bailouts and perhaps new regulatory regimes will increase risk aversion. Others believe that human nature and well-established cycles of market behavior guarantee a return to unbridled risk taking. (After a savings and loan crisis in the 1980s, a dot-com bubble in the 1990s, and a housing bubble in the 2000s, who can blame them?)

Risk aversion can be a legitimate defensive position, especially in conditions of extraordinary uncertainty. However, if risk aversion becomes indiscriminate and hampers the ability to innovate and seize opportunity, the enterprise will surely be at risk. Gaining competitive advantage demands active risk management, not just risk avoidance, as the discussion of rewarded and unrewarded risk in Chapter 3 explained.

In the oil industry in 2009, for example, many leading exploration and production enterprises bought back stock and reduced their debt. This strategy bucks the tradition of such firms of investing in their own operations and developing new capacity and reserves. It also leaves the risk, work, and potential rewards of tapping new oil fields to smaller competitors.

Voice of Experience

"Some companies have defined and disciplined their risk management to such an extent that they have a zero-tolerance risk policy. That can scare the entrepreneurial spirit right out of people in the belief that there's no longer any reward for taking even an intelligent risk.

"As a person who still has a large part of my entrepreneurial DNA intact, I like people with entrepreneurial instinct. So long as it's intelligent, and not cowboy-ish or bravado, risk is a wonderful thing for enhancing profit.

(Continued)

(*Continued*)

"I worry about those businesses that have screwed it down so tight and so formulaically that it's almost a career nonstarter for somebody to come up with an idea that pushes the risk envelope. You're not breeding the right sort of future leadership by doing that."

—Richard Slater, Director

The central question does not hinge on whether to adopt a risk-taking or risk-averse strategy, but on which specific risks are worth taking and which the enterprise should be averse toward. In other words, all risks are not created equal.

Is It Worth the Risk?

One basic calculation that must accompany any decision is that of whether the potential size of the reward exceeds the potential costs and the potential for loss. This brings us back to the concepts of unrewarded and rewarded risks.

Regarding unrewarded risk, risk aversion makes sense as a matter of policy. It only stands to reason that a risk that holds no ethical reward—or, as is often the case, the risk of actual punishment in the form of fines, censure, judgments, and even jail terms, in addition to a ruined reputation—is not worth incurring. Other unrewarded risks may come in less explicit guises. Operations, reporting, and compliance failures, for example, have no potential for reward and present only a downside. They should be avoided to prevent loss or harm. However, an enterprise must dedicate resources to minimizing risks in operations, reporting, and compliance that could be put elsewhere. So even here the enterprise faces trade-offs.

The risk of poor quality presents an interesting example. Even enterprises dedicated to "zero defects" see that as something of an ideal—a target, but not one that is necessarily worth the costs of achieving. (Yet one story, perhaps apocryphal, from quality improvement lore says that some years ago a Japanese supplier of a component to a U.S. company had to intentionally create defects in three out of every 10,000 units because that was the level of quality that the U.S. company had specified.)

The cost of poor quality can actually be calculated for specific defects, in terms of warranty claims, customer service interactions, replacement units, replacement parts, service calls, and even sales lost through bad word of mouth. These defects can be prioritized for elimination in terms of those costs (and the costs of eliminating them).

Perhaps not every operational defect should be corrected, only those that create enough costs and unrewarded risks for the company. What is enough? That is up to management to decide on a cost-benefit basis.

The main message again is that these decisions regarding unrewarded risks, like all decisions about risk, should be made explicitly. In any event, revenue growth comes from rewarded risks—the pursuit of value in innovating new processes, products, and services and in developing new markets. Some enterprises simply do not take enough of these kinds of risks. An enterprise cannot shrink its way to greatness.

The (Human) Nature of Risk Aversion

Why are some people more risk averse than others? Some of the difference appears to be cultural—both organizational and national. For example, an international study of consumers found that U.S. shoppers are the most open-minded and French shoppers the most risk-averse, while Germany accounted for the most committed information seekers.[2] Most of the reasons for risk aversion come down to specific individuals and their experiences and psychological makeup, and to the specific enterprise and situation in which they find themselves—and even to one's definition of risk aversion.

For instance, rational fear is not risk aversion. Mountain climber Jamie Clarke says, "Fear is a good thing. It should help keep things in perspective. No fear, and you're a danger to yourself and others. Too much fear, and you can become paralyzed. Fear is good—it's a warning, a reminder that what you are doing is dangerous and it keeps you alert. You need to understand your limitations and recognize your comfort zone. You need to stay in your comfort zone but increase your comfort zone by conditioning and preparation."[3]

CAUSES AND CONSEQUENCES OF RISK AVERSION Officers and executives become risk averse for many reasons, including:

- Focusing on short-term goals, such as quarterly earnings
- Setting the bar low enough to ensure that goals are met
- Avoiding being associated with a failure
- Fearing they'll be seen as "different" or not fitting into the culture
- Avoiding perceived or real punishment for taking risks

Risk aversion can have wide-ranging consequences. A risk-averse culture inhibits innovation, initiative, and even the exercise of responsibility. Risk aversion can foster mediocrity as well as a tendency to hide actual failures and to "game" the system. Instances of the latter include sales managers and reps always setting sales goals low enough to be achieved and managers overbudgeting expenses in order to come in below budgeted costs.

Also, people who want to take risks and innovate will avoid or leave a risk-averse organization. Risk aversion erodes trust within the enterprise. If people are punished for good-faith efforts and innovations that resulted in short-term failure, others may become much less likely to put their jobs and futures on the line. Lack of trust contributes to poor upward communication of problems and risks. However, risk aversion in an enterprise can be addressed.

Risk Intelligence Skill #9: Taking Enough of the Right Risks

An overly risk-averse enterprise will promote risk minimization—an approach associated with conventional risk management. Such enterprises tend to be bypassed or driven out of business by more aggressive competitors. Newer, smaller enterprises are typically far less risk averse, far more prone to take risks than larger, well-established ones.

The smaller companies have several advantages in this arena. First, they have far less to lose by virtually every measure—sales, profits, customers, even reputation and brand equity—compared with their larger brethren. Second, they are not hampered by a record of success and therefore don't automatically continue to do what made them successful in the first place. Third, they often tend to be managed and owned by young people, and the young tend to be more prone to take risks. Finally, these companies are often in business by virtue of their innovativeness and new markets. Thus they almost have to "make it up as they go along" and must take risks because they actually have no other choice.

In the 1970s and early 1980s, to ask an IBM to act like an Apple would have been absurd. Yet Digital Equipment Corporation (DEC), the company that pioneered the minicomputer to resounding success, stopped making computers smaller and left that task to the Apples and Compaqs of the world. Couldn't DEC have acted like an Apple? (The remnants of DEC were acquired by Compaq in 1998, which was acquired by Hewlett-Packard in 2002.) Why did DEC stop taking risks when it once challenged IBM? See the previous paragraph for the answer—it became a large, established, successful company.

However, Apple's continual innovation, led by Steve Jobs, still exemplifies the harnessing of creative destruction. From its early success and its 1980 IPO, Apple's share of the operating systems market began to fall until it reached about 5 percent. This eventually led to Jobs' departure in 1985. He returned to Apple in 1997, fresh from his success with Pixar, and he began to drop products such as Newton, Cyberdog, and Opendoc. Rather than launch a frontal attack on Microsoft, Apple "bet the farm" on its skills in graphics and design and targeted what it saw as an undefended space: consumer electronics and music distribution.

In 1997, Apple's market value was $1.7 billion. Apple introduced the iPod in 2001, and the iTunes music store in 2003. By 2006, one billion songs had sold on iTunes, and Apple's market value had grown to $72.9 billion. When the iPhone was announced in January 2007, Apple's market value had grown to $173 billion.[4] Apple makes its own products obsolete, moving, for example, from the iPod mini to the iPod nano in only 11 months.

To remain competitive, a company must take the right risks. This is neither an exercise in risk minimization nor risk maximization, but rather the pursuit of an optimum balance between risk and reward, between short-term gains and long-term survival and success.

Voice of Experience

"Unrewarded risks have to be managed by people who are expert at putting control processes and resources into place. But the risks that offer rewards have to be handled carefully to avoid stifling creativity. I've seen situations where just an idea for a new business had to be reviewed by the tax department, risk management, the lawyers, HR, and on and on.

"Every deal got killed because everyone had to prove how smart they were and weigh in on what the problems could be. When the CEO looked at it he'd say, 'Oh my God. We can't do this. This can't be done.'

"Obviously there ought to be deal-stoppers, but risk review cannot be so heavily weighted toward the corporate risk and control functions that innovation and entrepreneurship come to a halt."

—Lynn Krominga, Director

Robert Goddard, a pioneering rocket scientist, conducted research on liquid-fueled rocketry in the 1920s and ventured so far from the conventional thinking of his time as to propose rocket flight to the moon. One of his harshest critics was the *New York Times*. In 1969, 49 years after Goddard's work was published and one day after Apollo 11 was launched, the *New York Times* published a retraction: "It is now definitely established that a rocket can function in a vacuum as well as in an atmosphere. *The Times* regrets the error."[5] Though many of his ideas were dismissed during his lifetime, Goddard is considered one of the fathers of modern rocketry.

Wernher von Braun said, "It takes sixty-five thousand errors before you are qualified to make a rocket." Aerospace experimentation and exploration is rife with examples of rewarded risk. While testing a hybrid rocket and jet, Chuck Yeager, a war hero and highly respected pilot, was seriously burned as he set a new altitude record. But as a result of the sacrifices that he and other pioneering test pilots made and the risks they took, aviation and space programs have led to tremendous technological breakthroughs.

Intelligent Risk Taking

The decision to take a risk for reward ought to be explicit, conscious, and calculated. In the process of making the decision, a number of questions must be answered:

- What is the exposure? How will it be managed?
- What are the alternatives? What is the risk of inaction?
- Is the exposure acceptable? Is it within the appetite of the enterprise?
- What is the measure of success? Has the risk of failure been considered?
- What is the acceptable difference between actual and expected performance?
- Has a maximum allowable loss been determined? How will we know if that limit is being approached? What is the exit strategy?

Take, for example, the controversial 2009 decision by Massimo D'Amore, CEO of PepsiCo Americas, to rebrand the entire lineup of the company's most recognizable beverage brands. Facing an industry-wide decline in consumer preference for carbonated beverages and the recession's overall impact, D'Amore launched a program of "creative destruction" to tear down and then rebuild Pepsi's flagship brands, including Pepsi, Mountain Dew, Gatorade, and Tropicana.

Reporting on the move in the April 17, 2009, issue of *Business-Week*, industry observer Burt Helm queried in his headline, "Creative destruction—or just destruction?" Helm also said, "If he [D'Amore] fails, his tactics may well have ripped apart a storied marketing department and made PepsiCo weaker. If he succeeds, he'll have strengthened a famous brand and made himself a contender to succeed PepsiCo CEO Indra K. Nooyi."[6]

Even for PepsiCo Americas, this was a big bet, a controversial decision, and a calculated risk that will have at least begun to pay off—or not—by the time you read this. However, it was made explicitly and with the knowledge that the potential risk of inaction outweighed the risks of this action.

Voice of Experience

"Losing money does not necessarily mean that the process is flawed. Was the risk understood? Was it dimensioned properly? Was the outcome within the range of stress tests, or was it a complete surprise? These are different questions than simply, 'Was the outcome positive or negative?'"[7]

—Dan Mudge, CEO, docGENIX

Tools to Use in Taking the Right Risks

Risk takes many forms: strategic, operational, financial, credit, foreign exchange, regulatory, reputational, and political, among others. Various tools in the risk management toolbox can be applied to each of them. Some tools, such as scenario analysis and sensitivity analysis, can be applied to most risks. Others, such as financial ratio analysis (in making loan or credit decisions), are specific to the type of risk. In this section, we examine examples of both types of tools, beginning with a brief summary of country risk analysis.

Voice of Experience

"We manufacture heavily in several countries in Asia. There are certain risks with manufacturing in less economically developed countries. We try to identify what those risks are and go in with our eyes wide open.

"For example, if we saw a high risk with our plants in a particular country, we'd consider having backup plants located in other, more economically developed countries. It becomes a sort of cost benefit analysis of how much 'insurance' you want to buy for manufacturing. You can build a plant and leave it empty, and the day a given plant has a problem, you have another plant to go to. That's a pretty costly insurance policy, but those are the kinds of discussions we have to face."[8]

—Bob Eckert, Chairman and CEO, Mattel, Inc.

TOOL #1: COUNTRY RISK ANALYSIS A number of developing or emerging economies present significant business potential, as markets, as bases of operations, or both. While not a new item on the business agenda, emerging markets are now integral to nearly every major enterprise's strategy. Yet despite the opportunities in these markets, a surprising number of companies fall short of their goals. A 2007 Deloitte study[9] found that less than half of the executives surveyed said their companies had been extremely or very successful in meeting their operational goals or their revenue goals in emerging markets.

What was preventing so many companies from fulfilling their goals even when the global economy was booming? One factor was the increasing complexity that characterizes emerging market operations. As companies develop products and markets in emerging economies and locate more sophisticated activities in them, they must continually rethink their approaches and better manage complex risks. They must develop an organizational structure and culture that confers autonomy while building on the strengths that headquarters can provide.

At the same time, some companies native to emerging markets are taking the opportunity to acquire their weakened North American and European competitors. So they may be courting risks and challenges similar to those that enterprises in developed nations face in emerging markets. However, the risks and challenges of emerging markets remain formidable, not simply because they are "foreign" but because certain risks—for example, to supply chains and intellectual property, as well as legal and political risks—are more pronounced.

Thus a robust assessment of the operating environment and its risks—particularly in an emerging market—is essential. Such assessments should be performed before entering the market *and* regularly refreshed. When does a company need actual country risk management? When at least one of the following applies:

- Its foreign capital-at-risk and/or revenues represent more than 10 percent of total capital and/or revenues.
- It has a presence on two or more continents or in three or more countries.
- It is considering expanding into foreign markets, for example, through an acquisition, joint venture, or wholly owned subsidiary.
- A pivotal event occurs within the country or region in question.
- A significant change in the foreign operations' performance or situation occurs, such as decreasing (or increasing) sales or profits, or higher taxes.
- A significant change occurs in the risk profile of the parent organization or the foreign operation.

Exhibit 12.1 lists some of the elements to consider in a country risk assessment. It is intended to be illustrative rather than exhaustive. Specific assessment criteria will depend on the industry and the investment model. A more consistent approach to assessing country risk—or any other type of risk—can increase the effectiveness and efficiency of risk management and of the enterprise itself. The greater the risk, the more robust risk assessment and risk management should be.

The Deloitte study cited previously found that only slightly more than half of executives said their companies conduct a very rigorous risk assessment before entering an emerging market. Even when companies did conduct such assessments, they often failed to carefully analyze the full range of risks they would face, as evidenced by the following findings of the study:

- Most companies did not conduct a rigorous assessment of intellectual property risks, security risks, and geopolitical risks.
- Most companies did not integrate separate risk assessments conducted across their companies into a single, comprehensive view before investing in an emerging market.
- Seventy percent did not assess the risks of terrorism or natural disasters.

On the other hand, some companies used a variety of strategies to manage their risks in emerging markets. These included keeping high-value activities in developed markets, sourcing components from multiple emerging markets, and distributing production across multiple emerging markets. These companies also conducted rigorous risk assessments on an ongoing basis rather than only when first entering the market.

A thorough understanding of local regulatory requirements and operating conditions can improve chances of success. For example, retailers in emerging markets should carefully consider the following:

- Regulatory restrictions on sale of items below cost, hours of operation, use of loss leaders, size of operations, and requirements and limits for joint ventures, product selection, and number of brands
- Proximity to consumers and logistics costs for dispersed operations
- Purchasing power related to country scale
- Local requirements and preferences of consumers of that type of product

TOOL #2: CHOICE OF OPERATING MODELS An enterprise's choice of operating model when entering any new market or business also presents risks—and an opportunity to manage them. By "operating model" in this context we mean greenfield models as well as strategic alliances, joint ventures, channel partners, or other third-party arrangements. Such choices ought to weigh the complexity of the operation, size of required investment, time to market, market opportunity, and regulatory requirements. Also, a potential partner may be a potential competitor from the beginning of the relationship.

Each strategy has its uses, costs, benefits, advantages, and disadvantages. For instance, greenfield investments, especially if they involve a core competency and proprietary processes or technologies, generally use newly constructed, wholly owned subsidiaries. The potential benefits include increased control, greater upside potential, quicker decision making, and reduced intellectual property and other risks. While greenfield investments

EXHIBIT 12.1 Example Country Risk Assessment Criteria

- Types of investments
  - Greenfield (entering without assistance of a company already there)
  - Joint venture or other strategic alliance
  - Distributor or licensee
  - Acquisition
  - Outsourcing (e.g., sales channel, contract manufacturer)
- Financing/capital structure
  - Currency exchange
  - Stability of banking institutions
  - Creditworthiness
  - Liquidity risk
- Financial operations
  - Capability of personnel
  - Effectiveness of controls
- Fiscal environment
  - Effective tax rates
  - Ability to repatriate cash
- Regulatory environment/political stability
  - Potential for nationalization of company assets
  - Adverse change in regulatory regime
- Operating conditions
  - Reliability of suppliers and logistics
  - Reliance on suppliers to manage risk (quality/labor)
  - Restrictions on hours of operations or size of operations
- Legal and governmental protection
  - Intellectual property protections
  - Rule of law
  - Risk of nationalization
- Security and continuity of operations
  - Personnel and facilities
  - Risk of terrorism/civil unrest
  - Exposure to natural disasters and disruption
- Business reputation
  - National culture/corruption
  - Potential organizational and cultural differences
  - Potential for negative impact on the brand
- Labor conditions
  - Ability to attract and retain sufficient skilled workforce
  - Labor codes, restrictions of employment and termination
  - Propensity for human rights abuses
  - Strength of unions/potential for unionization

generally require more money and present greater risks, they also provide potentially greater returns.

Third-party operating models have their pros and cons as well. Among the potential benefits are lower upfront investment, often lower operating costs, greater flexibility, faster scalability, local knowledge, and potentially greater expertise. The disadvantages stem from the lack of control, which can bring higher risks to intellectual property, and often having to compete with the third party's other commitments. Typically, the upside potential is reduced by the fact that the third party will share in that upside.

In sum, considering and choosing an operating model as a means of expanding domestically or internationally represents a major decision with often far-reaching consequences and a range of risks that must be understood and managed.

TOOL #3: STRATEGIC SIMULATION Risk management must determine whether a risk has been properly understood and managed. If, in the event, results vary significantly from expectations or repeatedly fail to unacceptable degrees, then the decision criteria, the decision-making process, and the decision makers ought to be reevaluated.

A Strategic Simulation (as shown in Exhibit 12.2) is a tool for organizing the tactical measures of the costs and risks of an initiative or decision to promote discussion and understanding of the initiative's objectives and risks. Some objectives may compete or be mutually exclusive; therefore, the tool and its ranking system should account for that.

Using the example of a bank and trust company, the chart from John Segerstrom shown in Exhibit 12.2 demonstrates that decisions to increase or decrease an individual risk simultaneously increase or decrease exposure to other risks. These relationships must be well understood. If, after considering all these factors carefully, the enterprise determines that the risk is worth taking, then the decision makers are proceeding on the basis of a thorough analysis. This analysis, of course, provides no guarantee that the reward will be obtained or losses will not be incurred. The issue is that the risk was understood. Management should explicitly note its acceptance of the risk exposure.

The risk management policies of the enterprise should define its risk appetite—the *types* of risk it is willing to take or wishes to avoid. Next, executives and directors should determine *how much* of these types of risk the enterprise is willing to take. They should decide on the maximum allowable loss or risk tolerance, that is, the size of the bet and of the enterprise's collective bets. Then they should verify how much risk has actually been taken.

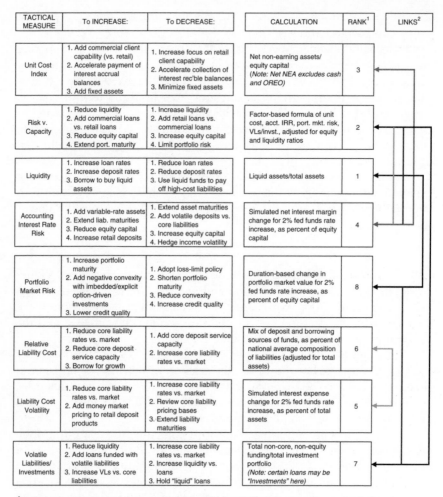

TACTICAL MEASURE	To INCREASE:	To DECREASE:	CALCULATION	RANK[1]	LINKS[2]
Unit Cost Index	1. Add commercial client capability (vs. retail) 2. Accelerate payment of interest accrual balances 3. Add fixed assets	1. Increase focus on retail client capability 2. Accelerate collection of interest rec'ble balances 3. Minimize fixed assets	Net non-earning assets/ equity capital (Note: Net NEA excludes cash and OREO)	3	
Risk v. Capacity	1. Reduce liquidity 2. Add commercial loans vs. retail loans 3. Reduce equity capital 4. Extend port. maturity	1. Increase liquidity 2. Add retail loans vs. commercial loans 3. Increase equity capital 4. Limit portfolio risk	Factor-based formula of unit cost, acct. IRR, port. mkt. risk, VLs/invst., adjusted for equity and liquidity ratios	2	
Liquidity	1. Increase loan rates 2. Increase deposit rates 3. Borrow to buy liquid assets	1. Reduce loan rates 2. Reduce deposit rates 3. Use liquid funds to pay off high-cost liabilities	Liquid assets/total assets	1	
Accounting Interest Rate Risk	1. Add variable-rate assets 2. Extend liab. maturities 3. Reduce equity capital 4. Increase retail deposits	1. Extend asset maturities 2. Add volatile deposits vs. core liabilities 3. Increase equity capital 4. Hedge income volatility	Simulated net interest margin change for 2% fed funds rate increase, as percent of equity capital	4	
Portfolio Market Risk	1. Increase portfolio maturity 2. Add negative convexity with imbedded/explicit option-driven investments 3. Lower credit quality	1. Adopt loss-limit policy 2. Shorten portfolio maturity 3. Reduce convexity 4. Increase credit quality	Duration-based change in portfolio market value for 2% fed funds rate increase, as percent of equity capital	8	
Relative Liability Cost	1. Reduce core liability rates vs. market 2. Reduce core deposit service capacity 3. Borrow for growth	1. Add core deposit service capacity 2. Increase core liability rates vs. market	Mix of deposit and borrowing sources of funds, as percent of national average composition of liabilities (adjusted for total assets)	6	
Liability Cost Volatility	1. Reduce core liability rates vs. market 2. Add money market pricing to retail deposit products	1. Increase core liability rates vs. market 2. Review core liability pricing bases 3. Extend liability maturities	Simulated interest expense change for 2% fed funds rate increase, as percent of total assets	5	
Volatile Liabilities/ Investments	1. Reduce liquidity 2. Add loans funded with volatile liabilities 3. Increase VLs vs. core liabilities	1. Increase core liability rates vs. market 2. Increase liquidity vs. loans 3. Hold "liquid" loans	Total non-core, non-equity funding/total investment portfolio (Note: certain loans may be "Investments" here)	7	

[1]RANK sets the priority of solution, for example, because Liquidity is ranked "1," no lower-ranked tactical initiative will force liquidity outside the bank's Focus Guide limits.
[2]LINKS shows relationships between TACTICs. A "link" between two tactical measures implies that changing either of them will cause a change in the other. In addition, any tactical change will be reflected in overall strategic direction, and may alter the strategic Focus Guides (changing other tactics' relative position).

EXHIBIT 12.2 Strategic Simulation Analysis

Basing the enterprise's entire diet on risk aversion is unhealthy and will lead to the eventual loss of competitive capability. The enterprise must achieve the right balance between risk aversion and risk taking, between risks it is not willing to take and those it must take to achieve and sustain competitiveness. The underlying assumptions of strategies should also be stress-tested under different scenarios for the implications and effects on both resilience and agility.

Voice of Experience

"Risks can be opportunities. There are so many right risks. Which ones do I give up on, and which do I take? Daring to pass up on some of the right risks may be a bigger problem than not daring to take any risk at all. If you have a real dearth of good ideas, you're in a dying business. But for ours, we have too many good opportunities, so our challenge is sorting through those, and then daring to take them and stick with them ... and pass up others."

— Eric Krasnoff, Chairman and CEO, Pall Corporation

No Risk, No Reward

Enterprises must recognize that the biggest risk of all may well be the one they don't take. As markets and business models change, the enterprises most at risk are those that stand still. Because "fear of failure" was discouraging research efforts, Chinese lawmakers proposed legislation to promote risk taking among China's scientific community. According to Xinhua News Agency, "Scientists and technicians who have initiated research with a high risk of failure will still have their expenses covered if they can provide evidence that they have tried their best when they failed to achieve their goals."[10]

Greg Page, chief executive officer of design consultancy IDEO, tries not to try to eliminate failure, but to capitalize on it. In product development, IDEO lives by the mantra "Fail early, fail often." By adopting this philosophy, IDEO flags and irons out mistakes earlier in the process, when they're less expensive to fix.

Who dares wins!

— *British Special Air Services Motto*

For the enterprise to survive and thrive, directors and executives must take certain risks and manage them properly. They must also avoid risks that offer no reward. So, which risks should leaders take? The ones that can bring about innovation that results in new processes, products, services, markets, acquisitions, and business models.

Not every risk with a potential reward will pay off, so you need a requisite variety of options. When the enterprise takes a risk in the expectation of a reward, it must actively manage that risk and manage the initiative so as to achieve the intended result and reward. It must also be able to absorb the potential loss should failure occur. For example, in an acquisition, how will the enterprise have the liquidity to pay back the debt incurred if performance falls short of expectations?

Voice of Experience

"I would encourage all decision makers who are trying to come up with a working enterprise strategy for risk and reward to do what we've done: Take the time to actually sit back and think, what does that mean? How do we go about actually doing that? And how could we fail?"

—James Hambrick, Chairman and CEO, The Lubrizol Corporation

No enterprise always makes the right decision, and the cost of eliminating all risk is too high even to consider. That's why enterprises need to know what risks they are taking, how to calculate whether the potential reward warrants the risk, and how to manage those risks to improve the chances of survival and success.

Questions to Ask about Taking Enough of the Right Risks

- Has the risk of failure been properly considered?
- Is the risk worth incurring, given the potential reward?
- Is it within our risk appetite?
- How will the exposure be actively managed? Are there alternatives?
- What are the trade-offs and interactions?
- What is the acceptable difference between actual and expected performance?
- Has a maximum allowable loss been determined?
- How will we know if that limit is being approached?
- What is our stop-loss and exit strategy?

CHAPTER 13

Sustain Operational Discipline

Well done is better than well said.

— Benjamin Franklin

To instill operational discipline and accountability, the Romans insisted that engineers stand under the arches they designed when the supporting wooden trusses were removed. That may explain why some of those arches have stood for more than 2,000 years. In the U.S. military, parachute packers are randomly selected to jump with parachutes they have packed. While most enterprises do not insist on such high-stakes demonstrations of one's competence, most do—or at least should—insist on a deep commitment to operational discipline.

As noted in the other chapters in Part II, you will tend to find these skills practiced most diligently in endeavors that pose high risk of immediate and often fatal consequences. Although it is virtually impossible to duplicate those conditions (legally) in a business or not-for-profit enterprise, it would no doubt be beneficial from a risk management perspective.

Operational discipline represents the final, vital risk intelligence skill because without it, risk management cannot be implemented as intended. Without it, warning signals will not be detected and transmitted, potential causes of failure will not be addressed, sources will not be verified, information will not be corroborated, safety margins will not be maintained, and responses to elevated risks or even crises will not occur.

Just as the first risk intelligence skill—check your assumptions at the door—enables leaders to develop and exercise the next eight skills, this skill enables the enterprise to carry out the leaders' risk management plan and program. Thus, the first and tenth skills bookend the practice of risk intelligence at the action level.

This chapter opens with an example from the military, where operational discipline is a matter of life and death. Then we turn to the reasons—the root causes—for operational discipline failing to take hold or for its breaking down. Then we demonstrate the skill of sustaining operational discipline by focusing on the ways in which E.I. du Pont de Nemours and Company achieves it.

Case Example: The U.S. Submarine Force

The U.S. Submarine Force has a risk aware, conservative culture. Yet its commanding officers must know how to take risks or the force could not operate at high speed, under pressure, during military conflicts, with limited visibility and with a nuclear reactor on board. Therefore, members of the submarine force take operational discipline, risk management, and preparedness extremely seriously. According to Matt Scharf, a former junior officer in the force, "If the risks aren't well managed, a lot of people can die."[1]

Scharf continues, "The operating environment is extremely complex, so information needs to be distilled and simplified. Human beings are not usually well suited to take multiple inputs and process them. Especially under stress, they can freeze up or make big mistakes. To manage this, the submarine force tries to identify a vital few indicators and establish conservative 'tactical tripwires' based on those indicators. For example, when tracking an enemy, it's very important to know how far away that enemy is to evade detection. Tactical tripwires are set appropriate to a given situation. For example, 'If the range is less than a 1,000 yards, then we will do x, y, z.' Everyone must know the tripwires and if one is tripped, we must immediately institute the contingency plan or standard operating procedures."

Four things the U.S. Submarine Force does exceptionally well are standard operating procedures, training and drills, after action reviews, and a "Roman-style" safety measure. Again, in the words of Matt Scharf:

- *Standardize operating procedures.* "Responses of people to the environment can be simplified or optimized by constantly training and preparing them. In the engine room, it was all about nuclear safety. It's not possible to have a standard operating procedure (SOP) for everything, but 99 percent of the potential major problems with the nuclear power plant were defined and had detailed SOPs to address them. There was intense training on the key indicators of a potential uncommon event, the immediate actions to take, and a follow-up set of actions."
- *Maintain constant vigilance.* "I've never gotten less sleep than I did during submarine duty. We were training constantly and by training I don't mean just sitting around in a classroom memorizing stuff. Even

when you're sleeping, you wake up to a fire drill and run around to fight the fake fire. It's just train, train, and train. It's painful, and everybody knows it. But it's totally appropriate for a nuclear powered submarine, and everyone knows that too. I think using drills and rehearsal in the private sector could be an excellent way to develop greater vigilance and discipline around defining and managing our key risks. You just need to be selective about when you do it."

- *Conduct after action reviews.* "The force has a structured process called After Action Review (AAR) for analyzing what happened, why it happened, and the lessons to improve future responses. We did a good job analyzing our performance. Some organizations don't. But the nature of any learning organization, especially one that is operating in a high-risk environment, is to recognize quickly that you've failed, or that you don't know everything. The captain would go through the AAR and then we would publish it so the whole ship would understand what happened and why and what we should do different next time. We didn't do that just with an extreme event—it was done with routine training or routine maintenance."

- *Establish a comprehensive program.* Perhaps taking a page from the Romans' book, "Sometimes you need to make that connection tighter. For example, as part of the Submarine Safety Program, introduced after the loss of the USS *Thresher* in 1963, the first time a newly built submarine goes to sea, representatives from the shipyard that constructed the submarine must accompany the crew. In a perfect world, a person who makes the decision about how much risk the organization is going to take would be exposed to the negative effects of what that risk could bring. When that relationship doesn't exist, I think you get the potential for bad decisions."[2]

Here is another example from the military:

Captain Christopher Baker of the USAF 21st Space Wing Legal Office says, "When there is insufficient respect for and attention to the need for discipline as a first principle, military operations can be expected to fail."[3] Baker lists a small set of examples of what happens when there is a lack of discipline in the armed forces. All of them had severe consequences for those involved, as described by Baker in the following passages. On August 30, 2007, "Six AGM-129 ACM cruise missiles, each loaded with a W80-1 variable yield nuclear warhead, were mistakenly loaded on a United States Air Force B-52H at Minot and transported to Barksdale. The following errors were made:

- The nuclear warheads in the missiles were supposed to have been removed before taking the missiles from storage.

- Although the crew in the weapons storage had begun to inspect the missiles, an early arriving transport crew hooked up the pylons [structures to support the missiles] and towed the missiles away without inspecting them or ensuring that the missiles had been inspected or cleared for removal.
- The munitions control center failed to verify that the pylon had received proper clearance and inspection, but approved the pylon for loading on the B-52 aircraft at 09:25.
- The missiles with the nuclear warheads were not reported missing and remained mounted to the aircraft at both Minot and Barksdale for a period of 36 hours."[4]

How does operational discipline apply in the corporate environment? For the answer, let's examine the fatal flaw of lack of operational discipline.

Voice of Experience

"Lack of operational discipline often has to do with knowing what needs to be done, but not actually doing it. Boards don't always hold management's feet to the fire by insisting on subsequent information about how things actually work out.

"Recently, I've seen boards paying a lot more attention to actual results compared to the expected. They're saying, 'We assumed such and such. Please tell us how this has worked out.' But I just don't think it's being done in all cases.

"Here's something else you don't often see discussed on the front end. If there's an entry strategy, what is that exit strategy and conditions? Companies make a case for doing something, but they don't really make a case for also getting out or pulling the plug when it's reasonable to do so."

—Denny Beresford, Director and Professor, J.M. Tull School of Accounting

---

Fatal Flaw #10: Lack of Operational Discipline

The consequences of a lack of operational discipline can range from loss of life, failure to reach military objectives, and breaches of security in the armed services, to monetary losses, legal exposure, and bankruptcy in business enterprises. For instance, according to the Coca-Cola Retailing Research Council, Europe, most corporate strategies fail because of a lack of operational discipline and the lack of courage on the part of leadership to stick it out.[5] In other words, strategies fail slowly over an extended period of time as lack of discipline results in poor implementation, execution, and follow-through.

Lack of operational discipline often generates problems that are more corrosive than explosive in nature. Bernie Price of Polaris Veritas, Inc, defines cluster failures as "the simultaneous damage of minor items of equipment." Price notes that these types of failures "often go unreported because they don't cause major equipment damage or product loss. The root cause can be some external failure, but, in our experience, it is much more likely to be due to some lack of operational discipline, that is, failure to stay inside the operating envelope or failure to accurately follow operating procedures."[6]

Price also defines the lack of operational discipline as errors caused by "deficient operating procedures, deficient training, conflicting priorities, inadequate labeling of equipment and instruments, or lack of effective administrative controls" rather than a deliberate act.[7] At the root of many such failures is lack of dedication and commitment by every person to carry out each task in the right way every time. Without that, programs remain on paper rather than being translated into organizational realities.

A Look at Root Causes

Given the consequences, it's essential to develop and sustain a high level of operational discipline. Toward that end, let's examine 11 root causes of a lack of operational discipline, which are the antithesis of DuPont's 11-point model for operational discipline described later in this chapter:

Root cause #1: Lack of "felt" leadership. Leadership determines the enterprise's values, goals, incentives, and system of accountability. People in an organization notice and are affected by leaders' shortcomings in any of these areas. Do leaders mean what they say? Leaders' decisions and behaviors answer that question and demonstrate management's true priorities. Leaders who do not consistently "walk the talk" fail to create the appropriate tone and level of vigilance despite slogans and speeches.

An official report on a fatal diving accident aboard the USCGC Healy, in which several lives were lost, identified 26 causal and 48 contributory factors to the fatalities. The report stated, "Central themes were a lack of appropriate supervision, a lack of risk assessment, which led to poor decision making, and a lack of operational discipline on the part of the individuals involved"[8]

Root cause #2: Insufficient resources to support operation. Lack of operational discipline may be rooted in inadequate or absent planning, procedures, training, preventive maintenance, and other support. Given pressures to cut costs, the highly visible costs of good risk management are always under pressure. Such pressures can even affect national and international security. A November 15, 2008, *Washington Post* article notes that the global economic downturn could weaken pro-Western governments, decrease foreign aid and defense spending, and thus create new vulnerabilities.[9]

Root cause #3: Employees not engaged in improving the business. Fear, lack of incentives, and command and control management can all leave employees disengaged from the organization. In his book *The Best Damn Ship in the Navy*,[10] former U.S. Naval Commander Captain Michael Abrashoff cited ways to encourage crewmembers to identify problems and empower them to make improvements. After all, he says, "It's your ship."

Abrashoff adds, "When people feel they own an organization, they perform with greater care and devotion. They want to do the right things right the first time, and they don't have accidents by taking shortcuts for the sake of expedience ... I am absolutely convinced that with good leadership, freedom does not weaken discipline—it strengthens it. Free people have a powerful incentive not to screw up."[11]

Root cause #4: Ineffective lines of communication. If the enterprise lacks a common language and keeps bad news from traveling fast, lessons are not learned or shared, and coordinated responses become difficult or impossible. On August 4, 1949, a lightning induced "smoker" (a firefighter's term) broke out along the south ridge of Mann Gulch, about 20 miles north of Helena, Montana. The fire was spotted the next day, and a team of 15 smoke jumpers was dispatched.

The plan was to proceed down the north slope and attack the fire from its rear flank using the Missouri River as an escape route. Unknown to the crew, the fire had jumped across Mann Gulch, eliminating the path to safety. Foreman Wagner Dodge ordered the team to reverse direction, but the fast-moving fire caught up to them. Dodge lit an intentional burn zone, or "escape fire," and urged his men to take refuge. The team ignored Dodge as discipline shattered and "every man for himself" prevailed. Dodge survived, along with two others who made it over the ridge safely. The rest, overtaken by the fire, perished.

An investigation into the causes of the tragedy cited "Inadequate overall smoke-jumper management approach, including lack of discipline and inadequate training. The web of causes included no formal team development or training, inexperience with intentional burn zones, failure to obey leadership, and failed communication."[12]

Root cause #5: Lack of strong teamwork. Strong teamwork depends on common objectives, incentives, and language. During Hurricane Katrina, the lack of adequately trained personnel became a major impediment to using the Incident Command System (ICS) described in Chapter 6 and to effectively managing state and federal resources. Scott Wells, the federal coordinating officer for Hurricanes Katrina and Rita, testified before Congress that state personnel lacked a number of key factors in appropriate crisis response and management, including overall discipline, clear control lines of authority, a clearly understood command structure, and consistency in operational procedures.[13]

Root cause #6: Lack of shared values. Values provide an essential frame of reference for decision making and responses. Without common values, the enterprise has no North Star by which to navigate. One might assume that members of the armed services would share a common purpose and values, but that's not always so. William Thomas, a U.S. Air Force major, refers to Charles Moskos's model of institutional and occupational attitudes in the military.

In Moskos's model, individuals with *institutional* attitudes are bound by a sense of shared values and perceive that their identity is defined by that membership; they focus on their role in that organization. Those with *occupational* attitudes are uncertain about organizational values and look to people outside the organization who exhibit qualities similar to their own.

Major Thomas suggests that the Air Force's emphasis on technology leaves it vulnerable to occupational attitudes. Technical specialists tend to focus on values and beliefs associated with their specialty, rather than on those of the Air Force. The more technical the service, the easier it is for specialists to relate to their civilian counterparts more than to fellow military in different specialties. Major Thomas believes this poses significant potential consequences.[14]

Root cause #7: Outdated documentation. When documentation of procedures, records, and recommendations is poor, best practices are lost and work processes suffer. Outdated or inadequate documentation increases inconsistency, failure rates, and costs. The financial markets in 2008 demonstrated how wrong things can go. As early as 2005, Sir Andrew Large, deputy governor of the Bank of England, noted that he had observed that a lack of operational discipline in some markets was leading to documentation backlogs and uncertainty over the enforceability of the transfer of risks. He saw the relaxation of the lending criteria in the leveraged buyout market, the increased reliance on potentially illiquid instruments in trading strategies, and the questionable quality in some initial public offerings as posing some significant risk.[15]

Root cause #8: Failure to practice what you preach. When management communicates "Do as I say, not as I do," operational discipline breaks down. No one is perfect, and experts often fail to follow their own advice, says *Wall Street Journal* columnist Jason Zweig.[16] Zweig once asked the 1990 Economics Nobel Laureate Harry Markowitz how he diversified his portfolio. Markowitz had conducted studies of the correlation between risk diversification and return, and he published his pioneering article "Portfolio Selection" in the *Journal of Finance*.

Following his own breakthroughs, Markowitz should have made intricate calculations based on historical averages to determine the optimal trade-off between risk and return. Instead, he visualized his grief if the stock market skyrocketed, and he wasn't in it—or if it tanked, and he was all in. His intention was to minimize his future regret, so he simply split 50-50 between bonds and equities.[17] Leaders of enterprises, however, must do as they say or those they lead will not be led.

Root cause #9: A proliferation of shortcuts. When people take shortcuts, they do their jobs quickly and easily, but not necessarily correctly. This results in incidents, accidents, waste, and rework. Similarly, most mountaineering accidents happen on the way down. As mountaineer Colwill notes, "Many deaths or serious accidents in mountaineering are not the result of extreme events or of a very serious error. They're usually the result of very little things happening—just a couple of circumstances that aren't quite right."

She adds, "It's often about the simple things like how you treat your harness and ropes. Normally you have a double system of clipping into ropes, and sometimes when climbers are descending, after a successful ascent, they want to go fast and they just use a single safety system. Especially after they have made several successful ascents, complacency creeps in, but the terrain hasn't changed. So they relax, they change systems a bit here and a bit there, and then something goes wrong, and suddenly it's over."

Root cause #10: Poor housekeeping. Disorderliness, inconsistency, and lack of attention to detail all create problems sooner or later, often with serious consequences. In the commercial truck and bus industry, many believed that most accidents and incidents of erratic driving were due to some sort of physical, emotional, or substance-related impairment. Instead, one safety manager suggested lack of operational discipline as the cause. According to his view, a major goal of management was to establish driving rules and policies and to ensure that drivers follow them.[18]

Root cause #11: Lack of pride in the organization. Lack of pride develops as a result of weaknesses in other operational discipline characteristics. These previous ten conditions, if they become common and serious enough, lead people to feel that "Nobody else seems to care, so why should I?"

Although this statement goes against many people's notions of leadership, the fact is that operational discipline cannot be instilled by order, or only by issuing policies and procedures and punishing breaches of discipline. Instead, operational discipline begins with—and depends upon—the discipline of the leaders themselves. Leaders who are undisciplined cannot develop and sustain operational discipline in their organizations. They cannot model discipline, nor can they instill it in others because they actually don't value or even understand operational discipline. So the "skill" of developing and sustaining operational discipline is not simply a skill but also a philosophy of and an approach to leadership and to organizational life itself.

Risk Intelligence Skill #10: Develop and Sustain Operational Discipline

Keeping a system stable and functioning properly, particularly when it contains a significant human component, takes consistent effort. Establishing operational discipline where it has been missing or waning can be even more of a challenge, but at least it presents clear leadership imperatives. For example, Captain Mike Abrashoff tells of his experience in turnaround leadership. As he took command of the USS Benfold, Abrashoff came to realize that performance was lacking because the previous leadership had been woefully out of touch with the crew.

After assessing the trouble spots, Abrashoff set about seeing the ship through his crew's eyes to better understand how to reengage his team. Unable to control compensation or to offer monetary incentives, Abrashoff set out to change the ship's culture to one in which people took ownership, became engaged, and worked hard because they felt valued and appreciated. He succeeded in that endeavor given four principles he has developed in his years of leadership experience:

1. *Question every rule.* When an officer or sailor came to Abrashoff for approval on anything, he would always ask why the activity or process was done in a particular way—and always ask whether there was a better way.
2. *Build trust through responsibility.* Train people properly, then give them responsibility and push decision making down the chain of command. Allow team members at all levels to respond by performing at higher than expected levels, and to fail occasionally.
3. *Thank the messenger.* Because mistakes, accidents, and failures will occur, leaders need to express their vision and set goals, but must also have the confidence to encourage reporting of problems and to accept honest appraisals of their own decisions.
4. *Promote risk takers.* Improvement occurs in an organization only through bravery, brainstorming, innovation, and taking the right risks, even if mistakes occur.[19] Those who take risks should be rewarded for doing so when they pay off, and not being punished when they fail to pan out.

As Captain Abrashoff's principles indicate, establishing and sustaining operational discipline does not depend on rigid control, nor is it an exercise in cheerleading. Operational discipline results when people understand the mission and values of the organization, commit themselves to supporting that mission and those values, and exert effort to ensure that the operation achieves the mission and enacts those values.

They do this because they know that their efforts are worthwhile and are recognized as such by the leadership. Neither the leaders nor the team can fake these beliefs and actions. They must understand and be prepared for their responsibilities, and accept accountability—both within themselves and within the organizational structure—for carrying them out.

Operational Discipline at DuPont

Founded in 1802, E. I. du Pont de Nemours and Company (DuPont) operates primarily in the chemicals, materials, textiles, coatings, nutrition, pesticides, packaging, safety, and electronics industries. Clearly, operational discipline is paramount in a company with operations in more than 70 countries, revenues of over $30 billion, some 60,000 employees, and more than 75 laboratories in 12 countries.[20] Indeed, it's a long tradition, particularly given the potentially dangerous processes involved in producing and distributing many of the company's products. In fact, one of DuPont's first operating policies, established by founder E. I. du Pont de Nemours, was that no gunpowder mill could go into operation without having first been operated by a family member and later by a senior executive.

DuPont defines operational discipline as "deeply rooted dedication and ongoing commitment by every person to carry out each task the right way every time. Our operational goal is to transform paper programs into real and tangible results."[21] DuPont's approach is a system that requires all of its parts to function effectively.

The remainder of this chapter describes DuPont's approach to risk management and to establishing operational discipline across the enterprise. These descriptions are in the words of Chief Engineer and Vice President of Engineering and Operations Jim Porter, now retired.[22]

AN INTEGRATED VIEW OF RISK MANAGEMENT   "Risk management is basically about the whole business trying to transform itself to deliver optimum business results, by optimizing positive opportunities and eliminating or minimizing negative risks. As you would expect, we used a variety of risk management tools. But we tried to re-orient traditional risk management to focus more on the enterprise. In the old days, we thought about risk as individual hazards. But then we thought of risk management as a holistic strategy and made sure that everybody in the company understood that it was not just the responsibility of the head office or of the internal controls people or finance or safety. It was everybody's responsibility on a day-to-day basis."

SECURITY AND SAFETY "Security is an aspect of risk management and integrated security is more than just physical security. It's not just about fences and cameras. It's about the whole concept of looking at security from a standpoint of information, the security of people and their safety, intellectual property, and so on.

"We based our security practices on our safety model so that it flowed through the line organization in a consistent way. The line organization was accountable for these things because they had to run the businesses, and they had to manage the risk."

OPERATING DISCIPLINE "Operating discipline becomes such a critical component of your fundamental safety net against unwanted incidents. I was in the engineering end of the business, so operating discipline for me was helping the company understand what assets we wanted to build, where we would want them, and how much we could afford to pay for them. Once those decisions were made, we executed the work processes to design and construct operating facilities.

"Engineers are the transformers in the company. We transformed the science of our chemists, biologists, physicists, and mathematicians into a commercial reality. Our operating discipline was based on engineering first principles and best practices developed from decades of experience. In this sense, operational discipline was the most effective and efficient way to do our work."

DEALING WITH COMPLEXITY "When you talk about complexity, a major, publicly held, fully integrated operating firm like the DuPont Company is about as complex as you can get—not because leadership tried to make it that way, but because it operates in environments that impose so many constraints. This high level of complexity is compounded by uncertainty because it is almost impossible to know if something will have a positive or a negative effect before the fact. We created a risk map to identify all the places where we could be impacted. It would never be complete because risks are comprised of interdependent variables requiring a continuous dynamic analysis to enable true risk-based decision making. Rarely are they independent variables."

DuPont's MAP OF RISK DOMAINS DuPont's risk map, shown in Exhibit 13.1, provided a visual representation of types and range of risks that DuPont had to address. The diagram captured and organized the complexities of the company's operations and risk. Says Jim Porter, "Our risk map attempted to show all our risk domains so we could put work processes and systems in place to give us an early warning. Once you've been warned, you can develop the best response. We tried to be proactive and responsive, not reactive, and to leverage our learning."

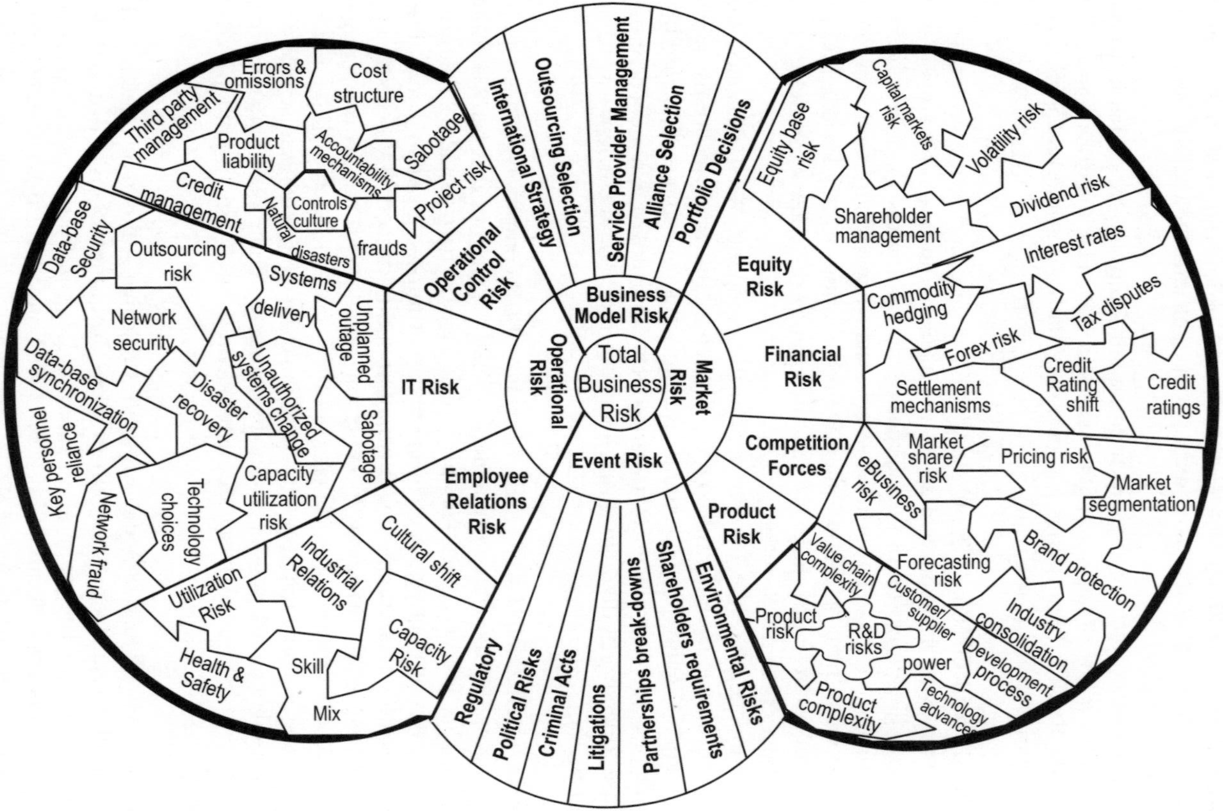

EXHIBIT 13.1 DuPont Company Risk Domains

230

CAPTURING THE LESSONS "There was another benefit to the learnings that came from dealing with complexity. You can leverage them for the future. That's a key underpinning of another value of operational discipline: learning and leveraging the lessons to avoid the mistakes of the past and ensure future successes.

"As far back as there's been an army in the United States, it has always tried to capture its learnings in field manuals, which represent the best guidance because it's based on experience. For example, the field manual would tell an infantry unit that you don't lift or shift your supporting artillery fire until you're actually on top of the target or until you start to take casualties from your own incoming artillery.

"That's a very hard lesson for someone to learn firsthand, but using it increases your potential to achieve your objective with minimum casualties. If you maintain operating discipline, you will accomplish what you intend more frequently than you will fail, and the net cost will be less than if you didn't follow the rule."

THE ADVANTAGE OF RESILIENCE "Operating discipline has always been a critical component of day-to-day business success, and it's also essential for resilience. If you do everything—operate your manufacturing facilities, conduct your R&D, evaluate your supply chain, manage your customer relationships—in a very disciplined, orderly, and best-practices way, your likelihood of sustaining your enterprise is much higher than if you don't. In the end, resilience is about being able to cope successfully with the unexpected. It's also about doing the right things in ways that allow you to remain sustainable."

THE ADVANTAGE OF AGILITY "In a marketplace where the customers ultimately are likely to change their mind fairly rapidly about what it is they really want, speed is really key. There is little or no warning today. Things happen so fast that you can be out of business in a heartbeat. If you don't have operational discipline, even if you have the best policies and practices in place, but don't actually use them, it doesn't do you any good."

SUSTAINABILITY: BURNING IT IN "It's not just about operating discipline per se. It's about operating discipline that's been 'burned' into the organization. It's a part of the culture. It's something that people value so much that they don't deviate from it just because they think something might be done in a different or better way. Once you can get it embedded into the culture like that, you're in better shape.

"Work process design is one of the more important pieces, and we became very disciplined about that. If you map a work process, you can determine the most efficient and effective way to do things. Then you can design a system to lock it in place, and the most efficient structure necessary to run it. Many other companies seem to change their organizational structures to improve business performance. That usually just ends up in sub-optimization at best. If you design your work processes first and then burn in a system, it makes operating discipline easier and much more sustainable.

"But life changes, so you've got to continue to look at your processes. You can't say, 'I've got the best' and just leave it that way. Continuous improvement and effective management of change are necessary."

VALUES ARE THE CORNERSTONE   "You've got to have core values—a culture built around the right things. In DuPont's case, it's around safety, with a committed goal of 'zero injuries.' It's around protecting the environment. It's around treating all people respectfully—and it's around maintaining the highest ethics. Our goal was zero incidents for anything to do with injuries. It was the same with adverse environmental impact, with ethics, or with the way we treated people. That goal underpinned everything we did in running our business and how we worked together. Operational discipline gets built-in a lot easier when everyone shares the same values.

"Of course, you can't take a zero incidents approach to creativity, but we used rigorous processes to manage the innovation process. Innovation was 'gated' in a way that put no boundary around how you worked or what you could work on. But you had to pass through gates and get approval to move the work forward. Strong operating discipline can prevent an initiative from becoming a very expensive R&D program or, in later stages, pilot plants or ultimately a capital appropriation for a full-scale plant that won't deliver positive business results.

"We usually brought in a panel of individuals who weren't directly involved in the project but who had the technical, managerial, or business competence to assess a project, just to get some additional viewpoints around it. The real key was to start small and scale fast."

CRISIS MANAGEMENT: YOUR BACKSTOP   "Despite your best efforts, eventually something is not going to go to plan. So when it doesn't, how do you deal with it? In our case, we had a very well-developed crisis management process led by the CEO. For example, if we had a hurricane in the Gulf, and we had a plant potentially in harm's way, we initiated our crisis management process. Five days out from land-fall, we started to track it. If the storm came ashore near our plant, we didn't want to be running when the storm hit. But we didn't want to shut down a plant and lose production if it wasn't necessary.

"Crisis management becomes your backstop. Of course, you try to prevent a crisis by having the right goals, managing your information well, operating in a very disciplined way, laying out all your processes, and embedding your experience in what you're doing. But there are many things beyond your control that you can't prevent. That's when you need a well-developed, operating discipline-based crisis management process."

KNOWLEDGE MANAGEMENT AND LONG-TERM MEMORY "Another critical component of operational discipline is effective knowledge-management systems. We managed our existing knowledge well and in ways that could be efficiently re-used and used to create new knowledge from it.

"Resiliency encompasses being able to use what you've already paid for in a way where you can create new value. In DuPont's case, we had thousands of employees with enormous knowledge based on experience. If we didn't capture that knowledge, we were going to have to pay to have it developed again.

"Anytime someone retired from DuPont Engineering, we had a team of knowledge stewards who 'downloaded' them into a database. For example, when my administrative assistant, who had worked for DuPont Company for 40 years, retired, they 'downloaded' her because of her vast knowledge of how work gets done."

THE RIGHT FUTURE GOALS "Having future goals along with your core values, of course, is critical to enterprise resilience. They are the ground you stand on. They provide direction. Just doing what you did yesterday and hoping for different results, as we all know, falls into the definition of insanity. You've also got to have all the *right* future goals. The right goals about how you are going to run the business, how well you're going to serve your shareholders, how well you're going to serve the other stakeholders—your customers, your employees, and the community that you operate in. That gives you the right direction."

Operate with Discipline

We have quoted Jim Porter at length because he provides such an overarching yet down-to-earth perspective on risk management practices at a major industrial company, with an eye particularly on operational discipline. As the example of Jim Porter's experience at DuPont illustrates, a company with a strong culture and a serious commitment to risk management can instill operational discipline into the enterprise's processes and practices in a very real way.

Operational discipline enables the enterprise to embed each of the other nine risk intelligence skills in its ongoing performance. The absence of operational discipline can undermine or even destroy a successful enterprise, but most enterprises do not attain success without a high level of operational discipline.

In fact, very often enterprises know what needs to be done but they cannot seem to do it with consistent competence, usually due to a lack of operational discipline. It is, however, operational discipline that enables organizations to survive crises and to maintain high standards of performance and integrity when experiencing extraordinary success.

Questions to Ask about Operational Discipline

- Is leadership felt by employees? Are there clear examples of "walking the talk" in a consistent manner?
- Are resources sufficient to support operations and manage the related risks?
- Are employees actively involved and engaged in running the business and improving it?
- Are the lines of communication working—up, down, and across the organization—like a central nervous system?
- Is teamwork strong, with collaboration, cooperation, and common objectives at all levels?
- Does everyone share common values about matters such as ethics, the environment, and health and safety?
- Is documentation of procedures, records, and recommendations up to date?
- Does leadership practice what it preaches? Are practices consistent with procedures? Are tasks completed as written and planned?
- Do staff avoid shortcuts? Do they do their jobs the right way every time?
- Does excellent housekeeping ensure orderliness and consistency in all areas?
- Is there pride in the enterprise?

PART III

Creating the Risk Intelligent Enterprise

CHAPTER 14

Risk Intelligence Is Free

Quality is free. But it is not a gift.

—Philip B. Crosby, *Quality Is Free*

In his 1979 book of the same name, Philip Crosby made the case that "quality is free." The statement refers to product quality achieved through process improvement methodologies. Essentially, Crosby said that investments made to improve quality fund themselves through the monetary benefits they generate. Those benefits include minimizing or eliminating the costs of waste, rework, and rejects, along with the costs of returns, service calls, and other costs that quality problems create for companies that don't get it right the first time.

As Crosby put it in his book, "It is much less expensive to prevent errors than to rework, scrap, or service them." He also placed responsibility for achieving quality squarely on management's shoulders, stating that it was up to management to develop work processes and procedures that attain and maintain desired levels of quality.

We posit a notion similar to Crosby's in this chapter—risk intelligence is free. Risk intelligence is free in the sense that, much like quality, it pays for itself in the form of costs prevented *and* revenues and profits gained. That last part, about gains, is important. Paralleling many executives' approach to risk as risk avoidance, some early proponents of quality tended to focus on costs avoided—waste, rework, and scrapped materials—to the neglect of the revenue potential associated with quality.

As Toyota, GE, Motorola, and many other companies have proven, the competitive advantages of quality translate to revenue and market share gains, as well as to cost savings.

Part of the payoff for becoming more risk intelligent includes the prevention of unrewarded risks to the extent practical and more cost-effective mitigation of those risks when they do occur. For instance, harmonizing controls and compliance procedures reduces their costs, as does consciously deciding where risk management resources should be allocated.

But the larger payoff by far lies in the gains from risk intelligent risk taking for reward. Think back to cases in this book such as Apple's iPods, Thomson's move to corroborated information, Royal Dutch Shell's shift from expanding capacity to improving inputs, and Goldman Sachs's overriding the company's risk models. Think too of the many companies that had no effective system of calculated risk taking for reward in the 2000s—not just in financial services, but in the real estate, automotive, retail, restaurant, and other industries.

We believe the business case for enterprises to become more risk intelligent is extremely strong. This chapter presents that case in terms of its monetary costs and benefits. We kick off Part III with this chapter because the business case for any initiative must be compelling and understandable to management and the board.

The value of preventing unrewarded risk and improving crisis preparedness should now be apparent, but we realize that we have not yet expressed that value in explicit monetary terms. Nor have we provided an analysis that most CFOs could get excited about (except perhaps the part about avoiding regulatory censure, citations, fines, congressional hearings, or even jail). Therefore, in this chapter we make explicit the cost of risk—and the benefits of risk intelligence—by monetizing them. In doing so, we follow the logic and example of quality improvement proponents and examine costs of failure that can be prevented *and* the costs that must be incurred to achieve the goal.

In the case of risk intelligence, the goal is to reduce the cost of failure (both direct and indirect) and, to the extent possible, to eventually reduce the costs of prevention and preparation. We can measure actual levels of losses, from fraud, inventory shrinkage, natural disasters, and theft, and the explicit costs of noncompliance with regulations. We can also measure the costs of a failed product launch or market entry or a failed acquisition.

Getting a reasonably accurate picture is not easy but it is important. Obviously, there are also nonfinancial impacts, such as negative media attention and regulatory scrutiny, which can affect an enterprise's reputation. But ultimately, these nonfinancial considerations manifest themselves in financial results.

In this chapter, we focus on the costs associated with risk and on the notion that risk intelligence, like quality, is free. We also refer you to the quote at the start of this chapter: "Quality is free. But it is not a gift." Quality is free in the sense that it pays for itself, but people must work hard to achieve quality. Similarly, risk intelligence is free but people must work hard to achieve it. Neither quality nor risk intelligence comes about by accident or on its own.

A Closer Look at Costs

The questions that were being asked about quality decades ago—What is the value? What will it cost? Doesn't higher quality mean higher costs? Where are the additional resources? Who is responsible? Why should this be a priority?—are the same as those being asked about risk management today. Back then, quality was poorly defined, as were the ways in which it might be achieved. Quality was often seen as related to exception management, in which a "quality assurance" professional inspected and then either accepted or rejected a finished product—or the company merely awaited customer complaints and then resolved them as they occurred. The longer it took to detect a quality problem, the more expensive and time consuming it became to fix it.

Similarly, risk is currently not well measured and tools for controlling it are still in development. Questions about the value, costs, and priorities regarding risk management abound, and the business case must be made on an enterprise-by-enterprise basis in monetary terms.

Two Types of Returns

As we've mentioned, discussion of value and risk are inseparable. To discuss one in isolation from the other is not practical, meaningful, or wise. The enterprise has two principal sources of value: first, its existing assets, tangible and intangible, which it must protect to secure a return *of* investment; and, second, future growth, which requires innovation and aggressive initiatives to obtain a return *on* investment.

Risk is the potential for failure to protect existing assets or failure to achieve future growth. Failure is an unacceptable difference between actual and expected performance. There are many risks to existing assets. Understanding and managing these risks has been the domain of conventional risk management—of insurance, business continuity, internal control, and so on. There are also risks to future growth and prosperity. Because future growth requires calculated risk taking, the risks to growth and prosperity must also be well understood and managed.

So, when considering the financial aspects of risk intelligence, bear in mind that return *of* investment and return *on* investment represent the twin objectives. The former focuses on asset and revenue preservation, while the latter focuses on asset and revenue growth—and both are essential if the enterprise is to survive and thrive.

The Cost of Quality

The U.S. quality movement gained traction in the early 1980s, shortly after the publication of Philip Crosby's *Quality Is Free*. That book, as well as the work of other researchers, translated "quality" into terms that general managers and financial executives could relate to—that is, into monetary terms. Without cost justification, quality improvement could have remained an arcane process management methodology, never coming to the attention of senior executives.

In 1980, Joseph M. Juran, a pioneer in managing for quality (whose *Quality Control Handbook* was first published in 1951), and Frank M. Gryna set out to measure the total cost of quality. Up until then, many managers thought of the cost of quality mainly as the cost of poor quality—the costs that arise from producing defects (such as the cost of waste, scrapped goods, rework, delays, downtime, customer complaints, warranty claims, and lost sales).

Juran and Gryna, as did Philip Crosby, expanded the definition to include the cost of *good quality*. The costs are as follows:

- The *cost of poor quality* includes internal and external failure costs. Internal failure costs arise *before* the products are delivered to customers and include rework, scrapped goods, delays, downtime, redesign, failure analysis, and retesting.
- External failure costs arise *after* the products are delivered to customers and include customer complaints, warranty claims, repairs, service calls, and sales lost due to customer dissatisfaction and bad word of mouth.
- These are the costs of response and recovery from a quality failure. It's been recognized for some time that many of the costs of poor quality are hard to identify by casual observation and can be difficult to measure. Some of the costs of poor quality such as waste, scrap, rejects, returns, recalls, and testing are quite visible and readily measurable.
- Others are less visible but are nonetheless very real. These indirect costs of poor quality include factors such as delays, paperwork, excess inventory, and the cost of developing failed products. There are usually significant opportunities to reduce those "hidden" costs in most organizations.
- The *cost of good quality* includes all expenses incurred to prevent defects and errors from occurring in products or services in the first place (prevention costs), *and* all expenses incurred to control quality by ensuring that products or services conform to quality standards and performance requirements (appraisal costs).

- *Prevention costs* include quality planning, supplier evaluation, new product review, error proofing, and quality improvement team meetings, projects, and training.
- *Appraisal costs* include process and materials control and testing, checking and testing products and services, field testing, process audits, and calibration of measuring and testing equipment. These are the costs of advance preparation and preventing quality problems.

The cost of poor quality plus the cost of good quality equal the total cost of quality, expressed as follows:

> **Total cost of quality** (TCOQ) = **Cost of poor quality** (all the internal and external costs resulting from failure to achieve desired levels of quality in process, product, or service) + **Cost of good quality** (the costs of activities and processes that achieve desired quality in a process, product, or service)

In other words, if the process, product, or service works perfectly, all of these costs would be eliminated. Juran and Gryna found that, over time, quality improvement programs can reduce the total cost of quality by half if the costs haven't been systematically addressed previously.[1] They also found that most of the problems resulted from relatively few causes, the ubiquitous 80/20 rule—80 percent of the problems resulted from 20 percent of the causes. This, again, points us toward the need to distinguish between "the vital few and the trivial many."

The traditional management view of the relationship between the cost of poor quality and the cost of good quality is that in reducing the cost of poor quality the organization necessarily increases the cost of good quality. For example, to reduce waste and rejected materials, production managers must meet with suppliers and increase quality control efforts on inputs. To reduce rework, the company must spend more on process control, improved training, and closer supervision.

Such efforts do increase costs, but only up to a point. That's because by designing better processes and using better inputs, over time you can drive down not only the costs of poor quality but also the costs of good quality. Better processes generate lower prevention and quality control costs—costs of good quality. Those costs cannot be eliminated, but they can be reduced as processes improve.[2]

The Total Cost of Risk

Like decisions to invest in quality improvement, decisions to invest in risk intelligence should be based on the returns. Management must consider the cost of risk in terms of financial impact. This means the amount of revenue the enterprise would have to bring in, or the amount of savings it would have to achieve, to replace the amount lost should the risk occur. We have found that these numbers generally prove that an ounce of prevention is indeed worth several pounds of cure.

To consider the amount to be invested, management must know the total cost of risk (TCOR). The total cost of risk consists of two sets of costs—the cost of failure (COF) and the cost of risk management (CORM).

The cost of failure (COF) includes direct and indirect costs associated with a failure (again, we use the term "failure" as quality improvement uses the term "defect"). Direct costs are the costs of response and recovery from failures of quality, products, projects, acquisitions, alliances, or market entry attempts.

Direct costs of failure also include the losses and costs associated with response and recovery from events such as regulatory actions, product recalls, warranty claims, disruption to supply chains or operations, seizure of assets by a foreign power, and natural and manmade disasters. COF also includes indirect costs ("collateral damage") such as opportunity costs, lost opportunities, and damage to reputation or brand equity. The cost of failure is the sum of these direct and indirect costs, expressed in monetary terms.

Cost of risk management (CORM) includes direct expenses associated with preparation for, and prevention and control of, risks. Direct expenses include, for example, the costs of risk management functions; board and management time; training; review, monitoring, and control; early detection and response capabilities; insurance premiums; and internal and external audit and other assurance functions. Indirect costs of risk management also include any burden on the business, such as compliance and procedural tasks, and unnecessary approval levels. The cost of risk management (CORM) is the sum of the direct and indirect costs of good risk management.

The total cost of risk calculation, roughly equivalent to the total cost of quality, is:

Total cost of risk (TCOR) = **Cost of failure** (COF, the direct and indirect costs associated with losses due to failures and the costs of response and recovery) + **Cost of risk management** (CORM, the direct and indirect costs of risk management activities, processes, and personnel that support prevention and preparation for potential failure, i.e., risk)

Some of these costs, particularly costs of failure, can be hard to calculate. But it is possible and it is certainly worth the effort. In fact, quantifying risk in monetary terms is essential because it:

- Helps management to prioritize risks in monetary terms using a common denominator and thus enables normalization of risk impact across all business units
- Enables measurement of mitigation by the amount of the reduction in risk or cost of failure
- Provides thresholds for reporting and escalating communication of risks
- Enables management to make cost-benefit calculations to determine the return on investment in improving risk management.

In addition, measuring risk in monetary terms allows risks that are common to multiple business units to be aggregated into enterprise-wide impacts. Money is the language of business and monetary terms provide a readily understandable means for communicating the size of risks and the benefits of improved risk management. The costs of risk can be quite clearly conceived in terms of insurance. When buying insurance, companies evaluate the cost of failure (the potential loss) and the costs of risk management (the cost of the premium) and then decide accordingly.

Exhibit 14.1 portrays the costs of risk management as an iceberg. The entire iceberg represents the TCOR. That cost includes the CORM, which are the smaller but more visible tip of the iceberg. The COF are much larger, but they remain hidden, until they occur. Our goal is to identify, understand, anticipate, and better manage all those costs and eventually shrink the entire iceberg.

Determining COF can be difficult. In most enterprises, accounting systems do not readily provide cost of failure information for failed product

Cost of Risk Management

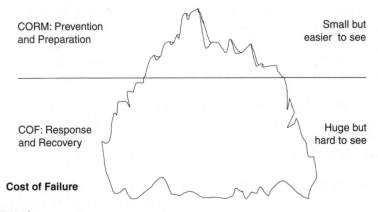

EXHIBIT 14.1 Cost of Risk Management

launches, market entries, acquisitions, or opportunity costs. Nor do they provide the costs for failing to protect existing assets. With the exception of headline-making catastrophes, failures often become some of the enterprise's best-kept secrets. Yet keeping such information hidden, especially hidden from the board and senior executives, can prove highly disadvantageous, for several reasons:

- If COF is not well understood, gaining support to allocate the resources required to drive corrective action will remain difficult.
- If COF is not measured, improvement in risk management, and thus value, cannot be demonstrated.
- CORM is generally more visible than COF, so there will always likely be downward pressure to reduce CORM and improve efficiency without fully considering the COF.

Just because management doesn't know the cost of failure doesn't mean it should not. In fact, a true assessment of the potential magnitude of failure should be conducted across the entire enterprise, including the extended enterprise.

The cost of risk management will generally be easier to develop. A number of the costs, such as compensation of risk functions, insurance premiums, training expenses, and auditors' fees, are explicit. Others can be developed. The burden on the business is often one of the most difficult aspects to quantify and yet it often accounts for the greatest resistance on the part of the business to a more systematic approach to risk management.

Exhibit 14.2 presents the basic components of TCOR. On the left side are the components of COF, in which failure is an unacceptable difference between actual and expected performance.[3] The components of COF include the hard costs of recovery and correction plus any collateral damage, such as tarnished brand and reputation. The right-hand side describes some of the elements of CORM such as awareness and training, prevention, review, preparedness, monitoring, early detection, early response, internal and external audit, and other forms of assurance and independent reassurance.

TCOR equals the COF plus CORM. To minimize TCOR, the ideal objective would be to minimize both COF and CORM. However, bringing down the total cost of risk may actually mean having to make a greater investment in the cost of risk management.

THE RULE OF INVERSE PRECISION   Extreme precision in these measures is not the goal. That is particularly so if there have been limited (or no) efforts in the past to develop these numbers. When it comes to initial estimates, generally the bigger the number, the less precise you have to be. The value

EXHIBIT 14.2 Total Cost of Risk (TCOR)

Total Cost of Failure (COF)		Total Costs of Risk Management (CORM)	
Direct Costs of Failure (Response & Recovery)	$	**Direct Costs of Risk Management (Prevention, Preparation & Control)**	$
Quality failures		All risk functions	
Failed products		(e.g., legal, treasury, insurance, business continuity, etc).	
Failed projects		Awareness and training	
Failed acquisitions		Review, monitoring and control	
Failed market entry		Early detection and early response	
Response		Assurance and independent	
Recovery		reassurance (internal and external)	
Indirect Costs/Collateral Damage		**Indirect Costs**	
Lost opportunity		Burden on the business	
Reputation		Potential for growth in bureaucracy	
Total Cost of Failure		**Total Cost of Risk Management**	
Bottom-line impact and top-line revenue equivalency		Estimated ROI for TCORM investment	

of knowing whether the potential costs in direct expenses and lost sales of, say, a two-week shutdown of a production or distribution facility is $6.2 million or $6.3 million will usually not be that important.

It will be easier to determine potential impact on existing assets such as inventories of goods at risk of spoilage or buildings exposed to potential destruction. The same applies to calculations of overtime incurred due to shutdowns, increased costs of rush orders, and even the value of specific customer relationships. All should be available from records or from knowledgeable personnel.

The value (or replacement value) of equipment and other real property is available from records and vendors. The cost impact of downtime and of late deliveries can come from records and from seasoned employees. More elusive will be potential damage to intangibles such as goodwill, reputation, and brand equity. However, the impact of substitute products on future growth and customer retention can be calculated.

The estimates need only to provide a credible idea of the potential impact of various risk events, and thus their priority and their impact relative to the expense of avoidance or mitigation. The figures will also serve as benchmarks by which to gauge impact, velocity, and momentum. That is, if the costs associated with an event rise more quickly or slowly than anticipated or if the mass is larger or smaller, you can gauge velocity and momentum. That in turn will tell you how much, if anything, to spend to keep pace with or to get ahead of the crisis or event. Experience can then be used to corroborate whether those initial estimates were reasonably accurate and, if not, to recalibrate.

Where to Begin?

SEC regulations[4] require publicly listed companies in the United States to disclose significant or material factors associated with their securities. Without delving into the accounting meanings of "significant" and "material," we can say that determinations of materiality for purposes of disclosure[5] are *generally* interpreted as 5 percent of net income. Applying this guidance, each disclosed risk factor has the potential to adversely impact net operating results by at least 5 percent.

An unpublished 2005 Deloitte study of a sample of more than 300 publicly listed enterprises across 45 industry segments revealed that they disclosed a combined total of 246 individual risk factors. On average, a single company disclosed about 32 risk factors. The 10 most frequently disclosed are listed in Exhibit 14.3. Note that most of these risks are not preventable, and therefore you must be prepared for those risks in particular.

The preceding discussion and Exhibit 14.3 addresses hypothetical situations. To relate this analysis to your enterprise, complete Exhibit 14.4 by estimating the cost of failure associated with the risk factors specific to your enterprise.

EXHIBIT 14.3 Most Frequent Publicly Disclosed Risks (in a sample of 300+ companies)*

Rank	Disclosed Risk	Frequency
1	Economic conditions/trends	294
2	Adverse legal/regulatory/environmental changes	288
3	Competitors and competitive actions	281
4	Business interruption (e.g., supply interruption and natural disasters/severe weather)	277
5	Litigation/intellectual capital issues	213
6	M&A strategy/execution/integration	192
7	Political stability/country risk	189
8	Unanticipated changes in consumer demands/preferences	187
9	Inability to develop/market new products	156
10	Terrorist activities/war/civil unrest	149

*Unpublished research of 10-Q, 10-K, and 20-F filings; Deloitte 2005.

EXHIBIT 14.4 Estimated Cost of Failure Template

Frequently Disclosed 10-K Risk Factors	COF ($)
Economic downturn/recession/credit/liquidity	_____
Adverse changes in laws/regulations	_____
New competitors/competitors' actions	_____
Litigation and intellectual property protection	_____
Political instability/country risk	_____
Failed M&A strategy, execution/integration	_____
Changes in consumer demand/preferences	_____
Disruptions to supply chain (stability, sourcing, cost)	_____
Terrorist activities/war/civil unrest	_____
Cost/availability of capital	_____
Other	_____
Cost of missed opportunities (usually not a 10-K factor)	_____
Cost of Failure	

Many of these factors are external to the enterprise. Some may say these risks are not within the enterprise's control. While it may be true that the causes of these factors are not within the direct control of the enterprise, the enterprise can and must develop responses to mitigate the effects of these risks. To do otherwise would be like saying you are responsible for the engine room but not the successful navigation of turbulent waters because storms are not within your control.

After selecting your enterprise's risk factors and adding your own, complete the COF column with your best estimate of the cost of these failures, including direct and indirect costs. Again, the larger the number, the less precise you need to be. The real question is, how big does a failure need to be for it to be unacceptable?

To get to the TCOR, you can't simply stop at the cost of failure. You must also calculate CORM, which includes all costs to prevent or prepare for a potential risk and the costs of control and monitoring. Exhibit 14.5 offers some examples.

Many of these numbers will be easier to gather than those for COF. For those that aren't, a best guess will still render a high-level view of CORM. From there, calculating TCOR is just a matter of adding COF to CORM.

You probably won't like the size of the resulting number. So your goal then becomes to reduce TCOR by optimizing the cost of risk management and, as a result, reducing the cost of failure. Will it work? Will improved risk management actually reduce the cost of failure to the point where risk management outlays produce a worthwhile return?

EXHIBIT 14.5 Cost of Risk Management (CORM)

	CORM ($)
COST OF PREVENTION/PREPARATION	
Planning and communications	_____
Risk assessments (such as for new products, country, and physical and cyber security)	_____
Training and professional development	_____
Process and systems controls	_____
Performance data acquisition and analysis	_____
Backup data	_____
Inventory buffers	_____
Failure/loss experience reporting	_____
Research on emerging risks	_____
Improvement projects	_____
Insurance/risk financing	_____
Other prevention and preparation costs	_____
COST OF CONTROL AND MONITORING	
Risk and compliance monitoring	_____
Internal review processes (such as legal, security, and finance)	_____
Inspections, tests, and reviews (such as SOX and internal and external audit)	_____
Business burden (time required to comply)	_____
Maintaining accuracy of testing equipment/reliability of reporting	_____
Use of risk and control consultants	_____
Materials and staff time consumed	_____
Other monitoring and control costs	
Cost of Risk Management (CORM)	▬▬▬▬▬▬

Recall that if the record of quality improvement efforts is any indication, the answer is yes. But there does come a point where further investments in risk management may not be justified. Juran and Gryna illustrated this point by plotting three curves, similar to those shown in Exhibit 14.6, where we show the costs of risk management.

- The cost of failure (COF) is represented by the large-dash line. COF can never be reduced to zero, but it decreases as risk management effectiveness (on the horizontal axis) increases. Ineffective risk management can cause the cost of failure to theoretically rise to infinity—that is, to the point at which the enterprise itself fails.
- The cost of risk management (CORM) is represented by the dot-and-dash curve. If things are working properly, as the cost of risk management increases so does the effectiveness of risk management. Note that

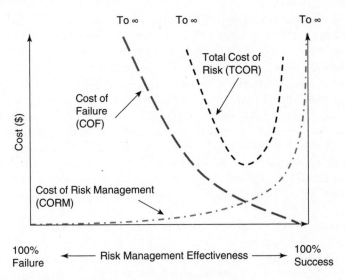

EXHIBIT 14.6 TCOR and Risk Management Effectiveness

100 percent success is not possible, but can be approached (more so in limited areas of quality improvement than in risk management).

- The total cost of risk (TCOR) is depicted by the U-shaped short-dash curve, and it is the sum of the cost of failure plus the cost of risk management.

Note that TCOR falls as the cost of risk management rises—but only up to a point! What does this mean? It means that TCOR begins to rise at the point where the marginal expenditure on risk management equals the marginal reduction in the cost of failure. That is the point of negative marginal returns—the optimal point for expenditures on risk management. After that point, increased expenditures on risk management will still produce decreases in the cost of failure, but the increased expenditure will outweigh the decreased risk.

The goal therefore is to find that optimum point. Of course, we recognize that this is something of a theoretical construct with regard to risk management as opposed to quality improvement. Risk is a moving target—subject to far more dynamic forces than the quality of a tangible product. But this construct makes two points. First, it is worthwhile for most enterprises to step up their risk management efforts if they have not taken an integrated, systematic, enterprise-wide approach. Second, generally speaking, risk management should not become an obsession to the point where you try to eliminate every potential failure. That would be antithetical to risk intelligence.

Translating Juran and Gryna's recommendations regarding quality improvement initiatives into risk management terms, it would be best to begin with "breakthrough" projects where the COF is greatest and the CORM is least. If no such improvement opportunities can be identified, then focus on control and efficiency improvements to reduce CORM. With the exception of risks for which the enterprise has zero tolerance, such as health and safety, management should avoid further investments in risk mitigation where the costs of mitigation exceed the costs of failure and thus simply add to TCOR. The best opportunities to improve effectiveness should be addressed first, and then the best opportunities to improve efficiency.

Henry Ford said, "Failure is the opportunity to begin again more intelligently." Learning from failure is often at the heart of success and innovation. Outside of certain zero tolerance areas a certain level of failure must not only be expected and tolerated but actually encouraged. What is the range of failure that is acceptable and to be expected?

There is no such thing as perfect prevention, and failure cannot be eliminated. Efforts to eliminate the risk of failure will likely result in loss of innovation and erosion of competitiveness. Furthermore, you should avoid improvements that just create bureaucracy. Finally, estimates of the costs of risk should be credible and avoid either over- or understatement.

MORE LESSONS FROM QUALITY IMPROVEMENT A major lesson from quality improvement that is quite germane to risk management is that "If no systematic approach has previously been employed, it is possible to achieve a 50 percent reduction in the cost of poor quality"[6] and, by extension, the cost of failure. Applying Juran and Gryna's quality prescriptions to risk management and substituting concepts of risk intelligence and risk management for those of quality, it ought to be evident that:

1. Prevention, preparation, control, and monitoring are less expensive than response and recovery, provided the risk is relevant to the business and presents significant potential for loss, harm, or missed opportunity.
2. If you don't know how much it is costing you to fail, you will have a hard time proving the value of preventing failure.
3. The enterprise requires a risk intelligent system of governance and risk management that includes:
   a. The entire enterprise, including the extended enterprise, the supply chain, and the lifecycle of its products or services
   b. A common and consistent vocabulary of risk terms

    c. A comprehensive management process that includes planning, orga-
       nizing, staffing, controlling, monitoring, and continuous improve-
       ment.
4. Once identified, the cost of failure will usually be high enough to get
   senior management's attention.
5. The cost of failure is usually found in the "vital few versus the trivial many"—that is, most of the cost of failure will likely be caused by
   relatively few factors.
6. You must make the cost of failure real to management by expressing it
   in monetary terms such as:
    a. Percentage of top-line revenue required to compensate for a failure
    b. Impact on operating margin
    c. Comparability to the cost of current risk management

Case Example: Quantification   One company uses four measures to develop a
sense of the value of their risk management efforts:

1. *Risk exposure reductions.* These are the effects of the mitigations. The
   initial, inherent impact (cost of the risk event) is determined during
   the original assessment of the risk. When mitigations are effective,
   the new, residual impact is usually lower than the inherent impact.
   The difference (the amount by which the risk exposure is reduced) is
   tracked.
2. *Risk events.* All risk events that occur throughout the year are tracked.
   The impact of the event is recorded and compared with the risk assessment (and whether it was assessed) and then reported.
3. *Actual savings.* The company calculates the cost savings that accrue as
   a direct result of improved risk management and includes items such
   as insurance premium reductions. This calculation includes realized
   reductions in exposure for an actual risk event when risk management
   reduced the exposure and the actual cost came in lower than originally
   assessed.
4. *The cost of risk mitigation.* Understanding the cost of risk mitigation
   is an important part of the decision-making process especially when
   prioritizing responses.

    Exhibit 14.7 shows a sample calculation of the risk exposure reduction
for a number of identified risks and a comparison to the cost of achieving
that reduction.
    Scenarios are used to define the risk and to quantify the impact based
on the severity and speed of impact. The scenarios are locked down during
the assessment so that subsequent assessments can be compared with the

EXHIBIT 14.7 Reductions in Risk Exposure*

Risk Name	Inherent Impact ($m)	Residual Impact ($m)	Risk Exposure Reduction ($m)	Cost of Risk Reduction ($m)
Risk A	1,000	200	800	40
Risk B	900	400	500	20
Risk C	650	300	350	20
Risk D	700	450	250	15
Risk E	150	25	125	5
Risk F	300	190	110	6
Risk G	300	200	100	4
Risk H	100	10	90	4
Risk I	150	60	90	5
Risk J	125	40	85	5
Risk K	220	145	75	5
Risk L	80	5	75	3
Risk M	180	130	50	4
Risk N	75	45	30	2
Risk O	30	5	25	2
Risk P	25	5	20	1
20 other risks <$10m each, totaling $100m	150	50	100	6
	$5,135	**$2,260**	**$2,875**	**147**

*Savings are realized if/when the risk event occurs.

initial assessment to determine the reduction of impact based only upon the mitigations.

Probabilistic estimates are not used at this point in calculating inherent risk. That's because they may distort perceptions of inherent risks as being unlikely and thus as not requiring mitigation, when they do require it.

THE VALUE OF RISK EXPOSURE REDUCTION   The relationship between the inherent risk value and the residual risk value is important. An analysis of this relationship underscores the importance of the mitigations being applied. The inherent risk impact of an event is the gross risk impact before risk management; the residual risk impact is the net risk impact of the event after risk management.

The difference between inherent risk impact and residual risk impact is the reduction in risk exposure. It's also essential to weigh the impact of the risk event if the mitigations fail. For example, if the gross risk (inherent risk) is $800 million and the net risk (residual risk) is $10 million, the net risk might seem small, but the mitigated value is $790 million (the difference between $800 million and $10 million). If the mitigations were to fail, the risk event would generate far more loss than the current net risk of $10 million, perhaps closer to the $800 million. Therefore, assurance and independent reassurance that the risk mitigations are effective become essential.

When confronted with equivalent net exposures and limited resources, the enterprise must make difficult choices in prioritizing its risk mitigation responses. At this point, it is appropriate to consider estimates of probability. Decisions to allocate resources to reduce net exposures based on their probability should be an informed choice. If certain net exposures are seen as more likely and worth further mitigation, then other, less likely net exposures are consciously accepted.

As noted, some risk assessments fail because they falsely assume that high-impact, low-likelihood events won't occur. But as we've all seen, extreme events happen all the time. A more prudent approach identifies the risks that are highly relevant to the business and that pose the greatest threat to the enterprise. The board should then seek reasonable assurances from management that these risks have been understood and mitigated *independent of their likelihood*. After all, if the risk is relevant and high impact, the company ought to have a plan to manage it.

The Rewards of Risk Intelligence

This chapter focuses on the cost-benefit calculus required to make the case for risk intelligence. But the rewards of risk intelligence take many forms, virtually all of which, we believe, translate to financial returns. Those rewards include:

- Improved ability to prevent, detect, correct, and escalate critical risk issues and incidents
- Reduced burden on business operations by standardizing risk management principles and language
- Improved sharing of risk information and better integration of existing risk management functions
- Improved ability to rely on one another's work rather than to repeat it
- Improved resilience and agility built into core processes in strategic planning, product development, treasury management, IT security, and virtually every other enterprise activity, and a greater range of strategic responses to threats and opportunities

- Improved strategic flexibility for upside and downside scenarios, due to identification of "black swans" and through development of requisite variety
- Improved speed of response and recovery from crisis and better damage control
- Greater ability to show the board and other stakeholders that management understands and is managing the full range of risks the enterprise faces, with critical interdependencies identified and appropriate margins of safety established

These may seem somewhat "soft" to some readers, so we mention them at the end of this chapter, after making the financial case. However, we have found that these rewards, although perhaps harder to quantify, are every bit as real and beneficial as the measurable monetary returns of risk intelligence.

Making the Case

Executives must make decisions regarding risk management initiatives and practices the same way they make every other decision—on the basis of costs and benefits. This chapter has illustrated the importance of understanding the total cost of risk, which includes the cost of failure and the cost of risk management, so that the enterprise can make calculated, rational decisions regarding expenditures to improve risk intelligence and competitive advantage.

This chapter drew upon concepts, tools, and methods from quality improvement because the considerations, challenges, and decisions are very similar. However, the figures upon which quality calculations are based are usually more precise than those involved in risk management.

That said, approaching risk intelligence in this way provides a logical framework and a systematic approach to the issue. Also, again drawing a parallel to quality improvement, risk intelligence is free in the sense that well-chosen expenditures on risk management can produce benefits that completely offset the costs. Moreover, it's quite possible that the benefits of avoiding or mitigating failures will more than outweigh the costs of risk management. If not, at least the board and management made a risk intelligent decision.

Demonstrating the value of prevention can be difficult, even with cost-of-failure calculations; after all, few of us go through the day considering the monetary value of all of the problems we've avoided, let alone considering avoiding them to be profitable. But the benefits of risk intelligence go well beyond avoiding the cost of failure, to include capabilities that enhance both operations and competitive advantage.

Questions to Ask about the Costs and Benefits of Risk Intelligence

- What is our current cost of failure?
- What is our current cost of risk management?
- What is our current total cost of risk?
- Where are the opportunities for breakthrough improvements?
- What level of investment is required to significantly reduce the total cost of risk?

CHAPTER 15

Risk Intelligent Governance

*The challenge for our leaders is to respond to risk with the right mix
of daring and reason... For this we need the best information we
can get, the best judgment we can summon, and the best advice we
can find.*

—Madeleine Albright[1]

Surviving and thriving in uncertainty require the enterprise to be risk
intelligent—to anticipate, detect, and respond effectively to change,
whether it be sudden and violent or slow and subtle. Leadership needs
to be intelligent about the risks the enterprise should take to be competitive
and the risks it should prevent or avoid. After all, as Jamie Clarke, a mountaineer who has successfully climbed Mt. Everest, says, "Who wants to be
risk stupid?"[2]

Recall that discussions of value and risk are inseparable. Risk, including
the risk of inaction, attends every attempt to protect and create value. Superior decision making and thus competitive advantage demands intelligence
and insight into potential rewards and the related risks. As noted in the preceding chapter, just like quality, the marginally increased cost of improved
risk management typically will be more than offset by the reduced cost of
failure.

Let's start with the decision-making roles and responsibilities of the
board and its committees. Most discussions of governance—roles, responsibilities, tasks, and structures—focus on what the board is supposed to
do but not how to go about doing it. The business literature abounds
with "how-to" advice for executives but offers relatively little for directors.
Similarly, well-developed systems of operating management exist, but little has been done to create a systematic approach to governance for the
board.

Most boards would benefit from such a system, and risk intelligence provides a framework for systematically establishing and executing board-level risk-related responsibilities, as it does for all risk-related activities. From governance of strategic risk to operational decisions to reporting and compliance activities, risk intelligence can be and should be woven into all core business and decision-making processes.

For these reasons, risk management must not become a discrete activity—something you do when you are done with your day job. Conventional risk management is too often perceived by directors and executives as someone else's job. Building risk intelligence into core processes embeds awareness, management, and control of risk at all levels, thus improving effectiveness and efficiency.

This chapter focuses specifically on the board's governance activities, particularly with regard to value and risk oversight. It examines the board's responsibilities for value and risk and provides practical ways by which the board can interact with senior executives in executing their respective risk-related responsibilities.

The Risk Intelligent Board

Governance is ultimately about decision making and execution. What are the key decisions? Who gets to make them? What insights and intelligence do they need to make a superior decision under the circumstances? How is the decision enacted and with what results? Based on the results, should we stay the course or change course? Effective governance provides the appropriate level of direction and control in determining the goals of the enterprise, the means of pursuing those goals, and the risks attendant to that pursuit.

In other words, effective governance is risk intelligent. Although the board is ultimately responsible and accountable for the survival and success of the enterprise, it delegates decision authority to its various committees and to the CEO. The CEO, in turn, delegates to other executives, who delegate down the chain of command.

The board should determine which decisions (opportunities and risks) it wants to come to its attention. For those decisions, the board can judge firsthand the quality and capability of risk management. In most enterprises, board members know they are responsible for governance, both to safeguard shareholders' interests and to support sustained growth and success.

They also know they are ultimately accountable for matters related to risk oversight. Yet, as noted, boards often don't know how to establish a framework and a process that will enable them to execute their role in governance. Indeed, many boards have dealt with the new demands around risk through ad hoc approaches that address specific risks at certain times but fail to provide a reliable, comprehensive process of risk intelligent governance.

Nonetheless, executives are responsible for managing the business and all the associated risks and providing reasonable assurance to the board that there are capable people, processes, and systems to do so. This is especially the case for those decisions, risks, and opportunities that do not need to come to the board.

Thus, a risk intelligent board:

1. Provides insight and advice, not just oversight
2. Establishes the character of the enterprise
3. Balances long-term and short-term considerations
4. Approves the risk appetite and tolerances of the enterprise
5. Defines the decisions (opportunities and risks) that require the board's attention
6. Obtains reasonable assurance from management as well as independent reassurance
7. Ensures the enterprise is prepared for crises

The following sections address each of these capabilities.

Provide Insight and Advice, Not Just Oversight

Few would dispute that oversight is the primary responsibility of the full board of directors, although they might disagree about what oversight means. As earlier chapters noted, CEOs want boards to also provide insight. In both cases, the challenge for many boards is how to gain a line of sight into enterprises that are increasingly complex, diverse, and opaque. Don Rice, a CEO and director, says, "When reviewing strategic plans with management, boards should ask questions that contribute to strategy and not just conduct operational reviews"[3]

Not all directors agree that in-depth knowledge of operations is essential. Leslie Rahl, president and founder of Capital Market Risk Advisors of New York and also a director says, "Risk management is a board issue . . . The real role of the board is to ask the right questions. I think this does not require in-depth knowledge but rather good judgment."[4]

The essence of governance is decision making and oversight of the execution of those decisions—while responsibility for execution rests with senior management and the business units. Given those realities, what are the board's oversight responsibilities?

Generally, they are to set the tone, elevate risk as a priority, and initiate the communication and activities that lead to sound enterprise management.

This means ensuring management has created a cohesive risk management process across the organization, in which risk-related interdependencies are routinely investigated, evaluated, understood, and effectively managed.

Voice of Experience

"The number one challenge facing some boards today is a lack of courage to ask and follow-up with the difficult question. For example, 'How can we be making loans with no documentation and expect that we're going to get paid?' Management may say, 'Well, that's because you don't understand the issue. Let me explain to you why we think it's going to be okay.' Then the directors may not have the courage to ask probing 'second' questions.

"So it's a lack of courage or maybe a lack of directors feeling empowered to ask the tough questions without feeling that they are impinging on management. That's an important dynamic, which we need more of. There's no forum for constructive challenge, especially when people are making a lot of money.

"The next challenge is accountability. Show me a map of the risks, show me who is responsible for the management of the risk, and what committee of the board is responsible for the oversight of the management of the risk. Many organizations do not have clear accountability for the management and oversight of risk from beginning to end."

—Ken Daly, CEO, National Association of Corporate Directors

Directors should be a sounding board for the CEO and a source of constructive challenge of key decisions and directions. The board ought to be one of the CEO's most valuable resources. Yet many directors complain that much of their time is consumed by a focus on compliance. Many CEOs also privately lament that they are not getting the kinds of insight and advice they need from their boards on strategic issues. They are also quick to add that they ought to be careful what they wish for.

Directors should, therefore, first gain insight into the threats and opportunities critical to the future survival and success of the enterprise; second, understand and approve the business strategy and structure for future growth and protection of existing assets; and, third, approve the range of acceptable outcomes in terms of enterprise franchise value (that is, define success and failure).

On that last point, the board can be better prepared by defining criteria for success and failure in advance, that is, its risk appetite and tolerances.

With such criteria, the board can make better determinations regarding both margins of safety and stop-loss provisions for specific major transactions. The matter of risk appetite is discussed further below.

Voice of Experience

"When I start getting involved in a new situation, I will say, 'I don't understand the business model here. What are the drivers of this business?' I believe it can take a year or more on a board to even get to the point where we can ask the right questions. You can have a good business background and so forth, but until you really understand the values of the organization, what the business drivers are of the organization, what kind of strategy they have in place (if they have a strategy in place), and how they execute, it's going to be difficult to really add a lot of value as a director.

"One of the things that needs to happen on boards is to make sure that people understand the strategy, understand the drivers, understand the values, because values create the behavior and create the culture. If you've got that kind of understanding, then you can say, 'All right, I want to see the capital structure. I want to see what affects the capital structure, what affects their earnings, the revenues, what kind of risks are we looking at?'"

—David Meuse, Director

The board should also thoroughly understand the enterprise strategy and its risks. Moreover, strategy development should be a collaborative process between management and the board. Directors and officers should mutually agree on the process to be used to develop the strategy and on their respective roles in strategy development. As noted earlier, without clear understanding and alignment between directors and officers, an otherwise sound strategy may be reversed or an otherwise capable leadership displaced when difficulties are experienced.

To ensure more active involvement in strategy, boards should make the discussion of strategy a part of their standing agenda. This can be supplemented by regular reviews of strategy and special board retreats. A number of directors have expressed the concern that strategic issues are often given too little time on meeting agendas or left until everyone is dashing to catch their planes.

How can directors prevent management from simply telling them what they want to hear? Professor Ray Reilly says, "Having a solid framework is a great starting position. The framework should be used to structure periodic consideration by the board of the key elements of the firm's corporate and business strategies. Management is responsible for providing a clear and current picture of each element and the interrelationships among them. Board members should use their understanding and insight to ask the difficult questions and to identify and challenge critical assumptions. They should provide an alternative view from their unique perspectives. Fulfilling this role requires board members with highly developed business acumen."[5]

As part of its oversight responsibilities, the board should continually monitor the implementation of strategies against key performance metrics and monitor the major risks and opportunities that may affect the strategy. Oversight also means ensuring that course corrections are made as required. That is, directors must be able to recognize the need for a change in strategic direction when circumstances require and have the will to voice their concerns and demand action.

Voice of Experience

"Both companies and boards tend to dwell too long on more problematic situations. It's sort of like the old story of the individual investor: They keep hoping that things will work out better. They are really good at knowing when to buy stocks, but they are terrible at knowing when to sell them. Many companies share that kind of experience—they stay way too long with things that just aren't going to work out in the long run."

—Denny Beresford, Director and Professor, J.M. Tull School of Accounting

Another area of governance that could benefit from increased board insight is the growing divergence of board, shareholder, and stakeholder expectations and the challenges involved in trying to manage and meet those expectations. This is especially important as the board itself is no longer a monolith. But it doesn't stop there. Various types of shareholders and key stakeholders often have sharply different expectations, interests, and views that the board should make a special effort to understand.

Professor Ira Millstein notes that since the 1960s, patterns of share ownership have changed and have become much more concentrated. From individual investors to institutional investors, such as mutual funds and pension funds, to hedge funds and private equity and more recently, sovereign wealth funds, and direct government ownership, these changes may have "balkanized" the boardroom.[6]

Each of these shareholders may have different objectives and expectations regarding investments, time horizons, executive compensation, nomination of directors, corporate social responsibility, or defensive positions to potential threats or offensive positions to exploit opportunities.

All of these factors make it even more crucial that there be a proactive communication process for understanding and responding to diverse shareholder and stakeholder interests. (See also the discussion on guidance policy in Chapter 11, "Set Your Enterprise Time Horizons.")

Establish the Character of the Enterprise

One of the most important roles of the board, if not the most important, is to select the CEO based on the individual's attributes, including values, passion, and understanding of the business. That selection goes a long way toward defining the character of the enterprise. The commitment to the core values of the firm, its ethical conduct, and sustainable growth begin with the appointment of the CEO, which sets the tone at the top. But the process does not end there.

The board should ensure that the desired character and culture of the entire enterprise is being appropriately developed and nurtured. Site visits and employee opinion surveys can be used to help gain insight into the corporate culture. Executives must be accountable for their actions, and this includes specific assignment of responsibility for the management of key dimensions of value and risk. It is the board that either holds senior executives accountable, or fails to do so, and thus establishes the true character of the enterprise.

WHAT DOES THE BOARD DELEGATE—AND NOT DELEGATE? The enterprise's delegation of authority (DoA) policy should be considered one of the foundational policies for enterprise management. It should ensure the cohesive and consistent character of the enterprise and clear accountability. Through the DoA, the board delegates certain authorities and responsibilities to the CEO. Although authority will be further delegated within the company, accountability for managing the enterprise's property, assets, and human resources rests with the CEO. Yet the DoA cannot substitute for good judgment, particularly when it comes to risk.

The importance of a well-defined DoA was brought home to an international consumer products company with operations in South America. The country board was composed of local nationals, including the CEO and the CFO. To reduce the impact of a potential devaluation of the currency on their compensation, management revised their retirement plans with the approval of the local national board—but not corporate. When the devaluation occurred, the effect was an increase in retirement benefits beyond those of the global CEO and CFO.

When corporate discovered this, it demanded that these benefits be rescinded. The local national board refused. When corporate took action to terminate the local CEO and CFO, a clause was triggered such that all of their benefits became immediately due and payable in cash. It cost the company millions of dollars to terminate those executives. The specific lesson is that all country policies must be subject to review and approval by corporate before they can be considered binding. But the broader lesson is that there should be a process in place to intentionally provide delegations of authority only after appropriate risks have been considered.

In addition to its powers as specified in the enterprise's certificate of incorporation and by-laws, the board should reserve to itself all authority not specifically delegated under the DoA. This typically includes:

- All matters related to corporate governance
- All public disclosures
- Significant financial decisions and the size of risks and opportunities requiring the attention of the board or its committees
- Accounting policies and principles and audit and nonaudit services and changes in accounting principles
- Executive compensation; appointment and termination of officers
- Waivers to corporate policies related to personal use of corporate assets or exemptions from the company's code of ethics and conduct (such as conflicts)
- Strategic plan and annual business plan
- Major capital expenditures, including IT, above a set dollar limit
- Business development: acquisitions and divestitures, investments in joint ventures and strategic alliances, and equity injections
- Officer and executive personnel matters
- Major borrowings and credit extensions
- Entering and exiting major business activities
- Major contractual commitments, leases and guarantees, expenditures on branding and marketing and on legal and tax settlements
- Any other matter that the board may choose to review

Obviously, what constitutes the meaning of "major" must be defined by the board. This is discussed further below.

Balance Long-Term and Short-Term Considerations

Sustainable enterprise strategies balance short-term and long-term considerations, as Chapter 11, "Set Your Enterprise Time Horizons," described.

Pressures to maximize short-term stock price performance have partly diminished the strategic role of the board, but a board can resist this trend. It can do so by the way it structures executive compensation and tenure. When executives' compensation depends on short-term performance and they see their tenure as limited, their decisions will reflect those facts. It is up to the board to think about the long-term interests of the enterprise and to ensure that executives act in those interests.

We recognize the difficulty of resisting short-termism. Doing so requires strong alignment on strategy between directors and officers. That alignment requires both directors and management to understand one another's positions regarding the business model and strategy, the required degrees of strategic flexibility, and the risk appetite and approach to risk management. This in turn suggests agreement and a unified focus on:

- Optimizing shareholder value rather than merely maximizing it in the short term
- Working toward long-term success rather than just short-term survival
- Considering the interests of all stakeholders, and not just shareholders

Michael Raynor has developed a simple chart (Exhibit 15.1) that depicts these responsibilities and the related considerations and questions.

Exhibit 15.1 relates to the same time horizon considerations raised in Chapter 11, which pointed out that certain levels of management should be focused on specific issues related to selected time horizons. The board must concern itself with the long-term success of the company. Long-term success depends on "strategic flexibility" and on the organization's ability to adapt and evolve as the environment changes. The board should also pay particular attention to the long-term unintended consequences of short-term decisions.

Approve the Risk Appetite and Tolerances of the Enterprise

Recall that risk is the potential for failure and that failure is an unacceptable difference between actual and expected performance. Some level of failure is to be expected and even desired. After all, experimentation and innovation by their very nature must involve latitude for failure. But at what point does that level of failure become unacceptable or pose the threat of ruin?

This must be a board decision and therefore, the board must approve the enterprise risk appetite. The risk appetite is the maximum allowable loss by type of risk and overall for the enterprise. Risk appetite should also describe the level of acceptable variability or tolerance for variability in expected outcomes whether they be in regard to goals and objectives, the strategy and its execution, operations, reporting, or compliance.

Organizational Level	Time Horizon	Risk/Return Focus	Strategic Question	Strategic Stance
Board Corporate	10 yrs to ∞			
Group	5 to 20 yrs		What could affect our status as an ongoing concern?	Strategic flexibility
Business unit	3 to 5 yrs		What could cause our strategy to fall short of our goals?	Strategic hedging
Function	1 to 3 yrs		What could cause our project to fail?	Strategic learning

EXHIBIT 15.1 Strategic Flexibility

The risk appetite policy should describe the enterprise appetite for various classes of risk and how much of that type of risk can be taken without endangering the enterprise. Risk appetite should vary according to the type of risk, i.e., whether risks are rewarded or unrewarded.

Making a clear distinction between rewarded and unrewarded risks is essential. As GM Vice Chairman Bob Lutz said, "We have to continue to fight the tendency that's in any large organization to be risk averse. That kind of thinking generates predictable mediocrity."[7]

The amount you are willing to bet on an acquisition and the acceptable level of variability will be different from your appetite for non-compliance with environmental regulations, unethical conduct, or health and safety violations. While there is no balance sheet approach that can produce an overall number for the enterprise across all types of risk, the aggregates of specific classes of risk should be understood. Adjusting the risk level of one type of risk may affect others. Therefore, these interactions and interdependencies need to be well understood as previously described in Exhibit 12.2.

The key then is to understand the capacity of the enterprise to effectively manage all of these risk classes simultaneously and to establish common policies regarding how risk will be monitored and managed. When the enterprise's capability is stretched too thinly, there is no margin for error.

Directors and management must be aligned on the risk appetite, particularly when executive turnover occurs, business conditions change, or new strategies are considered. When short-term performance considerations rule decisions, the inevitable bumps in the road may cause directors to prematurely abandon otherwise sound leadership or strategies.

As one director put it: "Management knows a lot more about the company and its strategy than directors do. But directors should know it and understand it just as well. We need to be able to check management's judgments and conclusions. They need to be patient with us while we do that. We have to have the same understanding so we can look them in the face and say, 'Go for it' because we believe it is right."

In developing the risk appetite policy, the board should ask and answer the following questions:

- How much do you expect to make by taking this risk and how much can you afford to lose?
- How much are you willing or unwilling to bet by type of risk without running the overall risk of ruin?

- What is the maximum allowable loss on any single bet and all aggregated bets in respective risk classes?
- What level of variation or failure do you expect and will you tolerate before it becomes unacceptable?
- Do you really understand how much overall risk you are taking?
- Is the enterprise capable of taking on this overall level of risk?
- Have you built in an appropriate margin of safety?
- What mechanisms are in place to signal approaching limits?
- How will you know that these limits are being observed?
- Are there stop losses in place?

In sum, the enterprise's risk appetite should describe the kinds and amounts of risks that the organization is willing and unwilling to take. It should express the amount of risk it can take without endangering the enterprise and, therefore, which risks warrant serious and continuing consideration.

The development of the enterprise risk appetite is not formulaic and involves considerable judgment. As circumstances inevitably change, it is also likely to be an iterative and dynamic process.

Define the Decisions that Require the Board's Attention

Many decisions (opportunities and risks) need not come to the board's attention because management and employees address them in the course of their daily work. The board should nonetheless periodically satisfy itself that capable people, processes, and information systems are in place to manage these everyday decisions. Then the board should avoid involvement in decisions that do not require its attention. But what size risk or opportunity—in terms of financial or nonfinancial impacts—do require the board's attention? Unfortunately, many boards have not explicitly answered that question.

To remedy this, the board should clearly define its expectations of the type and level of information that must come to their attention. The board should define its intelligence needs, including thresholds and escalation triggers for the major classifications of opportunity and risk and areas of impact on the enterprise. Sample areas of impact might include:

- *Financial.* Potential impact on revenues, earnings, or capital expressed as a percentage or monetary amount (plus or minus)
- *Reputation.* Potential for sustained positive or negative media attention at local, regional, national, or international levels and potential effects on brand equity and sales

- *Key stakeholders.* Parties with the potential to affect the enterprise, or be affected by a development within it, which might include customers, employees, suppliers, communities, pressure groups, and non-governmental organizations
- *Legal/regulatory.* Potential for sudden, adverse changes in laws and regulations or for major federal or state investigations and any potential fines, penalties, or adverse reputational impact
- *Health and safety.* Potential for impact on the environment, public health, or the safety of employees
- *Industry or enterprise specific.* Customer, supplier, or labor disruptions that are critical to the firm's strategy and scope of operations.

The preceding are only examples. Each board should define the type and magnitude of the potential impacts—and the areas of impact—with which it must be concerned. Financial metrics should be consistent with those the enterprise uses to measure its success. Since many companies use percentage of net income as a materiality threshold for items requiring disclosure, it may make sense to use a similar metric for other risks and opportunities. The threshold then should be defined for determining how big a risk or an opportunity must be to warrant the full board's or its committees' attention.

Obtain Reasonable Assurance from Management and Independent Reassurance

As part of its risk-related responsibilities, the board should obtain reasonable (but not absolute) assurance from management that there are capable people, processes, and systems in place to manage risks that do not need to come to its attention.

In 1996, the Delaware Chancery Court decision regarding Caremark reinforced the concept of reasonableness.[8] The court ruled, "The board is under a duty to attempt in good faith to assure that a corporate information and reporting system, which the board concludes is adequate, exists ... for such a compliance system to be adequate, it must be reasonably designed to provide to senior management and to the board itself timely, accurate information sufficient to allow management and the board, each within its scope, to reach informed judgments concerning both the corporation's compliance with law and its business performance."

By the same token, it is management's responsibility to provide assurance to the board and to third parties that risks are appropriately addressed and within the risk appetite of the enterprise. This is consistent with the requirements of sections 302 and 404 of Sarbanes-Oxley and, if applied on a broader scale, begins to address concerns raised about the effectiveness of risk management in general.

As noted earlier, internal audit plays an important role in assurance. But how does internal audit's assurance responsibility differ from management's? We find it helpful to describe internal audit's role as providing reasonable independent "reassurance" to executive management and the board that management's reports regarding all key risks are reliable. In a sense, reassurance better describes internal audit's role, given that management provides assurance.

Also, while improving effectiveness is important, many enterprises (particularly in highly regulated industries) also want to improve efficiencies and reduce governance, compliance, and risk-management costs. Internal audit can support those goals by:

- Broadening its independent activities to include facilitating identification and evaluation of all risks across the enterprise
- Coaching management in appropriate responses to risks
- Reporting on consolidated risks and management's responses
- Championing risk intelligent practices

After spending much of the 2000s coping with regulatory compliance, most internal audit functions are eager to contribute to value-adding risk management activities. That said, internal audit should not assume risk-management responsibilities. For instance, internal audit should not set the risk appetite, impose risk management processes, assume accountability for risk management, perform management's assurance role, or make decisions regarding risk taking, although independent recommendations on risk responses ought to be encouraged.

Ensure the Enterprise Is Prepared for Crises

Sooner or later, nearly every board encounters a crisis. The success of the outcome depends greatly on the quality of the organizational response and especially the response of its leadership.[9] (Also see Chapter 6 for a further discussion of preparedness and crisis management.) The board should ensure that management has a crisis management process in place for all types of crises. Hopgood and Tankersley[10] identify a number of common types of crisis:

- Balance sheet or income statement
- Liquidity and capital structure
- People
- Legal

- Environmental
- Reputation
- Leadership and governance

The board is particularly responsible for planning for "leadership and governance" crises. These could include short-, intermediate-, and long-term succession plans for the CEO and other key executives who may suddenly become unavailable for any number of reasons.

More generally, the board's crisis response process should include director call-trees, pre-arranged access to crisis advisors and legal counsel, and communication plans. However, the board cannot actually conduct crisis management. As Hopgood and Tankersley note, "Directors are often too far from the front line to be able to foresee the very large number of practical issues that a given crisis scenario may present... Directors should ensure good management [but] they should not provide it."[11]

The board should obtain reasonable assurance that the company has the necessary crisis management capabilities in place and that they include:

- A comprehensive risk management process that includes risk identification, assessment, response, monitoring, and continuous improvement
- A list of key stakeholders, their communication requirements, and plans to address those requirements
- An executive with overall responsibility for coordinating crisis planning and response
- A multidisciplinary crisis-response team
- Regularly updated crisis-response skills training, including media relations
- Crisis response drills to test preparedness for a variety of crisis scenarios
- A documented, company crisis response plan, a legal response plan, and a crisis communications plan[12]

Committees of the Board and Risk Intelligence

The New York Stock Exchange requires three standing committees of the board:

1. Compensation committee
2. Nominating and governance committee
3. Audit committee

Sarbanes-Oxley, the U.S. legislation following accounting and finance scandals in the nation in the early 2000s, increased attention on the audit committee's role and responsibilities. The global credit crisis later in the decade shifted attention to the roles and responsibilities of the nominating and governance committee and the compensation committee.

Therefore—and given generally increasing levels of risk—boards and their committees should systematically consider risk as part of every key decision that comes before them. The following sections discuss risk intelligent approaches for these three committees and the potential value of adding a risk committee to the roster of board committees. The latter was recommended in 2009 by New York Senator Charles Schumer in his proposed Shareholder Bill of Rights.

Systematic consideration of risk and reward is not the exclusive purview of any single committee. A regular dialogue between directors and officers is essential to success. A "check the box" approach to risk and value must be avoided. Boards and their committees must be able to demonstrate that they understand the key risks and there are capable people, processes, and systems in place to effectively manage those risks.

It is essential that committees of the board share insights and intelligence that emerge from their specific areas of responsibility that may have impact on the entire enterprise. This is frequently accomplished informally because committee members often sit on several committees. However, the chairs of the committees should mutually agree on those issues and risks that must come to their specific committees and which should be shared with each other and the board as a whole.

Voice of Experience

"Unfortunately, today oversight has often become a bureaucratic process. The risk manager comes in and says the same things at every board meeting and there's nothing real challenging in that. They're giving reports, and reports put me and everybody else to sleep. Not literally, but board members are so used to 'Well, here it comes again and we're going to expect this and this and this. But if instead we used the report as the starting point for a dialogue that would be really great.'"

—David Meuse, Director

The Risk Intelligent Compensation Committee

Few issues provoke as much public outrage as executive compensation. The controversy was ignited in the early 1990s when senior executive pay in the United States started to outstrip that of rank-and-file employees by far greater multiples than in other nations and with the publication of *In Search of Excess: The Overcompensation of American Executives* by executive pay consultant Graef Crystal. The events of the 2000s, particularly the back-dating of employee stock options in a number of companies and certain bonuses paid to executives in the financial sector, only fanned the flames.

Compensation committees must understand the risks associated with such issues and approve the design of compensation packages that encourage short- and long-term performance, retain key employees, and discourage poor performance and reckless decisions. Essentially, compensation linked to performance must reflect the enterprise's business strategy, because executives will focus on the factors that drive their compensation.

Compensation must—or rather will—also reflect the values and culture of the company and its priorities. Richard Floersch, executive vice president of McDonald's Corp. and chairman of the Center on Executive Compensation, suggests that the following questions be addressed:[13]

- Does your company have incentive measures that address both company performance and its sustainability? A focus on revenue growth means little if the results will have negative long-term effects or result in massive write-downs.
- Are the potential payouts under your annual incentive program capped at a reasonable level to minimize 'swinging for the fences' at the expense of long-term company viability?
- Does your compensation committee have discretion to adjust payouts that, while reflective of actual performance, do not appear fair in the broader context?
- Does your compensation committee place a higher priority on doing what's right for the company in the long term instead of just copying what competitors and other companies are doing?
- Are your company's stock ownership and/or retention policies sufficiently rigorous to require executives to own substantial company stock over their careers, and hold it for long periods of time to align pay with shareholder interests?
- Does your company have a meaningful 'clawback' policy? More than 64 percent of the Fortune 100 companies have such policies. If a company doesn't perform as well as originally believed, then why pay executives as if it did?

Floersch also cites Equilar Inc. data that show that "Roughly 70 percent of total compensation for S&P 500 CEOs was in the form of long-term incentives, typically earned over three years or more and predominantly tied to shareholder return."[14] While quantitative performance measures such as earnings per share and return on investment are important, nonquantitative measures such as reputation and brand equity ought to be considered as well.

The Risk Intelligent Nominating and Governance Committee

As the name implies, the nominating and governance committee formulates and recommends governance principles and policies. In addition to recommending the selection of the CEO, this committee works to enhance the quality of nominees to the board and ensure the integrity of the nominating process. The latter responsibilities have become increasingly important given the intensifying focus on board composition and diversity, director elections, and proxy access.

Traditionally, board vacancies have been filled by the CEO. More recently, the NYSE listing standards require companies to establish a separate nominating committee or to delegate the responsibilities to another separate committee composed entirely of independent directors.

A risk intelligent enterprise selects directors for their expertise and for their potential contribution to the company's strategic success. The National Association of Corporate Directors (NACD) Blue Ribbon Commission's 2006 report, "The Role of the Board in Corporate Strategy" notes that recruitment and selection criteria should target specific qualifications that align with the enterprise's strategic requirements. It also states that director education should focus on key elements of the strategy and that compensation should require a substantial target for stock ownership and pay in stock.[15]

The committee must also consider the competing responsibilities and time commitments of candidates. Indeed, directors are also reassessing their commitments in view of increasing duties. As a result, some boards are encountering increased difficulty in attracting directors, particularly candidates whose experience and skills match the strategic needs of the enterprise. This committee must also plan for CEO succession, an increasing challenge in light of the facts noted in Chapter 1—higher executive turnover, increased demands for accountability, and often diminished power.

As noted earlier in this chapter, NYSE listing requires that "management succession planning include policies and principles for CEO selection and performance review, as well as policies regarding succession in the event of an emergency or the retirement of the CEO."

The Risk Intelligent Audit Committee

The audit committee's three principal roles are to:

- Understand the major financial risks to the organization and the policies and guidelines for assessing and managing major financial exposures
- Obtain reasonable assurance from management that the financial statements are accurate and reliable
- Obtain independent reassurance that management's reports can be relied upon

NYSE corporate governance listing standards require the audit committee to discuss the company's risk assessment and management policies and process with management. The commentary accompanying the standards clarifies that, although senior management is responsible for assessing and managing the company's risks, the audit committee should focus on areas of major financial risk exposure and discuss the guidelines and policies for addressing these areas.

Risk belongs on the audit committee agenda, but many audit committees are already overloaded with their existing responsibilities. Also, although the audit committee must obtain reasonable assurance about risk-related policies, processes, and systems, many directors doubt that the audit committee should be more deeply involved in business risks not directly related to the integrity of the reports and financial statements. Therefore, some boards (mainly in financial services) have established a separate risk committee, discussed below.

Traditionally, audit committees focus on the company's financial reporting and the related risk management programs. They are also now trying to understand broader risks affecting the company, and the company's overall risk management program. The NYSE requirements relate to *financial risk* exposures, which are often a consequence of other sources of risk, such as those discussed in the company's 10-Ks and 10-Qs. These may include strategy, operations, and compliance with environmental, health, safety, legal, and regulatory requirements.

So what is the appropriate role for the audit committee when it comes to risk oversight? There appear to be two primary schools of thought:

- Because the audit committee already oversees risks related to the integrity of the enterprise's financial statements, it should also have oversight of all risks.
- While the audit committee has oversight of financial statement risk, it cannot oversee all business risks; therefore, oversight of business risks

should be the responsibility of the full board or perhaps a risk committee of the board.

Ultimately, the full board has final responsibility for risk oversight. Depending on its workload, the audit committee could develop an enterprise-wide view of risk management capabilities to enable the board to assess whether these are appropriate and functioning properly. In this way, the audit committee can obtain the reasonable assurance required to fulfill the board's fiduciary responsibilities.

Risk Committee of the Board

A number of enterprises have been prompted to increase the scope and intensity of risk oversight at the board level. One way to do this is by establishing a board-level risk committee. Susan Martyn, professor of law at the University of Toledo, advises companies to create such committees: "If you don't have it now, you should have it at the board level."[16]

A survey by the NACD indicates that relatively few companies have actually established board committees exclusively focused on risk oversight. According to its survey, only 4.5 percent of respondents reported that their board had a risk committee.[17] Ken Daly, CEO of the NACD, says, "There is no single board committee that has the time or competencies to really do the right job performing oversight of a company's risk. Risk management is a team sport . . . company boards that rush to set up dedicated risk committees may create more problems than they solve . . . If you only set up a risk committee and don't follow through, it might actually be detrimental to a company's long-term interests."[18]

In October 2009, the NACD released a report entitled "Risk Governance: Balancing Risk and Reward" that included an example charter for a risk committee. However, regardless of the committee structure the board employs, directors must ensure the adequacy of director expertise with regard to risk awareness and management. Directors should evaluate their expertise (individually and collectively) and determine gaps, individually and collectively, and attract and retain directors with the requisite expertise.

Directors are likely to be busier at their own companies during tough economic times, particularly during a crisis. A director serving on a large number of boards may not have enough time to serve well, especially if his or her own company is having problems. For example, many directors reassessed their commitments in light of their increased duties after the credit crisis and the recession of the 2000s. Clearly, director recruitment must be a dynamic and ongoing process.

Where Does Risk Oversight End and Risk Management Begin?

Alternatively, where does oversight end and interference begin? The question is frequently raised, although it ought to be obvious that risk oversight is the board's responsibility and management is responsible for managing the business and the associated risks. Unfortunately, there is no clear bright line but a matter of judgment for directors and executives.

The right balance depends on the organization's circumstance, culture, and structure. One director offered a way to consider where the right balance lies when he asked, "How well do you think the general public and shareholders are going to accept the excuse that we didn't want to probe too deeply and get in the way of management? That'll be a wimpy damn excuse and it ought not be one we use."

Nose In, Hands Off

Directors who probe and challenge to gain insight and to exercise oversight should not be viewed as trying to manage the business. Management should help the board understand how value is created and destroyed in the business. It should also make the assumptions underlying the business model explicit, so they can be constructively challenged.

Many directors believe that it takes a year or more for them to begin to really understand the business. Therefore, management should develop ways to help directors come up the learning curve faster. Given the limitations on board time and industry-specific knowledge, management should continually educate the board so it can more quickly understand the enterprise and the key drivers of success, remembering that shift inexorably happens.

Good governance essentially hinges on sound decision making. Rigorous attention to the nuances of corporate governance and risk management can only boost investors' confidence and that of all other stakeholders. In fact, the days when the board could "go through the motions" of governance are largely over. Today's enterprises are too large and complex, the risks they face are too numerous and potentially damaging, and the stakeholders are too exposed and demanding for business as usual to continue.

This chapter has focused on governance primarily from the standpoint of the board's risk-related oversight responsibilities. The next chapter addresses the roles and responsibilities of executive management, the emerging role of the Chief Risk Officer, the role of risk councils or committees, and the means to build risk intelligence into the fabric of the enterprise.

Questions to Ask about Governance

Roles and Responsibilities

- How does the board establish the character of the enterprise and set the appropriate tone at the top?
- How does the board separate board and management responsibilities in risk management?
- Should the board have a separate risk committee?
- Has the enterprise risk appetite been approved by the board?
- How big does a risk or opportunity need to be to get on the agenda of the board and its committees?
- Conversely, what kinds and levels of risk and opportunities ought not to come to the attention of the board and its committees?
- How does the board gain assurance and reassurance that the risks that do not come to its attention are being appropriately managed?
- Does the board have its own preparedness plans specifically for leadership and governance crises?

Strategy

- How does the board gain insight into the strategies for value creation and value protection and the attendant risks?
- How does the board assess the short- and long-term implications of its decisions?
- What are the key strategies and what are the milestones and budgets associated with those strategies?
- What are the key business assumptions, and what if they are wrong?
- What could cause discontinuities in the business, such as changes in technology, business models, and demographics?
- How can the enterprise better align company resources with the needs of its customers? Who are its customers today? Who are the customers of the future?
- What are the risks *of* this strategy? How could the strategy itself be wrong?
- What are the risks *to* this strategy? What could cause it to fail?
  - People factors?
  - Process factors?
  - Systems factors?
  - External factors?

- How fast could it fail? What would be the effects of such failure? How can its impacts be measured in:
  - Revenue growth?
  - Operating margin?
  - Asset efficiency?
  - Expectations/reputation?
- What can be done to prevent or better prepare for, respond to, and recover from such failure?
- Which executive(s) are responsible for managing specific risks?
- How will we monitor performance? How often?
- What is our stop-loss position on specific strategies?
- If we need to exit, how will we be able to do that? What are our assumptions about our ability to exit?

Risk Intelligent Enterprise Management

For those decisions that must come to its attention, the board has the opportunity to judge firsthand the quality and capability of management. Executives are then responsible for executing those decisions, managing the business and the associated risks, and providing reasonable assurance to the board. This is especially the case for those other decisions that need not come to the attention of the board.

Executives can thus improve their support of the oversight role of the board by:

- Better understanding their information and intelligence requirements to facilitate greater insight and better advice, oversight, and decision making
- Paying close attention to the risks associated with delegations of authority
- Orchestrating the risk identification, assessment, response, and monitoring activities across existing silos

- Highlighting the potential long-term consequences of short-term decisions
- Recommending a risk appetite policy for board approval and then establishing appropriate controls and monitoring mechanisms to stay within those limits
- Providing reasonable assurance to the board regarding the effectiveness of risk mitigation and the areas of greatest vulnerability
- Developing and rehearsing crisis preparedness plans

The challenge, of course, is how best to accomplish this. While these needs are not new, there is a much greater sense of urgency. This perhaps accounts, in large part, for the emergence of Enterprise Risk Management (ERM) as a means to address them.

ERM and Risk Intelligence

ERM means various things to various people. In general, the term indicates a framework for risk management that integrates planning, operational, and control functions, and/or the processes and methods that enable risk identification, monitoring, assessment, and control in the enterprise. In the mid-1990s, a number of U.S. companies, mostly in financial services and energy, began to adopt ERM, but nearly all of them lacked an authoritative framework.

As a result, their approaches were often nonsystematic and focused mainly on market risk. By 2001, a recession triggered by the bursting of the dot-com bubble put an end to many of these initiatives, at least temporarily, and left behind a great deal of confusion about ERM and its value.

Various missteps and false starts generated widespread criticism of ERM, some deserved and some not. In efforts to address the situation, several organizations, including the Casualty Actuarial Society, the Committee of Sponsoring Organizations of the Treadway Commission (COSO), and the Treasury Board of Canada Secretariat, developed ERM frameworks or elements of frameworks. However, as of this writing, many companies have yet to adopt an integrated ERM framework. Many have yet to rationalize and harmonize risk assessment criteria and processes. Many have yet to improve the effectiveness and efficiency of risk management in a systematic manner.

Despite the number and severity of risk management failures, some executives remain unconvinced of the business case for improved risk management. Some still doubt the value of prevention and preparation, particularly for events that fall into the "black swan" category. Some even continue to believe in their invincibility or immunity to risk. Prevention receives low priority when profits are under pressure and resources are scarce, as they were in the latter half of the 2000s in many organizations.

Even when they grasp the value of sound risk management, executives who want to implement a systematic approach may not know how to go about it. This can be devastating because early wins demonstrate value, and to many observers their absence demonstrates the opposite. Attempts to implement ERM as a "standalone" initiative or a project apart from other strategic or operational processes generally fail. People tend to perceive such efforts as bureaucratic, burdensome, and temporary, rather than serious, systematic, and sustainable.

Different perceptions of risk and risk management among various specialists in various silos can generate a lack of cross-functional alignment and coordination. ERM will surely fail without sound program management and a team effort characterized by committed leadership, realistic goals and expectations, specific milestones and metrics, solid communication, and sufficient resources.

One Size Fits One

ERM frameworks include those developed by COSO to the Australia/New Zealand standard 4360, the Risk and Insurance Management Society (RIMS), and more recently those introduced by the rating agencies such as Standard & Poor's and Moody's. The International Standards Organization (ISO) has also turned its attention to the matter. This proliferation of frameworks can splinter and confuse rather than unify and harmonize. Ultimately, the enterprise must choose or develop the framework that best suits its specific and unique needs.

The goal is not to adopt a framework for its own sake (although some framework may be preferable to none). To be of real value, the framework must fulfill its function, which is to help gather and reconcile viewpoints, and identify ways and means of dealing with risk by providing comprehensive, cohesive intelligence and insights to decision makers.

Given that every enterprise has its unique culture and practices, any framework must be translated into terms that are meaningful to its people. The more closely the framework matches the culture and practices of the enterprise, the greater its chances of survival and success. Indeed, as countless implementations of enterprise resource planning (ERP) software have demonstrated, it's essential to ensure that the framework fits the enterprise rather than to attempt to fit the enterprise to the framework.

Every effort must be made to "build it in" rather than "bolt it on," because the former integrates risk management into decision making and work processes, while the latter sets it up as separate from the conduct of business.

That's the value of risk intelligence. It can serve as a framework or as the "operating system" to which another framework, including one of the enterprise's own design, can be "downloaded." In that way the enterprise can build risk intelligence into the fabric of the business.

Voice of Experience

"The concept of EM (Enterprise Management) versus ERM resonates with us. Our board certainly is apprehensive about operational risk, day-to-day risk. We're a specialty chemical company and there's inherent danger. Therefore, the board is obviously interested to make sure we have all the programs and processes and methodologies in place to mitigate and minimize those types of risk. But they also understand strategic risk, which is something different all together.

"My management team recognized the value of looking at enterprise management, not just enterprise risk management, based on its own experience. They have already begun to wrestle with the fact that a bottom-up approach to operational risk is fine. This is really a long-standing competence in the company and we're pretty good at that.

"The formalization of proper enterprise management at a strategic level in a better way is something we have been purposefully trying to improve. In fact, despite having what you might call an enterprise risk management superstructure, we've already started working on multiple individual initiatives that really address enterprise management at the strategic level."

—James Hambrick, Chairman and CEO, The Lubrizol Corporation

Developing Risk Intelligent Enterprise Management

Before management can begin transforming the organization into a risk intelligent enterprise, it must understand the business case for doing so. It must see the cost of failure, the cost of risk management, and the total cost of risk. It must see that past failures or perhaps rising compliance and risk management costs, indicate that changes must be made.

Leadership must see that risks pose very real monetary threats and that risk-averse decisions have hampered or will hamper risk taking for reward and generate unacceptable levels of performance and growth. Ideally, the leaders will see that the enterprise's resilience and agility and its ability to survive and thrive will be compromised unless it becomes more risk intelligent.

In any mature enterprise, there are already numerous risk management functions both explicitly and implicitly. Everyone has a risk management role. For some, however, risk management is one of their primary responsibilities. These include, for example, insurance, legal, business continuity, and security (physical and cyber). The focus in the following pages is not on these traditional functions but on emerging functions such as the chief risk officer and risk councils.

Although effective risk intelligence requires neither a chief risk officer (CRO) nor a risk management committee, both have become more common over the past decade (here we are referring to management bodies and *not* those at the board level). The following section describes the functions and growing prevalence of CROs and risk management committees or councils.

The Chief Risk Officer

In many organizations, the CEO is the de facto chief risk officer. However, more companies are beginning to appoint CROs to assume primary responsibility for enterprise risk management in order to give risk management greater priority and focus. In a 2007 survey by Deloitte,[2] one-quarter of the respondents indicated that primary responsibility for ERM rests with their CRO, while just over a third said their CFO had the responsibility, in line with the traditional view of this function.

These findings may signal a movement toward more focused oversight of ERM, especially considering that, in combination, CROs and directors of ERM comprised 32 percent of responses. The study also showed that 32 percent of CROs report to the CFO and 27 percent to the CEO. High accountability and organizational visibility for the CRO may reflect a commitment to ERM from the top and set the stage for successful ERM programs.

What does the CRO do? While the research provided no conclusive consensus, in a risk intelligent enterprise, the individual holding the title of CRO ideally would:

- Lead the establishment of a capable process for managing enterprise-wide risks in an integrated, systematic manner
- Orchestrate the harmonization, synchronization, and rationalization of existing risk management specializations, goals, processes, and systems
- Serve as a central source of strategy, methods, skills, and tools for supporting risk management
- Maintain close reporting ties to the CFO, CEO, and the board and have indirect ("dotted-line") reporting from the heads of the major risk management functions, including internal audit, ethics, compliance, legal, health and safety, and loss prevention

- Serve as the reporting line for risk committees developed within the organization, including for IT, internal audit, market risk, credit risk, insurance, ethics, and strategy
- Develop risk intelligence capabilities: people, processes, and systems

For the board especially, a CRO can supply some previously identified missing links in risk intelligence and can:

- Increase board and management confidence in the reliability of management reports about current operations and the effectiveness of risk management
- Facilitate proactive thinking about future risks and provide continuity and consistency in risk management capability development
- Develop a common and practical risk framework, policies, and measurement methodologies for improved decision making
- Help bridge the gaps and identify the redundancies that inevitably occur in an enterprise's risk management efforts
- Provide a solid foundation for developing and implementing a successful risk intelligence strategy, process, and culture

To be most effective, the CRO ought to be independent of management. This means that the CRO should not have direct responsibility for managing risk and probably not have risk management functions reporting directly to him or her. Such a reporting relationship could produce conflicts that might cause the CRO to defend rather than challenge risk management actions. For this reason, the CRO should also report directly to the CEO or the board rather than to the CFO, as is often the case.

CROs also must be credible so that their opinions carry sufficient weight and thus should be compensated appropriately. The CRO's compensation should also depend in part on business performance so that, as one director put it, the role does not simply become that of a "Dr. No" who refuses to accept any risk. Also, given the principles presented in this book, perhaps the CRO should be renamed the chief risk intelligence officer to more accurately reflect a decision-support role rather than being directly responsible for risk management.

Risk Intelligence Councils

A number of companies have created risk management committees or risk councils. A 2008 survey of nonfinancial companies by Deloitte[3] found that about 40 percent of the respondents had some form of risk committee, the majority of them (25 percent) at the management level and not at the board. A mere 2 percent had only a board-level risk committee at that time. Sixty percent of respondents had no risk committee. This may reflect that risk is managed by the executive team or that a specific individual, such as a CFO or a director of ERM, may be charged with overall risk management.

A well-structured risk committee can accelerate development of a common language and understanding of risk, and common risk assessment criteria and escalation triggers. A risk committee can also support the development of coordinated responses to enterprise-wide risks and opportunities.

Risk committees are often chaired by the CFO, CRO, or director of ERM. However, a key issue is the role and authority of such a committee. If the committee is responsible for risk management, this may undermine the responsibilities of the business units, unless the committee is composed of those responsible for managing both value and risk. Otherwise, it may be best to consider these committees as risk intelligence councils.

The purpose of a risk intelligence council, as distinct from a risk management committee, is not to manage risks but to:

- Harmonize, synchronize, and rationalize approaches to risk management
- Support the gathering of intelligence about risks for those who must manage them
- Share knowledge and lessons learned
- Act as a conduit for risk intelligence activities to improve the understanding of risk and thereby support superior decision making throughout the enterprise

Sometimes risk councils begin as "steering committees" that oversee the development of risk management programs. In such cases, the committee must have strong endorsement from senior executives.

Act as One

Much of the benefits of risk intelligence, both in cost savings and in improved detection of and response to risks, are the result of more integrated approaches to risk management. But what exactly does that mean? What is integration and how does it come about?

We have discussed ways of improving people's awareness of risk at all levels. To develop an integrated approach to risk management the board must:

- Make risk management a priority and impress the importance of it on the executive team

- Help develop a common language of risk
- Encourage measurement of the potential costs and impact of risk
- See that management gauges the unrewarded and rewarded risks of decisions and activities

This process can be accelerated by harmonizing, synchronizing, and rationalizing risk management goals, processes, and systems.

Harmonizing Risk Management

As does a woven fabric, an organization derives its durability not only from the tensile strength of the vertical strands—the warp—but also from the weft, or horizontal strands, that bind them together. In an organization, both the vertical hierarchical elements, such as policies, procedures, orders, and exemplary leadership, and the horizontal elements, such as communication, collegiality, and collaboration, are necessary for resiliency and agility. A risk intelligent enterprise increases the strength of these horizontal elements by increasing horizontal communication and coordination.

Applied to the enterprise, the vertical strands represent the different lines of businesses with P&L responsibilities, while the horizontal strands reflect the functional areas and specializations, and the locations in which they operate. Those vertical strands and the *hierarchy* that they represent provide the strength that comes from a clear sense of direction, a confident and trusted leadership team, and a unified public presence. The horizontal strands represent the commonalities that run *across* the enterprise—its culture, its shared values, its cross-organizational communications, and its shared functions, approaches, and systems.

While deep specialization must be maintained, there should be greater focus on improving cross-functional coordination. Unfortunately, many enterprises find themselves without a framework and the necessary connections. Even when frameworks and connections exist, they must be carefully maintained to counter the natural tendency toward disorder and devolution. The Office of Director of National Intelligence offers an example of how frameworks can be developed.

CASE EXAMPLE: OFFICE OF THE DIRECTOR OF NATIONAL INTELLIGENCE (ODNI)

To enable the rapid exchange of information, ODNI and the Department of Defense have developed information security certifications and accreditations that have since also been adopted by the Department of Justice and the Department of Homeland Security. The measures adopted by ODNI include [italics added]:

1. Define a *common set* of trust levels to share information and connect systems more easily.
2. Adopt *reciprocity agreements* to reduce systems development and approval time.
3. Define *common security controls* using the National Institute of Standards and Technology's Special Publication 800-5 as a starting point.
4. Agree to *common definitions and understanding of security terms*, starting with the Committee on National Security Systems 4009 glossary as a baseline.
5. Implement a *senior risk executive function* on which to base an enterprise view of all factors, including mission, IT, budget, and security.
6. Operate IT security within the enterprise operational requirements, *enabling situational awareness and command and control.*
7. Institute a *common process* to incorporate security engineering within the lifecycle processes.[4]

These certifications and accreditations emphasize the importance of developing a common approach wherever it makes sense to do so. It is worth reiterating, however, that the existence of these factors is not in itself sufficient to maintain the key connections. Consistent execution is required, also, as was discussed in Chapter 13, "Sustain Operational Discipline."

Synchronizing Risk Management

When specialists act autonomously, their timing may be convenient to their specific purposes but impose significant burdens on the business. Synchronization should aim to match closely the information requirements and responses to risk of specialists within the business from the standpoint of timing. People need to have information when it will do them the most good. For example, when an incident occurs, a decision is made, or a response is launched, the people who need to know must know and must, as required, synchronize their actions. This may mean acting simultaneously or sequentially, along a single line of activity or, more typically, with coordination among activities. Lack of synchronization can lead to delay, disruption, even disaster.

Exhibit 16.1 illustrates how one company gathered risk-related intelligence to match the timing of its key planning processes, strategy, capital, annual operational plans and reviews, and internal audit. Systematic discussion of risk is also part of the standing agenda of each monthly meeting of the executive team. Status reports are made at least annually to the board, and a risk-informed audit plan is reviewed and approved by the audit committee.

The company utilizes ERM coordinators, one in each business unit and a cross-functional council, to provide risk input to the ERM corporate team.

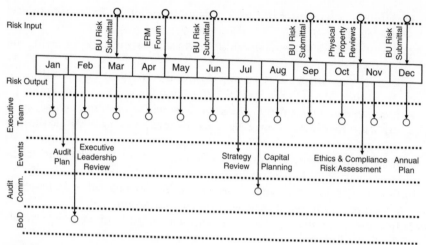

EXHIBIT 16.1 Building in Risk Intelligence

These are not full-time roles and perhaps use less than 10 percent of the person's available time. Nor are they a specified position. ERM coordinators are selected for their credibility and broad knowledge of the business unit and have access to management. They work with subject matter experts on each risk to develop the risk assessment. The coordinator brings the knowledge of the ERM process while the subject matter expert brings firsthand knowledge of the risk.

Occasionally, the coordinators work with the ERM corporate team to consult on specific risks and on related scenario development. They also collect the risk information and conduct the review with the business unit or council leadership for submission to the ERM corporate team each quarter.

Improving synchronization can:

- Help coordinate specializations for better anticipation, preparedness, response, and recovery; improved coordination of timing of requests for information can also smooth workload demands on the business units
- Increase the focus on hand-offs and information exchanges where intelligence could fall into the cracks, given that quality problems and failures in risk management often occur at the nexus or intersection of functions
- Facilitate the escalation of critical risks or decisions by establishing criteria for what should be escalated, who should escalate it, how should it be escalated, and how fast

Together, harmonization and synchronization largely address means of improving the effectiveness of risk management activities across specializations and of driving down the cost of failure, ultimately to reduce the total cost of risk. There are also opportunities to improve the efficiency of specializations through improved rationalization.

Rationalizing Risk Management

The goal of rationalization is to reduce costs while increasing effectiveness of controls by eliminating duplication, redundancies, and gaps in structures, processes, and controls. This must, however, be done while retaining the distinctive competencies and meeting the needs of the risk management and business specializations. Concerted efforts can reduce or eliminate duplication of effort related to assessment, testing, reporting, and control. Such efforts will also help lessen the burden on the business and related costs created by "piling on" requests for risk-related information.

In this context, "rationalize" essentially means that each process and each part of each process is examined for its purpose, effectiveness, uniqueness, costs, and results. Then, on that basis, it is justified, modified, or eliminated. For example, controls rationalization in an enterprise ideally occurs in a four-phase approach:

1. *Phase 1.* Apply a top-down, risk-based approach to rescoping controls
2. *Phase 2.* Rationalize existing process-level controls
3. *Phase 3.* Leverage automated controls and enabling technology
4. *Phase 4.* Standardize and centralize processes where it makes sense

In Phases 1 and 2, you can realize near-term reductions in costs, identify future potential improvements, and create a foundation for a sustainable control program. In Phases 3 and 4, you can implement that sustainable program by building greater efficiency and effectiveness into the control environment. The latter two phases may require greater investment of resources than the first two, but they will lower the risk profile of the enterprise while generating increased long-term savings.

A New Way of Doing Business

The more risk management is perceived to be discrete from the ways in which the business is actually run, the greater the potential for failure. By integrating risk intelligence into the enterprise's core decision-making processes, executive leadership can improve its support for the board and the enterprise's overall chances of success. When executives and directors see the discussion of value and risk as an intrinsic element of successful enterprise management, the transformation has begun.

How then does an enterprise transform itself? What are the challenges? What needs to be done? These are the subjects of the next and final chapter.

Questions to Ask about Risk Intelligent Enterprise Management

- Has the systematic consideration of risk been built into all core decision-making processes?
- Have specific executives been assigned specific ownership for the end-to-end management of specific risks?
- Has a common language of risk been adopted by all risk specializations, e.g., IT, legal, HR, internal audit, insurance and business continuity, etc.?
- Has there been a systematic effort to harmonize, synchronize, and rationalize risk specializations?
- Do compensation programs consider risk management effectiveness and efficiency?

CHAPTER 17

The Way Forward
Creating the Risk Intelligent Enterprise

To win you have to risk loss.
— Jean-Claude Killy, champion Alpine ski racer

In the "good old days" of the post-World War II era, buffers of space and time gave organizations more leeway to react and adapt. Events in remote places seemed to have little impact and were more insulated. Information was available to a relative few, whose power came from their specialized knowledge. Centralized systems of management and control seemed to work. Problems could be reduced to their components and managed separately. Most assets were thought to be tangible and could be protected. Most risks were thought to be known or knowable, and their likelihood predictable. Risks appeared to be far less interdependent.

Conventional risk management focused on asset-protection, typically in the form of insurance. It was also believed that risks could be identified and managed within silos and that risk aversion would maximize shareholder value. Risk was typically seen as a cost, not as an opportunity. Risk management programs took "one size fits all" forms. For these and many other reasons, conventional risk management has failed.

In the turbulent and uncertain 21st century, the buffers of space and time no longer exist. Information has become instantly available. It still confers power, but now everyone has it. Communities of interest can form overnight. Centralized control often fails in the face of turbulence. Fixing pieces no longer solves problems. Many assets are now intangible and cannot be protected in traditional ways. Many risk events are unknown and perhaps unknowable.

Surviving and thriving in uncertainty and turbulence requires unconventional thinking and calculated risk taking. The enterprise must be understood

293

holistically and seen as a living organism. Risks must also be understood as opportunities that can be optimized or exploited, not just as costs. Risks must be viewed as interconnected and difficult to contain. Like wildfires, they cross boundaries and must be managed accordingly. If a risk is relevant and potentially life threatening, be prepared for it.

Everything has changed but human nature. Judgment will always be difficult. The 21st century enterprise must develop a 21st century view of risk and risk management. Nearly all enterprises have certain characteristics in common. They all operate to a large degree in the same macro-economic environment. The "fatal flaws" and corresponding "risk intelligence skills" described in Part II apply almost universally.

That said, every enterprise is also unique and differs from all others in key ways. Every enterprise operates at a different stage of development. It possesses different skills, understanding, awareness, and culture. Each of these unique characteristics must be considered carefully by leaders trying to improve risk intelligence, along with the unique benefits the enterprise can realize through that improvement.

The Benefits of Improved Risk Intelligence

Demonstrating the value of prevention is often difficult. It should be intuitively obvious that the improved ability to protect existing assets while more effectively managing the risks to future growth ought to improve the enterprise's chances of survival and success. The enterprise that builds risk intelligence into the core ways of running its business can improve its resilience and agility and should realize the following benefits:

- Challenging basic business assumptions (White Swans) can identify Black Swans and provide first-mover advantage.
- Defining the corporate risk appetite and risk tolerances can help reduce the risk of ruin.
- Improving signal detection can provide advance warning and enable more proactive responses.
- Identifying mission-critical interdependencies can help establish an appropriate margin of safety.
- Anticipating potential causes of failure can improve chances of survival and success through improved preparedness.
- Factoring in momentum and velocity can improve speed of response and recovery.
- Verifying your sources and corroborating the reliability of information can improve insights for decision making and thus the quality of decisions.

- Taking a longer-term perspective can aid in identifying the potential unintended consequences of short-term decisions.
- Improving operational discipline helps sustain success.
- Understanding the Total Cost of Risk can help demonstrate the value proposition and reduce the Cost of Failure while improving risk intelligent enterprise management.

If these benefits are seen as worthwhile, how do you get started and what are some of the pitfalls to avoid? Before deciding where you need to go, first take the measure of where you are right now. Why not start with a quick snapshot of your current Risk Intelligence Quotient or Risk IQ?

What's Your Enterprise Risk IQ?

The following is an informal guide to help you to consider your current state of risk intelligence. We present it more as a tool for structuring your thinking and discussing your current methods than as a scientific diagnostic. It can, however, help you pinpoint problem areas. To use the tool, rate your enterprise's capabilities in each of the following areas on a scale of 1 to 5, with the values representing capabilities as follows:

1. Lacking the capability
2. Somewhat capable
3. Fairly capable
4. Quite capable
5. Highly capable

Risk Intelligence Practices	Capability
Decision-makers have the information and insights needed to make timely and informed decisions.	1 2 3 4 5
We have consistent, aligned corporate values, culture, and rewards.	1 2 3 4 5
We effectively develop and deploy strategies for value creation and protection.	1 2 3 4 5
Executives explicitly own and manage value and risk.	1 2 3 4 5
We have a systematic and disciplined approach to value creation and risk management.	1 2 3 4 5
People are risk aware, not just risk averse.	1 2 3 4 5
Risk management considerations are built into all key decisions, business processes, and work activities.	1 2 3 4 5
Executives provide reasonable assurance that we have the required capabilities—people, processes, and systems—to protect and grow our business.	1 2 3 4 5

(Continued)

(Continued)

Risk Intelligence Practices	Capability
Directors obtain independent reassurance that management's reports are robust and reliable.	1 2 3 4 5
We understand our total cost of risk (TCOR).	1 2 3 4 5

Risk Intelligence Skills	Capability
We regularly challenge our fundamental business assumptions.	1 2 3 4 5
We maintain high levels of vigilance for threats and opportunities in our operating environment.	1 2 3 4 5
We factor velocity and momentum into our risk assessments.	1 2 3 4 5
We understand the key connections among our critical dependencies.	1 2 3 4 5
We constructively anticipate potential causes of failure.	1 2 3 4 5
We verify our sources and corroborate the information they provide.	1 2 3 4 5
We maintain an acceptable margin of safety to ensure our survival.	1 2 3 4 5
We set enterprise-wide short-, intermediate-, and long-term performance time horizons.	1 2 3 4 5
We take enough of the right risks to promote innovation and growth.	1 2 3 4 5
We sustain operational discipline at every level of the organization.	1 2 3 4 5
Total Risk IQ (out of a possible 100)	_____

The ratings for your enterprise roughly translate into the following descriptions:

20–36 = *Initial.* An "Initial"-stage enterprise is characterized by:
- Ad hoc or chaotic responses to risk
- Possibly strong verbal traditions, but few clearly defined policies and procedures
- Record of missed opportunities and inconsistent responses to recurring problems
- Responses based on individual heroics, capabilities, and verbal traditions
- Little or no learning captured from experience
- Survival may be at risk

37–53 = *Fragmented.* The "Fragmented" enterprise is characterized by:
- Individual and/or specialist reactions to adverse events and opportunities
- Discrete management roles established for a small set of risks
- Lack of coordinated response
- Lack of common language of risk and value

- Learning occurs primarily within silos, with little knowledge sharing
- Potential to experience multiple crises, often moving from one to the next
- Potential to survive but unlikely to thrive in the long term

54–70 = Top-Down. The "Top-Down" enterprise is characterized by:

- Good tone set at the top and clear values
- A well-defined and communicated framework for policies, procedures, and risk authorities
- Defined business-function responsibilities for risk management
- Primarily qualitative risk assessments
- Largely reactive but some shared learning and proactive responses
- Improved chances of surviving and thriving

71–86 = Integrated. In addition to the characteristics of the "Top-Down" enterprise, the "Integrated" enterprise is also characterized by:

- Integrated proactive responses to both adverse and opportunistic events
- Performance-linked risk and value metrics (qualitative and quantitative)
- Timely and rapid escalation of risks and opportunities to decision makers
- Cultural transformation underway
- Bottom-up as well as top-down communications
- Strong chances of survival and sustainability

87–100 = Risk Intelligent. In addition to the characteristics of the "Top-Down" and "Integrated" enterprise, the "Risk Intelligent" enterprise is characterized by:

- "Felt" leadership and the right tone at top, middle, and bottom
- Key risk and value factors built into all key decision-making processes (risk management and value creation is everyone's job)
- Common adoption of risk intelligence skills and a resulting high state of vigilance and preparedness
- Effective signal detection of potential shifts in the environment or business
- Risk interactions managed with incentives
- Sustainable business model and risk management practices that improve chances of survival and success

We strongly suggest that you rate your enterprise not only by yourself, but that you also solicit ratings from other executives and board members. This way, you can start to develop a shared understanding of the enterprise's current capabilities. A common view is necessary if you are to determine priorities and plan your transformation to improve risk intelligence.

While this simple exercise can provide a quick snapshot of your enterprise's Risk IQ, more sophisticated, comprehensive, and systematic methods and tools are available for evaluating your risk intelligence capabilities. For example, Deloitte has developed an in-depth model to help assess an enterprise's current capabilities and define the level of capability required to survive and thrive in turbulence.

Making the Transformation

Once the enterprise understands its current state of risk intelligence and the best opportunities for improvement, it needs a plan to close the gap and to transform the way it comprehends and manages risks to value. It takes time and effort to become a risk intelligent enterprise.

Risk intelligence is not a status or designation that can be attained and then enjoyed ever more. Rather, it is a way of making better decisions amid uncertainty and under turbulent conditions. Thus, risk intelligence is not an end in itself but a way of doing business, not a goal but a developmental journey. By the same token, improving risk intelligence must be a deliberate and sustainable enterprise process, rather than a mere project.

Voice of Experience

"To be successful, risk management has to be a core process of managing the enterprise, not merely a project. A lot of directors seem to think that because they devise a 'strategy' to deal with known risk, they've got a good handle on risk. My perception is that they don't. Too often, all they want to do is identify the top ten risks based on what people know. It's a project approach—and that's not what's really needed. A systematized approach of understanding the most basic business assumptions has more long-lasting potential."

—Larry Rittenberg, Professor and Chairman Emeritus, Committee of Sponsoring Organizations of the Treadway Commission (COSO)

Developing and applying the necessary supporting processes, systems, and tools enterprise-wide requires a "fractal" approach, in which any part of the whole embodies the properties of the whole. That implies that skills, processes, systems, and tools are common at every organizational level.

To be effective, these processes, systems, and tools must be deployed throughout the enterprise and applied with discipline. Although they will be applied differently at different levels, if the skills, processes, systems, and tools work for the senior executives and the board, then directors and executives should have confidence that they will work elsewhere. Also, as with any skills, the more you practice, the better you become—provided you practice properly and maintain discipline.

At its best, risk intelligence informs every area of the business at every level such that the practices become part of every function, strategy, initiative, decision, activity, and job. This entails making risk intelligence an organizational value on the order of practicing true customer focus or achieving high quality through zero defects.

Such values do not come about by themselves or by executive decree or through a one-shot training initiative, a short-term project, or a "check the box" approach. They come about because the board and management views them as worthwhile, practices them publicly, recognizes them in compensation programs, and embeds them in core processes and systems.

The Transformation Challenge

In many organizations, despite the number and severity of risk management failures, executives still remain unconvinced of the business case for improved risk intelligence and thus risk management. Given this, there are several possible explanations as to why transformation efforts may fail.

For starters, even though the greatest value of risk management is prevention and preparation, demonstrating their value in advance often proves daunting. People may say, "That can't happen here," or "It can't happen again," or "We're too smart to let that happen to us."

Voice of Experience

"People don't see the need for prevention until it's too late. Obviously when a crisis occurs, everyone recognizes the need; it's self-evident. It ought to be obvious that prevention is less expensive and more effective than response and recovery.

"I've tried to create recognition of the need for prevention in stages by starting with a risk scan. Let's make sure we understand the risks that we have in the organization and the need to take some actions to mitigate the risk, understand it more, to be more involved in what this looks like.

(Continued)

(Continued)

"It's a process of moving from financial risk to operating risk to unintended consequences to compensation risk, to culture, ethics, and the much broader global impacts and competition. Our risk scan is much broader today than two or three years ago, when it was all financially based. So it's in a step-by-step mode."

—Suzanne Hopgood, Director

Prevention, therefore, is much less likely to receive priority, especially when resources are scarce. A clear statement of the TCOR may be required to demonstrate the value of improved prevention and preparation. Even when executives are convinced of the value, those who try to implement a systematic approach may experience flawed or prolonged execution.

Generally, it is best to aim for rapid implementation by building more systematic consideration of risk to value directly into the core business processes. Early wins are important to demonstrate value. Nothing succeeds like success, and word of mouth can aid implementation.

Lack of program management such as specific milestones and metrics as well as a failure to recognize the level of effort required can contribute to failed implementation. The implementation may also fail if the implementation team lacks dedicated, credible, and capable resources; if the vision and expectations are poorly communicated; and if the enterprise lacks a common language of risk. Difficulties in reconciling the different perspectives of various specialist silos also can result in a lack of cross-functional alignment and coordination.

Transformation Success Factors

Improving risk intelligence is the result of systematic, deliberate effort. It is not a project, but certain steps and deliverables can be defined and monitored for progress toward the goal.

CREATE THE RIGHT TONE AT THE TOP   Boards are taking corporate risk personally, and that's a good thing. Boards are demanding increased transparency about how value is created and how value can be destroyed. Risk is now a main topic on most board agendas, especially regarding how to better anticipate and prepare for the unexpected. These heightened expectations and those of other stakeholders, such as regulators and rating agencies, are driving increased demands for improvements in the ways key risks are understood and managed.

Directors must continue to raise the bar in terms of developing a risk intelligent understanding of the business. Businesses must take certain risks if they are to be competitive and achieve future growth such as new product development and new market entry while they must be averse to other risks such as noncompliance and health and safety.

Directors should fully understand the enterprise's key strategies for value creation and value protection and the key risks. Without clear board expectations of improved transparency, risk management program efforts may fail. Thus, the board should establish a clear mandate regarding the importance of intelligent risk management.

ASSIGN EXECUTIVE OWNERSHIP Senior executive commitment and active involvement in the intelligent management of risk are essential. Without them, no systematic and sustainable change is possible. Risk management policies and programs will remain mere paper exercises in the absence of real executive commitment. Generating commitment is an iterative process in which value is consistently demonstrated.

Value must be measured in terms of the ability to protect existing assets and enable future growth. The process must be nonbureaucratic and part of all key decision-making processes. Executives also need to be measured on the basis of risk-adjusted performance. Executive ownership needs to be made explicit, and executives need to be accountable for the reliability of their risk assessments and the effectiveness of risk mitigation on a cross-functional basis.

Because business is risky, the organization needs all of its senses and sensors working effectively. Management should be directly responsible for reporting the results of their risk assessments. This, in turn, requires accurate and timely risk intelligence and reports. It also requires an internal environment that promotes the open, timely, and honest communication that drives out fear.

LEVERAGE THE BEST OF THE EXISTING ORGANIZATIONAL CULTURE The culture of every enterprise is unique, and successful risk intelligence must fit the culture. For example, if your enterprise uses Six Sigma, then perhaps you should make risk intelligence a part of the Six Sigma program. Use the example of your most successful transformation and leverage the lessons learned. Some companies have leveraged the success of their environment, health and safety, Sarbanes-Oxley, corporate compliance, quality, sustainability, or resilience programs to design and launch their risk intelligence program.

Make risk intelligence an essential part of the unique culture of the enterprise. When benchmarking how others have successfully implemented programs, make every effort to understand those programs as systems rather than just as a collection of various parts.

Also be cognizant of the problems of benchmarking. Just because someone reports they are doing something does not necessarily make it so. Even if many have adopted a particular practice or set of practices, it doesn't mean that it is right for your organization or even that it is a best practice. Mere program transplants without translation will likely fail. Most programs require translation to make them meaningful to the unique culture of the enterprise.

BUILD RISK INTELLIGENCE INTO CORE BUSINESS PROCESSES   Build risk intelligence into the ways of doing business; do not "bolt it on." Integrating risk intelligence into the strategic and operational planning and budgeting processes is especially important and should be part of annual and quarterly reviews. Risk and reward should be made an explicit consideration in every major decision-making process, calendarized, and tied to compensation metrics.

ADOPT A DISCIPLINED CHANGE MANAGEMENT PROCESS   Never let a crisis go to waste. If the enterprise has experienced severe failures, then these can be constructively used to drive needed change. It is often much more difficult to produce change in organizations that perceive themselves as successful. Ultimately, successful change is about capturing the minds and hearts of the people who make decisions and must execute those decisions.

Change management programs need to systematically consider the culture and values of the enterprise and leverage those values to demonstrate how a different approach can help the organization survive and thrive. Build risk intelligence into everyone's job. Help people become risk aware, not just risk averse. Adopt a systematic and disciplined approach.

LINK METRICS TO COMPENSATION AND PERFORMANCE MANAGEMENT   People will do what they get measured on and compensated for. The design of compensation systems needs to carefully consider potential unintended consequences. In a growing number of companies, such systems are now being designed to produce a better balance between short-, intermediate-, and long-term performance and to emphasize not only the results obtained but the process used to achieve them. Change efforts will fail if they are not aligned with and supported by the compensation system.

FOCUS ON THE "VITAL FEW," NOT THE "TRIVIAL MANY"   Many programs fail because they attempt to "boil the ocean." Especially when a program is being newly introduced, it is important to focus on the "killer" risks and the "gigantic" opportunities. Certainly, it is important to gain a full understanding of the nature of risks the company faces. However, there are many ways to begin.

Some companies choose to conduct a high-level survey of risks (i.e., to cast a broad net and then to prioritize responses). Others, knowing that certain risks pose a real and imminent threat to the viability of company, simply choose to start with those as priorities and then expand the scope.

However, trying to take on too many issues at the same time is likely to fail. Organizations usually can focus constructively only on a few priorities at any one time. The key is to find the "vital few" issues as distinct from the "trivial many." If everything is a priority, nothing really is.

IMPROVE CROSS-FUNCTIONAL PREPAREDNESS AND COORDINATION Provide timely, shared intelligence across silos for continual learning. Where numerous specializations are involved in risk management, the real challenge often becomes sharing intelligence and lessons learned. Each specialization often has its own specialist language and its own criteria for assessing and reporting risk. Often insulated from one another, they lack a common language and a means of coordination.

Developing a common language of risk, including common assessment criteria, is often an essential first step in improving cross-functional coordination. Synchronizing the timing of the involvement of the specialists as they interact with the business units can effectively reduce the burden on the business. Using common criteria and common processes can also help leverage one another's work and can produce significant savings. A chief risk officer can play an important role in helping to build cross-functional capabilities and in harmonizing, synchronizing, and rationalizing the various risk specializations.

DEMAND DISCIPLINE AND ACCOUNTABILITY IN EXECUTION A robust and consistent risk intelligence process requires sustained operational discipline. Assign specific ownership for specific risks. The board should define which risks should be addressed by its various committees, including those that are reserved for the full board. The board should also require executive accountability by assigning specific executive responsibilities for various classes of risks—for example, strategy, operations, reporting, and compliance. Those executives should, in turn, assign and require specific accountability for individual risks within those risk classes.

INSIST ON REASONABLE ASSURANCE AND INDEPENDENT REASSURANCE FOR THE MOST RELEVANT AND HIGHEST IMPACT RISKS Some risk assessments have failed because they falsely assumed that high-impact, low-likelihood events would not occur. Executives tend to dismiss extreme events as implausible. A more prudent approach is to identify those risks that are highly relevant (intrinsic) to the business and pose the greatest threat to the enterprise.

Reasonable assurances should then be sought from management that these key risks have been appropriately understood and mitigated, independent of their likelihood. After all, if the risk is relevant and high impact, the company ought to have a plan to manage it. Independent reassurance from internal audit and others should be sought to determine whether management's reports are robust and reliable.

Responsible executives should then assess and provide assurances regarding the effectiveness of risk management. Those independent of management (e.g., internal audit or a chief risk officer) can then comment on the reliability of those assurances and the robustness of the processes and systems deployed.

ACT ON YOUR KNOWLEDGE AND ADAPT   Unfortunately, too many risk assessments identify potential causes of failure that go unheeded. Clearly, resource constraints and priorities must be determined to allocate scarce resources, but there is little point in doing a risk assessment and then ignoring the result.

The process of adaptation to turbulence and the forces of creative destruction come through both continuous and discontinuous improvement. The organization must become a learning organization that constantly improves its ability to survive and thrive in the face of rapidly changing circumstances.

Conclusion

The first part of this book addressed the reality that conventional risk management has failed. The 21st century enterprise requires an unconventional approach to the understanding and management of risk to value in times of uncertainty and turbulence. Because turbulence cannot be predicted or modeled, the enterprise needs to improve its vigilance and preparedness.

The second part of the book described ten risk intelligence skills that ought to be common to directors, officers, and employees even if the challenges and decisions they must make will be different. The development of these ten skills is, of course, no absolute guarantee of success. However, their absence is likely a harbinger of fatal flaws that could lead to the demise of the enterprise.

The third part of the book described the characteristics of the Risk Intelligent Enterprise and the responsibilities of directors, officers, and employees. It outlined the steps to be taken to improve risk intelligence. It also discussed some of the missteps that ought to be avoided.

While all of these parts when taken together may seem to be onerous and costly, the reality is that decisions that affect the enterprise's survival and success are made every day at every level of the enterprise. This is enterprise management.

Improved risk intelligence can help improve the quality of decision making and, thus, the chances of enterprise survival and success. As in the case of quality, the marginally increased cost of improved risk management will be more than offset by the savings achieved by reducing the cost of failure. The enterprise that is able to make and then execute superior decisions about which risks to take to create future value and which risks to avoid in order to protect existing assets will find itself in a superior competitive position.

Notes

Chapter 1

1. Douglas J. Futuyma, *Evolutionary Biology,* 3rd ed. (Sunderland: Sinaur Associates, 1998), PBS, www.pbs.org/wgbh/evolution/library/03/2/l_032_01.html (Accessed 4 May 2009).

2. Arie De Geus. *The Living Company: Habits for Survival in a Turbulent Environment* (Cambridge, MA: Harvard Business School Press, 1997), 1.

3. Dane Hamilton, "Peloton Hedge Funds Liquidating; Will Close," Reuters.com, http://uk.reuters.com/article/businessNews/idUKN0563971020080305 (Accessed 5 March 2008).

4. Roddy Boyd, "The Last Days of Bear Stearns: It Took Only a Few Days, a Rising Sense of Panic—and a Critical E-Mail—to Spell the End of the 85-Year-Old Investment Bank," CNNMoney.com, http://money.cnn.com/2008/03/28/magazines/fortune/boyd_bear.fortune/ (Accessed 31 March 2008).

5. The Mortgage Lender Implode-O-Meter, http://ml-implode.com (Accessed 4 May 2009).

6. Federal Deposit Insurance Corporation, "FDIC Statistics at a Glance," www.fdic.gov/bank/statistical/stats/2009sep/fdic.html (Accessed 6 December 2009).

7. RealtyTrac 2008 U.S. Foreclosure Market Report, RealtyTrac.com, www.realtytrac.com/foreclosure/foreclosure-rates.html (Accessed 4 May 2009).

8. Ibid.

9. Joshua Brockman, "CEOs Crushed by Credit Crunch," NPR.org, 17 June 2008, www.npr.org/templates/story/story.php?storyId=91584662 (Accessed 4 May 2009).

10. Joann S. Lublin, "CEO Firings on the Rise as Downturn Gains Steam," *Wall Street Journal,* 13 January 2009.

11. CFO Research Services in Collaboration with SAP, "The Renewed Finance Function—Extending Performance Management Beyond Finance," November 2007 (Boston: CFO Publishing Corporation, 2007), 20.

12. Ibid.

13. USC Center for Effective Organizations and Heidrick & Struggles, "10th Annual Corporate Board Effectiveness Study 2006-2007," Hendrick.com, June 2007, www.heidrick.com/NR/rdonlyres/723D125E-9746-4486-829A-D49A8AF0832B/0/HS_BoardEffectivenessStudy0607.pdf (Accessed 4 May 2009).

14. Interview with Jeff Cunningham.

15. Ibid.

16. Robert F. Felton and Pamela Keenan Fritz, *McKinsey Quarterly 2005, Special Edition, Value and Performance* (March 2005), 54–55.

17. USC Center for Effective Organizations; Heidrick & Struggles, Board Effectiveness Study.

18. Joann S. Lublin and Cari Tuna, "Anticipating Corporate Crisis: Boards Intensify Efforts to Review Risks and Dodge Disasters," *Wall Street Journal*, 22 September 2008, B5.

19. Interview with Jeff Cunningham.

20. John L. Colley Jr. et al., *Corporate Governance* (New York: McGraw Hill, 2003), 14–24.

21. Richard Leblanc and James Gillies, *Inside the Boardroom: How Boards Really Work and the Coming Revolution in Corporate Governance* (Hoboken, NJ: John Wiley & Sons, 2005), 3.

22. Deloitte and Economist Intelligence Unit, "In the Dark: What Boards and Executives Don't Know About the Health of Their Businesses," Deloitte Touche Tohmatsu, October 2004, www.deloitte.com/dtt/whitepaper/0,1017,sid%253D1007%2526cid%253D62386,00.html (Accessed 4 May 2009).

23. Deloitte and Economist Intelligence Unit, "In the Dark II: What Many Boards and Executives Still Don't Know about the Health of Their Business," Deloitte Touche Tohmatsu, October 2007, www.deloitte.com/dtt/article/0,1002,cid=146837,00.html?WT.mc_id=dtthomeflash_IntheDark5_theme (Accessed 4 May 2009).

24. Lloyd's in Association with the Economist Intelligence Unit, "Taking Risk on Board: How Global Business Leaders View Risk," 2005, www.lloyds.com/NR/rdonlyres/48FC5495-1313-4616-AD83-AA2C1BA5C952/0/Takingriskonboard.pdf (Accessed 4 May 2009).

25. USC Center for Effective Organizations; Heidrick & Struggles, Board Effectiveness Study.

26. Interview with Professor Ray Reilly.

27. Keith B. Meyer and Robert S. Rollo, "Boards Think They're Doing a Good Job . . . But CEOs Disagree: What Directors Can Do to Bridge That Disconnect." Heidrick and Struggles Governance Letter, in *Directors & Boards* (Chicago: Heidrick and Struggles International, 22 March 2008), www.heidrick.com/NR/rdonlyres/B533E66E-C1F3-4396-A8E3-E8DDF66BE84A/0/DB2008Q2GovernanceLetterBoardsThinkMeyerRollo.pdf (Accessed 4 May 2009).

28. McKinsey Global Surveys: "How Companies Make Good Decisions," *McKinsey Quarterly*, January 2009, www.mckinseyquarterly.com/How_companies_make_good_decisions_McKinsey_Global_Survey_Results_2282 (Accessed 4 May 2009).

29. McKinsey Global Surveys: "Flaws in Strategic Decision Making," January, 2009, *McKinsey Quarterly*, www.mckinseyquarterly.com/Flaws_in_strategic_decision_making_McKinsey_Global_Survey_Results_2284 (Accessed 4 May 2009).

30. Meyer and Rollo, "Boards Think They're Doing a Good Job."

31. Ibid.

32. U.S. Council on Competitiveness, "Manage Risk and Achieve Resilience," www.compete.org/explore/risk-resilience/ (Accessed 4 May 2009).

33. Interview with Esther Colwill.

34. Interview with Jim Porter. Mr. Porter's comments reflect his opinions and may not necessarily reflect those of the DuPont Company.

35. Mary Buffett and David Clark. *The Tao of Warren Buffett: Warren Buffett's Words of Wisdom, Quotations and Interpretations to Guide You to Billionaire Wealth and Enlightened Business Management* (New York: Scribner, 2006), 89.

36. W. Ross Ashby, *An Introduction to Cybernetics* (London: Chapman & Hall, 1956).

37. "Culling the Herd," May 2009, www.darwinawards.com (Accessed 4 May 2009).

38. Interview with Jim Porter. Mr. Porter's comments reflect his opinions and may not necessarily reflect those of the DuPont Company.

Chapter 2

1. Federal Reserve System Board of Governors, "Intended Federal Funds Rate, Change and Level, 1990 to Present," FederalReserve.gov, www.federalreserve.gov/fomc/fundsrate.htm (Accessed 4 May 2009).

2. Federal Reserve System Board of Governors, Division of Banking Supervision and Regulation, "SUBJECT: Lending Standards for Commercial Loan," FederalReserve.gov, SR 98-18, June 23, 1998, www.federalreserve.gov/boarddocs/SRLetters/1998/sr9818.htm (Accessed 4 May 2009).

3. Robert J. Shiller, "'Irrational Exuberance'—Again: Remember the Stock Bubble? Yale Economist Robert Shiller Says We're Just as Mad for Real Estate," *CNNMoney.com*, 25 January 2005, http://money.cnn.com/2005/01/13/real_estate/realestate_shiller1_0502/index.htm (Accessed 4 May 2009).

4. "Update 1—Bernstein sees higher 2008-2010 loan losses at US banks" Reuters, 8 January 2009, http://reuters.com/article/marketsnews/idESBNG12776520090108?rpc=33 (Accessed 10 May 2009).

5. Andrew Ross Sorkin and Vikas Bajaj, "Shift for Goldman and Morgan Marks the End of an Era," *New York Times*, 21 September 2008, www.nytimes.com/2008/09/22/business/22bank.html. A1.

6. Charles Goodhart and Avinash Persaud,"How to Avoid the Next Crash," *Financial Times*, 30 January 2008, http://us.ft.com/ftgateway/superpage.ft?news_id=fto013020081447575749 (Accessed 10 May, 2009).

7. Zvi Griliches and Michael D. Intriligator, *Handbook of Econometrics, Volume I* (North-Holland: Elsevier, 1983).

8. Nassim Nicholas Taleb, *Fooled by Randomness: The Hidden Role of Randomness in the Markets and in Life*, 2nd Ed. (New York: Random House Trade Paperbacks, 2000).

9. Nassim Nicholas Taleb, *The Black Swan: The Impact of the Highly Improbable* (New York: Random House, 2007).

10. Benoit B. Mandelbrot and Richard L. Hudson, Richard, *The (Mis)-Behavior of Markets: A Fractal View of Risk, Ruin and Reward* (New York: Basic Books, 2004).

11. Ibid., 13.

12. Karl Pearson, "The Problem of the Random Walk," *Nature* 72, p. 294 (1905), www
.nature.com/physics/looking-back/pearson/index.html (Accessed 4 May, 2009).

13. Eugene Fama, "The Behavior of Stock Market Prices," *Journal of Business*,
Vol. 38, No. 1, January 1965, University of Chicago Press, JSTOR, www.
jstor.org/pss/2350752 (Accessed 1 June 2009).

14. Bruno Porro and Werner Schaad, "The Risk Landscape of the Future," Swiss Re,
2004.

15. William A Sherden, *The Fortune Sellers: The Big Business of Buying and Selling
Predictions* (Hoboken, NJ: John Wiley & Sons, 1997).

16. Ibid.

17. BusinessWeek, "The Next Big One: Where America Is Most Vulnerable and
How the Nation Can Better Manage the Risks Ahead," www.businessweek.
com/magazine/content/05_38/b3951001.htm (Accessed 2 July 2009).

18. Richard Bookstaber, *A Demon of Our Own Design: Markets, Hedge Funds, and
the Perils of Financial Innovation* (Hoboken, NJ: John Wiley & Sons, 2007),
145.

19. Ibid., 155.

20. Ibid., 161.

21. Ibid. 25–26

22. Mandelbrot and Hudson, *The (Mis)-Behavior of Markets,* 4.

Chapter 3

1. Clayton M. Christensen, *The Innovator's Dilemma: When New Technologies Cause
Great Firms to Fail.* (Boston: Harvard Business School Press, 1997) xiii.

2. Rolf Skjong, "Risk: A Word from Ancient Greece," DNV Managing Risk
DNV.com, 25 February 2005, www.dnv.com/focus/risk_management/more_
information/risk_origin/ (Accessed 1 June 2009).

3. Body of Knowledge Committee of the Committee of Academic Prereq-
uisites for Professional Practice "Civil Engineering Body of Knowledge
for the 21st Century: Preparing the Civil Engineer for the Future 2nd
ed." ASCE, American Society of Civil Engineers, 2008, www.asce.org/files/
pdf/professional/BOK2E_(ASCE_2008)_ebook.pdf?CFID=175792795&CFTOKEN=
b8732dfdb6b0ecc2-059C554A-ECAC-86A3-111272F7AC3F2B44&jsessionid=cc303
352111245634647370 (Accessed 5 July 2009).

4. Interview with Mario Andretti.

5. Senior Supervisors Group, "Observations on Risk Management Practices during
the Recent Market Turbulence," NewYorkFed.org, 6 March 2008, www.newyork-
fed.org/newsevents/news/banking/2008/ssg_risk_mgt_doc_final.pdf (Accessed 1
June 2009).

6. Ibid.

7. Douglas Powell, *An Introduction to Risk Communications and the Perception
of Risk* (Guelph: University of Guelph, 1996); P. M. Sandman, "Communicating
Risks: Some Basics," *Health and Environment Digest*, Vol. 1, No. 11 (1987): 3–4;
Paul Slovic, "Trust, Emotion, Sex, Politics, and Science: Surveying the Risk Assessment Battlefield," *Risk Analysis*, Vol. 19, No. 4 (1999): 689–701; V. Covello and

Paul Sandman, "Risk Communication: Evolution and Revolution" in A. Wolbarst (ed.): *Solutions to an Environment in Peril* (Baltimore: John Hopkins University Press, 2001), 164–178.

8. Deloitte Research, "Disarming the Value Killers," 2007.

9. Gennaro Bernile, Gregg A. Jarrell, and Howard Mulcahey, "The Effect of the Options Backdating Scandal on the Stock-Price Performance of 110 Accused Companies," Simon School Working Paper No. FR 06-10, 21 December 2006.

10. New York State, Office of the State Comptroller, "Impact of the Corporate Scandals on New York State," Office of the State Comptroller, August 2003, www.osc.state.ny.us/press/releases/aug03/corpgovernrpt.pdf (Accessed 1 June 2009).

11. Kevin Hendricks and Vinod R. Singhal, "The Effect of Supply Chain Disruptions on Long-Term Shareholder Value, Profitability, and Share Price Volatility," Georgia Institute of Technology, June 2005, www.loginstitute.ca/pdf/singhal_scm_report.pdf (Accessed 4 May 2009).

12. Identity Theft Resource Center of San Diego, "Breaches Blast 2007 Record: As of August 22, ITRC's List Surpasses 446 Documented Breaches" Posted in: Press Releases, ITRC Surveys & Studies By ITRC, 15 June 2009, www.idtheftcenter.org/artman2/publish/m_press/Breaches_Blast_2007_Record.shtml (Accessed 16 June 2009).

13. Ross Kerber, "Cost of Data Breach at TJX Soars to $256m," *Boston Globe*, 15 August 2007, www.boston.com/business/globe/articles/2007/08/15/cost_of_data_breach_at_tjx_soars_to_256m/ (Accessed 1 June, 2009).

14. Lisa R. Anderson and Jennifer M. Mellor, "Predicting Heath Behaviors with and Experimental Measure of Risk Preference," Vol. 27, Issue 5, *Journal of Health Economics*, Abstract:doi:10.1016/j.jhealeco.2008.05.11, www.sciencedirect.com/science?_ob=ArticleURL&_udi=B6V8K-4SPC0K7-1&_user=10&_rdoc=1&_fmt=&_orig=search&_sort=d&view=c&_acct=C000050221&_version=1&_urlVersion=0&_userid=10&md5=a37c09303276a702aab6067a5fd6b899 (Accessed June 1 2009).

Chapter 4

1. Andrew S. Grove, *Only the Paranoid Survive* (New York: Currency/Doubleday, 1996), 3.

2. Joseph Schumpeter, *Capitalism, Socialism and Democracy* (New York: Harper, 1975 [orig. pub. 1942]), 82–85.

3. Jean Charles Rochet, *Why Are There So Many Banking Crises? The Politics and Policy of Bank Regulation* (Princeton: Princeton University Press, 2000), 1.

4. Charles P. Kindleberger. *Manias, Panics and Crashes: A History of Financial Crises*, 5th ed. (Hoboken, NJ: John Wiley & Sons, 2000).

5. Robert J. Shiller, *Irrational Exuberance, 2nd ed.* (Princeton: Princeton University Press, 2005), 60–61.

6. Ibid., 67–68.

7. Charles P. Kindleberger. *Manias, Panics and Crashes: A History of Financial Crises*, 5th ed. (Hoboken, NJ: John Wiley & Sons, 2000), 14.

8. Ibid., 17.

9. Philip S. Russel and Violet M. Torbey, "The Efficient Market Hypothesis on Trial: A Survey," *Quest: A Journal of Applied Topics in Business and Economics*, 2002, www.westga.edu/~bquest/2002/market.htm (Accessed 1 June 2009).

10. David N. James, "The Trouble I've Seen," in *Harvard Business Review on Leading in Turbulent Times*, ed. Harvard Business School, Adrian Slywatsky and Joseph L. Badaracco Jr. (Boston: Harvard Business School Publishing Company, 2003), 99.

11. David Olive, "Rumours of Newspapers' Demise ..." *Toronto Star*, 8 April 2007, thestar.com, www.thestar.com/Business/article/200650 (Accessed 1 May 2009).

12. Ibid.

13. Eric Alterman, "Out of Print: The Death and Life of the American Newspaper," *New Yorker*, 31 March 2008, www.newyorker.com/reporting/2008/03/31/080331fa_fact_alterman (Accessed 1 May 2009).

14. The Pew Research Center for People and the Press, "Online Readership Modestly Boost Newspaper Readership: Maturing Internet News Audience Broader than Deep," people-press.org, 30 July 2006, http://people-press.org/report/282/online-papers-modestly-boost-newspaper-readership (Accessed 1 May 2009).

15. Dawn Kawamoto, "Online Newspaper Readership Climbs 16%," Digital Media-CNET news, 27 January 2009, http://news.cnet.com/8301-1023_3-10150884-93.html (Accessed 5 May 2009).

16. Alterman, "Out of Print."

17. Institute of Practitioners in Advertising and Future Foundation, "Social Media Futures—The Future of Advertising and Agencies in a Networked Society: A 10-Year Perspective," 19 January 2009, www.ipa.co.uk/Content/Social-Media-Futures-report (Accessed 1 June 2009).

18. Olive, "Rumours of Newspapers' Demise ..."

19. Matthew Karnitschnig and Russell Adams, "Billionaire Reaches Deal on Funding for Times Co." WSJ.com, 20 January 2009, http://online.wsj.com/article/SB123224568644693653.html (Accessed 1 June 2009).

20. Alterman, "Out of Print."

21. Nassim Nicholas Taleb, *The Black Swan: The Impact of the Highly Improbable* (New York: Random House Publishers, 2007).

22. Cassell Bryan-Low, "Thomson Evolution Takes Next Step," Media Channel and *Wall Street Journal*, 12 June 2007, www.mediachannel.org/wordpress/2007/06/12/thomson-evolution-takes-next-step/ (Accessed 5 July 2009).

23. Ibid.

24. Ibid.

25. Ibid.

26. Ibid.

27. Richard Harrington, "You Say You Want a Revolution?" *CEO Perspectives*, December 2005/January 2006.

28. John McCormick, "Projects: Management—Harrington: The Transformer," Baseline, 11 April 2006, www.baselinemag.com/c/a/Projects-Management/Richard-Harrington-The-Transformer/ (Accessed 1 May 2009).

29. Harrington, "You Say You Want a Revolution?"

30. John Blossom, "Thomson's Harrington: The Fire Hose vs. the Sprinkler," Shore, www.shore.com/commentary/weblogs/2005/0/thomsons-harrington-fire-hose-vs/html (Accessed 1 May 2009).

31. Howard Marks, "Volatility + Leverage =Dynamite" (Memo to Oaktree Clients, 17 December 2008), 9.
32. Paul Raspin and Siri Terjesen, "What Have We Learned About Forecasting the Future?" *Business Strategy Series*. Vol. 8, No. 2, (2007): 116–121.
33. Senior Supervisors' Group (SSG), "Observations on Risk Management Practices during the Recent Market Turbulence," ny.frg.org, 6 March 2008, www.ny.frb .org/newsevents/news/banking/2008/SSG_Risk_Mgt_doc_final.pdf, 17 (Accessed 1 June 2009).
34. Ibid., 17.

Chapter 5

1. D. G. Jones and M. R. Endsley, "Sources of Situation Awareness Errors in Aviation" *Aviation, Space and Environmental Medicine*, 67(6), www.asma.org/ journal/abstracts/v67n6/67-507.htm, 507–512 (Accessed 6 July 2009).
2. Daniel Simons, "Visual Cognition Lab of the University of Illinois," Viscog.beckman.uiuc.edu, http://viscog.beckman.illinois.edu/flashmovie/15.php (Accessed 6 December 2009).
3. Gretchen Morgenson, "The Reckoning: Behind Insurer's Crisis, Blind Eye to a Web of Risk" *New York Times,* 28 September 2008, www.nytimes.com/2008/09/ 28/business/28melt.html?scp=2&sq=morgenson%20september%2028%202008&st =cse (Accessed 1 July 2009).
4. Davis Goldman, "Where AIG's New Bailout Ranks," CNNMoney.com, November 10, 2008, www.money.cnn.com/2008/11/10/news/economy/aig_ bailout_comparison/index.htm?postversion=2008111012; New York News, "AIG to Get Up to $30 Billion More in Bailout Funds," NBCNewYork.com, 2 March 2009, www.nbcnewyork.com/news/us_world/AIG-to-Get-.html (Accessed 1 July 2009).
5. Ulrike Malmendier and Geoffrey Tate, "Superstar CEOs," Social Science Research Network (SSRN), 15 March 2007, http://papers.ssrn.com/sol3/ papers.cfm?abstract_id=972725 (Accessed 1 July 2009).
6. Military History Encyclopedia on the Web, www.historyofwar.org/articles/ battles_arnhem.html; Niall Cherry, "Operation Market Garden: Last Stand at an Arnhem Schoolhouse," Historynet.com, www.historynet.com/operation-market-garden-last-stand-at-an-arnhem-schoolhouse (both accessed 5 July 2009).
7. Reuters, "Swiss Bank UBP Had Early Warnings on Madoff—WSJ," January 14, 2009, Reuters.com, www.reuters.com/article/americasIpoNews/idUSLE655-2320090114 (Accessed 1 July 2009).
8. Jones and Endsley, "Sources of Situation Awareness Errors."
9. Marcia S. Smith and National Aeronautics Safety Administration (NASA), "NASA's Space Shuttle Columbia: Synopsis of the Report of the Columbia Accident Investigation Board," CRS Report for Congress, 2 September 2003 CRS, 195, http://history.nasa.gov/columbia/Troxell/Columbia%20Web%20Site/Documents/ Congress/CRS%20Summary%20of%20CAIB%20Report.pdf (Accessed 1 July 2009).
10. Turo Uskali, PhD, "Paying Attention to Weak Signals," *Innovation Journalism*, Vol.2, No.11 (30 Aug 2005).

11. Igor Ansoff and Edward McDonnell, *Implanting Strategic Management*, 2nd edition (Upper Saddle River, NJ: Prentice Hall International, 1990).

12. Kees van der Heijden, *Scenarios: The Art of Strategic Conversation* (Hoboken, NJ: John Wiley & Sons, 1996).

13. Ibid., 19.

14. Interview with Bob Eckert.

15. Senior Supervisors Group, "Observations on Risk Management Practices during the Recent Market Turbulence," Senior Supervisors Group Report, 6 March 2008, www.sec.gov/news/press/2008/report030608.pdf, 3 (Accessed 1 July 2009).

16. Ibid.

17. Joe Nocera, "Risk Mismanagement—What Led to the Financial Meltdown"—NYTimes.com, 4 January 2009, www.nytimes.com/2009/01/04/magazine/04risk-t.html?ex=1388725200&en=18b73c4ac71854f7&ei=5124&partner=digg&exprod=digg (Accessed 1 July 2009).

18. Roy MacGregor, *Total Gretzky: The Magic, the Legend, the Numbers* (Toronto: McClelland and Stewart, 1999), 19–20.

19. Joan Makara, "Managing Financial Risk in a Global Enterprise" (in Management and Finance of Hard and Soft Risk: ERM Symposium Session C-3), 2 May 2005, www.ermsymposium.org/2005/erm2005/c3_bk.pdf (Accessed 1 July 2009).

Chapter 6

1. George Gilder, "Metcalf's Law and Legacy," *Forbes Magazine,* 13 September 1993.

2. Richard Bookstaber, *A Demon of Our Own Design: Markets, Hedge Funds, and the Perils of Financial Innovation* (Hoboken, NJ: John Wiley & Sons, 2007), p. 144.

3. Interview with William O. McCabe.

4. Suzanne Hopgood and Michael Tankersley, *Board Leadership for the Company in Crisis* (Washington, D.C.: National Association of Corporate Directors, 2005), 26.

5. Domain-B Newsletter, "Top Ore Miners Hit by Chinese Steel Production Cut," Domain-b.com, 14 October 2008, www.domain-b.com/industry/Steel/20081014_chinese_steel.html (Accessed 1 May 2009).

6. Conference Board, "Business Continuity Planning," Conference-Board.org, Webcast October 2005 www.conference-board.org/cgi-bin/MsmGo.exe?grab_id=0&EXTRA_ARG=&SCOPE=Public&host_id=42&page_id=6237&query=crisis%20preparation%20recovery&hiword=CRISISA%20PREPARATORY%20RECOVERYS%20RECOVERS%20PREPARATIONS%20RECOVERING%20PREPARING%20PREP-ARES%20RECOVERIES%20preparation%20RECOVERED%20recovery%20RECO-VER%20PREPARED%20PREPARE%20crisis%20 (Accessed 1 June 2009).

7. Deborah J. Pretty, PhD, "Catastrophes, Reputation and Shareholder Value," Templeton College, Oxford, 21 September 2000, and www.erisk.com/Resource Center/Viewpoint/QADeborahPretty-OxfordMet.asp (Accessed 6 July 2009).

8. Rory F. Knight and Deborah J. Pretty, "The Impact of Catastrophes on Shareholder Value—A Research Report Sponsored by Sedgewick Group" (Oxford: Templeton College, University of Oxford, 1996), www.nrf.com/Attachments.asp?id=12546; Rory F. Knight and Deborah J. Pretty, "Reputation and Value: The Case of

Corporate Catastrophes," in *Improving Risk Quality to Drive Value*, fmglobal.com, 2001, www.fmglobal.com/pdfs/oxfordmetrica.pdf; Rory F. Knight and Deborah J. Pretty, "Protecting Value in the Face of Mass Fatality Events," Oxfordmetricacom, 2005, www.oxfordmetrica.com/pdf/OMMassFatalitiesBriefing.pdf (Accessed 6 July 2009).

9. Knight and Pretty, "Protecting Value," 24.
10. Interview with Bob Eckert.
11. Incident Command Management System Department of Homeland Security, "National Incident Management System (NIMS): National Standard Curriculum Training Development Guidance FY07," 2004, www.fema.gov/pdf/ emergency/nims/nims_tsctdg_0307v2.pdf, 9–12; Federal Emergency Management Agency (FEMA), NIMS Resource Center, "Incident Command Management System, FEMA.gov, 2007, www.fema.gov/emergency/nims/Incident CommandSystem.shtm, 45–47 (Accessed 6 July 2009).

Chapter 7

1. *USA Today,* "Biofuel Boom Raises Beer Prices in Germany," May 28, 2007, USATODAY.com, www.usatoday.com/news/world/2007-05-28-biofuel-beer_N.htm (Accessed 1 June 2009).
2. Wyn Grant, "Commentary on the Common Agricultural Policy of the EU," Common Agricultural Policy at Blogspot, 4 March 2007, http://commonagpolicy. blogspot.com/2007/03/biofuels-may-push-up-beer-prices.html (Accessed 1 June 2009).
3. Deutsche Welle, "Germany's Cheap Beer Tradition Under Threat From Biofuels," DW-World.de, 23 April 2007, www.dw-world.de/dw/article/ 0,2144,2451025,00.html (Accessed 5 May 2009).
4. Dr. Jacques Diouf, "Press Conference on Soaring Food Prices and Action Needed," Food and Agriculture Organization of the United Nations, (Press Conference Given in Rome, 17 December 2007), www.fao.org/newsroom/ common/ecg/1000733/en/facts99.pdf (Accessed 5 June 2009).
5. CNW Group, "ScotiaBank/Economic Reports: Scotiabank's Commodity Price Index Leaps in October," 28 November 2007, Newswire.ca, www.newswire .ca/en/releases/archive/November2007/28/c5206.html (Accessed 5 May 2009).
6. BBC News/Americas, "Mexicans stage tortilla protest," BBC News, 1 February 2007, http://news.bbc.co.uk/go/pr/fr/-/2/hi/americas/6319093.stm, (Accessed 5 May 2009).
7. Richard A. Bookstaber, *A Demon of Our Own Design* (Hoboken, NJ: John Wiley & Sons, 2007), 157.
8. Ian Dobson et al., "Complex Systems Analysis of Series of Blackouts: Cascading Failure, Criticality, and Self-Organization, Bulk Power System Dynamics and Control—VI," Presented: Cortina d'Ampezzo, Italy, 22–27 August, 2004, www.ornl.gov/sci/fed/Theory/publication/pub2004/dobsonIREP04.pdf (Accessed 6 July 2009).
9. Henry Petroski, *Success through Failure: The Paradox of Design* (Princeton: Princeton University Press, 2006).

10. Paul Ormerod, *Why Most Things Fail: Evolution, Extinction and Economics* (Hoboken, NJ: John Wiley & Sons, 2006), 35.
11. Network Centric Operations Industry Consortium (NCOIC), "Accelerating Network Centric Systems Through Industry Collaboration," NCIOC Brochure, www.ncoic.org/about/Brochure.pdf.
12. Siobhan Gorman, "Electricity Grid in U.S. Penetrated By Spies." WSJ.com, 8 April 2009, http://online.wsj.com/article/SB123914805204099085.html (Accessed 5 May 2009).
13. Siobhan Gorman, August Cole, and Yochi Dreazen, "Computer Spies Breach Fighter-Jet Project," WSJ.com, 21 April 2009, http://online.wsj.com/article/SB124027491029837401.html (Accessed 5 May 2009).
14. Jonathan Byrnes, "Learning to Manage Complexity," Harvard Business School: Working Knowledge for Business Leaders Archive, 7 November 2005, http://hbswk.hbs.edu/archive/5079.html (Accessed 5 June 2009).
15. W. Ross Ashby, *An Introduction to Cybernetics* (London: Chapman and Hall, 1956), 207.
16. Michael E. Raynor, *The Strategy Paradox* (New York: Doubleday, 2007), 4.
17. Karl E. Weick, "Educational Organizations as Loosely Coupled Systems," *Administrative Sciences Quarterly*. Vol.21(1) March 1976 (Ithaca, NY: Cornell University Press, 1976), 1.
18. Terry Winograd, PhD, and Fernando Flores, PhD, *Understanding Computers and Cognition: A New Foundation for Design* (Upper Saddle River, NJ: Addison-Wesley/Pearson Educational Publications, 1988).

Chapter 8

1. Shelby Foote, *The Civil War, A Narrative: Red River to Appomattox* (New York: Random House, 1974), 203.
2. CNBC, "Fed Chairman: Some Small US Banks May Go Under," CNBC.com with Reuters and AP, 28 February 2008, www.cnbc.com/id/23390252 (Accessed 1 June 2009).
3. Charles Koch, *The Science of Success* (Hoboken, NJ: John Wiley & Sons, Inc. 2007), 151.
4. American Society of Civil Engineers, Definition cited by Technical Council on Forensic Engineering, www.ascetcfe.org/ (Accessed 5 July 2009).
5. Interview with Howard Marks.
6. Caroline Alexander, *The Endurance: Shackleton's Legendary Antarctic Expedition* (New York: Alfred A. Knopf, 1998).
7. Senior Supervisors Group, "Observations on Risk Management Practices during the Recent Market Turbulence," March 2008.
8. Ziva Kunda, "The Case for Motivated Reasoning," *Psychological Bulletin*, 108, 1990; Shelly E. Taylor, *Positive Illusions: Creative Self-Deception and the Healthy Mind* (New York: Basic Books, 1989).
9. David M. DeJoy, "The Optimism Bias and Traffic Accident Risk Perception," *Accident Analysis and Prevention*, August 21(4), 1989: 333–40.
10. David A. Armor and Shelley E. Taylor, "When Predictions Fail: The Dilemma of Unrealistic Optimism," in *Heuristics and Biases: The Psychology of Intuitive*

Judgment, Thomas Gilovich et al., ed. (Cambridge, UK: Cambridge University Press, 2002).

11. Ellen Goodman, "The Gospel According to Moral Hazard," *Boston Globe,* March 21, 2008, www.boston.com/bostonglobe/editorial_opinion/oped/articles/2008/03/21/the_gospel_according_to_moral_hazard/ (Accessed 17 October 2009).

12. David N. James, "The Trouble I've Seen," *Harvard Business Review*, March 1, 2002. Author's Note: Writing in the *Harvard Business Review*, David N. James, a professional crisis manager who rescues enterprises on the verge of bankruptcy, says that freeing an enterprise from its past obligations "places it at a huge advantage relative to businesses that have to pay their creditors in full." He goes on to say, "the profitability of the whole industry declines, creating a real risk that the trouble will spread to other corporations."

13. Karin Thorburn, "Bankruptcy Auctions: A Viable Alternative to Chapter 11," *Tuck Forum*, V(2), Spring 2001.

14. Phil Cohen, "Deming's 14 Points," hci.com, www.hci.com.au/hcisite2/articles/deming.htm (Accessed 1 June 2009).

15. Interview with Lynn Krominga.

16. Derek Lundy, *The Godforsaken Sea: Racing the World's Most Dangerous Water* (New York: Alfred A. Knopf, 1998), 7.

Chapter 9

1. Management and Leadership Quotes, www.management-quotes.net/quote/37358, and Deming.org, http://deming.org/index.cfm?.comtent.

2. History Commons, "Context of December 2002: CIA Torn over Curveball's Reliability," HistoryCommons.org, www.historycommons.org/context.jsp?item=complete_timeline_of_the_2003_invasion_of_iraq_1176 (Accessed 6 July 2009).

3. Innocence Project, "Lessons Not Learned: An Innocence Project Report," Innocenceproject.org and Benjamin N. Cardozzo School of Law, Yeshiva University, www.innocenceproject.org/docs/NY_innocence_report.pdf (Accessed 1 July 2009).

4. Mark S. Beasley, Joseph V. Carcello, and Dana R. Hermanson, "COSO's New Fraud Study: What It Means for CPAs," *Journal of Accountancy*, Vol. 187, 1999, www.allbusiness.com/accounting-reporting/reports-statements/260736-1.html (Accessed 1 July 2009).

5. Alan Feuer and Christine Haughney, "Standing Accused: A Pillar of Finance and Charity," *New York Times,* December 13, 2008, www.timesdaily.com/article/20081213/ZNYT01/812133011/-1/NEWS30?Title=Standing_Accused_A_Pillar_of_Finance_and_Charity*(Accessed 1 June 2009).*

6. Cara Scanell, "Madoff Chasers Dug for Years, to No Avail," WSJ.com, 5 January 2009, http://online.wsj.com/article/SB123111743915052731.html?mod=rss_whats_news_us (Accessed 1 June 2009).

7. Binyamin Applebaum, David S. Hilzenrath, and Amir R. Paley, "All Just One Big Lie," www.washingtonpost.com/wp-dyn/content/article/2008/12/12/AR2008121203970.html.

8. Alex Berenson and Diana B. Henriques, "Look at Wall Street Wizard Finds Magic Had Skeptics," *New York Times,* 12 December 2008, www.nytimes.com/2008/12/13/business/13fraud.html?em (Accessed 1 June 2009).

9. Mark S. Beasley, Joseph V. Carcello, and Dana R. Hermanson, "Top 10 Audit Deficiencies: Lessons from Fraud-Related SEC Cases," *Journal of Accountancy,* April 2001, 63–66.

10. Tom Ridge, "Managing Risk before It Manages You" (Speech delivered to the Institute of Internal Auditors, New Orleans, 2006).

11. Activity Based Risk Evaluation Model of Auditing, (ABREMA), Abrema.net, www.abrema.net/home_framework.html (*Accessed 1 June 2009*).

12. Senior Supervisors Group (SSG), Observations on Risk Management Practices during Recent Market Turbulence, SSG, 6 March 2008, 3, www.ny.frb.org/newsevents/news/banking/2008/SSG_Risk_Mgt_doc_final.pdf (Accessed 1 June 2009).

13. Ibid., 3.

14. Joe Nocera, "Risk Mismanagement—What Led to the Financial Meltdown," NYTimes.com, 4 January 2009, www.nytimes.com/2009/01/04/magazine/04risk-t.html?ex=1388725200&en=18b73c4ac71854f7&ei=5124&partner=digg&exprod=digg (Accessed 1 July 2009).

15. Ben Z. Gottesman and Konstantinos Karagiannis, "A False Sense of Security," *PC Magazine,* 2 February 2005.

16. Deloitte Development LLC, "Perspectives on ERM and the Risk Intelligent Enterprise: Enterprise Risk Management Benchmark Study," Deloitte Development LLC, March 2008, www.deloitte.com/view/en_US/us/Services/audit-enterprise-risk-services/governance-regulatory-risk-strategies/Enterprise-Risk-Management/article/7491942e84ffd110VgnVCM100000ba42f00aRCRD.htm (Accessed 6 December 2009).

17. U.S. Department of Defense, "News Transcript, Presenter: Secretary of Defense Donald H. Rumsfeld," Defenselink.mil, 12 February 2002, www.defenselink.mil/transcripts/transcript.aspx?transcriptid=2636 (Accessed 23 July 2009).

18. Guy Bloom, "Understanding Giving and Receiving Information: Explanation of the Johari Window of Joseph Luft and Harry Ingram," 12 Manage: The Executive Fast Track, www.12manage.com/methods_luft_ingham_johari_window.html (Accessed 6 June 2009).

19. Irving Janis, *Victims of Groupthink: A Psychological Study of Foreign-Policy Decisions and Fiascoes* (Boston: Houghton Mifflin Enterprise, 1972).

20. Ibid., 9.

21. Ibid., 148–149.

22. Pew Research Center's Project for Excellence in Journalism.

Chapter 10

1. Benjamin Graham, *The Intelligent Investor,* 4th rev. ed. (New York: Harper and Row, 1973), 287.

2. Interview with Mario Andretti.

3. Interview with Esther Colwill.

4. Federal Deposit Insurance Corporation Financial Institutions Letter, "Liquidity Risk Management," August 26, 2008.
5. David N. James, "The Trouble I've Seen," *Harvard Business Review*, March 1, 2002, 100.
6. Bank for International Settlements, "Principles for Sound Liquidity Risk Management and Supervision," Basel Committee on Banking Supervision, 92-9131-767-5. P. 2, June 2008, www.bis.org/publ/bcbs138.htm (Accessed 6 June 2009).
7. Michael Lewis, "The End," *Portfolio*, November 2008.
8. Stephen Greenspan, *Annals of Gullibility: Why We Get Duped and How to Avoid It* (Westport, CT: Praeger, 2008).

Chapter 11

1. The Economist Research Tools, "Economics A-Z, Definition of Short-Termism," Economist.com, www.economist.com/research/Economics/alphabetic.cfm?letter=S#short-termism (Accessed 6 June 2009).
2. Matteo Tonello, "Revisiting Stock Market Short-Termism," Conference Board, April 2006, www.conferenceboard.ca/documents.aspx?did=1617 (Accessed 6 June 2009).
3. Lenny T. Mendonca and Jeremy Oppenheim, "Investing in Sustainability: An Interview with Al Gore and David Blood," *McKinsey Quarterly*, May 2007.
4. Leo Hindery, *It Takes a CEO: It's Time to Lead with Integrity* (New York: Free Press, 2005).
5. Ira Millstein, "When Boards Speak to Their Shareholders," Corporate Board, Millstein Center for Corporate Governance and Performance, Yale School of Management, May/June 2008, http://millstein.som.yale.edu/media/may_june08.shtml (Accessed 6 June 2009).
6. Duke University and CFO Business Outlook, "Survey: CFO Outlook Improves; Capitol Spending, Hiring Expected to Increase," Office of News and Communication, Duke University and *CFO Business Outlook*, 7 March 2007, www.dukenews.duke.edu/2007/03/cfo_survey.html (Accessed 6 June 2009).
7. Scott Newquist and Max Russell, *Putting Investors First: Real Solutions for Better Corporate Governance* (New Jersey: Bloomberg Press, 2003), 72.
8. Tom Stevenson, "Short-termism Is a Future Menace," *Telegraph*, March 15, 2007.
9. Duke University and CFO Business Outlook, "Survey: CFO Outlook Improves."
10. Newquist and Russell, *Putting Investors First,* 44.
11. USC Center for Effective Organizations and Heidrick & Struggles, "10th Annual Corporate Board Effectiveness Study 2006-2007", Hendrick.com, June 2007, www.heidrick.com/NR/rdonlyres/723D125E-9746-4486-829A-D49A8AF0832B/0/HS_BoardEffectivenessStudy0607.pdf.
12. Nick Wingfield and Jessica Hodgeson, "Ballmer Defends R&D, Seeks Yahoo Talks," WSJ.com 25 February 2009, http://online.wsj.com/article/SB123548426979759217.html?mod=yahoo_hs&ru=yahoo (Accessed 6 June 2009).
13. Ibid.
14. Elliott Jaques, *The Requisite Organization: The CEO's Guide to Creative Structure and Leadership.* (Fleming Island, FL: Cason Hall 1989), 20.
15. Michael E. Raynor, *The Strategy Paradox* (New York: Doubleday, 2007).

16. Aspen Institute, "Long-Term Value Creation: Guiding Principles for Corporations and Investors," Aspeninstitute.org, 18 June 2007, www.aspeninstitute.org/sites/default/files/content/docs/pubs/Aspen_Principles_with_signers_April_09.pdf (Accessed 6 June 2009).
17. Ibid.
18. Stephen Taub, "Welcome Back, Guidance," CFO.com, 28 May 2008, www.cfo.com/article.cfm/11449859/c_11442040?f=archives&origin=archive (Accessed 20 June 2009).
19. Interview with Robert Dannhauser and Matt Orsagh.
20. Ibid.
21. Lee Scott, "Twenty First Century Leadership" (Presented on October 24, 2005), Walmart, http://walmartwatch.com/img/documents/21st_Century_Leadership.pdf (Accessed 20 June 2009).
22. Ibid.
23. World Business Council for Sustainable Development, "Investing in Doing Good Can Be Good Risk Management," FT.com, 3 November 2008, www.wbcsd.org/plugins/DocSearch/details.asp?type=DocDet&ObjectId=MzIxOTM (Accessed 20 June 2009).

Chapter 12

1. John F. Kennedy, www.quotesandpoem.com/quotes/showquotes/subject/action/3441 (Accessed 20 June 2009).
2. Kath Straub, "One Size Fits All Doesn't Fit," e-Newsletter, Insights from Human Factors International, Humanfactors.com, February 2008, www.humanfactors.com/library/feb08uc.htm#kath (Accessed 20 June 2009).
3. Interview with Jamie Clarke.
4. Yukari Iwatani Kane, "Apple's Jobs Takes Medical Leave," *Wall Street Journal*, 15 January 2009, A2.
5. "The Times Regrets the Error: A Correction," *New York Times*, July 17, 1969,"
6. Burt Helm, "Blowing Up Pepsi," *BusinessWeek*. 16 April 2009.
7. Interview with Dan Mudge.
8. Interview with Bob Eckert.
9. Deloitte Touche Tohmatsu, "Innovation in Emerging Markets," 2007, www.deloitte.com/view/en_CA/ca/industries/manufacturing/article/1da65de9542fb110VgnVCM100000ba42f00aRCRD.htm (Accessed 16 October, 2009)
10. Xinhua News Agency, www.china-embassy.org/eng/gyzg/t356238.htm

Chapter 13

1. Interview with Matt Scharf.
2. Ibid.
3. Capt. Christopher Baker, "History Shows Examples of Failure to Discipline," 21st Space Wing Legal Office Peterson Air Force Base, Colorado, 21 October 2008, www.peterson.af.mil/news/story.asp?id=123120640 (Accessed 20 June 2009).

4. Ibid.
5. The Coca-Cola Retailing Research Council—Europe, "The Inflection Point: Critical Pathways in Food Retailing," Project XII 2007, WPP.com, June 2007, www.wpp.com/NR/rdonlyres/95D45A46-A669-4C5A-B31B-E6BBDF63A513/0/WPP_CCRRCE_TheInflectionPoint_Jun07v2.pdf (Accessed 1 July 2009).
6. Bernie Price, "Reliability Reality in Process Plants: The Archimedean Leap from the 'Bathtub'" (Presented at the 2004 International Maintenance Conference), Polaris Veritas, www.reliabilityweb.com/art05/reliability_reality.htm (Accessed 1 July 2009).
7. Ibid.
8. Coast Guard News, "Coast Guard Announces Results of Healy Investigation," 12 January 2007, Coastguardnews.com, http://coastguardnews.com/coast-guard-announces-results-of-healy-investigation/2007/01/12/ (Accessed 1 July 2009).
9. Breitbart, "U.S. Intelligence Believes Crisis Could Increase Risk of Terror," Breitbart.com, 15 November 2008, www.breitbart.com/article.php?id=081115185533.5saifzy6&show_article=1&catnum=3 (Accessed 1 July 2009).
10. Captain D. Michael Abrashoff, *It's Your Ship: Management Techniques from the Best Damn Ship in the Navy* (New York: Warner Books, 2002).
11. Ibid., 62.
12. Bryan O'Connor, "Rocky Mountain Death Trap: The Mann Gulch Fire," July 2007, NASA, http://pbma.nasa.gov/docs/public/pbma/images/msm/mann_gulch_vits.pdf (Accessed 1 July 2009).
13. Scott Wells, Federal Coordinating Officer, Louisiana Hurricanes Katrina & Rita, in Testimony Before the Senate Homeland Security and Governmental Affairs Committee on Hurricane Katrina: Perspectives of FEMA's Operations Professionals, 8 December 2005, www.agiweb.org/gap/legis109/katrina_hearings.html#dec8 (Accessed 1 July 2009).
14. Major William C. Thomas, "The Cultural Identity of The United States Air Force," 30 January 2004, *Air and Space Power Journal—Chronicles Online Journal*, www.airpower.maxwell.af.mil/airchronicles/cc/thomas.html (Accessed 1 July 2009).
15. Sir Andrew Large, "Financial Stability: Managing Liquidity Risk in a Global System," Speech presented at the Fourteenth City of London Central Banking and Regulatory Conference, National Liberal Club, London, 28 November 2005. www.bis.org/review/r051208e.pdf (Accessed 1 July 2009).
16. Jason Zweig, "Investing Experts Urge 'Do as I Say, Not as I Do'," Intelligent Investor, WSJ.com, 3 January 2009, http://online.wsj.com/article/SB123093692433550093.html (Accessed 1 July 2009).
17. Ibid.
18. Ronald Kipling, Jeffrey Scott Hickman, and Gene Bergoffen, "Effective Commercial Truck and Bus Safety Management Techniques," Commercial Truck and Safety Synthesis Program (U.S.), Federal Motor Carrier Safety Administration, February 2007, www.fmcsa.dot.gov/facts-research/research-technology/tech/Truck-and-Bus-Safety-Management-feb-2007.pdf (Accessed 1 July 2009).
19. Abrashoff, *It's Your Ship*.

20. DuPont Home Page: "Company at a Glance," www2.dupont.com/Our_Company/en_US/glance/index.html (Accessed 7 July 2009).
21. James A. Klein and Bruce K. Vaughen, "The Next Generation Approach to Operational Discipline at DuPont," Aiche.confex.com, 23 April 2007, http://aiche.confex.com/aiche/s07/techprogram/P80873.HTM (Accessed 20 June 2009).
22. The opinions expressed are those of Mr. Porter and may not necessarily reflect those of the DuPont Company.

Chapter 14

1. Frank M. Gryna and J. M. Juran, *Quality Planning and Analysis: From Product Development through Use,* 2nd ed. (Columbus: McGraw-Hill, 1980).
2. Ibid.
3. Technical Council on Forensic Engineering of the American Society of Civil Engineers, (TCOR), www.ascetcfe.org/; K.K. Phoon and G.L. Sivakumar Babu, "Potential Role of Reliability on Forensic Geotechnical Engineering," Geoengineer.org, http://reliability.geoengineer.org/TC40/13ARC_Phoon.pdf (Accessed 8 July 2009).
4. U.S. Security and Exchange Commission, (SEC), "SEC Disclosure Item: Item 503 (c) of Regulation S-K," Lawyer Links Advantage, LLC, http://content.lawyerlinks.com/default.htm#http://content.lawyerlinks.com/sec/S_K/sk_503c.htm (Accessed 8 July 2009).
5. U.S. Security and Exchange Commission, (SEC), "Proposed Rule: Disclosure Required by Sections 404, 406 and 407 of the Sarbanes-Oxley Act of 2002," www.sec.gov/rules/proposed/33-8138.htm; Tim J. Leech, "Sarbanes-Oxley Sections 302 and 404: A White Paper Proposing Practical, Cost Effective Compliance Strategies," www.sec.gov/rules/proposed/s74002/card941503 (Accessed 8 July 2009).
6. Frank M. Gryna and J. M. Juran, *Quality Planning and Analysis: From Product Development through Use,* 2nd ed. (New York: McGraw-Hill, 1980).

Chapter 15

1. Madeleine Albright, "Risk Management Report," FT.com, 10 September 2007, www.ft.com/reports/riskmgmtsep2007 (Accessed 8 July 2009).
2. Interview with Jamie Clarke.
3. Agenda and Don Rice, "Wells Fargo Director on Reviewing Strategic Plans," Video Presentation on 10 November 2008. Agendaweek.com, http://money-media.feedroom.com/?fr_story=44d21a7af8093d56051a3722956473850bc78df6&rf (Accessed 8 July 2009).
4. Agenda and Leslie Rahl, "Risk Management: Ask the Right Questions: Transcript and Video Presentation," Agendaweek.com, 13 October 2008, www.agendaweek.com/articles/20081013/risk_mgmt_right_questions_transcript. and http://money-media.feedroom.com/?fr_story=d8d7b985f8433b85241876ea915a2b06b174857b&rf (Accessed 8 July 2009).
5. Interview with Professor Ray Reilly.

6. Ira Millstein, "When Boards Speak to Their Shareholders," Corporate Board, Millstein Center for Corporate Governance and Performance Yale School of Management, May/June 2008, http://millstein.som.yale.edu/media/may_june08.shtml.

7. *Wall Street Journal.* 3 December 2009. B1.

8. *In re Caremark Int'l Inc. Deriv Litig.,* 698 A.2d 959, 1996 WL 549894, p. 7 (Del. Ch. 1996).

9. Rory F. Knight and Deborah J. Pretty, "The Impact of Catastrophes on Shareholder Value—A Research Report Sponsored by Sedgewick Group," (Oxford: Templeton College, Oxford University, 1996), www.nrf.com/Attachments.asp?id=12546 (Accessed 8 July 2009).

10. Suzanne Hopgood and Michael Tankersley, *Board Leadership for the Company in Crisis* (Washington, D.C.: National Association of Corporate Directors, 2005), 102–106.

11. Ibid. 12–13.

12. Ibid. 15.

13. Richard R. Floersch, "The Right Way to Determine Executive Pay," *Wall Street Journal,* 5 March 2009.

14. Ibid.

15. National Association of Corporate Directors, (NACD), *Blue Ribbon Commission Report: Report of the NACD Blue Ribbon Commission on the Role of the Board in Corporate Strategy* (Washington D.C.: NACD, 2006).

16. Josh Martin, "Financial Crisis Underscores Need for Risk Committees," Agendaweek.com, 24 November 2008, www.agendaweek.com/articles/20081124/financial_crisis_underscores_need_risk_committees (Accessed 8 July 2009).

17. Ibid.

18. Ibid.

Chapter 16

1. Interview with Bob Eckert.

2. Deloitte Development LLC, Perspectives on ERM and the Risk Intelligent Enterprise: Enterprise Risk Management Benchmark Survey, Deloitte.com, 18 November 2008, www.deloitte.com/dtt/article/0,1002,cid%253D231429,00.html (Accessed 8 July 2009).

3. Ibid.

4. Jason Miller, "DOD Must Fix Product Security Evaluation Process, Officials Say," *Federal Computer Week,* FCW.com, 22 January 2008, http://fcw.com/articles/2008/01/22/dod-must-fix-product-security-evaluation-process-officials-say.aspx; Jason Miller, "ODNI, DOD Detail 7 Areas of IT Security to Make Standard" *Federal Computer Week,* FCW.com, 27 March 2007, www.fcw.com/online/news/98068-1.html (No longer available on server) (both Accessed 8 July 2009).

About the Authors

Frederick (Rick) Funston is a principal with Deloitte & Touche LLP. Rick has more than thirty years of experience in working with directors and officers in small-, mid-, and large-cap companies across a broad range of industry sectors, including aerospace and defense, automotive, financial services, energy and utilities, consumer business, telecommunications, and technology, as well as in the public sector. Rick has also trained hostage negotiators.

In 2000, Rick created the concept of risk intelligence for both value creation and value protection. He works with boards of directors and senior executives on means to improve the effectiveness and efficiency of governance, risk, and compliance processes. He is a frequent speaker on creating and sustaining risk intelligence for competitive advantage in complex, global organizations, and he has written numerous articles on ERM and risk intelligence.

Rick has a master's degree in social work from Tulane University. His interests include scuba diving, martial arts, photography, and golf. He lives with his wife, Irina, in Bloomfield Hills, MI.

Steve Wagner is a nationally recognized thought leader on the governance and oversight practices of corporate boards. On May 30, 2009, Steve retired as the managing partner of Deloitte LLP's Center for Corporate Governance, where he led the firm's integrated strategy for governance services. Steve is a frequent speaker at governance conferences and directors' colleges throughout the United States and has authored and been quoted in numerous articles on the subjects of governance and risk. From 2005 until his retirement, Steve hosted Deloitte's innovative Corporate Governance Debriefs series, which provides education on corporate governance topics to financial executives. He is also the co-founder of Deloitte's Directors' Series, which convenes large numbers of corporate directors semi-annually to engage in open discussion on critical governance issues. In 2008, Steve was named to the Directorship 100 most influential people on the subject of corporate governance and in the board room.

Steve received a B.S.B.A. from Babson College. He is a member of the AICPA, and is actively engaged in a number of community organizations in the greater Boston area, including the United Way, the Boston Youth Symphony Orchestras, Brigham and Women's Hospital, and Milton Academy. Steve enjoys golfing, kayaking, boating, and long-distance running.

Index